Thomas Henry Huxley, William Jay Youmans

The elements of physiology and hygiene; a text-book for educational institutions

Revised Edition

Thomas Henry Huxley, William Jay Youmans

The elements of physiology and hygiene; a text-book for educational institutions
Revised Edition

ISBN/EAN: 9783337215323

Printed in Europe, USA, Canada, Australia, Japan

Cover: Foto ©Andreas Hilbeck / pixelio.de

More available books at **www.hansebooks.com**

THE ELEMENTS

OF

PHYSIOLOGY AND HYGIENE;

A TEXT-BOOK

FOR EDUCATIONAL INSTITUTIONS,

BY

THOS. H. HUXLEY, LL. D., F. R. S.

AND

WM. JAY YOUMANS, M. D.

REVISED EDITION,

WITH MANY NEW ILLUSTRATIONS.

NEW YORK:
D. APPLETON AND COMPANY,
1, 3, AND 5 BOND STREET.
1884.

PREFACE

———•••———

IN the preface to the first American edition of this work, published in 1867, its joint authorship was thus explained : " My friend and teacher, Professor Huxley, having been for a considerable time engaged in the preparation of an elementary work on Physiology, at such brief intervals as he could snatch from his laborious scientific researches, and it having been suggested to him that its republication in this country might be desirable, he confided the early sheets of the work to me, to make such additions of matter and modifications of form as might be thought proper to adapt it to the circumstances and requirements of American education." I accordingly revised the form, without disturbing Professor Huxley's text, and added several chapters on Practical Hygiene.

The author's aim in the preparation of the volume was explained in the following passages :

" My object in writing it has been to set down, in plain and concise language, that which any person who desires to become acquainted with the principles of Human Physi-

ology may learn, with a fair prospect of having but little
to unlearn as our knowledge widens.

"It is only by inadvertence, or from an error in judgment, therefore, that the work contains any statement, or
doctrine, which cannot be regarded as the common property of all physiologists. I have endeavored simply to
play the part of a sieve, and to separate the well-estab-
lished and the essential from the doubtful and the unim-
portant portions of the vast mass of knowledge and opinion
we call Human Physiology."

Professor Huxley's work has been thoroughly tested.
It has gone through many impressions in England, has
been translated into several of the Continental languages,
has been extensively used in this country; and the general
verdict of men of science, and of eminent educators, has
been that it is the most valuable and authentic digest of
the elementary facts and principles of Physiology that
is anywhere to be found.

There was, nevertheless, one fault in the first edition
of Professor Huxley's book, which grew out of the fact
that he was a man of conscience as well as a man of science, and recognized a duty to the subject he was treating.
Offended by that looseness of style and inaccurate representation which mark the popular manuals of the subject,
and feeling that there can be no real educational benefit
in scientific study without mental exertion, he wrote with
a conciseness and a compression which made parts of his
book too difficult for average pupils. The present edition
has, therefore, been carefully revised and much of it re-
written with more fullness of illustration and simplicity
of statement; while familiar words have been substituted

for technical terms as far as is consistent with precision. Professor Huxley stands high as a master of pointed and forcible English, and, in this respect, his volume may now be offered as without rival among the books of its class.

A large number of new engravings have been introduced into the volume, and a chapter has been added on the "Physiological Constants," that will be of value to the student in recapitulating and combining the general results of the science. That the dimensions of the book might not be increased, the first chapter of the former edition has been omitted, together with the section on the forms of mental impairment. Some important additions have, however, been made to the chapter on "Air and Health."

The eminent claim of Professor Huxley's "Elementary Physiology" is, that, while up to the times, it is trustworthy in its presentation of the subject; while rejecting discredited doctrines and doubtful speculations, it embodies the latest results that are established, and represents the present actual state of physiological knowledge.

Probably, the most important advance which has been lately made in the field of science consists in the establishment of the great principle of the correlation and conservation of forces. Accordingly, regarding Physiology as strictly the science of vital actions or living forces, Professor Huxley tacitly conforms the whole plan of his work to this fundamental principle. Committing himself to no unsettled theories respecting the transformations of energy, he nevertheless views the living organism *dynamically*, as a problem of the disturbance and restoration of equilibrium between the receipt and expenditure of matter

and force. The functions of alimentation, circulation, respiration, and secretion, and the exercise of physical and
mental power, are considered in the light of losses and
gains to the system, and with constant reference to the
physiological balance of forces.

My own additions to the volume have been made in
response to a growing demand that the subject of Hygiene,
in both its bodily and mental aspects, shall receive increasing attention in general education. I trust that the acknowledged importance of this subject, as well as the advantage of dealing with it separately, after the Physiology
has been mastered, will in some degree promote the favorable reception of the work by the teachers of the country.

W. J. Y.

New York, *August*, 1873.

CONTENTS.

PART I.

ELEMENTARY PHYSIOLOGY.

CHAPTER I.

PART II.

ELEMENTARY HYGIENE.

CHAPTER XIV.

CHAPTER XV.

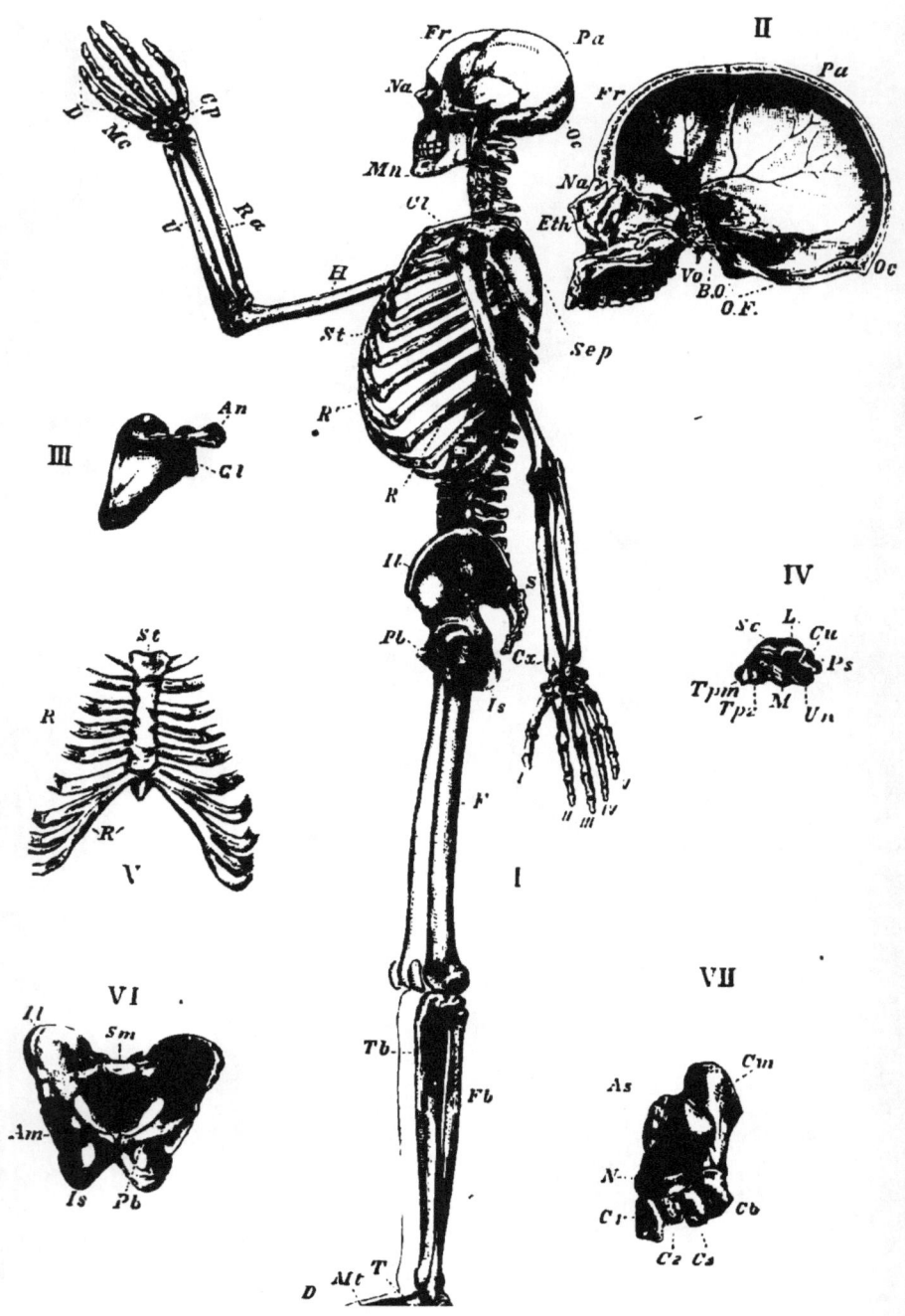

EXPLANATION OF THE PLATE.

Fig. I.—The Human Skeleton in Profile.

Na. The Nasal bones.
Fr. The Frontal bone.
Pa. The Parietal bones.
Oc. The Occipital bone. } In the Skull.
Mn. The Mandible or Lower Jaw.
St. The Sternum.
R. The Ribs.
R'. The Cartilages of the Ribs. } In the Thorax.
S. The Sacrum.
Cx. The Coccyx.
Scp. The Scapula, or Shoulder-Blade.
Cl. The Clavicle, or Collar-Bone.
H. The Humerus.
Ra. The Radius.
U. The Ulna.
Cp. The Carpus. } In the Arm.

Mc. The Metacarpus.
D. The Phalanges of the Fingers or Digits of the Hand. } In the Arm.
i, ii, iii, iv, v. The Thumb, or Pollex, and the succeeding Fingers.
Il. The Ilium.
Pb. The Pubis.
Is. The Ischium. } Which together form the Haunch-bone, or Os innominatum.
F. The Femur.
Tb. The Tibia.
Fb. The Fibula.
T. The Tarsus.
Mt. The Metatarsus.
D. The Phalanges of the Toes, or Digits of the Foot. } In the Leg.

Fig. II —Longitudinal and Vertical Section of the Skull.

The section passes a little to the left of the middle line. The letters as before, except:

Eth. The Ethmoid bone.
Vo. The Vomer.

B.O. Part of the Occipital bone.
O.F. The Occipital Foramen.

The branching lines are the impressions left by the arteries of the membranes of the brain upon the inner surface of the wall of the cavity, which lodges the cerebrum.

Fig. III.—The Right Scapula.

An. Acromion process.

Gl. Glenoidal cavity.

Fig. IV. The Dorsal Aspect of the Bones of the Carpus of the Left Hand.

Sc. Scaphoides.
Tpm. Trapezium.
L. Semilunare.

Tpz. Trapezoides.
Cu. Cuneiforme.
M. Magnum.

Ps. Pisiforme.
Un. Unciforme.

Fig. V.

A front view of the Sternum, *St.*, with the Cartilages of the Ribs, *R'*, and part of the Ribs themselves, *R.*

Fig. VI.—A Front View of the Pelvis.

Sm. The Sacrum.

Am. The Acetabulum.

Il., Pb., Is., as before.

Fig. VII.—The Dorsal Aspect of the Tarsus of the Left Foot.

Cm Calcaneum.
As. Astragalus.
N. Naviculare.

C1, C2, C3. The three Cuneiform bones.
Cb. The Cuboid.

PART I.

ELEMENTARY PHYSIOLOGY.

CHAPTER I.

A GENERAL VIEW OF THE STRUCTURE AND FUNCTIONS OF THE HUMAN BODY.

Section I.—*The Bodily Actions.*

1. How Bodily Actions are Studied.—The body of a living man performs a great diversity of actions, some of which are quite obvious; others require more or less careful observation; and yet others can be detected only by the employment of the most delicate appliances of science.

Thus, some part of the body of a living man is plainly always in motion. Even in sleep, when the limbs, head, and eyelids may be still, the incessant rise and fall of the chest continue to remind us that we are viewing slumber and not death.

More careful observation, however, is needed to detect the motion of the heart; or the pulsation of the arteries; or the changes in the size of the pupil of the eye with varying light; or to ascertain that the air which is breathed out of the body is hotter and damper than the air which is taken in by breathing.

And lastly, when we try to ascertain what happens in the eye when that organ is adjusted to different distances : or what in a nerve when it is excited : or of what materials flesh and blood are made : or in virtue of what mechanism it is that a sudden pain makes one start—we have to call into operation all the methods of inductive and deductive logic; all the resources of physics and chemistry; and all the delicacies of the art of experiment.

2. Scope of Human Physiology.—The sum of the facts and generalizations at which we arrive by these various modes of inquiry, be they simple or be they refined, concerning the actions of the body and the manner in which those actions are brought about, constitutes the science of Human Physiology. An elementary outline of this science, and of so much anatomy as is incidentally necessary, is the subject of the following chapters; of which I shall devote the present to an account of so much of the structure and such of the actions (or, as they are technically called, "functions") of the body, as can be ascertained by easy observation; or might be so ascertained if the bodies of men were as easily procured, examined, and subjected to experiment, as those of animals.

SECTION II.— *Work and Waste.*

3. Bodily Loss or Expenditure. — Suppose a chamber, with walls of ice, through which a current of pure ice-cold air passes; the walls of the chamber will of course remain unmelted.

Now, having weighed a healthy living man with great care, let him walk up and down the chamber for an hour. In doing this he will obviously exercise a great amount of mechanical force; as much, at least, as would be required to lift his weight as high and as often as he has raised himself at every step. But, in addition, a certain quantity of the ice will be melted, or converted into water; showing that the man has given off heat in abundance. Furthermore, if the air which enters the chamber be made to pass through lime-water, it will cause no cloudy white precipitate of carbonate of lime, because the quantity of carbonic acid in ordinary air is so small as to be inappreciable in this way. But if the air which passes out is made to take the same course, the lime-water will soon become milky, from the precipitation of carbonate of lime, showing the presence of carbonic acid, which, like the heat, is given off by the man.

Again, even if the air be quite dry as it enters the chamber (and the chamber be lined with some material so as to shut out all vapor from the melting ice-walls), that which is breathed out of the man, and that which is given off from his skin, will exhibit clouds of vapor; which vapor, therefore, is derived from the body.

After the expiration of the hour during which the experiment has lasted, let the man be released and weighed once more. He will be found to have lost weight.

Thus a living, active, man constantly exerts *mechanical force*, gives off *heat*, evolves *carbonic acid* and *water*, and undergoes a *loss of substance*.

4. A Physiological Income indispensable.—Plainly, this state of things could not continue for an unlimited period, or the man would dwindle to nothing. But long before the effects of this gradual diminution of substance become apparent to a by-stander, they are felt by the subject of the experiment in the form of the two imperious sensations called hunger and thirst. To still these cravings, to restore the weight of the body to its former amount, to enable it to continue giving out heat, water, and carbonic acid, at the same rate, for an indefinite period, it is absolutely necessary that the body should be supplied with each of three things, and with three only. These are, firstly, fresh air; secondly, drink — consisting of water in some shape or other, however much it may be adulterated; thirdly, food. That compound known to chemists as *proteid* matter, and which contains carbon, hydrogen, oxygen, and nitrogen, must form a part of this food, if it is to sustain life indefinitely; and fatty, starchy, or saccharine matters ought to be contained in the food, if it is to sustain life conveniently.

5. Forms of Excretions.—A certain proportion of the matter taken in as food either cannot be, or at any rate, is not, used; and leaves the body, as *excrementitious matter*, having simply passed through the alimentary canal without undergoing much change, and without ever being incorporated with the actual substance of the body. But, under healthy conditions, and when only so much food as is necessary is taken, no important proportion of either proteid matter, or fat, or starchy or saccharine food, passes out of the body as such. Almost all real food leaves the body in the form either of *water*, or of *carbonic acid*, or of a third substance called *urea*, or of certain *saline* compounds.

6. Absorption of Oxygen.—Chemists have determined that these products which are thrown out of the body and are called *excretions*, contain, if taken altogether, far more oxygen than the food and water taken into the body. Now, the only possible source whence the body can obtain oxygen, except from food and water, is the air which surrounds it.[1] And careful investigation of the air which leaves the chamber in the imaginary experiment described above would show, not only that it has gained carbonic acid *from* the man, but that it has lost *oxygen* in equal or rather greater amount *to* him.

7. Variation of the Physiological Balance.—Thus, if a man is neither gaining nor losing weight, the sum of the weights of all the substances above enumerated which leave the body, ought to be exactly equal to the weight of the food and water which enter it, together with that of

[1] Fresh country air contains in every 100 parts nearly 21 of oxygen and 79 of nitrogen gas, together with a small fraction of a part of carbonic acid, a minute uncertain proportion of ammonia, and a variable quantity of watery vapor. (*See* 103.)

the oxygen which it absorbs from the air. And this is proved to be the case.

Hence it follows that a man in health, and "neither gaining nor losing flesh," is *incessantly* oxidating and wasting away, and *periodically* making good the loss. So that if, in his average condition, he could be confined in the scale-pan of a delicate spring balance, like that used for weighing letters, the scale-pan would descend at every meal, and ascend in the intervals, oscillating to equal distances on each side of the average position, which would never be maintained for longer than a few minutes. There is, therefore, no such thing as a stationary condition of the weight of the body, and what we call such is simply a condition of variation within narrow limits—a condition in which the gains and losses of the numerous daily transactions of the economy balance one another.

8. Conditions of this Balance.—Suppose this diurnally-balanced physiological state to be reached, it can be maintained only so long as the quantity of the mechanical work done, and of heat, or other force evolved, remains absolutely unchanged.

Let such a physiologically-balanced man lift a heavy body from the ground, and the loss of weight which he would have undergone without that exertion will be immediately increased by a definite amount, which cannot be made good unless a proportionate amount of extra food be supplied to him. Let the temperature of the air fall, and the same result will occur, if his body remains as warm as before.

On the other hand, diminish his exertion and lower his production of heat, and either he will gain weight, or some of his food will remain unused.

9. Equation of Food and Force.—Thus, in a properly-nourished man, a stream of food is constantly entering the body in the shape of complex compounds containing comparatively little oxygen; as constantly, the elements of the food (whether before or after they have formed part of the living substance) are leaving the body, combined with more oxygen. And the incessant breaking down and oxidation of the complex compounds which enter the body are definitely proportioned to the amount of force the body exerts, whether in the shape of heat or otherwise; just in the same way as the amount of work to be got out of a steam-engine, and the amount of heat it and its furnace give off, bear a strict proportion to its consumption of fuel.

SECTION III.— *Outlines of the Bodily Structure.*

10. Structure of the Vital Mechanism.—From these general considerations regarding the nature of life, considered as physiological work, we may turn for the purpose of taking a like broad survey of the apparatus which does the work. We have seen the general performance of the engine, we may now look at its build.

The human body is obviously separable into *head, trunk*, and *limbs*. In the head, the brain-case or *skull* is distinguishable from the *face*. The trunk is naturally divided into the chest or *thorax*, and the belly or *abdomen*. Of the limbs there are two pairs—the upper, or *arms*, and the lower, or *legs ;* and legs and arms again are subdivided by their joints into parts which obviously exhibit a rough correspondence—*thigh* and *upper arm*, *leg* and *forearm*, *ankle* and *wrist*, *fingers* and *toes*, plainly answering to one another. And the two last, in fact, are so similar that they receive the same name of *digits ;* while the several joints of the fingers and toes have the common denomination of *phalanges*.

The whole body thus composed (without the viscera) is seen to be bilaterally symmetrical; that is to say, if it were split lengthways by a great knife, which should be made to pass along the middle line of both the dorsal and ventral (or back and front) aspects, the two halves would almost exactly resemble one another.

11. The Vertebral Column.—One-half of the body, divided in the manner described (Fig. 1), would exhibit, in the trunk, the cut faces of thirty-three bones, joined together by a very strong and tough substance into a long column, which lies much nearer the *dorsal* (or back) than the *ventral* (or front) aspect of the body. The bones thus cut through are called the *bodies* of the *vertebræ*. They separate a long, narrow canal, called the *spinal canal*, which is placed upon their dorsal side, from the spacious chamber of the chest and abdomen, which lies upon their ventral side. There is no direct communication between the dorsal canal and the ventral cavity.

12. Internal Organs.—The spinal canal contains a long white cord—the *spinal cord*—which is an important part of the nervous system. The ventral chamber is divided into the two subordinate cavities of the thorax and abdomen by a remarkable, partly fleshy and partly membranous, partition, the *diaphragm* (Fig. 1, *D*), which is concave toward the abdomen, and convex toward the thorax. The *alimentary canal* (Fig. 1, *Al.*), traverses these cavities from one end to the other, piercing the diaphragm. So does a long double series of distinct masses of nervous substance, which are called *ganglia*, are connected together by nervous cords, and constitute the so-called *sympathetic* (Fig. 1, *Sy.*). The abdomen contains, in addition to these parts, the two *kidneys*, one placed against each side of the vertebral column, the *liver*, the *pancreas* or "sweetbread," and the *spleen*. The thorax incloses, besides its segment of the alimentary canal and of the sympathetic, the *heart* and the two *lungs*. The latter are placed one on each side of the heart, which lies nearly in the middle of the thorax.

13. The Head and Brain.—Where the body is succeeded by the head, the uppermost of the thirty-three vertebral bodies is followed by a continuous mass of bone, which extends through the whole length of the head, and, like the

spinal column, separates a dorsal chamber from a ventral
one. The dorsal chamber, or *cavity of the skull*, opens
into the spinal canal. It contains a mass of nervous matter
called the *brain*, which is continuous with the spinal cord,
the brain and the spinal cord together constituting what is
termed the *cerebro-spinal* axis (Fig. 1, *C.S.*, *C.S.*). The

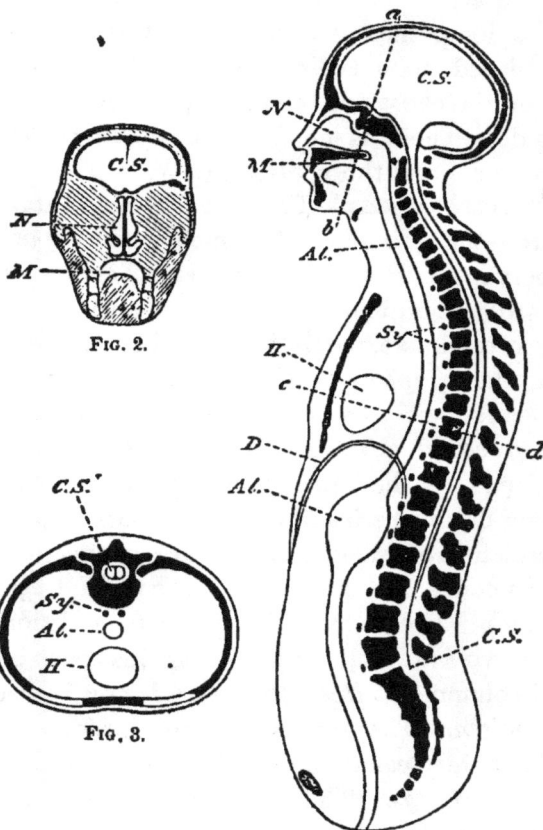

FIG. 2.

FIG. 3.

FIG. 1.

Fig. 1.—A diagrammatic section of the human body taken vertically through the
median plane. *C.S.*, the cerebro-spinal nervous system; *N.*, the cavity of the nose;
M., that of the mouth; *Al. Al.*, the alimentary canal represented as a simple straight
tube; *H.*, the heart; *D.*, the diaphragm; *Sy.*, the sympathetic ganglia.
Fig. 2.—A transverse vertical section of the head taken along the line *a b*, Fig. 1;
letters as before.
Fig. 3.—A transverse section taken along the line *c d*, Fig. 1; letters as before.

ventral chamber, or *cavity of the face*, is almost entirely occupied by the *mouth* and *pharynx*, into which last the upper end of the alimentary canal (called gullet or *œsophagus*) opens.

14. The Human Body a Double Tube.—Thus, the study of a longitudinal section shows us that the human body is a double tube, the two tubes being completely separated by the spinal column and the bony axis of the skull, which form the floor of the one tube and the roof of the other. The dorsal tube contains the cerebro-spinal axis; the ventral, the alimentary canal, the sympathetic nervous system, and the heart, besides other organs.

Transverse sections, taken perpendicularly to the axis of the vertebral column, or to that of the skull, show still more clearly that this is the fundamental structure of the human body, and that the great apparent difference between the head and the trunk is due to the different size of the dorsal cavity relatively to the ventral. In the head the former cavity is very large in proportion to the size of the latter (Fig. 2); in the thorax, or abdomen, it is very small (Fig. 3).

The limbs contain no such chambers as are found in the body and the head; but, with the exception of certain branching tubes filled with fluid, which are called *bloodvessels* and *lymphatics*, are solid or semi-solid throughout.

Section IV.—*The Bodily Tissues.*

15. The Skin.—Such being the general character and arrangement of the parts of the human body, it will next be well to consider into what constituents it may be separated by the aid of no better means of discrimination than the eye and the anatomist's knife.

With no more elaborate aids than these, it becomes easy to separate that tough membrane which invests the whole body, and is called the skin, or *integument*, from the parts which lie beneath it. Furthermore, it is readily

enough ascertained that this integument consists of two
portions: a superficial layer, which is constantly being shed
in the form of powder or scales, composed of minute particles of horny matter, and is called the *epidermis ;* and the
deeper part, the *dermis*, which is dense and fibrous (Fig.
40). The epidermis, if wounded, neither gives rise to pain
nor bleeds. The dermis, under like circumstances, is very
tender, and bleeds freely. A practical distinction is drawn
between the two in shaving, in the course of which operation the razor ought to cut only epidermic structures; for
if it go a shade deeper, it gives rise to pain and bleeding.

16. Mucous Membranes.—The skin can be readily enough
removed from all parts of the exterior, but at the margins
of the apertures of the body it seems to stop, and to be replaced by a layer which is much redder, more sensitive,
bleeds more readily, and which keeps itself continually
moist by giving out a more or less tenacious fluid, called
mucus. Hence, at these apertures, the skin is said to stop,
and to be replaced by *mucous membrane*, which lines all
those interior cavities, such as the alimentary canal, into
which the apertures open. But, in truth, the skin does not
really come to an end at these points, but is directly continued into the mucous membrane, which last is simply an
integument of greater delicacy, but consisting fundament-
ally of the same two layers—a deep, fibrous layer, containing blood-vessels and nerves, and a superficial, insensible,
and bloodless one, now called the *epithelium*. Thus every
part of the body might be said to be contained between
the walls of a double bag, formed by the epidermis, which
invests the outside of the body, and the epithelium, its continuation, which lines the internal cavities.

17. Connective Tissue.—The dermis, and the deep, san-
guine layer, which answers to it in the mucous membranes,
are chiefly made up of a filamentous substance, which yields
abundant *gelatine* on being boiled, and is the matter which
tans when hide is made into leather. This is called *areolar*,

fibrous, or, better, *connective* tissue.[1] The last name is the best, because this tissue is the great connecting medium by which the different parts of the body are held together. Thus it passes from the dermis between all the other organs, ensheathing the muscles, coating the bones and cartilages, and eventually reaching and entering into the mucous membranes. And so completely and thoroughly does the connective tissue permeate almost all parts of the body, that if every other tissue could be dissected away, a complete model of all the organs would be left composed of this tissue. Connective tissue varies very much in character; sometimes being very soft and tender, at others—as in the tendons and ligaments, which are almost wholly composed of it—attaining great strength and density.

18. The Muscles.—Among the most important of the tissues embedded in and ensheathed by the connective tissue, are some the presence and action of which can be readily determined during life.

If the upper arm of a man whose arm is stretched out be tightly grasped by another person, the latter, as the former bends up his forearm, will feel a great soft mass, which lies at the fore part of the upper arm, swell, harden, and become prominent. As the arm is extended again, the swelling and hardness vanish.

On removing the skin, the body which thus changes its configuration is found to be a mass of red flesh, sheathed in connective tissue. The sheath is continued at each end into a tendon, by which the muscle is attached, on the one hand, to the shoulder-bone, and, on the other, to one of the bones of the forearm. This mass of flesh is the *muscle* called *biceps*, and it has the peculiar property of changing its dimensions—shortening and becoming thick in proportion to its decrease in length—when influenced by the will as well as by some other causes,[2] and of returning to its

---

[1] Every such constituent of the body, as epidermis, cartilage or muscle, is called a " tissue." (*See* Chapter XII.) [2] Such causes are called *stimuli.*

original form when let alone. This temporary change in
the dimensions of a muscle, this shortening and becoming
thick, is spoken of as its *contraction*. It is by reason of
this property that muscular tissue becomes the great motor
agent of the body; the muscles being so disposed between
the systems of levers which support the body, that their
contraction necessitates the motion of one lever upon another.

19. The Cartilages and Bones.—These levers form part
of the system of hard tissues which constitute the *skeleton*.
The less hard of these are the *cartilages*, composed of a
dense, firm substance, ordinarily known as "gristle." The
harder are the *bones*, which are masses either of cartilage,
or of connective tissue, hardened by being impregnated
with *phosphate* and *carbonate of lime*. They are animal
tissues which have become, in a manner, naturally petrified;
and when the salts of lime are extracted, as they may be,
by the action of acids, a model of the bone in soft and flexible animal matter remains.

More than two hundred separate bones are ordinarily
reckoned in the human body, though the actual number of
distinct bones varies at different periods of life, many bones
which are separate in youth becoming united together in
old age. Thus there are originally, as we have seen, thirty-
three separate bodies of vertebræ in the spinal column, and
the upper twenty-four of these commonly remain distinct
throughout life. But the twenty-fifth, twenty-sixth, twenty-
seventh, twenty-eighth, and twenty-ninth early unite into
one great bone, called the *sacrum ;* and the four remaining
vertebræ often run into one bony mass called the *coccyx*.
In early adult life, the skull contains twenty-two naturally
separate bones, but in youth the number is much greater,
and in old age far less. Twenty-four ribs bound the chest
laterally, twelve on each side, and most of them are connected by cartilages with the breastbone. In the girdle
which supports the shoulder, two bones are always dis-

tinguishable as the *scapula* and *clavicle*. The *pelvis*, to which the legs are attached, consists of two separate bones called the *ossa innominata* in the adult; but each *os innominatum* is separable into three (called *pubis, ischium,* and *ilium*) in the young. There are thirty bones in each of the arms, and the same number in each of the legs, counting the *patella*, or knee-pan.

All these bones are fastened together by ligaments, or by cartilages; and, where they play freely over one another, a coat of cartilage furnishes the surfaces which come into contact. The cartilages which thus form part of a joint are called *articular* cartilages, and their free surfaces, by which they rub against each other, are lined by a delicate *synovial* membrane, which secretes a lubricating fluid —the *synovia*.

SECTION V.—*The Combination of Actions.*

20. How we stand upright.—Though the bones of the skeleton are all strongly enough connected together by ligaments and cartilages, the joints play so freely, and the centre of gravity of the body, when erect, is so high up, that it is impossible to make a skeleton or a dead body support itself in the upright position. That position, easy as it seems, is the result of the contraction of a multitude of muscles which oppose and balance one another. Thus, the foot affording the surface of support, the muscles of the calf (Fig. 4, I) must contract, or the legs and body would fall forward. But this action tends to bend the leg; and, to neutralize this and keep the leg straight, the great muscles in front of the thigh (Fig. 4, 2), must come into play. But these, by the same action, tend to bend the body forward on the legs; and, if the body is to be kept straight, they must be neutralized by the action of the muscles of the buttocks and of the back (Fig. 4, III).

The erect position, then, which we assume so easily and without thinking about it, is the result of the combined and accurately-proportioned action of a vast number of muscles. What is it that makes them work together in this way?

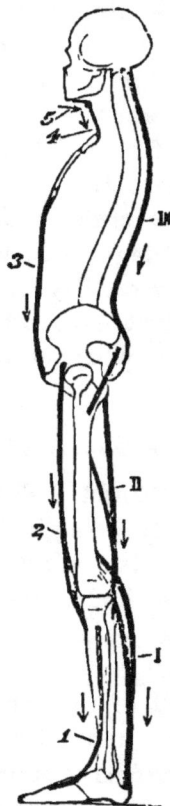

Fig. 4.

A Diagram illustrating the Attachments of some of the most important Muscles which keep the Body in the erect Posture.

I. The muscles of the calf. II. Those of the back of the thigh. III. Those of the spine. These tend to keep the body from falling forward.
1. The muscles of the front of the leg. 2. Those of the front of the thigh. 3. Those of the front of the abdomen. 4, 5. Those of the front of the neck. These tend to keep the body from falling backward.
The arrows indicate the direction of action of the muscles, the foot being fixed.

21. Relation of the Mind to the Muscles.—Let any person in the erect position receive a violent blow on the head, and you know what occurs. On the instant he drops prostrate, in a heap, with his limbs relaxed and powerless. What has happened to him? The blow may have been so inflicted as not to touch a single muscle of the body; it may not cause the loss of a drop of blood: and, indeed, if the "concussion," as it is called, has not been too severe, the sufferer, after a few moments of unconsciousness, will come to himself, and be as well as ever again. Clearly, therefore, no permanent injury has been done to any part of the body, least of all to the muscles, but an influence has been exerted upon a something which governs the muscles. And this influence may be the effect of very subtle causes. A strong mental emotion, and even a very bad smell, will, in some people, produce the same effect as a blow.

These observations might lead to the conclusion that it is the mind which directly governs the muscles, but a little further inquiry will show that such is not the case. For people have been so stabbed, or shot in the back, as to cut the spinal cord, without any considerable injury to other parts: and then they have lost the power of standing upright as much as before, though their minds may have remained perfectly clear. And not only have they lost the power of standing upright under these circumstances, but they no longer retain any power of either feeling what is going on in their legs, or, by an act of their volition, causing motion in them.

22. The Spinal Cord converts Impressions into Movements.—And yet, though the mind is thus cut off from the lower limbs, a controlling and governing power over them still remains in the body. For, if the soles of the disabled feet be tickled, though no sensation will reach the body, the legs will be jerked up, just as would be the case in an uninjured person. Again, if a series of galvanic shocks be· sent along the spinal cord, the legs will perform movements even more powerful than those which the will could produce in an uninjured person. And, finally, if the injury is of such a nature that the cord is crushed or profoundly dis-

2

organized, all these phenomena cease; tickling the soles, or sending galvanic shocks along the spine, will produce no effect upon the legs.

By examinations of this kind carried still further, we arrive at the remarkable result that the brain is the seat of all sensation and mental action, and the primary source of all voluntary muscular contractions; while the spinal cord is capable of receiving an impression from the exterior, and converting it not only into a simple muscular contraction, but into a combination of such actions.

Thus, in general terms, we may say of the cerebro-spinal nervous centres, that they have the power, when they receive certain impressions from without, of giving rise to simple or combined muscular contractions.

23. Special Sensations.—But you will further note that these impressions from without are of very different characters. Any part of the surface of the body may be so affected as to give rise to the sensations of contact, or of heat or cold; and any or every substance is able, under certain circumstances, to produce these sensations. But only very few and comparatively small portions of the bodily framework are competent to be affected in such a manner as to cause the sensations of taste or of smell, of sight or of hearing; and only a few substances, or particular kinds of vibrations, are able so to affect those regions. These very limited parts of the body, which put us in relation with particular kinds of substances, or forms of force, are what are termed *sensory organs*. There are two such organs for sight, two for hearing, two for smell, and one, or more strictly speaking two, for taste.

SECTION VI.—*Nutrition, Circulation, Excretion.*

24. Constant Renewal of Tissues.—And now that we have taken this brief view of the structure of the body, of the organs which support it, of the organs which move it, and of the organs which put it in relation with the surrounding world, or, in other words, enable it to move in harmony with influences from without, we must consider the means by which all this wonderful apparatus is kept in working order.

All work, as we have seen, implies waste. The work of the nervous system and that of the muscles, therefore, implies consumption either of their own substance, or of something else. And, as the organism can make nothing, it must possess the means of obtaining from without that which it wants, and of throwing off from itself that which it wastes; and we have seen that, in the gross, it does these things. The body feeds, and it excretes. But we must now pass from the broad fact to the mechanism by which the fact is brought about. The organs which convert food into nutriment are the organs of *alimentation;* those which distribute nutriment all over the body are organs of *circulation;* those which get rid of the waste products are organs of *excretion.*

25. Alimentary Apparatus.—The organs of alimentation are the mouth, pharynx, gullet, stomach, and intestines, with their appendages. What they do is, first to receive and grind the food. They then act upon it with chemical agents, of which they possess a store which is renewed as fast as it is wasted; and in this way separate it into a fluid containing nutritious matters in solution or suspension, and innutritious dregs or *fæces.*

26. Mechanism of Distribution.—A system of minute tubes, with very thin walls, termed *capillaries,* is distributed through the whole organism except the epidermis and its products, the epithelium, the cartilages, and the substance of the teeth. On all sides these tubes pass into others, which are called *arteries* and *veins;* while these, becoming larger and larger, at length open into the *heart,* an organ which, as we have seen, is placed in the thorax. During life, these tubes and the chambers of the heart, with which they are connected, are all full of liquid, which is, for the most part, that red fluid with which we are all familiar as *blood*.

The walls of the heart are muscular, and contract rhythmically, or at regular intervals. By means of these contractions the blood which its cavities contain is driven in jets out of these cavities into the arteries, and thence into the capillaries, whence it returns by the veins back into the heart.

This is the *circulation of the blood*.

27. Exchanges of the Blood.—Now the fluid containing the dissolved or suspended nutritive matters which are the result of the process of digestion, traverses the very thin layer of soft and permeable tissue which separates the cavity of the alimentary canal from the cavities of the innumerable capillary vessels which lie in the walls of that canal, and so enters the blood, with which those capillaries are filled. Whirled away by the torrent of the circulation, the blood, thus charged with nutritive matter, enters the heart, and is thence propelled into the organs of the body. To these organs it supplies the nutriment with which it is charged; from them it takes their waste products, and, finally, returns by the veins, loaded with useless and injurious excretions, which sooner or later take the form of water, carbonic acid, and urea.

28. Drainage of Waste Matters from the Body.—These excretionary matters are separated from the blood by the *excretory organs*, of which there are three—the *skin*, the *lungs*, and the *kidneys*.

Different as these organs may be in appearance, they are constructed upon one and the same principle. Each, in ultimate analysis, consists of a very thin sheet of tissue, like so much delicate blotting-paper, the one face of which is free, or lines a cavity in communication with the exterior of the body, while the other is in contact with the blood which has to be purified.

The excreted matters are, as it were, strained from the

blood, through this delicate layer of filtering-tissue, and on to its free surface, whence they make their escape.

Each of these organs is especially concerned in the elimination of one of the chief waste products—water, carbonic acid, and urea—though it may at the same time be a means of escape for the others. Thus the lungs are especially busied in getting rid of carbonic acid, but at the same time they give off a good deal of water. The duty of the kidneys is to excrete urea (together with other saline matters), but at the same time they pass away a large quantity of water and a trifling amount of carbonic acid; while the skin gives off much water, some amount of carbonic acid, and a certain quantity of saline matter, among which urea is, at all events, sometimes present.

29. Double Function of the Lungs.—Finally, the lungs play a double part, being not merely eliminators of waste, or excretionary, products, but importers into the economy of a substance which is not exactly either food or drink, but something as important as either—to wit, *oxygen*. It is oxygen which is the great sweeper of the economy. Introduced by the blood, into which it is absorbed, into all corners of the organism, it seizes upon those organic molecules which are disposable, lays hold of their elements, and combines with them into the new and simpler forms, carbonic acid, water, and urea.

The oxidation, or, in other words, the *burning* of these matters, gives rise to an amount of heat which is as efficient as a fire to raise the blood to a temperature of about 100°; and this hot fluid, incessantly renewed in all parts of the economy by the torrent of the circulation, warms the body, as a house is warmed by a hot-water apparatus.

30. Regulative Action of the Nerves.—But these alimentary, distributive or circulatory, excretory, and combustive processes would be worse than useless if they were not kept in strict proportion one to another. If the state of physiological balance is to be maintained, not only must the quantity of aliment taken be at least equivalent to the quantity of matter excreted ; but that aliment must be distributed with due rapidity to the seat of each local waste. The circulatory system is the commissariat of the physiological army.

Again, if the body is to be maintained at a tolerably even temperature, while that of the air is constantly varying, the condition of the hot-water apparatus must be most carefully regulated.

In other words, a *combining organ* must be added to the organs already mentioned, and this is found in the nervous system, which not only possesses the function already described of enabling us to move our bodies and to know what is going on in the external world ; but makes us aware of the need of food, enables us to discriminate nutritous from innutritious matters, and to exert the muscular actions needful for seizing, killing, and cooking ; guides the hand to the mouth, and governs all the movements of the jaws and of the alimentary canal. By it, the working of the heart is properly adjusted, and the calibres of the distributing pipes are regulated, so as indirectly to govern the excretory and combustive processes. And these are more directly affected by other actions of the nervous system.

Section VII.—*Life and Death.*

31. The Vital Actions.—The various functions which have been thus briefly indicated constitute the greater part of what are called the *vital actions* of the human body, and, so long as they are performed, the body is said to possess *life*. The cessation of the performance of these functions is what is ordinarily called *death*.

But there are really several kinds of death, which may, in the first place, be distinguished from one another under the two heads of *local* and of *general* death.

32. Local Death.—*Local death* is going on at every

moment, and in most, if not in all, parts of the living
body. Individual cells of the epidermis and of the epithelium are incessantly dying and being cast off, to be replaced by others which are, as constantly, coming into
separate existence. The like is true of blood-corpuscles,
and probably of many other elements of the tissues.

This form of local death is insensible to ourselves, and
is essential to the due maintenance of life. But, occasionally, local death occurs on a larger scale, as the result of
injury, or as the consequence of disease. A burn, for example, may suddenly kill more or less of the skin; or part
of the tissues of the skin may die, as in the case of the
slough which lies in the midst of a boil; or a whole limb
may die, and exhibit the strange phenomena of *mortifica-
tion.*

The local death of some tissues is followed by their
regeneration. Not only all the forms of epidermis and
epithelium, but nerve, connective tissue, bone, and, at any
rate, some muscles, may be thus reproduced, even on a
large scale. Cartilage, once destroyed, is said not to be
restored.

33. General Death.—*General death* is of two kinds—
death of the body as a whole, and *death of the tissues.* By
the former term is implied the absolute cessation of the
functions of the brain, of the circulatory, and of the respiratory organs; by the latter, the entire disappearance of the
vital actions of the ultimate structural constituents of the
body. When death takes place, the body, as a whole, dies
first, the death of the tissues sometimes not occurring until
after a considerable interval.

Hence it is that, for some little time after what is ordinarily called death, the muscles of an executed criminal may
be made to contract by the application of proper stimuli.
The muscles are not dead, though the man is.

34. Modes of Death.—The modes in which death is
brought about appear at first sight to be extremely varied.

We speak of natural death by old age, or by some of the endless forms of disease; of violent death by starvation, or by the innumerable varieties of injury, or poison.   But, in reality, the immediate cause of death is always the stoppage of the functions of one of three organs; the cerebro-spinal nervous centre, the lungs, or the heart. Thus, a man may be instantly killed by such an injury to a part of the brain which is called the *medulla oblongata* (*see* 332), as may be produced by hanging, or breaking the neck.

Or death may be the immediate result of suffocation by strangulation, smothering, or drowning; or, in other words, of stoppage of the respiratory functions.

Or, finally, death ensues at once when the heart ceases to propel blood.   These three organs—the brain, the lungs, and the heart—have been fancifully termed the *tripod of life.*

In ultimate analysis, however, life has but two legs to stand upon, the lungs and the heart, for death through the brain is always the effect of the secondary action of the injury to that organ upon the lungs or the heart.   The functions of the brain cease, when either respiration or circulation is at an end.   But if circulation and respiration are kept up artificially, the brain may be removed without causing death.   On the other hand, if the blood be not aërated, its circulation by the heart cannot preserve life; and, if the circulation be at an end, mere aëration of the blood in the lungs is equally ineffectual for the prevention of death.

35. Dissolution of the Body.—With the cessation of life, the every-day forces of the inorganic world no longer remain the servants of the bodily frame, as they were during life, but become its masters. Oxygen, the sweeper of the living organism, becomes the lord of the dead body.   Atom by atom, the complex molecules of the tissues are taken to pieces and reduced to simpler and more oxidized substances, until the soft parts are dissipated chiefly in the form of carbonic acid, ammonia, water, and soluble salts, and the bones and teeth alone remain. But not even these dense and earthy structures are competent to offer a permanent resistance to water and air. Sooner or later the animal basis which holds together the earthy salts decomposes and dissolves—the solid structures become friable, and break down into powder. Finally, they dissolve and are diffused among the waters of the surface of the globe, just as the gaseous products of decomposition are dissipated through its atmosphere.

It is impossible to follow, with any degree of certainty, wanderings more varied and more extensive than those imagined by the ancient sages who held the doctrine of transmigration; but the chances are that, sooner or later, some, if not all, of the scattered atoms will be gathered into new forms of life.

The sun's rays, acting through the vegetable world, build up some of the wandering molecules of carbonic acid, of water, of ammonia, and of salts, into the fabric of plants. The plants are devoured by animals, animals devour one another, man devours both plants and other animals; and hence it is very possible that atoms which once formed an integral part of the busy brain of Julius Cæsar may now enter into the composition of Cæsar the negro in Alabama, and of Cæsar the house-dog in an English homestead.

And thus there is sober truth in the words which Shakespeare puts into the mouth of *Hamlet :*

> " Imperial Cæsar, dead and turned to clay,
> Might stop a hole to keep the cold away;
> Oh that that earth, which kept the world in awe,
> Should patch a wall, 't expel the winter's flaw ! "

CHAPTER II.

SECTION I.—*The Vascular System.*

36. Capillary Vessels.—Almost all parts of the body are *vascular ;* that is to say, they are traversed by minute and very close-set canals, which open into one another só as to constitute a small-meshed net-work, and confer upon these parts a spongy texture. The canals, or rather tubes, are provided with distinct but very delicate walls, composed of a structureless membrane (Fig. 5, *a*), in which at intervals small oval bodies (Fig. 5, *b*), termed *nuclei* (*see* 340), are embedded.

These tubes are the *capillaries.* They vary in diameter from $\frac{1}{2000}$th to $\frac{1}{1500}$th of an inch; they are sometimes disposed in loops, sometimes in long, sometimes in wide, sometimes in narrow meshes; and the diameters of these meshes, or, in other words, the interspaces between the capillaries are sometimes hardly wider than the diameter of a capillary, sometimes many times as wide (*see* Figs. 19, 25, 26, 40, 41, 46). These interspaces are occupied by the substance of the tissue which the capillaries permeate (Fig. 5, *c*), so that the ultimate anatomical components of every part of the body are, strictly speaking, outside the vessels, or *extra-vascular.*

But there are certain parts which, in another and broader sense, are also said to be extra-vascular or non-vascular. These are the epidermis and epithelium, the nails and hairs, the substance of the teeth, and the cartilages; which may and do attain a very considerable thickness or length, and yet contain no vessels. However, as we have seen that all the tissues are really extra-vascular, these differ only in degree from the rest. The circumstance that all the tissues are outside the vessels by no means interferes with their being bathed by the fluid which is inside the vessels. In fact, the walls of the capillaries are so exceedingly thin

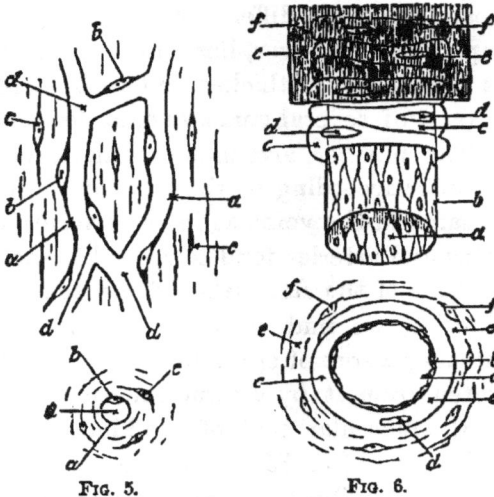

Fig. 5.

Fig. 6.

Fig. 5.—Diagrammatic representation of a capillary seen from above and in section: *a*, the wall of the capillary with *b*, the nuclei; *c*, nuclei belonging to the connective tissue in which the capillary is supposed to be lying; *d*, the canal of the capillary.

Fig. 6.—Diagrammatic representation of the structure of a small artery: *a*, epithelium; *b*, the so-called basement membrane; *c*, the circular non-striated muscular fibres, each with nucleus *d*; *e*, the coat of fibrous tissue with nuclei *f*.

that their fluid contents readily exude through the delicate membrane of which they are composed, and irrigate the tissues in which they lie.

37. The Smaller Arteries and Veins.—Of the capillary tubes thus described, one kind contains, during life, the red fluid, *blood*, while the others are filled with a pale, watery, or milky fluid, termed *lymph*, or *chyle*. The capillaries, which contain blood, are continued on different sides into somewhat larger tubes, with thicker walls, which are the smallest *arteries* and *veins*.

The mere fact that the walls of these vessels are thicker than those of the capillaries constitutes an important difference between the capillaries and the small arteries and veins; for the walls of the latter are thus rendered far less permeable to fluids, and that thorough irrigation of the tissues, which is effected by the capillaries, cannot be performed by them.

The most important difference between these vessels and the capillaries, however, lies in the circumstance that their walls are not only thicker, but also more complex, being composed of several coats, one, at least, of which is muscular. The number, arrangement, and even nature of these coats differ according to the size of the vessels, and are not the same in the veins as in the arteries, though the smallest veins and arteries tend to resemble each other.

38. Structure of the Arteries.—If we take one of the smallest arteries, we find, first, a very delicate lining of cells constituting a sort of epithelium (Fig. 6, *a*). Outside this (separated from it by a structureless membrane, Fig. 6, *b*) comes the muscular coat of the kind called *plain* or *non-striated* muscle (*see* 355), made up of flattened, spindle-shape bands or fibres, which are wrapped round the vessel (Fig. 6, *c*).

Outside the muscular coat is a sheath of fibrous or connective tissue (Fig. 6, *f*).

In the smallest arteries there is but a single layer of these muscular fibres, encircling the vessel like a series of rings; but, in the larger arteries, there are several layers of circular muscular fibres, variously bound together with fibrous and elastic tissue, though, as the vessels get larger, the quantity of muscular tissue in them gets *relatively* less.

39. Contractility of the Vascular Fibres.—Now, these plain muscular fibres possess that same power of contraction, or shortening in the long, and broadening in the narrow, directions which, as was stated in the preceding chapter, is the special property of muscular tissue. And, when they exercise this power, they, of course, narrow the calibre of the vessel, just as squeezing it in any other way would do; and this contraction may go so far as, in some cases, to reduce the cavity of the vessel almost to nothing, and to render it practically impervious.

40. Circulating Vessels controlled by Nerves.—The state of contraction of these muscles of the small arteries and veins is regulated, like that of other muscles, by their nerves; or, in other words, the nerves supplied to the vessels determine whether the passage through these tubes should be wide and free, or narrow and obstructed. Thus, while the small arteries and veins lose the function, which the capillaries possess, of directly irrigating the tissues by transudation, they gain that of regulating the supply of fluid to the irrigators, or capillaries themselves. The contraction, or dilatation, of the arteries which supply a set of capillaries, comes to the same result as lowering or raising the sluice-gates of a system of irrigation-canals.

41. Differences between Arteries and Veins.—The smaller arteries and veins severally unite into, or are branches of, larger arterial or venous trunks, which again spring from or unite into still larger ones, and these, at length, communicate by a few principal arterial and venous trunks with the heart.

The smallest arteries and veins, as we have seen, are similar in structure, but the larger arteries and veins differ widely; for the larger arteries have walls so thick and stout that they do not sink together when empty; and this thickness and stoutness arises from the circumstance that not only is the muscular coat very thick, but that, in addition, and more especially, several layers of a highly-elastic, strong, fibrous substance become mixed up with the muscular layers. Thus, when a large artery is pulled out and let go, it stretches and returns to its primitive dimensions, almost like a piece of India-rubber. .

The larger veins, on the other hand, contain but little of either elastic or muscular tissue. Hence, their walls are thin, and they collapse when empty.

This is one great difference between the larger arteries

and the veins; the other is the presence of what are termed *valves* in a great many of the veins, especially in those which lie in muscular parts of the body. They are absent in the largest trunks, and in the smallest branches, and in all the divisions of the portal, pulmonary, and cerebral veins.

42. Action of the Valves of the Veins.—These valves are pouch-like folds of the inner wall of the vein. The bottom of the pouch is turned towards those capillaries from which the vein springs. The free edge of the pouch is directed the other way, or towards the heart. The action of these pouches is to impede the passage of any fluid from the heart towards the capillaries, while they do not interfere with fluid passing in the opposite direction (Fig. 7). The working of some of these valves may be very easily demonstrated in the living body. When the arm is bared, blue veins may be seen running from the hand, under the skin, to the upper arm. The diameter of these veins is pretty even, and diminishes regularly towards the hand, so long as the current of the blood, which is running in them, from the hand to the upper arm, is uninterrupted.

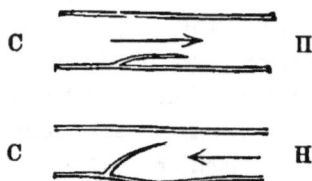

Fig. 7.

DIAGRAMMATIC SECTIONS OF VEINS WITH VALVES.

In the upper, the blood is supposed to be flowing in the direction of the arrow, toward the heart; in the lower, the reverse way. C, capillary side; H, heart side.

But, if a finger be pressed upon the upper part of one of these veins, and then passed downwards along it, so as to drive the blood which it contains backwards, sundry swellings, like little knots, will suddenly make their appearance at several points in the length of the vein, where nothing of the kind was visible before. These swellings are simply dilatations of the wall of the vein, caused by the pressure of the blood on that wall, above a valve which opposes its backward progress. The moment the backward impulse ceases, the blood flows on again; the valve, swinging back towards the wall of the vein, affords no obstacle to its progress, and the distention caused by its pressure disappears (Fig. 7).

The only arteries which possess valves are the primary trunks — the aorta and pulmonary artery — which spring from the heart, and they will be best considered with the latter organ.

43. The Lymphatics.—Besides the capillary net-work and the trunks connected with it, which constitute the blood-vascular system, all parts of the body which possess blood-capillaries—except the brain and spinal cord, the eyeball, the gristles, tendons, and perhaps the bones [1]— also contain another set of what are termed *lymphatic* capillaries, mixed up with those of the blood-vascular system, but not directly communicating with them, and, in addition, differing from the blood-capillaries in being connected with larger vessels of only one kind. That is to say, they open only into trunks which carry fluid away from them, there being no large vessels which bring any thing to them.

These trunks further resemble the small veins in being abundantly provided with valves, which freely allow of the passage of liquid from the lymphatic capillaries, but obstruct the flow of any thing the other way. But the lymphatic trunks differ from the veins, in that they do not rapidly unite into larger and larger trunks, which present a continually increasing calibre, and allow of a flow without interruption to the heart.

[1] It is probable that these exceptions are apparent rather than real, but the question is not yet satisfactorily decided.

On the contrary, remaining nearly of the same size, they, at intervals, enter and ramify in rounded bodies called *lymphatic glands*, whence new lymphatic trunks arise (Fig. 8).   In these glands the lymphatic capillaries and passages are closely interlaced with blood-capillaries.

Fig. 8.

THE LYMPHATICS OF THE FRONT OF THE RIGHT ARM.

g Lymphatic glands, or *ganglia*, as they are sometimes called.   These *ganglia* are not to be confounded with nervous *ganglia*.

Sooner or later, however, the great majority of the smaller lymphatic trunks pour their contents into a tube, which is about as large as a crow-quill, lies in front of the backbone, and is called the *thoracic duct*.   This opens at the root of the neck into the conjoined trunks of the great veins which bring back the blood from the left side of the head and the left arm (Fig. 9).   The remaining lymphatics are connected by a common canal with the corresponding vein on the right side.

Where the principal trunks of the lymphatic system open into the veins, valves are placed, which allow of the

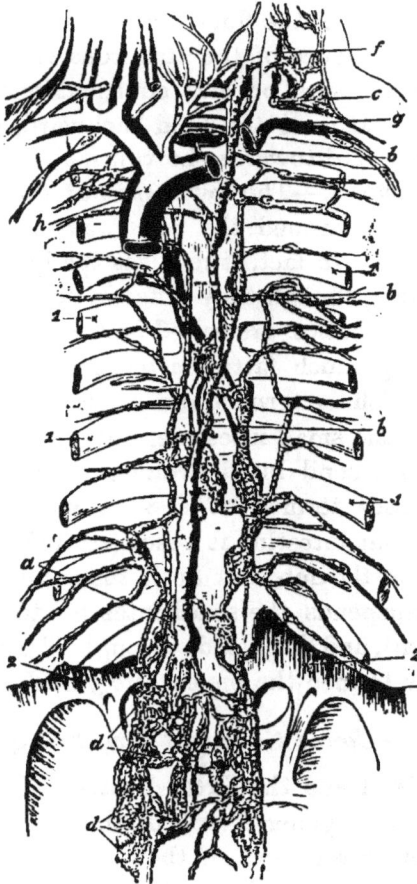

FIG. 9.

THE THORACIC DUCT.

The **Thoracic Duct** occupies the middle of the figure. It lies upon the spinal column, at the sides of which are seen portions of the ribs (1).

a, the receptacle of the chyle; *b*, the trunk of the thoracic duct, opening at *c* into the junction of the left jugular (*f*) and subclavian (*g*) veins as they unite into the left innominate vein, which has been cut across to show the thoracic duct running behind it; *d*, lymphatic glands placed in the lumbar regions; *h*, the superior vena cava formed by the junction of the right and left innominate veins.

passage of fluid only from the lymphatic to the vein. Thus the lymphatic vessels are, as it were, a part of the venous system, though, by reason of these valves, the fluid which is contained in the veins cannot get into the lymphatics. On the other hand, every facility is afforded for the passage into the veins of the fluid contained in the lymphatics. Indeed, in consequence of the numerous valves in the lymphatics, every pressure on and contraction of their walls, not being able to send the fluid backward, must drive it more or less forward towards the veins.

44. The Lacteals.—The lower part of the thoracic duct is dilated, and is termed the *receptacle*, or *cistern*, of the *chyle* (*a*, Fig. 9). In fact, it receives the lymphatics of the intestines, which, though they differ in no essential respect from other lymphatics, are called *lacteals*, because, after a meal containing much fatty matter, they are filled with a milky fluid, which is termed the *chyle*. The lacteals, or lymphatics of the small intestine, not only form net-works in its walls, but send blind prolongations into the little velvety processes termed *villi*, with which the mucous membrane of that intestine is beset (*see* 189). The trunks which open into the net-work lie in the *mesentery* (or membrane which suspends the small intestine to the back wall of the abdomen), and the glands through which these trunks lead are hence termed the *mesenteric glands*.

SECTION II.— *Connections and Structure of the Heart.*

45. The Heart and the Great Vessels.—It will now be desirable to take a general view of the arrangement of all these different vessels, and of their relations to the great central organ of the vascular system—the heart (Fig. 10).

All the veins of every part of the body, except the lungs, the heart itself, and certain viscera of the abdomen, join together into larger veins, which, sooner or later, open into one of two great trunks (Fig. 10, *V. C.S.*, *V. C.I.*), termed the *superior* and the *inferior vena cava*, which

debouch into the upper, or broad end of the right half of
the heart.

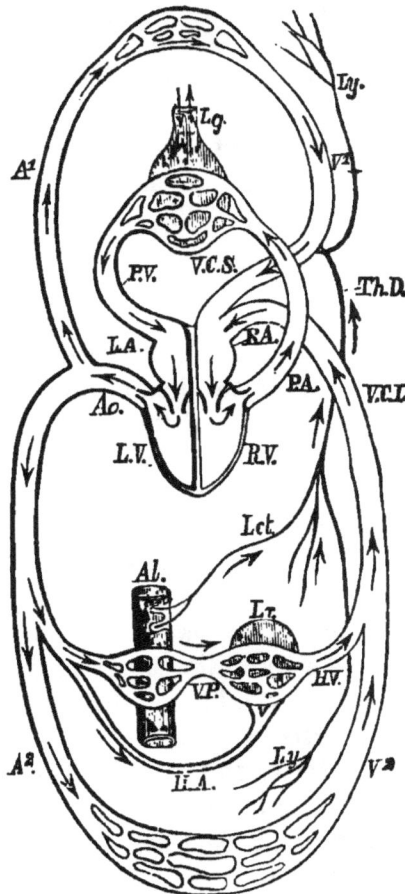

FIG. 10.

DIAGRAM OF THE HEART AND VESSELS, WITH THE COURSE OF THE CIRCULATION,
VIEWED FROM BEHIND, SO THAT THE PROPER LEFT OF THE OBSERVER CORRE-
SPONDS WITH THE LEFT SIDE OF THE HEART IN THE DIAGRAM.

L.A., left auricle; *L. V.*, left ventricle; *Ao.*, aorta; *A*[1], arteries to the upper part of
the body; *A*[2], arteries to the lower part of the body; *H.A.*, hepatic artery, which supplies the liver with part of its blood; *V*[1], veins of the upper part of the body; *V*[2],
veins of the lower part of the body; *V.P.*, vena portæ; *H.V.*, hepatic vein; *V.C.I.*, inferior vena cava; *V.C.S.*, superior vena cava; *R.A.*, right auricle; *R. V.*, right ventricle;
P.A., pulmonary artery; *Lg.*, lung; *P. V.*, pulmonary vein; *Lct.*, lacteals; *Ly.*, lymphatics; *Th.D.*, thoracic duct; *Al.*, alimentary canal; *Lr.*, liver. The arrows indicate
the course of the blood, lymph, and chyle. The vessels which contain arterial blood
have dark contours, while those which carry venous blood have light contours.

All the arteries of every part of the body, except the lungs, are more or less remote branches of one great trunk —the *aorta* (Fig. 10, *Ao.*), which springs from the lower division of the left half of the heart.

The arteries of the lungs are branches of a great trunk (Fig. 10, *P.A.*), springing from the lower division of the right side of the heart. The veins of the lungs, on the contrary, open by four trunks into the upper part of the left side of the heart (Fig. 10, *P. V.*).

Thus the venous trunks open into the upper division of each half of the heart; those of the body in general into that of the right half; those of the lungs into that of the left half; while the arterial trunks spring from the lower moieties of each half of the heart, that for the body in general from the left side, and that for the lungs from the right side.

Hence it follows that the great artery of the body, and the great veins of the body, are connected with opposite sides of the heart; and the great artery of the lungs, and the great veins of the lungs also, with opposite sides of that organ. On the other hand, the veins of the body open into the same side of the heart as the artery of the lungs, and the veins of the lungs open into the same side of the heart as the artery of the body.

46. Coronary Arteries and Vein. — The arteries which open into the capillaries of the substance of the heart are called *coronary arteries*, and arise, like the other arteries, from the aorta, but quite close to its origin, just beyond the semilunar valves. But the *coronary vein*, which is formed by the union of the small veins which arise from the capillaries of the heart, does not open into either of the venæ cavæ, but pours the blood which it contains directly into the division of the heart into which these cavæ open; that is to say, into the right upper division (Fig. 17, *b*).

47. Hepatic Vessels. — The abdominal viscera referred to above, the veins of which do not take the usual course, are the stomach, the intestines, the spleen, and the pancreas. These veins all combine into a single trunk, which is termed the *vena portæ* (Fig. 10, *V.P.*), but this trunk does not open into the *vena cava inferior*. On the contrary, having reached the liver, it enters the substance of that organ, and breaks up into an immense multitude of capillaries, which ramify through the liver, and become connected with those into which the artery of the liver, called the *hepatic artery* (Fig. 10, *H.A.*), branches. From this common capillary mesh-work veins arise, and unite, at length, into a single trunk, the *hepatic vein* (Fig. 10, *H. V.*), which emerges from the liver, and opens into the *inferior vena cava*. The portal vein is the only great vein in the body which branches out and becomes continuous with the capillaries of an organ, like an artery.

48. The Heart.—The heart (Figs. 11 and 13), to which all the vessels in the body have now been directly or indirectly traced, is an organ, the size of which is usually roughly estimated as equal to that of the closed fist of the person to whom it belongs, and which has a broad end turned upwards and backwards, and rather to the right side, called its *base;* and a pointed end, which is called its *apex*, turned downwards and forwards, and to the left side, so as to lie opposite the interval between the fifth and sixth ribs.

It is lodged between the lungs, nearer the front than the back wall of the chest, and is inclosed in a sort of double bag—the *pericardium* (Fig. 12, *p.*). One-half of the double bag is closely adherent to the heart itself, forming a thin coat upon its outer surface. At the base of the heart, this half of the bag passes on to the great vessels which spring from, or open into, that organ; and becomes continuous with the other half, which loosely envelops the heart and the adherent half of the bag. Between the two layers of the pericardium, consequently, there is a completely-closed, narrow cavity, lined by an epithelium, and secreting into its interior a small quantity of clear fluid.[1]

FIG. 11.

HEART OF SHEEP, AS SEEN AFTER REMOVAL FROM THE BODY, LYING UPON THE TWO LUNGS. THE PERICARDIUM HAS BEEN CUT AWAY, BUT NO OTHER DISSECTION MADE.

R.A., auricular appendage of right auricle; *L.A.,* auricular appendage of left auricle: *R.V.,* right ventricle; *L.V.,* left ventricle; *S.V.C.,* superior vena cava; *I.V.C.,* inferior vena cava; *P.A.,* pulmonary artery; *Ao.,* aorta; *A'o'.,* innominate branch from aorta dividing into subclavian and carotid arteries; *L.,* lung; *Tr.,* trachea. 1. Solid cord often present, the remnant of a once open communication between the pulmonary artery and aorta. 2. Masses of fat at the bases of the ventricle hiding from view the greater part of the auricles. 3. Line of fat marking the division between the two ventricles. 4. Mass of fat covering end of trachea.

[1] This fluid, like that contained in the peritoneum, pleura, and other shut sacs of a similar character to the pericardium, is sometimes called *serum;* whence the membranes forming the walls of these sacs are frequently termed *serous membranes.*

The outer layer of the pericardium is firmly connected below with the upper surface of the diaphragm.

But the heart cannot be said to depend altogether upon the diaphragm for support, inasmuch as the great vessels

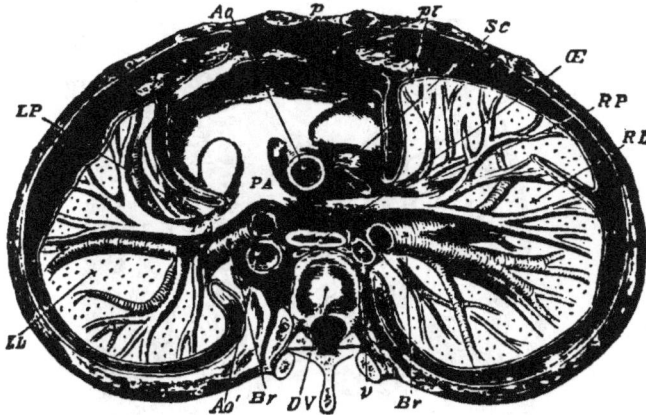

FIG. 12.

TRANSVERSE SECTION OF THE CHEST, WITH THE HEART AND LUNGS IN PLACE.
(A little diagrammatic.)

D. V., dorsal vertebra, or joint of the backbone; *Ao., Ao'*, aorta, the top of its arch being cut away in this section; *S.C.*, superior vena cava; *P.A.*, pulmonary artery, divided into a branch for each lung; *L.P., R.P.*, left and right pulmonary veins; *Br.*, bronchi; *R.L., L.L.*, right and left lungs; *Œ.*, the gullet or œsophagus; *p.*, outer bag of pericardium; *pl.*, the two layers of pleura; *v.*, azygos vein.

which issue from or enter it—and for the most part pass upwards from its base—help to suspend and keep it in place.

49. The Auricles and Ventricles.—Thus the heart is coated, outside, by one layer of the pericardium. Inside, it contains two great cavities or "divisions," as they have been termed above, completely separated by a fixed partition which extends from the base to the apex of the heart; and, consequently, having no direct communication with one another. Each of these two great cavities is further subdivided, not longitudinally but transversely, by a movable partition. The cavity above the transverse partition, on each side, is called the *auricle;* the cavity below, the *ventricle*—right or left as the case may be.

Each of the four cavities has the same capacity, and is capable of containing from four to six cubic inches of water. The walls of the auricles are much thinner than those of the ventricles. The wall of the left ventricle is much

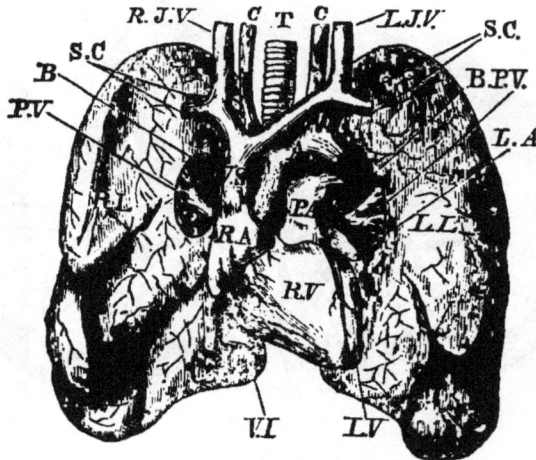

FIG. 13.

THE HEART, GREAT VESSELS, AND LUNGS. (Front View.)

R.V., right ventricle; *L.V.*, left ventricle; *R.A.*, right auricle; *L.A.*, left auricle; *Ao.*, aorta; *P.A.*, pulmonary artery; *P.V.*, pulmonary veins; *R.L.*, right lung; *L.L.*, left lung; *V.S.*, vena cava superior; *S.C.*, subclavian vessels; *C.*, carotids; *R.J.V.*, and *L.J.V.*, right and left jugular veins; *V.I.*, vena cava inferior; *T.*, trachea; *B.*, bronchi. All the great vessels but those of the lungs are cut.

thicker than that of the right ventricle; but no such difference is perceptible between the two auricles (Figs. 14 and 15, 1 and 3).

50. Their Unequal Work.—In fact, as we shall see, the ventricles have more work to do than the auricles, and the left ventricle more to do than the right. Hence the ventricles have more muscular substance than the auricles, and the left ventricle than the right; and it is this excess of muscular substance which gives rise to the excess of thickness observed in the left ventricle.

51. Muscular Fibres and Fibrous Rings.—The muscular fibres of the heart are not smooth, nucleated bands, like those of the vessels, but are bundles of transversely-striped fibres, and resemble those of the chief muscles of the body, except that they have no sheath, or *sarcolemma*, such as we shall find to exist in the latter.

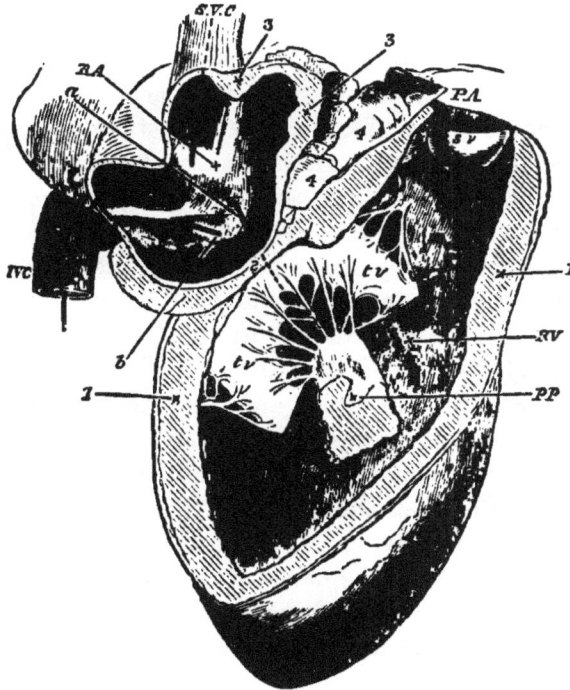

Fig. 14.

RIGHT SIDE OF THE HEART OF A SHEEP.

R.A., cavity of right auricle ; *S.V.C.*, superior vena cava ; *I.V.C.*, inferior vena cava (a style has been passed through each of these); *a.* a style passed from the auricle to the ventricle through the auriculo-ventricular orifice ; *b*, a style passed into the coronary vein. *R.V.*, cavity of right ventricle ; *t.v., t.v.*, two flaps of the tricuspid valve ; the third is dimly seen behind them, the style *a* passing between the three. Between the two flaps, and attached to them by *chordæ tendineæ*, is seen a papillary muscle, *pp.*, cut away from its attachment to that portion of the wall of the ventricle which has been removed. Above, the ventricle terminates somewhat like a funnel in the pulmonary artery, *P.A.* One of the pockets of the semilunar valve, *s.v.*, is seen in its entirety, another partially. 1. The wall of the ventricle cut across. 2. The position of the auriculo-ventricular ring. 3. The wall of the auricle. 4. Masses of fat lodged between the auricle and pulmonary artery.

Almost the whole mass of the heart is made up of these muscular fibres, which have a very remarkable and complex

3

arrangement. There is, however, an internal membranous
and epithelial lining, called the *endocardium ;* and, at the
junction between the auricles and ventricles, the apertures
of communication between their cavities, called the *auriculo-ventricular apertures*, are strengthened by *fibrous
rings*. To these rings the movable partitions, or *valves*,
between the auricles and ventricles, the arrangement of
which must next be considered, are attached.

52. Valves of the Heart; their Structure and Action.—
There are three of these partitions attached to the circumference of the right auriculo-ventricular aperture, and two
to that of the left (Figs. 14, 15, 16, 17, *t v, m v*). Each is
a broad, thin, but very tough and strong triangular fold of
the endocardium, attached by its base, which joins on to
its fellow, to the auriculo - ventricular fibrous ring; and
hanging with its point downwards into the ventricular cavity. On the right side there are, therefore, three of these
broad, pointed membranes, whence the whole apparatus is
called the *tricuspid valve*. On the left side there are but
two, which, when detached from all their connections but
the auriculo-ventricular ring, look something like a bishop's
mitre, and hence bear the name of the *mitral valve*.

The edges and apices of the valves are not completely
free and loose. On the contrary, a number of fine but
strong tendinous cords, called *chordæ tendineæ*, connect
them with some column-like elevations of the fleshy substance of the walls of the ventricle, which are termed
papillary muscles (Figs. 14 and 15, *pp*); similar column-
like elevations of the walls of the ventricles, but, having
no *chordæ tendineæ* attached to them, are called *columnæ
carneæ*.

It follows, from this arrangement, that the valves oppose no obstacle to the passage of fluid from the auricles
to the ventricles; but, if any should be forced the other
way, it will at once get between the valve and the wall
of the heart, and drive the valve backwards and upwards.

Partly because they soon meet in the middle and oppose one another's action, and partly because the *chordæ tendineæ* hold their edges and prevent them from going back too far, the valves, thus forced back, give rise to the formation of a complete transverse partition between the

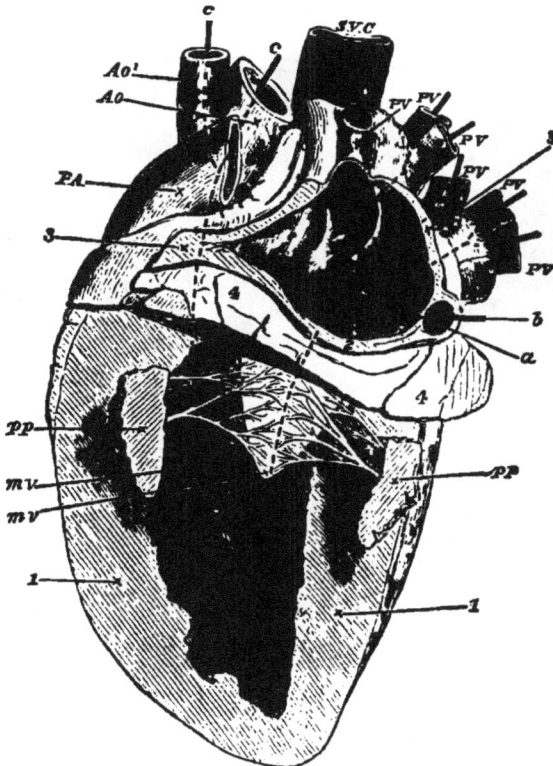

FIG. 15.

LEFT SIDE OF THE HEART OF A SHEEP (LAID OPEN).

P. ., pulmonary veins opening into the left auricle by four openings, as shown by the styles; *a*, a style passed from auricle into ventricle through the auriculo-ventricular orifice; *b*, a style passed into the coronary vein, which, though it has no connection with the left auricle, is, from its position, necessarily cut across in thus laying open the auricle· *m.v.*, the two flaps of the mitral valve (drawn somewhat diagrammatically; *pp*, papillary muscles, belonging, as before, to the part of the ventricle cut away; *c*, a style passed from ventricle in *Ao*, aorta; *Ao¹*, branch of aorta (*see* Fig. 11, *A'o'*); *P.A.*, pulmonary artery; *S.V.C.*, superior vena cava. 1. Wall of ventricle cut across. 2. Wall of auricle cut away around auriculo-ventricular orifice. 3. Other portions of auricular wall cut across. 4. Mass of fat around base of ventricle (*see* Fig. 11, 2).

ventricle and the auricle, through which no fluid can pass.
Where the aorta opens into the left ventricle, and where
the pulmonary artery opens into the right ventricle, another
valvular apparatus is placed, consisting, in each case, of
three pouch-like valves, called the *semilunar valves* (Fig.
14, *s.v.;* Figs. 16 and 17, *Ao. P.A.*), which are similar to those

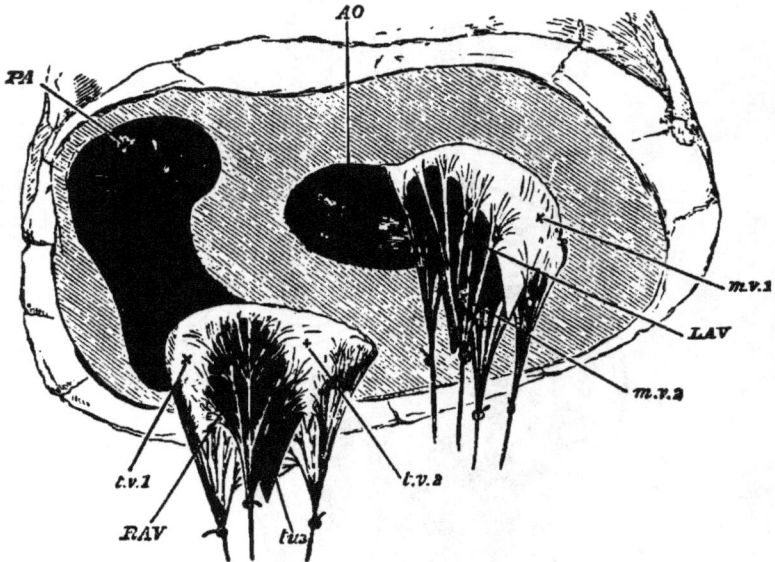

FIG. 16.

VIEW OF THE ORIFICES OF THE HEART FROM BELOW, THE WHOLE OF THE VENTRI-
CLES HAVING BEEN CUT AWAY.

R.A.V., right auriculo-ventricular orifice, surrounded by the three flaps *t.v.* 1, *t.v.* 2,
t.v. 3, of the tricuspid valve; these are stretched by weights attached to the *chordæ
tendineæ*. *L.A.V.*, left auriculo-ventricular orifice, surrounded in the same way by
the two flaps, *m.v.* 1, *m.v.* 2, of mitral valve; *P.A.*, the orifice of pulmonary artery,
the semilunar valves having met and closed together; *Ao.*, the orifice of the aorta,
with its semilunar valves. The shaded portion, leading from *R.A.V.* to *P.A.*, represents the funnel seen in Fig. 14.

of the veins. But, as they are placed on the same level and
meet in the middle line, they completely stop the passage
when any fluid is forced along the artery towards the heart.
On the other hand, these valves flap back, and allow any
fluid to pass from the heart into the artery, with the utmost
readiness.

The action of the auriculo-ventricular valves may be demonstrated with great ease on a sheep's heart, in which the aorta and pulmonary artery have been tied and the greater part of the auricles cut away, by pouring water into the ventricles through the auriculo-ventricular aperture. The tricuspid and mitral valves then usually become closed by the upward pressure of the water which gets behind them. Or, if the ventricles be nearly filled, the valves may be made to come together at once by gently squeezing the ventricles. In like manner, if the base of the aorta, or pulmonary artery, be cut out of the heart, so as not to in-

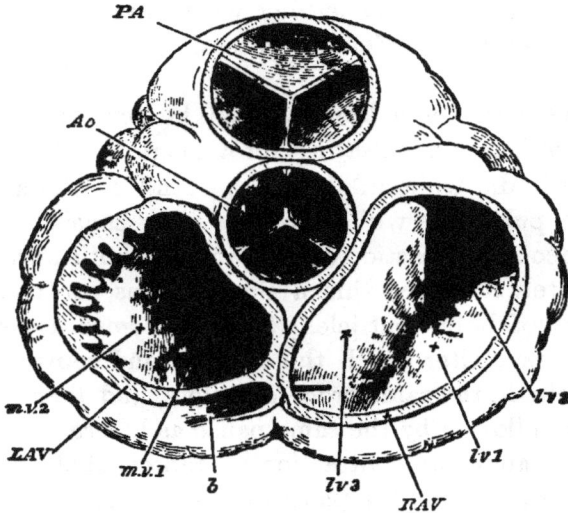

FIG. 17.

THE ORIFICES OF THE HEART SEEN FROM ABOVE, THE AURICLES AND GREAT VESSELS BEING CUT AWAY.

P.A., pulmonary artery, with its semilunar valves; *Ao.*, aorta, do. *R.A.V.*, right auriculo-ventricular orifice, with the three flaps (*lv.* 1, 2, 3) of tricuspid valve. *L.A.V.*, left auriculo-ventricular orifice, with *m.v.* 1 and 2, flaps of mitral valve; *b*, style passed into coronary vein. On the left part of *L.A.V.*, the section of the auricle is carried through the auricular appendage; hence the toothed appearance due to the portions in relief cut across.

jure the semilunar valves, water poured into the upper ends of the vessel will cause its valves to close tightly, and allow nothing to flow out after the first moment.

Thus the arrangement of the auriculo-ventricular valves is such, that any fluid contained in the chambers of the heart can be made to pass through the auriculo-ventricular apertures in only one direction: that is to say, from the auricles to the ventricles. On the other hand, the arrangement of the semilunar valves is such that the fluid contents of the ventricles pass easily into the aorta and pulmonary artery, while none can be made to travel the other way from the arterial trunks to the ventricles.

53. Rhythm of its Movement — Systole and Diastole. —Like all other muscular tissues, the substance of the heart is contractile; but, unlike most muscles, the heart contains within itself a something which causes its different parts to contract in a definite succession and at regular intervals.

If the heart of a living animal be removed from the body, it will go on pulsating for a longer or shorter time, much as it did while in the body. And careful attention to these pulsations will show that they consist of: 1. A simultaneous contraction of the walls of both auricles; 2. Immediately following this, a simultaneous contraction of the walls of both ventricles; 3. Then comes a pause, or state of rest; after which the auricles and ventricles contract again in the same order as before, and their contractions are followed by the same pause as before.

If the auricular contraction be represented by A˘, the ventricle by V˘, and the pauses by —, the series of actions will be as follows: A˘ V˘ —; A˘ V˘ —; A˘ V˘ —; etc. Thus, the contraction of the heart is *rhythmical*, two short contractions of its upper and lower halves respectively being followed by a pause of the whole, which occupies about as much time as the two contractions.

The state of contraction of the ventricle or auricle is called its *systole ;* the state of relaxation, during which it undergoes dilatation, its *diastole.*

SECTION III.— *Working of the Heart and Vessels.*

54. Working of the Heart. — Having now acquired a notion of the arrangement of the different pipes and reservoirs of the circulatory system, of the position of the valves, and of the rhythmical contractions of the heart, it will be easy to comprehend what must happen if, when the whole apparatus is full of blood, the first step in the pulsation of the heart occurs and the auricles contract.

By this action each auricle tends to squeeze the fluid which it contains out of itself in two directions—the one towards the great veins, the other towards the ventricles; and the direction which the blood, as a whole, will take, will depend upon the relative resistance offered to it in these two directions. Towards the great veins it is resisted by the mass of the blood contained in the veins. Towards the ventricles, on the contrary, there is no resistance worth mentioning, inasmuch as the valves are open, the walls of the ventricles, in their uncontracted state, are flaccid and easily distended, and the entire pressure of the arterial blood is taken off by the semilunar valves, which are necessarily closed.

Therefore, when the auricles contract, only a very little of the fluid which they contain will flow back into the veins, and the great proportion will pass into and distend the ventricles. As the ventricles fill and begin to resist further distention, the blood, getting behind the auriculo-ventricular valves, will push them towards one another, and almost shut them. The auricles now cease to contract, and immediately that their walls relax, fresh blood flows from the great veins and slowly distends them again.

But, the moment the auricular systole is over, the ventricular systole begins. The walls of each ventricle contract vigorously, and the first effect of that contraction is to shut the auriculo-ventricular valves completely and to stop all egress towards the auricle. The pressure upon the valves becomes very considerable, and they might even be driven upwards, if it were not for the *chordæ tendineæ* which hold down their edges.

As the contraction continues and the capacities of the ventricles become diminished, the points of the wall of the heart to which the *chordæ tendineæ* are attached approach the edges of the valves; and thus there is a tendency to allow of a slackening of these cords, which, if it really took place, might permit the edges of the valves to flap back and so destroy their utility. This tendency, however, is counteracted by the *chordæ tendineæ* being connected, not directly to the walls of the heart, but to those muscular pillars, the papillary muscles, which stand out from its substance. These muscular pillars shorten at the same time as the substance of the heart contracts; and thus, just so far as the contraction of the walls of the ventricles brings the papillary muscles nearer the valves, do they, by their own contraction, pull the *chordæ tendineæ* as tight as before.

By the means which have now been described, the fluid in the ventricle is debarred from passing back into the auricle; the whole force of the contraction of the ventricular walls is therefore expended in overcoming the resistance presented by the semilunar valves. This resistance has several sources, being the result, partly, of the weight of the vertical column of blood which the valves support; partly, of the reaction of the distended elastic walls of the great arteries, and partly, of the friction and inertia of the blood contained in the vessels.

It now becomes obvious why the ventricles have so much more to do than the auricles, and why valves are needed between the auricles and ventricles, while none are wanted between the auricles and the veins.

All that the auricles have to do is to fill the ventricles, which offer no active resistance to that process. Hence the thinness of the walls of the auricles, and hence the

needlessness of any auriculo-venous valve, the resistance
on the side of the ventricle being so insignificant that it
gives way, at once, before the pressure of the blood in the
veins.

On the other hand, the ventricles have to overcome a
great resistance in order to force fluid into elastic tubes
which are already full; and, if there were no auriculo-ventricular valves, the fluid in the ventricles would meet with
less obstacle in pushing its way backwards into the auricles
and thence into the veins, than in separating the semilunar
valves. Hence the necessity, firstly, of the auriculo-ventricular valves; and, secondly, of the thickness and strength
of the walls of the ventricles. And since the aorta, sys-
temic arteries, capillaries, and veins, form a much larger
system of tubes, containing more fluid and offering more
resistance than the pulmonary arteries, capillaries, and
veins, it follows that the left ventricle needs a thicker
muscular wall than the right.

55. The Working of the Arteries.—Thus, at every systole of the auricles, the ventricles are filled and the auricles
emptied, the latter being slowly refilled by the pressure of
the fluid in the great veins, which is amply sufficient to
overcome the passive resistance of the relaxed auricular
walls. And, at every systole of the ventricles, the arterial
systems of the body and lungs receive the contents of these
ventricles, and the nearly-emptied ventricles remain ready
to be refilled by the auricles.

We must now consider what happens in the arteries.
When the contents of the ventricles are suddenly forced
into these tubes (which, it must be recollected, are already
full), a shock is given to the entire mass of fluid which
they contain. This shock is propagated almost instanta-
neously throughout the fluid, becoming fainter and fainter
in proportion to the increase of the mass of the blood in the
capillaries, until it finally ceases to be discernible.

If the vessels were tubes of a rigid material, like gas-

pipes, the fluid which the arteries contain would be trans-
ported forward as far as this impulse was competent to
carry it, at the same instant as the shock, throughout their
whole extent.   And, as the arteries open into the capillaries, the capillaries into the veins, and these into the heart,
a quantity of fluid exactly equal to that driven out of the
ventricles would be returned to the auricles, almost at the
same moment that the ventricles contract.

However, the vessels are not rigid, but, on the contrary,
very yielding tubes; and the great arteries, as we have
seen, have especially elastic walls.   What happens, then,
when the ventricular systole takes place, is: firstly, the
production of the general slight and sudden shock already
mentioned; and, secondly, the dilatation of the great arteries by the pressure of the increased quantity of blood
forced into them.   .

But, when the systole is over, the force stored up in the
dilated arterial walls, in the shape of elastic tension, comes
into play and exerts a pressure on the fluid—the first effect
of which is to shut the semilunar valves; the second, to
drive a certain quantity of the fluid from the larger arteries
along the smaller ones.   These it dilates in the same fashion.   The fluid at length passing into the capillaries, the
ejection of a corresponding quantity of fluid from them into
the veins, and finally from the veins into the heart, is the
ultimate result of the ventricular systole.

56. The Beat of the Heart. — Several of the practical
results of the working of the heart and arteries just described now become intelligible.   For example, between
the fifth and sixth ribs, on the left side, a certain movement is perceptible by the finger and by the eye, which is
known as the *beating* of the heart.   It is the result of the
striking of the apex of the heart against the pericardium,
and, through it, on the inner wall of the chest, at this point,
at the moment of the systole of the ventricles.   When the
systole occurs, in fact, two things happen: in the first place,

as a result of the manner in which the muscular fibres of the heart are disposed, its apex bends upwards sharply; and, in the second place, its front face is thrown a little downwards and forwards, in consequence of the stretching and elongation of the aorta by the blood which is thrown into it. The result of one or other, or both of these actions combined, is the upward and forward blow of the apex of the heart which we feel.

57. The Sounds of the Heart.—Secondly, if the ear be applied over the heart, certain *sounds* are heard, which recur with great regularity, at intervals corresponding with those between every two beats. First comes a longish dull sound; then a short sharp sound; then a pause; then the long, then the sharp sound, then another pause; and so on. There are many different opinions as to the cause of the first sound, and perhaps physiologists are not yet at the bottom of the matter; though the more probable view is, that part of it is a muscular sound caused by the contraction of the muscular fibres of the ventricle, and part is due to the tension of the auriculo-ventricular valves; but the second sound is, without doubt, caused by the sudden closure of the semilunar valves when the ventricular systole ends. That such is the case has been proved experimentally, by hooking back the semilunar valves in a living animal, when the second sound ceases at once.

58. The Pulse.—Thirdly, if the finger be placed upon an artery, such as that at the wrist, what is termed the *pulse* will be felt; that is to say, the elastic artery dilates somewhat, at regular intervals, which answer to the beatings of the heart. The pulse which is felt by the finger, however, does not correspond precisely with the beat of the heart, but takes place a little after it, and the interval is longer the greater the distance of the artery from the heart. The beat of the artery on the inner side of the ankle, for example, is a little later than the beat of the artery in the temple.

The reason of this is that the sense of touch by finger is only delicate enough to distinguish the dilatation of the artery by the wave of blood, which is driven along it by the elastic reaction of the aorta, and is not competent to perceive the first shock caused by the systole. But, if, instead of the fingers, sufficiently delicate levers were made to rest upon any two arteries, it would be found that the pulse really begins at the same time in both, the shock of the systole making itself felt all over the vascular system at once; and that it is only the actual dilatation of the arterial walls, which, traveling in the form of a wave from the larger to the smaller arteries, takes longer to reach and distend the more distant branch.

59. Jetting of Blood from Cut Arteries.—Fourthly, when an artery is cut, the outflow of the fluid which it contains is increased by *jerks*, the intervals of which correspond with the intervals of the beats of the heart. The cause of this is plainly the same as that of the pulse; the force which would be employed in distending the walls of the artery, were the latter entire, is spent in jerking the fluid out when the artery is cut.

60. Why the Capillaries are pulseless.—Fifthly, under ordinary circumstances, the pulse is no longer to be detected in the capillaries, or in the veins. This arises from several circumstances. One of them is that the capacity of the branches of an artery is greater than the capacity of its trunk, and the capacity of the capillaries, as a whole, is greater than that of all the small arteries put together. Hence, supposing the capacity of the trunk to be 10, that of its branches 50, and that of the capillaries into which these open 100, it is clear that a quantity of fluid thrown into the trunk, sufficient to dilate it by one-tenth, and to produce a very considerable and obvious effect, could not distend each branch by more than $\frac{1}{50}$th, and each capillary by $\frac{1}{100}$th of its volume, an effect which might be quite imperceptible.

But this is not all. Did the pulse merely become in-distinguishable on account of its division and dispersion among so many capillaries, it ought to be felt again when the blood is once more gathered up into a few large venous trunks. But it is not. The pulse is definitely lost at the capillaries. There is, under ordinary circumstances, no pulse whatever in the veins, except sometimes a backward pulse from the heart along the great venous trunks; but this is quite another matter.

61. Cause of a Steady Capillary Flow.—This actual loss, or rather transformation of the pulse, is effected by means of the elasticity of the arterial walls, in the following manner:

In the first place, it must be borne in mind that, owing to the minute size of the capillaries and small arteries, the amount of friction taking place in their channels when the blood is passing through them is very great; in other words, they offer a very great resistance to the passage of the blood.

The consequence of this is, that the blood cannot get through the capillaries, in spite of the fact that their total area is so much greater than that of the aorta, into the veins so fast as it is thrown into the arteries by the heart. The whole arterial system, therefore, becomes over-distended with blood.

Now, we know by experiment that, under such conditions as these, an elastic tube has the power, if long enough and elastic enough, to change a jerked impulse into a continuous flow. If a syringe (or one of the elastic bottles now so frequently in use) be fastened to one end of a long glass tube, and water be pumped through the tube, it will flow from the far end in jerks, corresponding to the jerks of the syringe. This will be the case whether the tube be quite open at the far end, or drawn out to a fine point so as to offer great resistance to the outflow of the water. The glass tube is a rigid tube, and there is no elasticity to

be brought into play.   If now a long India-rubber tube be
substituted for the glass tube, it will be found to act differ-
ently, according as the opening at the far end is wide or
narrow.

If it is wide, the water flows out in jerks, nearly as distinct as those from the glass tube.   There is little resistance to the flow, little distention of the India-rubber tube,
little elasticity brought into play.

If, however, the opening be narrowed, as by fastening
to it a stopcock or a glass tube drawn to a point, or if a
piece of sponge be thrust into the end of the tube; if, in
fact, in any way resistance be offered to the outflow of the
water, the tube becomes distended, its elasticity is brought
into play, and the water flows out from the end, not in
jerks but in a stream, which is more and more completely
continuous the longer and more elastic the tube.

Substitute for the syringe the heart, for the stopcock
or sponge the capillaries and small arteries, for the India-
rubber tube the whole arterial system, and you have exactly the same result in the living body.   Through the
action of the elastic arterial walls the separate jets from
the heart are blended into one continuous stream.   The
whole force of each blow of the heart is not at once spent
in driving a quantity of blood out of the capillaries ; a part
only is thus spent, the rest goes to distend the elastic arteries.   But, during the interval between that beat and
the next, the distended arteries are narrowing again, by
virtue of their elasticity, and so are pressing the blood on
into the capillaries with as much force as they were themselves distended by the heart.   Then comes another beat,
and the same process is repeated.   At each stroke the
elastic arteries shelter the capillaries from part of the sudden blow, and then quietly and steadily pass on that part
of the blow to the capillaries during the interval between
the strokes.

The larger the amount of elastic arterial wall thus

brought into play, i. e., the greater the distance from the heart, the greater is the fraction of each heart's stroke which is thus converted into a steady elastic pressure between the beats. Thus the pulse becomes less and less marked the farther you go from the heart; any given length of the arterial system, so to speak, being sheltered by the lengths between it and the heart.

Every inch of the arterial system may, in fact, be considered as converting a small fraction of the heart's jerk into a steady pressure, and when all these fractions are summed up together in the total length of the arterial system no trace of the jerk is left.

As the effect of each systole becomes diminished in the smaller vessels by the causes above mentioned, that of this constant pressure becomes more obvious, and gives rise to a steady passage of the fluid from the arteries towards the veins. In this way, in fact, the arteries perform the same functions as the air-reservoir of a fire-engine, which converts the jerking impulse given by the pumps into the steady flow of the delivery-hose.

62, Velocity of the Blood Current.—Such is the general result of the mechanical conditions of the organs of the circulation combined with the rhythmical activity of the heart. This activity drives the fluid contained in these organs out of the heart into the arteries, thence to the capillaries, and from them through the veins back to the heart. And, in the course of these operations, it gives rise, incidentally, to the beating of the heart, the sounds of the heart, and the pulse.

It has been found, by experiment, that in the horse it takes about half a minute for any substance, as, for instance, a chemical body, whose presence in the blood can easily be recognized, to comple the circuit, ex. gr., to pass from the jugular vein down through the right side of the heart, the lungs, the left side of the heart, up through the arteries of the head and neck, and so back to the jugular vein.

By far the greater portion of this half-minute is taken up by the passage through the capillaries, where the blood moves, it is estimated, at the rate only of about one and a half inch in a *minute*, whereas through the carotid artery of a dog it flies along at the rate of about ten inches in a *second*.

Of course, to complete the circuit of the circulation, a blood-corpuscle need not have to go through so much as half of an inch of capillaries in either the lungs or any of the tissues of the body.

Inasmuch as the force which drives the blood on is (putting the other comparatively slight helps on one side) the beat of the heart and that alone, however much it may be modified, as we have seen, in character, it is obvious that the velocity with which the blood moves must be greatest in the aorta and diminish towards the capillaries.

For with each branching of the arteries the total area of the arterial system is increased, the total width of the capillary tubes, if they were all put together side by side, being very much greater than that of the aorta. Hence the blood, or a corpuscle, for instance, of the blood being driven by the same force, viz., the heart's beat, over the whole body, must pass much more rapidly through the aorta than through the capillary system or any part of that system.

It is not that the greater friction in any capillary causes the blood to flow more slowly there and there only. The resistance caused by the friction in the capillaries is thrown back upon the aorta, which indeed feels the resistance of the whole vascular system; and it is this total resistance which has to be overcome by the heart before the blood can move on at all.

The blood driven everywhere by the same force simply moves more and more slowly as it passes into wider and wider channels. When it is in the capillaries it is slowest; after escaping from the capillaries, as the veins unite into larger and larger trunks, and hence as the total venous area is getting less and less, the blood moves again faster and faster for just the same reason that in the arteries it moved slower and slower.

A very similar case is that of a river widening out in a plain into a lake and then contracting into a narrow stream again. The water is driven by one force throughout (that of gravity). The current is much slower in the lake than in the narrower river either before or behind.

SECTION IV.—*The General Circulation.*

63. The Course of the Circulation.—It is now necessary to trace the exact course of the circulation as a whole. And we may conveniently commence with a portion of the blood contained at any moment in the right auricle. The contraction of the right auricle drives that fluid into the right ventricle; the ventricle then contracts and forces it into the pulmonary artery; from hence it passes into the capillaries of the lungs. Leaving these, it returns by the four pulmonary veins to the left auricle; and the contraction of the left auricle drives it into the left ventricle.

The systole of the left ventricle forces the blood into the aorta. The branches of the aorta convey it into all parts of the body except the lungs; and from the capillaries of all these parts, except from those of the intestines and certain other viscera in the abdomen, it is conveyed, by vessels which gradually unite into larger and larger trunks, into either the superior or the inferior *vena cava*, which carry it to the right auricle once more.

But the blood brought to the capillaries of the stomach and intestines, spleen, and pancreas, is gathered into veins which unite into a single trunk—the *vena portæ*. The vena portæ distributes its blood to the liver, mingling with that supplied to the capillaries of the same organ by the hepatic artery. From these capillaries it is conveyed by small veins, which unite into a large trunk—the *hepatic vein,* which opens into the inferior vena cava. The flow of the blood from the abdominal viscera, through the liver, to the hepatic vein, is called the *portal circulation.*

The heart itself is supplied with blood by the two *coronary arteries* which spring from the root of the aorta just above two of the semilunar valves. The blood from the capillaries of the heart is carried back by the coronary vein, not to either vena cava, but to the right auricle. The opening of the coronary vein is protected by a valve, so as to prevent the right auricle from driving the venous blood which it contains back into the vessels of the heart.

64. Routes of the Travelling Blood-Particles.—Thus, the *shortest possible course* which any particle of the blood can take, in order to pass from one side of the heart to the other, is to leave the aorta by one of the coronary arteries, and return to the right auricle by the coronary vein. And, in order to pass through the *greatest possible number of capillaries* and return to the point from which it started, a particle of blood must leave the heart by the aorta and traverse the arteries which supply the alimentary canal, spleen, and pancreas. It then enters, firstly, the capillaries of these organs; secondly, the capillaries of the liver; and, thirdly, after passing through the right side of the heart, the capillaries of the lungs, from which it returns to the left side and eventually to the aorta.

Furthermore, from what has been said respecting the lymphatic system, it follows that any particle of matter which enters a lacteal of the intestine, will reach the right auricle by the superior cava, after passing through the lymph capillaries and channels of sundry lymphatic glands; while any thing which enters the adjacent blood-capillary in the wall of the intestine will reach the right auricle by the inferior cava, after passing through the blood-capillaries of the liver.

65. Nervous Control of the Circulation.—It has been shown above (40) that the small arteries may be directly

affected by the nervous system, which controls the state
of contraction of their muscular walls, and so regulates
their calibre. The effect of this power of the nervous system is to give it a certain control over the circulation in
particular spots, and to produce such a·state of affairs
that, although the force of the heart and the general condition of the vessels remain the same, the state of the circulation may be very different in different localities.

66. Explanation of Blushing.—*Blushing* is a purely
local modification of the circulation of this kind, and it will
be instructive to consider how a blush is brought about.
An emotion—sometimes pleasurable, sometimes painful—
takes possession of the mind : thereupon a hot flush is felt,
the skin grows red, and, according to the intensity of the
emotion, these changes are confined to the cheeks only, or
extend to the "roots of the hair," or "all over."

What is the cause of these changes? The blood is a
red and a hot fluid; the skin reddens and grows hot, because its vessels contain an increased quantity of this red
and hot fluid; and its vessels contain more, because the
small arteries suddenly dilate, the natural moderate contraction of their muscles being superseded by a state of
relaxation. In other words, the action of the nerves which
cause this muscular contraction is suspended.

On the other hand, in many people, extreme terror
causes the skin to grow cold, and the face to appear pale
and pinched. Under these circumstances, in fact, the
supply of blood to the skin is greatly diminished, in consequence of an excessive stimulation of the nerves of the
small arteries, which causes them to contract and so to cut
off the supply of blood more or less completely.

67. Experimental Proof of this.—That this is the real
state of the case may be proved experimentally upon rab-
bits. These animals may be made to blush artificially. If,
in a rabbit, the sympathetic nerve, which sends branches
to the vessels of the head, is cut, the ear of the rabbit,

which is covered by so delicate an integument that the changes in the vessels can be readily perceived, at once blushes. That is to say, the vessels dilate, fill with blood, and the ear becomes red and hot. The reason of this is, that when the sympathetic is cut, the nervous stimulus which is ordinarily sent along its branches is interrupted, and the muscles of the small vessels, which were slightly contracted, become altogether relaxed.

And now it is quite possible to produce pallor and cold in the rabbit's ear. To do this it is only necessary to irritate the cut end of the sympathetic which remains connected with the vessels. The nerve then becomes excited, so that the muscular fibres of the vessels are thrown into a violent state of contraction, which diminishes their calibre so much that the blood can hardly make its way through them. Consequently, the ear becomes pale and cold.

68. Relation of this Nervous Control to Disease. — The practical importance of this local control exerted by the nervous system is immense. When exposure to cold gives a man catarrh, or inflammation of the lungs, or diarrhœa, or some still more serious affection of the abdominal viscera, the disease is brought about through the nervous system. The impression made by the cold on the skin is conveyed to the nervous centres, and so influences the *vasomotor* nerves (as the nerves which govern the walls of the vessels are called) of the organ affected as to cause their partial paralysis, and produce that state of *congestion* (or undue distention of the vessels) which so commonly ends in inflammation. (*See* 327.)

69. Nervous Control over the Heart. — Is the heart, in like manner, under the contol of the central nervous system ?

As we all know, it is not under the direct influence of the will, but every one is no less familiar with the fact that the actions of the heart are wonderfully affected by all forms of emotion. Men and women often faint, and have sometimes been killed by sudden and violent joy or sorrow; and, when they faint or die in this way, they do so because the perturbation of the brain gives rise to a something which arrests the heart as dead as you stop a stopwatch with a spring. On the other hand, other emotions cause that extreme rapidity and violence of action which we call palpitation.

Now, there are three sets of nerves in the heart: one set are supplied by *ganglia*, or masses of nerve-cells, in its substance; another set come from the *sympathetic* nerve; a third set are branches of a remarkable nerve, which proceeds straight from the brain, and is called the *pneumogastric* nerve. There is every reason to believe that the regular rhythmical succession of the ordinary contractions of the heart depends upon the ganglia lodged in its substance. At any rate, it is certain that these movements depend neither on the sympathetic, nor on the pneumogastric, since they go on as well when the heart is removed from the body.

In the next place, there is much reason to believe that the influence which increases the rapidity of the heart's action is exerted through the sympathetic.

And, lastly, it is quite certain that the influence which arrests the heart's action is supplied by the pneumogastric. This may be demonstrated in animals, such as frogs, with great ease.

70. The Circulation directly observed. — If a frog be pithed, or its brain destroyed, so as to obliterate all sensibility, the animal will continue to live, and its circulation will go on perfectly well for an indefinite period. The body may be laid open without causing pain or other disturbance, and then the heart will be observed beating with great regularity. It is possible to make the heart move a long index backwards and forwards; and if frog and index are covered with a glass shade, the air under which is kept moist, the index will vibrate with great steadiness for a couple of days.

It is easy to adjust to the frog thus prepared a contriv-
ance by which electrical shocks may be sent through the
pneumogastric nerves, so as to irritate them. The moment

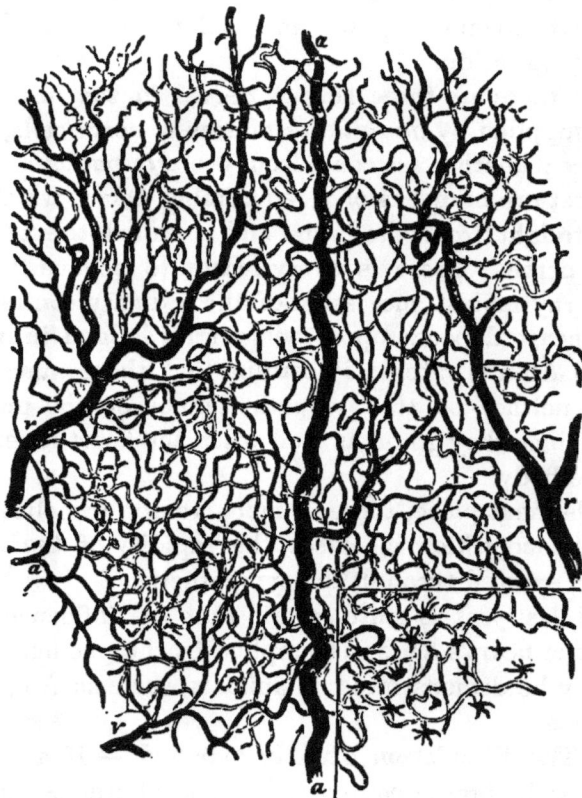

FIG. 18.

Portion of the web of a frog's foot seen under a low magnifying power, the blood-vessels only being represented except in the corner of the field, where in the portion
marked off the pigment spots are also drawn.

a., small arteries; *v.*, small veins: the minute tubes joining the arteries and the veins
are the capillaries. The arrows denote the direction of the circulation. The larger
artery running straight up in the middle line breaks up into capillaries at points higher
up than can be shown in the drawing.

this is done the index stops dead, and the heart will be
found quiescent, with relaxed and distended walls. After
a little time the influence of the pneumogastric passes off,

the heart recommences its work as vigorously as before, and the index vibrates through the same arc as formerly. With careful management, this experiment may be repeated very many times; and, after every arrest by the irritation of the pneumogastric, the heart resumes its work.

71. Proof of the Circulation in Man. — The evidence that the blood circulates in man, although perfectly conclusive, is almost all indirect. The most important points in the evidence are as follows:

In the first place, the disposition and structure of the organs of circulation, and more especially the arrangement of the various valves, will not, as was shown by Harvey, permit the blood to flow in any other direction than in the one described above. Moreover, we can easily with a syringe inject a fluid from the vena cava, for instance, through the right side of the heart, the lungs, the left side of the heart, the arteries, and capillaries, back to the vena cava; but not the other way. In the second place, we know that in the living body the blood is continually flowing in the arteries towards the capillaries, because when an artery is tied, in a living body, it swells up and pulsates on the side of the ligature nearest the heart, whereas on the other side it becomes empty, and the tissues supplied by the artery become pale from the want of a supply of blood to their capillaries. And when we cut an artery the blood is pumped out in jerks from the cut end nearest the heart, whereas little or no blood comes from the other end. When, however, we tie a vein the state of things is reversed, the swelling taking place on the side farthest from the heart, etc., etc., showing that in the veins the blood flows from the capillaries to the heart.

But certain of the lower animals, the whole, or parts, of the body of which are transparent, readily afford direct proof of the circulation, the blood visibly rushing from the arteries into the capillaries, and from the capillaries into the veins, so long as the animal is alive and its heart is at work. The animal in which the circulation can be most conveniently observed is the frog. The web between its

FIG. 19.

VERY SMALL PORTION OF FIG. 18, VERY HIGHLY MAGNIFIED.

A., walls of capillaries; *B.*, tissue of web lying between the capillaries; *C.*, cells of epidermis covering web (these are only shown in the right-hand and lower part of the field; in the other parts of the field the focus of the microscope lies below the epidermis); *D.*, nuclei of these epidermic cells; *E.*, pigment-cells contracted, not partially expanded as in Fig. 18; *F.*, red blood-corpuscle (oval in the frog) passing along capillary—nucleus not visible; *G.*, another corpuscle squeezing its way through a capillary, the canal of which is smaller than its own transverse diameter; *H.*, another bending as it slides round a corner; *K.*, corpuscle in capillary seen through the epidermis; *I.*, white blood-corpuscle.

toes is very transparent, and the particles suspended in its blood are so large that they can be readily seen as they slip swiftly along with the stream of blood, when the toes are fastened out, and the intervening web is examined under even a low magnifying power (Figs. 18 and 19).

CHAPTER III.

THE BLOOD AND THE LYMPH.

SECTION I.—*The Microscopical Elements of the Blood.*

72. How to examine it.—In order to become properly acquainted with the characters of the blood, it is necessary to examine it with a microscope magnifying at least three or four hundred diameters. Provided with this instrument, a hand-lens, and some slips of thick and thin glass, the student will be enabled to follow the present chapter.

The most convenient mode of obtaining small quantities of blood for examination is to twist a piece of string, pretty tightly, round the middle of the last joint of the middle, or ring-finger, of the left hand. The end of the finger will immediately swell a little, and become darker colored, in consequence of the obstruction to the return of the blood in the veins caused by the ligature. When in this condition, if it be slightly pricked with a sharp clean needle (an operation which causes hardly any pain), a good-sized drop of blood will at once exude. Let it be deposited on one of the slips of thick glass, and covered lightly and gently with a piece of the thin glass, so as to spread it out evenly into a thin layer. Let a second slide receive another drop, and, to keep it from drying, let it be put under an inverted watch-glass or wine-glass, with a bit of wet blotting-paper inside. Let a third drop be dealt with in

4

the same way, a few granules of common salt being first added to the drop.

73. Its Appearance when magnified.—To the naked eye the layer of blood upon the first slide will appear of a pale-reddish color, and quite clear and homogeneous. But on viewing it with even a pocket-lens its apparent homogeneity will disappear, and it will look like a mixture of excessively fine yellowish-red particles, like sand, or dust, with a watery, almost colorless, fluid. Immediately after the blood is drawn, the particles will appear to be scattered very evenly through the fluid, but by degrees they aggregate into minute patches, and the layer of blood becomes more or less spotty.

The " particles " are what are termed the *corpuscles* of the blood; the nearly colorless fluid in which they are suspended is the *plasma*.

The second slide may now be examined. The drop of blood will be unaltered in form, and may perhaps seem to have undergone no change. But, if the slide be inclined, it will be found that the drop no longer flows; and, indeed, the slide may be inverted without the disturbance of the drop, which has become solidified, and may be removed, with the point of a penknife, as a gelatinous mass. The mass is quite soft and moist, so that this setting, or *coagulation*, of a drop of blood is something very different from its drying.

On the third slide, this process of coagulation will be found not to have taken place, the blood remaining as fluid as it was when it left the body. The salt, therefore, has prevented the coagulation of the blood. Thus this very simple investigation teaches that blood is composed of a nearly colorless plasma, in which many colored corpuscles are suspended; that it has a remarkable power of coagulating; and that this coagulation may be prevented by artificial means, such as the addition of salt.

74. The Blood-Corpuscles.—If, instead of using the hand

lens, the drop of blood on the first slide be placed under
the microscope, the particles, or corpuscles, of the blood
will be found to be bodies with very definite characters,
and of two kinds, called respectively the *red corpuscles* and
the *colorless corpuscles.* The former are much more numerous than the latter, and have a yellowish-red tinge; while
the latter, somewhat larger than the red corpuscles, are, as
their name implies, pale and devoid of coloration.

75. Their Size, Form, and Appearance. — The corpuscles differ also in other and more important respects. The
red corpuscles (Fig. 20) are flattened circular disks, on an

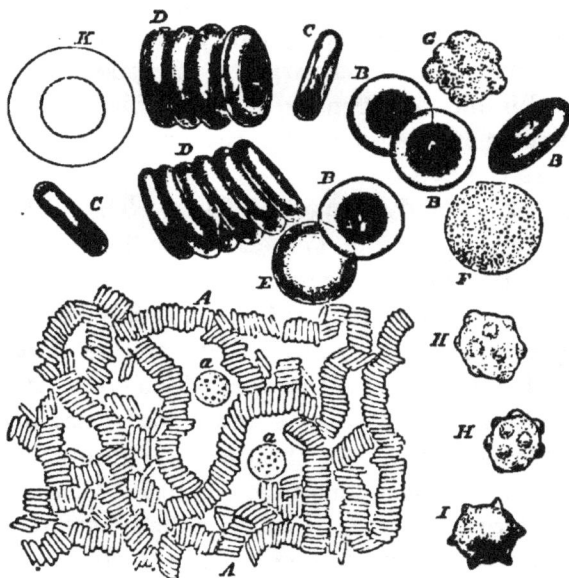

FIG. 20.

RED AND WHITE CORPUSCLES OF THE BLOOD MAGNIFIED.

A. Moderately magnified. The red corpuscles are seen lying in rouleaux; at *a*
and *a* are seen two white corpuscles.
    B. Red corpuscles much more highly magnified, seen in face; *C.,* ditto, seen in pro-
file; *D.,* ditto, in rouleaux, rather more highly magnified; *E.,* a red corpuscle swollen
into a sphere by imbibition of water.
    F. A white corpuscle magnified same as *B.; G.,* ditto, throwing out some blunt
processes; *K.,* ditto, treated with acetic acid, and showing nucleus magnified same
as *D.*
    H. Red corpuscles puckered or crenate all over.
    I. Ditto, at the edge only.

average $\frac{1}{3200}$th of an inch in diameter, and having about one-fourth of that thickness. It follows that rather more than ten millions of them will lie on a space one inch square, and that the volume of each corpuscle does not exceed $\frac{1}{120000000000000}$th of a cubic inch.

The broad faces of the disks are not flat, but somewhat concave, as if they were pushed in towards one another. Hence the corpuscle is thinner in the middle than at the edges, and when viewed under the microscope, by transmitted light, looks clear in the middle and darker at the edges, or dark in the middle and clear at the edges, according to circumstances. When, on the other hand, the disks roll over and present their edges to the eye, they look like rods. All these varieties of appearance may be made intelligible by turning a round biscuit or muffin, bodies similar in shape to the red corpuscles, in various ways before the eye.

76. Structure and Changes of Form.—The red corpuscles are very soft, flexible, and elastic bodies, so that they readily squeeze through apertures and passages narrower than their own diameters, and immediately resume their proper shapes (Fig. 19, *G.H.*). The exterior of each corpuscle is denser than its interior, which contains a semifluid, or quite fluid matter, of a red color, called *hæmoglobin*. By proper processes this may be resolved into an albuminous substance sometimes called *globulin*, and a peculiar coloring matter, which is called *hæmatin*. The interior substance presents no distinct structure.

From the density of the outer as compared with the inner substance of each corpuscle, they are, practically, small flattened bags, or sacs, the form of which may be changed by altering the density of the plasma. Thus, if it be made denser by dissolving saline substances, or sugar, in it, water is drawn from the contents of the corpuscle to the dense plasma, and the corpuscle becomes still more flattened, and very often much wrinkled. On the other hand, if the plasma be diluted with water, the latter forces itself into and dilutes the contents of the corpuscle, causing the latter to swell out, and even become spherical; and, by adding dense and weak solutions alternately, the corpuscles may be made to become successively spheroidal and discoidal.   Exposure to carbonic-acid gas seems to cause the corpuscles to swell out; oxygen gas, on the contrary, appears to flatten them.

77. The Colorless Corpuscles.—The *colorless corpuscles* (Fig. 20, *a a.*, *F. G. K.*) are larger than the red corpuscles, their average diameter being $\frac{1}{2600}$th of an inch.   They are further seen, at a glance, to differ from the red corpuscles by the extreme irregularity of their form, and by their tendency to attach themselves to the glass slide, while the red corpuscles float about and tumble freely over one another.

A still more remarkable feature of the colorless corpuscles than the irregularity of their form is the unceasing

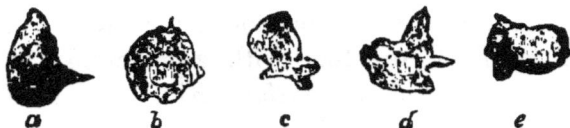

FIG. 21.

SUCCESSIVE FORMS ASSUMED BY COLORLESS CORPUSCLES OF HUMAN BLOOD.
(Magnified about six hundred diameters.)

The interval between the forms *a, b, c, d,* was a minute; between *d* and *e* two minutes; so that the whole series of changes from *a* to *e* took five minutes.

variation of shape which they exhibit.   The form of a red corpuscle is changed only by influences from without, such as pressure, or the like; that of the colorless corpuscle is undergoing constant alteration, as the result of changes taking place in its own substance.   To see these changes well, a microscope, with a magnifying power of five or six hundred diameters, is requisite; and, even then, they are so gradual that the best way to ascertain their existence is to make a drawing of a given colorless corpuscle at intervals of a minute or two. This is what has been done with the corpuscle represented in Fig. 21, in which *a* represents the form of the corpuscle when first observed; *b*, its form a minute afterwards; *c*, that at the end of the second; *d*, that at the end of the third; and *e*, that at the end of the fifth minute.

Careful watching of a colorless corpuscle, in fact, shows that every part of its surface is constantly changing—undergoing active contraction, or being passively dilated by the contraction of other parts. It exhibits *contractility* in its lowest and most primitive form.

78. Structure and Contractility.—While they are thus living and active, no correct notion can be formed of the structure of the colorless corpuscles. By diluting the blood with water, or, still better, with water acidulated with acetic acid, the corpuscles are killed, and become distended, so that their real nature is shown. They are then seen to be spheroidal bags, or sacs, with very thin walls; and to contain in their interior a fluid which is either clear or granular, together with a spheroidal vesicular body, which is called the *nucleus* (Fig. 20, *K*). It sometimes, though very rarely, happens that the nucleus has a red tint.

The sac-like colorless corpuscle, with its nucleus, is what is called a *nucleated cell.* It will be observed that it lives in a free state in the plasma of the blood, and that it exhibits an independent contractility. In fact, except that it is dependent for the conditions of its existence upon the plasma, it might be compared to one of those simple organisms which are met with in stagnant water, and are called *Amœbœ.*

79. Derivation of the Corpuscles.—That the red corpuscles are in some way or other derived from the colorless corpuscles may be regarded as certain: but the steps of the process have not been made out with perfect certainty.

There is very great reason, however, for believing that the red corpuscle is simply the nucleus of the colorless corpuscle somewhat enlarged; flattened from side to side; changed, by development within its interior of a red coloring-matter; and set free by the bursting of the sac or wall of the colorless corpuscle. In other words, the red corpuscle is a free nucleus.

The origin of the colorless corpuscles themselves is not certainly determined; but it is highly probable that they are constituent cells of particular parts of the solid substance of the body which have been detached and carried into the blood, and that this process is chiefly effected in what are called the *ductless glands* (*see* 155), from whence the detached cells pass, as *lymph-corpuscles*, directly, or indirectly, into the blood.

The following facts are of importance in their bearing on the relation between the different kinds of corpuscles:

(*a*) The invertebrate animals,[1] which have true blood-corpuscles, possess only such as resemble the colorless corpuscles of man.

(*b*) The lowest vertebrate animal, the lancelot (*Amphioxus*), possesses only colorless corpuscles; and the very young embryos [2] of all vertebrate animals have only colorless and nucleated corpuscles.

(*c*) All the vertebrated animals, the young of which are born from eggs,[3] have two kinds of corpuscles—colorless corpuscles, like those of man, and large red-colored corpuscles, which are generally oval, and further differ from those of man in presenting a nucleus. In fact, they are simply the colorless corpuscles enlarged and colored.

(*d*) All animals which suckle their young (or what are called mammals) have, like man, two kinds of corpuscles;

---

[1] Invertebrate animals are animals devoid of backbones, such as insects, snails, sea-anemones, etc. Vertebrate animals are fishes, amphibia, reptiles, birds, and mammals.

[2] An embryo is the rudimentary unborn young of any creature.

[3] These are fishes, amphibia, reptiles, and birds.

colorless ones, and small colored corpuscles — the latter being always flattened, and devoid of any nucleus. They are usually circular, but in the camel tribe they are elliptical. And it is worthy of remark that, in these animals, the nuclei of the colorless corpuscles become elliptical.

(*e*) The colorless corpuscles differ much less from one another in size and form, in the vertebrate series, than the colored. The latter are smallest in the little musk-deer, in which animal they are about a quarter as large as those of a man. On the other hand, the red corpuscles are largest in the *Amphibia* (or frogs and salamanders), in some of which animals they are ten times as long as in man.

80. Changes attending the Death of the Blood.—As the blood dies, its several constituents, which have now been described, undergo marked changes.

The *colorless corpuscles* lose their contractility, but otherwise undergo little alteration. They tend to cohere neither with one another, nor with the red corpuscles, but adhere to the glass plate on which they are placed.

It is quite otherwise with the *red corpuscles*, which at first, as has been said, float about and roll, or slide, over each other quite freely. After a short time (the length of which varies in different persons, but usually amounts to two or three minutes), they seem, as it were, to become sticky, and tend to cohere; and this tendency increases until, at length, the great majority of them become applied face to face, so as to form long series, like rolls of coin. The end of one roll cohering with the sides of another, a net-work of various degrees of closeness is produced (Fig. 20, *A*.).

The corpuscles remain thus coherent for a certain length of time, but eventually separate, and float freely again. The addition of a little water, or dilute acids or saline solutions, will at once cause the rolls to break up.

It is from this running of the corpuscles together into

patches of net-work that the change noted above in the appearances of the layer of blood, viewed with a lens, arises. So long as the corpuscles are separate, the sandy appearance lasts; but when they run together, the layer appears patchy or spotted.

The red corpuscles rarely, if ever, all run together into rolls, some always remaining free in the meshes of the net. In contact with air, or if subjected to pressure, many of the red corpuscles become covered with little knobs, so as to look like minute mulberries—an appearance which has been mistaken for a breaking up, or spontaneous division, of the corpuscles (Fig. 20, *H.K.*).

81. **Blood-Crystals.**—There is a still more remarkable change which the red blood-corpuscles occasionally undergo. Under certain circumstances, the peculiar red substance which forms the chief mass of their contents, and which has been called *hæmoglobin* (from its readily breaking up into globulin and hæmatin, 76), separates in a crystalline form. In man, these crystals have the shape of prisms; in other animals they take other forms. Human blood crystallizes with difficulty, but that of the Guinea-pig, rat, or dog, much more easily. The best way to see these *blood-crystals* is to take a little rat's blood, from which the fibrin has been removed, shake it up with a little ether, and let it stand in the cold for some hours. A sediment will form at the bottom, which, when examined with the microscope, will be found to consist of long, narrow crystals. Crystallization is much assisted by adding after the ether a small quantity of alcohol.

SECTION II.—*Properties of the Blood.*

82. **Its Coagulation.**—When the layer of blood has been drawn ten or fifteen minutes, the plasma will be seen to be no longer clear. It then exhibits multitudes of extremely delicate filaments of a substance called *Fibrin*, which have been deposited from it, and which traverse it in all direc-

tions, uniting with one another and with the corpuscles, and binding the whole into a semi-solid mass.

It is this deposition of fibrin which is the cause of the apparent solidification, or coagulation, of the drop upon the second slide; but the phenomena of coagulation, which are of very great importance, cannot be properly understood until the behavior of the blood, when drawn in larger quantity than a drop, has been studied.

83. Separation of its Constituents.—When, by the ordinary process of opening a vein with a lancet, a quantity of blood is collected into a basin, it is at first perfectly fluid: but in a very few minutes it becomes, through coagulation, a jelly-like mass, so solid that the basin may be turned upside-down without any of the blood being spilt. At first the clot is a uniform red jelly, but very soon drops of a clear, yellowish, watery-looking fluid make their appearance on the surface of the clot, and on the sides of the basin. These drops increase in number, and run together, and after a while it has become apparent that the originally uniform jelly has separated into two very different constituents — the one a clear, yellowish liquid; the other a red, semi-solid mass, which lies in the liquid, and at the surface is paler in color and firmer than in its deeper part.

The liquid is called the *serum ;* the semi-solid mass the clot, or *crassamentum.* Now, the clot obviously contains the corpuscles of the blood, bound together by some other substance; and this last, if a small part of the clot be examined microscopically, will be found to be that fibrous-looking matter, *fibrin*, which has been seen forming in the thin layer of blood. Thus the clot is equivalent to the corpuscles *plus* the fibrin of the plasma, while the serum is the plasma *minus* the fibrinous elements which it contained.

84. The Buffy-Coat.—The corpuscles of the blood are slightly heavier than the plasma, and therefore, when the blood is drawn, they sink very slowly towards the bottom. Hence the upper part of the clot contains fewer corpuscles, and is lighter in color, than the lower part—there being fewer corpuscles left in the upper layer of plasma for the fibrin to catch when it sets. And there are some conditions of the blood in which the corpuscles run together much more rapidly and in denser masses than usual. Hence they more readily overcome the resistance of the plasma to their falling, just as feathers stuck together in masses fall much more rapidly through the air than the same feathers when loose. When this is the case, the upper stratum of plasma is quite free from red corpuscles before the fibrin forms in it; and, consequently, the uppermost layer of the clot is nearly white: it receives the name of the *buffy-coat*.

After the clot is formed, the fibrin shrinks and squeezes out much of the serum contained within its meshes; and, other things being equal, it contracts the more the fewer corpuscles there are in the way of its shrinking. Hence, when the buffy-coat is formed, it usually contracts so much as to give the clot a cup-like upper surface.

Thus the buffy-coat is fibrin naturally separated from the red corpuscles; the same separation may be effected, artificially, by whipping the blood with twigs as soon as it is drawn, until its coagulation is complete. Under these circumstances the fibrin will collect upon the twigs, and a red fluid will be left behind, consisting of the serum *plus* the red corpuscles, and many of the colorless ones.

85. Conditions influencing Coagulation. — The coagulation of the blood is hastened, retarded, or temporarily prevented, by many circumstances.

(*a*) *Temperature.*—A high temperature accelerates the coagulation of the blood; a low one retards it very greatly; and some experimenters have stated that, when kept at a sufficiently low temperature, it does not coagulate at all.

(*b*) *The Addition of Soluble Matter to the Blood.*—Many

saline substances, and more especially sulphate of soda and common salt, dissolved in the blood in sufficient quantity, prevent its coagulation ; but coagulation sets in when water is added, so as to dilute the saline solution.

(c) *Contact with Living or not Living Matter.*—Contact with not living matter promotes the coagulation of the blood. Thus, blood drawn into a basin begins to coagulate first where it is in contact with the sides of the basin; and a wire introduced into a living vein will become coated with fibrin, although perfectly fluid blood surrounds it.

On the other hand, direct contact with living matter retards, or altogether prevents, the coagulation of the blood. Thus blood remains fluid for a very long time in a portion of a vein which is tied at each end.

The heart of a turtle remains alive for a lengthened period (many hours or even days) after it is extracted from the body; and, so long as it remains alive, the blood contained in it will not coagulate, though, if a portion of the same blood be removed from the heart, it will coagulate in a few minutes.

Blood taken from the body of the turtle, and kept from coagulating by cold for some time, may be poured into the separated, but still living, heart, and then will not coagulate.

Freshly-deposited fibrin acts somewhat like living matter, coagulable blood remaining fluid for a long time in tubes coated with such fibrin.

86. Nature of the Process of Coagulation.—The coagulation of the blood is an altogether physico chemical process, dependent upon the properties of certain of the constituents of the plasma, apart from the vitality of that fluid. This is proved by the fact that if blood-plasma be prevented from coagulating by cold, and greatly diluted, a current of carbonic acid passed through it will throw down a white powdery substance. If this white substance be dissolved in a weak solution of common salt, or in an extremely weak solution of potash or soda, it, after a while, coagulates, and yields a clot of true pure fibrin. It would be absurd to suppose that a substance which has been precipitated from its solution, and redissolved, still remains alive.

There are reasons for believing that this white substance consists of two constituents of very similar composition, which exist separately in living blood, and the union of which is the cause of the act of coagulation. These reasons may be briefly stated thus: The pericardium and other serous cavities in the body contain a clear fluid, which has exuded from the blood-vessels, and contains the elements of the blood without the blood-corpuscles. This fluid sometimes coagulates spontaneously, as the blood-plasma would do, but very often shows no disposition to spontaneous coagulation. When this is the case, it may nevertheless be made to coagulate, and yield a true fibrinous clot, by adding to it a little serum of blood.

Now, if serum of blood be largely diluted with water, and a current of carbonic-acid gas be passed through it, a white powdery substance will be thrown down; this, redissolved in a dilute saline, or extremely dilute alkaline solution, will, when added to the pericardial fluid, produce even as good a clot as that obtained with the original serum.

This white substance has been called *globulin*. It exists not only in serum, but also, though in smaller quantities, in connective tissue, in the cornea, in the humors of the eye, and in some other fluids of the body.

It possesses the same general chemical properties as the albuminous substance which enters so largely into the the composition of the red corpuscles (76), and hence, at present, bears the same name. But when treated with chemical reagents, even with such as do not produce any appreciable effect on its chemical composition, it very speedily loses its peculiar power of causing serous fluids to coagulate. For instance, this power is destroyed by an excess of alkali, or by the presence of acids.

Hence, though there is great reason to believe that the *fibrino-plastic globulin* (as it has been called) which exists in serum does really come from the red corpuscles, the globulin which is obtained in large quantities from these bodies, by the use of powerful reagents, has no coagulating effect at all on pericardial or other serous fluids.

Though globulin is so susceptible of change when in solution, it may be dried at a low temperature and kept in the form of powder for many months, without losing its coagulating power.

Thus *globulin*, added, under proper conditions, to serous effusion, is a coagulator of that effusion, giving rise to the development of fibrin in it.

It does so by its interaction with a substance contained in the serous effusion, which can be extracted by itself, and then plays just the same part towards a solution of globulin, as globulin does towards its solution. This substance has been called *fibrinogen*. It is exceedingly like globulin, and may be thrown down from serous exudation by carbonic acid, just as globulin may be precipitated from the serum of the blood. When redissolved in an alkaline solution, and added to any fluid containing globulin, it acts as a coagulator of that fluid, and gives rise to the development of a clot of fibrin in it. In accordance with what has just been stated, serum of blood which has completely coagulated may be kept in one vessel, and pericardial fluid in another, for an indefinite period, if spontaneous decomposition be prevented, without the coagulation of either. But let them be mixed, and coagulation sets in.

Thus it seems to be clear, that the coagulation of the blood, and the formation of fibrin, are caused primarily by the interaction of two substances (or two modifications of the same substance), *globulin* or *fibrinoplastin* and *fibrinogen*, the former of which may be obtained from the serum of the blood, and from some tissues of the body; while the latter is known, at present, only in the plasma of the blood, of the lymph, and of the chyle, and in fluids derived from them.

87. The Physical Qualities of the Blood.—The proverb that "blood is thicker than water" is literally true, as the blood is not only "thickened" by the corpuscles, of which it has been calculated that no fewer than 70,000,000,000 (eighty times the number of the human population of the globe) are contained in a cubic inch, but is rendered slightly viscid by the solid matters dissolved in the plasma. The blood is thus rendered heavier than water, its specific gravity being about 1055. In other words, twenty cubic inches of blood have about the same weight as twenty-one cubic inches of water.

The corpuscles are heavier than the plasma, and their volume is usually somewhat less than that of the plasma. Of colorless corpuscles there are usually not more than three or four for every thousand of red corpuscles; but the number varies very much, increasing shortly after food is taken, and diminishing in the intervals between meals.

The blood is hot, its temperature being about 100° Fahr.

88. The Chemical Composition of the Blood.—Considered chemically, the blood is an alkaline fluid, consisting of water, of solid and of gaseous matters.

The proportions of these several constituents vary according to age, sex, and condition, but the following statement holds good on the average :

In every 100 parts of the blood there are 79 parts of water and 21 parts of dry solids; in other words, the water and the solids of the blood stand to one another in about the same proportion as the nitrogen and the oxygen of the air. Roughly speaking, one-quarter of the blood is dry, solid matter; three-quarters water. Of the 21 parts of dry solids, 12 (= $\frac{4}{7}$ths) belong to the corpuscles. The remaining 9 are about two-thirds (6.7 parts = $\frac{2}{3}$ths) albumen (a substance like white of egg, coagulating by heat), and one-third ($=\frac{1}{4}$th of the whole solid matter) a mixture of saline, fatty, and saccharine matters, sundry products of the waste of the body, and fibrin. The quantity of the latter constituent is remarkably small in relation to the conspicuous part it plays in the act of coagulation. Healthy blood, in fact, yields in coagulating not more than from two to four parts in a thousand of its weight of fibrin.

The total quantity of gaseous matter contained in the blood is equal to rather less than half the *volume* of the blood; that is to say, 100 cubic inches of blood will contain rather less than 50 cubic inches of gases. These gaseous matters are carbonic acid, oxygen, and nitrogen; or, in other words, the same gases as those which exist in the atmosphere, but in totally different proportions; for whereas air contains nearly three-fourths nitrogen, one fourth oxygen, and a mere trace of carbonic acid, the average composition of the blood gases is nearly two-thirds carbonic acid, rather less than one-third oxygen, and not one-tenth nitrogen.

It is important to observe that blood contains much more oxygen gas than could be held in solution by pure water at the same temperature and pressure. This power of holding oxygen appears in some way to depend upon the corpuscles, firstly, because mere serum has no greater power of absorbing oxygen than pure water has; and, secondly, because red corpuscles suspended in water instead of serum absorb oxygen very readily. The oxygen thus held by the red corpuscles is readily given up by them for purposes of oxidation, and indeed can be removed from them by means of a mercurial gas-pump. It would appear that the connection between the oxygen and the red corpuscles is of a peculiar nature, being a sort of loose chemical combination with one of their constituents, that constituent being the hæmoglobin; for solutions of hæmoglobin behave towards oxygen exactly as blood does.

The corpuscles differ chemically from the plasma, in

containing a large proportion of the fats and phosphates, all the iron, and almost all the potash, of the blood; while the plasma, on the other hand, contains by far the greater part of the chlorine and the soda.

89. Influence of Age, Sex, and Food, upon the Blood.— The blood of adults contains a larger proportion of solid constituents than that of children, and that of men more than that of women; but the difference of sex is hardly at all exhibited by persons of flabby, or what is called lymphatic, constitution.

Animal diet tends to increase the quantity of the red corpuscles; a vegetable diet and abstinence to diminish them. Bleeding exercises the same influence in a still more marked degree, the quantity of red corpuscles being diminished thereby in a much greater proportion than that of the other solid constituents of the blood.

90. Total Quantity of Blood in the Body. — The total quantity of blood contained in the body varies at different times, and the precise ascertainment of its amount is very difficult. It may probably be estimated, on the average, at not less than one-tenth of the weight of the body.

91. Function of the Blood.—The function of the blood is to supply nourishment to, and take away waste matters from, all parts of the body. It is absolutely essential to the life of every part of the body that it should be in such relation with a current of blood, that matters can pass freely from the blood to it, and from it to the blood, by transudation through the walls of the vessels in which the blood is contained. And this vivifying influence depends upon the corpuscles of the blood. The proof of these statements lies in the following experiments: If the vessels of a limb of a living animal be tied in such a manner as to cut off the supply of blood from the limb, without affecting it in any other way, all the symptoms of death will set in. The limb will grow pale and cold, it will lose its sensibility, and volition will no longer have power over it; it will stiffen, and eventually mortify and decompose.

But, even when the death-stiffening has begun to set in, if the ligatures be removed, and the blood be allowed to flow into the limb, the stiffening speedily ceases, the temperature of the part rises, the sensibility of the skin returns, the will regains power over the muscles, and, in short, the part returns to its normal condition.

If, instead of simply allowing the blood of the animal operated upon to flow again, such blood, deprived of its fibrin by whipping, but containing its corpuscles, be artificially passed through the vessels, it will be found as effectual a restorative as entire blood; while, on the other hand, the serum (which is equivalent to whipped blood without its corpuscles) has no such effect.

It is not necessary that the blood thus artificially injected should be that of the subject of the experiment. Men, or dogs, bled to apparent death, may be at once and effectually revived by filling their veins with blood taken from another man, or dog; an operation which is known by the name of *transfusion*.

Nor is it absolutely necessary for the success of this operation that the blood used in transfusion should belong to an animal of the same species. The blood of a horse will permanently revive an ass, and, speaking generally, the blood of one animal may be replaced without injurious effects by that of another closely-allied species; while that of a very different animal will be more or less injurious, and may even cause immediate death.

92. The Lymph.—The *Lymph*, which fills the lymphatic vessels, is, like the blood, an alkaline fluid, consisting of a plasma and corpuscles, and coagulates by the separation of fibrin from the plasma. The lymph differs from the blood in its corpuscles being all of the colorless kind, and in the very small proportion of its solid constituents, which amount to only about five per cent. of its weight. Lymph may, in fact, be regarded as blood *minus* its red corpuscles, and diluted with water, so as to be somewhat less dense than the serum of blood, which contains about eight per cent. of solid matters.

A quantity of fluid equal to that of the blood is probably poured into the blood, daily, from the lymphatic system. This fluid is in great measure the mere overflow of the blood itself—plasma which has exuded from the capillaries into the tissues, and which has not been taken up again into the venous current; the rest is due to the absorption of chyle from the alimentary canal.

CHAPTER IV.

RESPIRATION.

SECTION I.—*Arterial and Venous Blood.*

93. High Complexity of the Blood.—The blood, the general nature and properties of which have been described in the preceding chapter, is the highly-complex product, not of any one organ or constituent of the body, but of all. Many of its features are doubtless given to it by its intrinsic and proper structural elements, the corpuscles; but the general character of the blood is also profoundly affected by the circumstance, that every other part of the body takes something from the blood and pours something into it. The blood may be compared to a river, the nature of the contents of which is largely determined by that of the head-waters, and by that of the animals which swim in it; but which is also very much affected by the soil over which it flows, by the water-weeds which cover its banks, and by affluents from distant regions; by irrigation-works which are supplied from it, and by drain-pipes which flow into it.

94. Blood rendered Venous in the Capillaries.—One of

the most remarkable and important of the changes effected
in the blood is that which results, in most parts of the
body, from its simply passing through capillaries, or, in
other words, through vessels the walls of which are thin
enough to permit a free exchange between the blood and
the fluids which permeate the adjacent tissues (36).

Thus, if blood be taken from the artery which supplies
a limb, it will be found to have a bright-scarlet color;
while blood drawn, at the same time, from the vein of the
limb, will be of a purplish hue, so dark that it is commonly called " black blood." And, as this contrast is met
with in the contents of the arteries and veins in general
(except the pulmonary artery and veins), the scarlet blood
is commonly known as *arterial*, and the black blood as
venous. This conversion of arterial into venous blood takes
place in most parts of the body, while life persists. Thus,
if a limb be cut off and scarlet blood be forced into its
arteries by a syringe, it will issue from the veins as black
blood.

95. Difference between Arterial and Venous Blood.—
When specimens of venous and of arterial blood are subjected to chemical examination, the differences presented
by their solid and fluid constituents are found to be very
small and inconstant. As a rule, there is rather more
water in arterial blood, and rather more fatty matter. But
the gaseous contents of the two kinds of blood differ widely
in the proportion which the carbonic-acid gas bears to the
oxygen; there being a smaller quantity of oxygen and a
greater quantity of carbonic acid, in venous than in arterial
blood.

And it may be experimentally demonstrated, that this
difference in their gaseous contents is the only essential
difference between venous and arterial blood. For if venous blood be shaken up with oxygen, or even with air, it
gains oxygen, loses carbonic acid, and takes on the color
and properties of arterial blood. Similarly, if arterial

blood be treated with carbonic acid so as to be thoroughly saturated with that gas, it gains carbonic acid, loses oxygen, and acquires the true properties of venous blood; though, for a reason to be mentioned below, the change is not so complete in this case as in the former. The same result is attained, though more slowly, if the blood, in either case, be received into a bladder, and then placed in the carbonic acid, or oxygen gas; the thin moist animal membrane allowing the change to be effected with perfect ease, and offering no serious impediment to the passage of either gas.

96. Diffusion of Gases.—The physico-chemical processes involved in the exchange of carbonic acid for oxygen when venous is converted into arterial blood, or the reverse, in the cases mentioned above, are not thoroughly understood, and are probably somewhat complex.

It is known (*a*) that gases, mechanically held by a fluid in a given proportion, tend to diffuse into any atmosphere to which they are exposed, until they occupy that atmosphere in corresponding proportions; and (*b*) that gases separated by a dry porous partition, or simply in contact, diffuse into one another with a rapidity which is inversely proportioned to the square roots of their densities. A knowledge of these physical principles does, in a rough way, lead us to see how the gases contained in the blood may effect an exchange with those in the air, whether the blood be freely exposed, or inclosed in a membrane.

But the application of these principles gives no more than this sort of general insight. For, in the first place, when arterialization takes place through the walls of a bladder, or any other thin animal membrane, the matter is complicated by the circumstance that moisture dissolves carbonic acid far more freely than it will oxygen; hence a wet bladder has a very different action upon carbonic acid from that which it has upon oxygen. A moist bladder, partially filled with oxygen, and suspended in carbonic-acid gas, becomes rapidly distended, in consequence of the carbonic-acid gas passing into it with much greater rapidity than the oxygen passes out. Secondly, the gases of the blood are not held in a merely mechanical way in it; the oxygen seems to be loosely combined with the red corpuscles (88), and there is reason to think that a great part, at least, of the carbonic acid, is chemically connected, in a similarly loose way, with certain saline constituents of the serum. Hence the arterialization of blood in the lungs seems to be a very mixed process, partly physical, and yet, to a certain extent, chemical, and consequently very difficult to analyze.

The same may also be said of the change from arterial to venous blood in the tissues. Owing to the peculiar relation of oxygen to the red blood-corpuscles, the process which takes place in the tissues is not a simple interchange by diffusion of the oxygen of the blood for the carbonic acid of the tissues; on the contrary, the oxygen is given up for purposes of oxidation, the demand being determined by the supply of oxidizable materials in the tissue, while the blood, poor in carbonic acid, takes up, apparently by an independent action, a quantity of that gas from the tissues rich in it.

Hence venous blood is characterized not only by the large amount of carbonic acid present, but also by the fact that the red corpuscles have given up a good deal of their oxygen for the purposes of oxidation, or, as the chemists would say, have become reduced. This is the reason why arterial blood is not so easily converted into venous blood by exposure to carbonic acid as venous blood into arterial by exposure to oxygen. There is, in the former case, a want of some oxidizable substance to carry off the oxygen from and so to reduce the red corpuscles. When such an oxidizable substance is added (as, for instance, a salt of iron), the blood at once and immediately becomes completely venous.

Practically we may say that the most important difference between venous and arterial blood is not so much the
relative quantities of carbonic acid as that the red corpuscles of venous blood have lost a good deal of oxygen, are
reduced, and ready at once to take up any oxygen offered
to them.

97. Cause of the Change of Color in Blood.—The cause
of the change of color of the blood—of its darkening when
exposed to carbonic acid, and its brightening when under
the influence of oxygen—is not thoroughly understood.
There is reason to think, however, that the red corpuscles
are rendered somewhat flatter by oxygen gas, while they
are distended by the action of carbonic acid (76). Under
the former circumstances they may, not improbably, reflect
the light more strongly, so as to give a more distinct coloration to the blood ; while, under the latter, they may reflect
less light, and, in that way, allow the blood to appear
darker and duller.

This, however, is not the whole of the matter; for solutions of hæmoglobin or of blood-crystals (81), even when
perfectly free from actual blood-corpuscles, change in color
from scarlet to purple, according as they gain or lose oxygen. It has already been stated (88) that oxygen most
probably exists in the blood in loose combination with
hæmoglobin. But, further, there is evidence to show that
a solution of hæmoglobin, when thus loosely combined
with oxygen, has a scarlet color, while a solution of
hæmoglobin, deprived of oxygen, has a purplish hue.
Hence arterial blood, in which the hæmoglobin is richly
provided with oxygen, would naturally be scarlet, while
venous blood, which not only contains an excess of carbonic acid, but whose hæmoglobin also has lost a great
deal of its oxygen, would be purple.

98. Conditions of its Chemical Changes.—Whatever may
be their explanation, however, the facts are certain (1),
that arterial blood, separated by only a thin membrane

from carbonic acid, or from a fluid containing a greater amount of carbonic acid than itself, and also carrying certain oxidizable materials, becomes venous; and (2) that venous blood, separated by only a thin membrane from oxygen, or a fluid containing a greater proportion of free oxygen than itself, becomes arterial.

In these facts lies the explanation of the conversion of scarlet blood into dark blood as it passes through the capillaries of the body, for the latter are bathed by the juices of the tissues, which contain carbonic acid, the product of their waste and combustion, in excess, together with highly-oxidizable matters. On the other hand, if we seek for the explanation of the conversion of the dark blood in the veins into the scarlet blood of the arteries, we find, first, that the blood remains dark in the right auricle, the right ventricle, and the pulmonary artery; second, that it is scarlet not only in the aorta, but in the left ventricle, the left auricle, and the pulmonary veins. -   -

Obviously, then, the change from venous to arterial takes place in the pulmonary capillaries, for these are the sole channels of communication between the pulmonary arteries and the pulmonary veins.

SECTION II.—*The Lungs and their Office.*

99. The Essence-nature of Respiration.—But what are the physical conditions to which the blood is exposed in the pulmonary capillaries?

These vessels are very wide, thin-walled, and closely set, so as to form a net-work with very small meshes, which is contained in the substance of an extremely thin membrane. This membrane is in contact with the air, so that the blood in each capillary of the lung is separated from the air by only a delicate pellicle formed by its own wall and the lung-membrane. Hence an exchange very readily takes place between the blood and the air; the latter gaining moisture and carbonic acid, and losing oxygen (28, 29).[1]

This is the essential step in respiration : that it really takes place may be demonstrated very readily, by the experiment described in the first Chapter, in which air expired was proved to differ from air inspired, by containing more heat, more water, more carbonic acid, and less oxygen; or, on the other hand, by putting a ligature on the windpipe of a living animal so as to prevent air from passing into or out of the lungs, and then examining the contents of the heart and great vessels. The blood on both sides of the heart, and in the pulmonary veins and aorta, will be found to be as completely venous as in the venæ cavæ and pulmonary artery.

But, though the passage of carbonic-acid gas and hot watery vapor out of the blood and of oxygen into it is the essence of the respiratory process—and thus a membrane with blood on one side, and air on the other, is all that is absolutely necessary to effect the purification of the blood —yet the accumulation of carbonic acid is so rapid, and the need for oxygen so incessant, in all parts of the human body, that the former could not be cleared away, nor the latter supplied, with adequate rapidity, without the aid of extensive and complicated accessory machinery—the arrangement and working of which must next be carefully studied.

100. Mechanism of Respiration.—The back of the mouth or *pharynx* communicates by two channels with the external air (*see* Fig. 49). One of these is formed by the nasal passages, which cannot be closed by any muscular apparatus of their own ; the other is presented by the mouth, which can be shut or opened at will.

[1] The student must guard himself against the idea that arterial blood contains no carbonic acid, and venous blood no oxygen. In passing through the lungs, venous blood loses only a part of its carbonic acid ; and arterial blood, in passing through the tissues, loses only a part of its oxygen. In blood, however venous, there is in health always some oxygen; and, in even the brightest arterial blood, there is actually more carbonic acid than oxygen.

Immediately behind the tongue, at the lower and front part of the pharynx, is an aperture—the *glottis* (Fig. 22, *Gl.*)—capable of being closed by a sort of lid—the *epiglottis*—or by the shutting together of its side boundaries, formed by the so-called *vocal chords*. The glottis opens into a chamber with cartilaginous walls—the *larynx ;* and, leading from the larynx downwards along the front part of the throat, where it may be very readily felt, is the *trachea*, or windpipe (Fig. 22, *Tr.*).

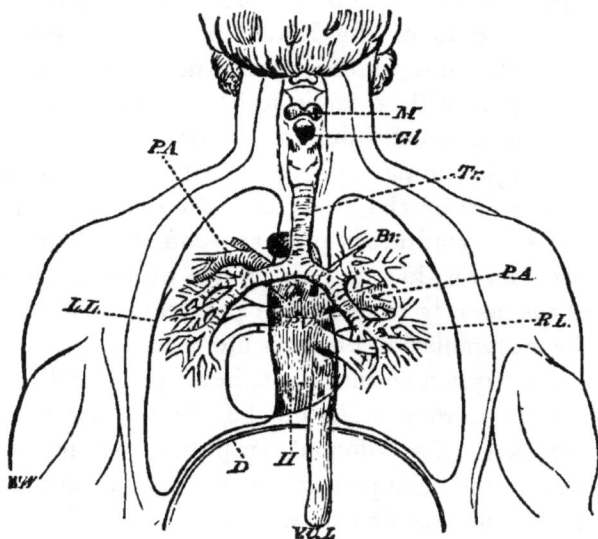

FIG. 22.

BACK VIEW OF THE NECK AND THORAX OF A HUMAN SUBJECT FROM WHICH THE VERTEBRAL COLUMN AND WHOLE POSTERIOR WALL OF THE CHEST ARE SUPPOSED TO BE REMOVED.

M., mouth; *Gl.*, glottis; *Tr.*, trachea; *L.L.*, left lung; *R.L.*, right lung; *Br.*, bronchus; *P.A.*, pulmonary artery; *P.V.*, pulmonary veins; *Ao.*, aorta; *D.*, diaphragm; *H.*, heart; *V.C.I.*, vena cava inferior.

If the trachea be handled through the skin, it will be found to be firm and resisting. Its walls are, in fact, strengthened by a series of cartilaginous hoops, which hoops are incomplete behind, their ends being united only by muscle and membrane, where the trachea comes into contact with the gullet, or *œsophagus*. The trachea passes into the thorax, and there divides into two branches, a right and a left, which are termed the *bronchi* (Fig. 22, *Br.*). Each bronchus enters the lung of its own side, and then breaks up into a great number of smaller branches, which are called the *bronchial tubes.* As these dimiuish in size, the cartilages, which are continued all through the bronchi and their large ramifications, become smaller and eventually disappear, so that the walls of the smallest bronchial tubes are entirely muscular or membranous. Thus, while

FIG. 23.

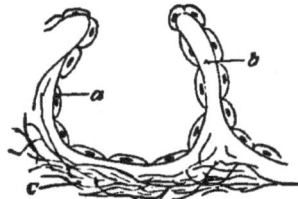

FIG. 24.

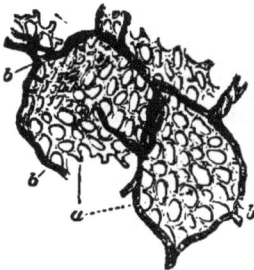

FIG. 25.

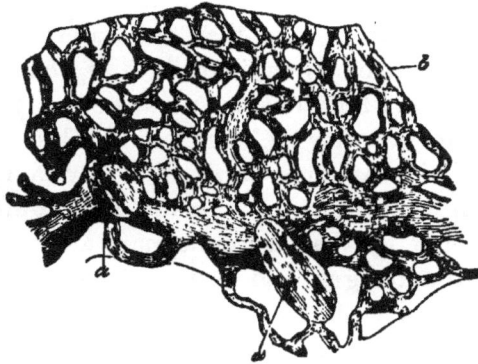

FIG. 26.

Fig. 23.—Two air-cells (*b*), with the ultimate bronchial tube (*a*) which opens into them. (Magnified twenty diameters.)

Fig. 24.—Diagrammatic view of an air-cell (Fig. 23) seen in section: *a*, epithelium; *b*, partition between two adjacent cells, in the thickness of which the capillaries run; *c*, fibres of elastic tissue.

Fig. 25.—Portion of injected lung magnified: *a*, the capillaries spread over the walls of two adjacent air-cells; *b*, small branches of arteries and veins.

Fig. 26.—Portions still more highly magnified.

the trachea and bronchi are kept permanently open and pervious to air by their cartilages, the smaller bronchial tubes may be almost closed by the contraction of their muscular walls.

The finer bronchial tubes end at length in elongated dilatations, about $\frac{1}{70}$th of an inch in diameter on the average (Fig. 23). Each of these dilatations is beset with, or perhaps rather is made up of, little sacs, which open irregularly into the cavity of the dilatation. These sacs are the *air-cells*. The very thin walls (Fig. 24) which separate these air-cells are supported by much delicate and highly-elastic tissue, and carry the wide and close-set capillaries into which the ultimate ramifications of the pulmonary artery pour its blood (Fig. 26). Thus, the blood contained in these capillaries is exposed on both sides to the air—being separated from the air-cell on either hand only by the very delicate pellicle which forms the wall of the capillary, and the lining of the air-sac.

101. The Provision for the Renewal of Air.—Hence no conditions can be more favorable to a ready exchange between the gaseous contents of the blood and those of the air in the air-cells, than the arrangements which obtain in the pulmonary capillaries; and, thus far, the structure of the lung fully enables us to understand how it is that the large quantity of blood poured through the pulmonary circulation becomes exposed in very thin streams, over a large surface, to the air. But the only result of this arrangement would be, that the pulmonary air would very speedily lose all its oxygen, and become completely saturated with carbonic acid, if special provision were not made for its being incessantly renewed.

102. Inspiration and Expiration.—If an adult man, breathing calmly in the sitting position, be watched, the respiratory act will be observed to be repeated thirteen to fifteen times every minute. Each act consists of certain components which succeed one another in a regular rhythmical order. First, the breath is drawn in, or *inspired;* immediately afterwards it is driven out, or *expired;* and these successive acts of *inspiration* and *expiration* are followed by a brief pause. Thus, just as in the rhythm of the heart the auricular systole, the ventricular systole, and then a pause, follow in regular order; so in the chest, the inspiration, the expiration, and then a pause, succeed one another. At each inspiration of an adult well-grown man, about thirty cubic inches of air are inspired; and at each expiration the same, or a slightly smaller, volume (allowing for the increase of temperature of the air so expired) is given out of the body.

103. Differences between Inspired and Expired Air.—
The expired air differs from the air inspired in the following particulars:

(*a*) Whatever the temperature of the external air is, that expired is nearly as hot as the blood, or has a temperature between 90° and 100°.

(*b*) However dry the external air may be, that expired is quite or nearly saturated with watery vapor.

(*c*) Though ordinary air contains nearly 2,100 parts of oxygen, and 7,900 of nitrogen, with not more than three parts of carbonic acid, in 10,000 parts, expired air contains about 470 parts of carbonic acid, and only between 1,500 and 1,600 parts of oxygen; while the quantity of nitrogen suffers little or no change. Speaking roughly, air which has been breathed once has gained five per cent. of carbonic acid, and lost five per cent. of oxygen.

The expired air contains, in addition, a greater or less quantity of animal matter of a highly-decomposable character.

(*d*) Very close analysis of the expired air shows, firstly, that the quantity of oxygen which disappears is always slightly in excess of the quantity of carbonic acid supplied; and, secondly, that the nitrogen is variable — the expired nitrogen being sometimes slightly in excess of, sometimes slightly less than that inspired, and sometimes remaining stationary.

104. The Amount of Work done by the Lungs.—From three hundred and fifty to four hundred cubic feet of air are thus passed through the lungs of an adult man taking little or no exercise, in the course of twenty-four hours; and are charged with carbonic acid, and deprived of oxygen, to the extent of nearly five per cent. This amounts to about eighteen cubic feet of the one gas taken in, and of the other given out. Thus, if a man be shut up in a close room, having the form of a cube seven feet in the side, every particle of air in that room will have passed through his lungs in twenty-four hours, and a fourth of the oxygen it contained will be replaced by carbonic acid.

The quantity of carbon eliminated in the twenty-four hours is pretty clearly represented by a piece of pure charcoal weighing eight ounces.

The quantity of water given off from the lungs in the twenty-four hours varies very much, but may be taken on the average as rather less than half a pint, or about nine ounces. It may fall below this amount, or increase to double or treble the quantity.

SECTION III.—*The Respiratory Mechanism.*

105. Mechanism of the Respiratory Movements. — The mechanical arrangements by which the respiratory movements, essential to the removal of the great mass of effete matters, and the importation of the large quantity of oxygen indicated, are effected, may be found in—(*a*) the elasticity of the lungs; (*b*) the mobility of the sides and bottom of the thoracic cavity in which the lungs are contained.

The thorax may be regarded as a completely shut conical box, with the small end turned upwards, the back of the box being formed by the spinal column, the sides by the ribs, the front by the breastbone, the bottom by the diaphragm, and the top by the root of the neck (Fig. 22).

The two lungs occupy almost all the cavity of this box which is not taken up by the heart. Each is inclosed in its serous membrane, the *pleura*, a double bag (very similar to the pericardium, the chief difference being that the outer bag of each pleura is, over the greater part of its extent, quite firmly adherent to the walls of the chest and the diaphragm (*see* Fig. 12), while the outer bag of the pericardium is for the most part loose), the inner bag closely covering the lung and the outer forming a lining to the cavity of the chest. So long as the walls of the thorax are entire, the cavity of each pleura is practically obliterated, that layer of the pleura which covers the lung being in close contact with that which lines the wall of the chest; but if a small opening be made into the pleura, the lung at once shrinks to a comparatively small size, and thus develops a great cavity between the two layers of the pleura. If a pipe be now fitted into the bronchus, and air blown through it, the lung is very readily distended to its full size; but, on being left to itself, it collapses, the air being driven out again with some force. The abundant elastic tissues of the walls of the air-cells are, in fact, so disposed as to be greatly stretched when the lungs are full; and, when the cause of the distention is removed, this elasticity comes into play and drives the greater part of the air out again.

The lungs are kept distended in the dead subject, so long as the walls of the chest are entire, by the pressure of the atmosphere. For though the elastic tissue is all the while pulling, as it were, at the layer of pleura which covers the lung, and attempting to separate it from that which lines the chest, it cannot produce such a separation without developing a vacuum between these two layers. To effect this, the elastic tissue must pull with a force greater than that of the external air (or fifteen pounds to the square inch), an effort far beyond its powers, which do not equal more than one-fourth of a pound on the square inch.

But the moment a hole is made in the pleura, the air enters into its cavity, the atmospheric pressure inside the lung is equalized by that outside it, and the elastic tissue, freed from its opponent, exerts its full power on the lung.

106. Walls of the Bronchial Tubes—Cilia. — The lungs are elastic, whether alive or dead. During life the air which they contain may be further affected by the contractility of the muscular walls of the bronchial tubes. If water is poured into the lungs of a recently-killed animal, and a series of electric shocks is then sent through the bronchial tubes, the latter contract, and the water is forced out. Lastly, during life a further source of motion in the bronchial tubes is provided by the *cilia*—minute filaments attached to the epithelium of the tubes, which incessantly vibrate backwards and forwards, and work in such a manner as to sweep liquid and solid matters outwards, or towards the trachea.

107. Movements of the Chest-Walls.—The ribs are attached to the spine, so as to be freely movable upon it; but, when left to themselves, they take a position which is inclined obliquely downwards and forwards.[1] Two sets of muscles, called *intercostals*, pass between the successive pairs of ribs on each side. The outer set, called *external intercostals* (Fig. 27, *A*), run from the rib above, obliquely downwards and forwards, to the rib below. The other set, *internal intercostals* (Fig. 27, *B*), cross these in direction, passing from the rib above, downwards and backwards, to the rib below.

The action of these muscles is somewhat puzzling at first, but is readily understood if the fact, that *when a muscle contracts it tends to make the distance between its two ends as short as possible*, be borne in mind. Let *a* and *b*, in Fig. 28, A, be two parallel bars, movable by their

---

[1] I purposely neglect the consideration of the cartilages of the ribs, and some other points, in order not to complicate the question unnecessarily. It may, however, be stated that those fibres of the internal intercostals which are situate between the cartilages act like the external, and raise the ribs.

ends upon the upright *c*, which may be regarded as at the
back of the apparatus, then a line directed from *x* to *y* will
be inclined downwards and forwards, and one from *w* to *z*
will be directed downwards and backwards. Now, it is
obvious that there is one position of the rods, and one only,
in which the points *x* and *y* are at the shortest possible distance, and one position only in which the points *w* and *z*
are at the shortest possible distance; and these are, for

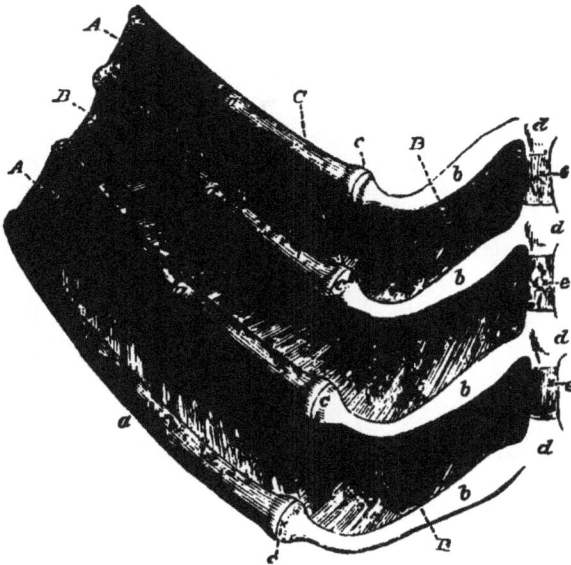

Fig. 27.

VIEW OF FOUR RIBS OF THE DOG WITH THE INTERCOSTAL MUSCLES.

a, the bony rib; *b*, the cartilage; *c*, the junction of bone and cartilage; *d*, un-
ossified, *e*, ossified, portions of the sternum. *A*, external intercostal muscle; *B*, internal intercostal muscle. In the middle interspace, the external intercostal has been
removed to show the internal intercostal beneath it.

x and *y* the position B, and for *w* and *z* the position C.
These positions are respectively such that the points *x*, *y*,
and *w*, *z*, are at the ends of straight lines perpendicular to
both rods.

Thus, to bring *x* and *y* into this position, the parallel

rods in A must move upwards; and, to bring w and z into it, they must move in the opposite way.

If the simple apparatus just described be made of wood, hooks being placed at the points x, y, and w, z; and an elastic band, as long when left to itself as the shortest dis-tance between these points, be provided with eyes which can be readily put on to or taken off these hooks: it will be found that when the bars are in the horizontal position, A, the elasticity of the band, when hooked on to x and y,

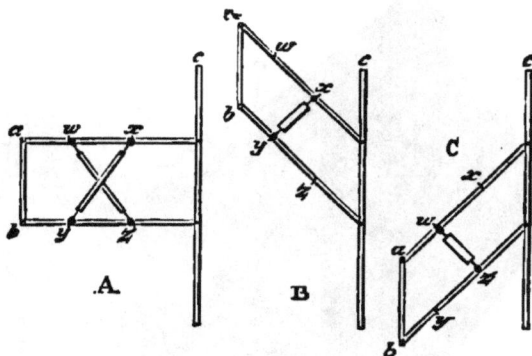

Fig. 28.

DIAGRAM OF MODELS ILLUSTRATING THE ACTION OF THE EXTERNAL AND INTERNAL INTERCOSTAL MUSCLES.

B, inspiratory elevation; C, expiratory depression.

will bring them up into the position shown in Fig. 28, B; while, if hooked on to w and z, it will force them down into the position shown in Fig. 28, C.

Substitute the contractility of the external and internal intercostal muscles for the elasticity of the band, and the latter will precisely exemplify their action; and it is thus proved that the external intercostals must raise, and the internal intercostals must depress, the bony ribs.

108. The Diaphragm.—The diaphragm is a great par-tition situated between the thorax and the abdomen, and always concave to the latter and convex to the former (Fig.

1, *D*). From its middle, which is tendinous, muscular fibres extend downwards and outwards to the ribs, and two, especially strong masses, which are called the *pillars of the diaphragm*, to the spinal column (Fig. 29). When these muscular fibres contract, therefore, they tend to make the diaphragm flatter, and to increase the capacity of the thorax at the expense of that of the abdomen, by pulling down the bottom of the thoracic box (Fig. 30).

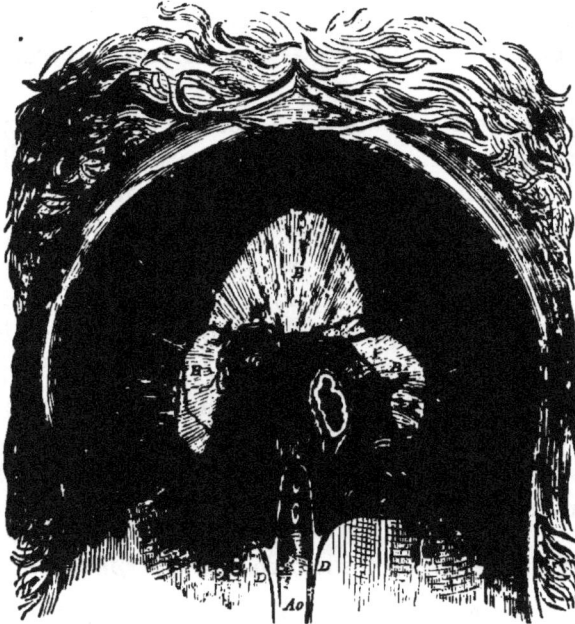

FIG. 29.

THE DIAPHRAGM OF A DOG VIEWED FROM THE LOWER OR ABDOMINAL SIDE.

V.C.I., the vena cava inferior; *O.*, the œsophagus; *Ao.*, the aorta; the broad white tendinous middle (*B*) is easily distinguished from the radiating muscular fibres (*A*) which pass down to the ribs and into the pillars (*C D*) in front of the vertebræ.

109. Action of Different Parts compared.—Let us now consider what would be the result of the action of the parts of the respiratory apparatus, which have been described, if the diaphragm alone should begin to contract at regular intervals.

When it contracts it increases the vertical dimensions of the thoracic cavity, and tends to pull away the lining of the bottom of the thoracic box from that which covers the bases of the lungs; but the air immediately rushing in at the trachea, proportionately increases the distention of the lungs, and prevents the formation of any vacuum between the two pleuræ of either lung in this region. When the diaphragm ceases to contract, so much of the elasticity of the lungs as was neutralized by the contraction of the diaphragm, comes into play, and the extra air taken in is driven out again. We have, in short, an *inspiration* and an *expiration*.

Suppose, on the other hand, that, the diaphragm being quiescent, the external intercostal muscles contract. The ribs will be raised from their oblique position, the antero-posterior dimensions of the thoracic cavity will be increased, and the lungs will be distended as before to balance the enlargement. If, now, the external intercostals relax, the action of gravity upon the ribs, the elasticity of the cartilages, and, more especially, that of the lungs, will alone suffice to bring back the ribs to their previous positions, and to drive out the extra air; but this expiratory action may be greatly aided by the contraction of the internal intercostals.

SECTION IV.—*Inspiration and Expiration.*

110. Accessory Muscles.—Thus it appears that we may have either *diaphragmatic respiration*, or *costal respiration*. As a general rule, however, not only do the two forms of respiration coincide and aid one another—the contraction of the diaphragm taking place at the same time with that of the external intercostals, and its relaxation with the contraction of the internal intercostals—but sundry other accessory agencies come into play. Thus, the muscles which connect the ribs with parts of the spine above them, and with the shoulder, may, more or less extensively, assist inspiration; while those which connect the ribs and breastbone with the pelvis, and form the front and side walls of the abdomen, are powerful aids to expiration. In fact, they assist expiration in two ways: first, directly, by pulling down the ribs; and next, indirectly, by pressing the viscera of the abdomen upwards against the under surface of the diaphragm, and so driving the floor of the thorax upwards.

It is for this reason that, whenever a violent expiratory effort is made, the walls of the abdomen are obviously flattened and driven towards the spine, the body being at the same time bent forwards.

In taking a deep inspiration, on the other hand, the walls of the abdomen are relaxed and become convex, the viscera being driven against them by the descent of the diaphragm—the spine is straightened, the head thrown back, and the shoulders outwards, so as to afford the greatest mechanical advantage to all the muscles which can elevate the ribs.

111. How Respiration differs in the Sexes.—It is a remarkable circumstance that the mechanism of respiration is somewhat different in the two sexes. In men, the diaphragm takes the larger share in the process, the upper ribs moving comparatively little; in women, the reverse is the case, the respiratory act being more largely the result of the movement of the ribs.

Sighing is a deep and prolonged inspiration. "*Sniffing*" is a more rapid inspiratory act, in which the mouth is kept shut, and the air made to pass through the nose. ·

Coughing is a violent expiratory act. A deep inspiration being first taken, the glottis is closed and then burst open by the violent compression of the air contained in the lungs by the contraction of the expiratory muscles, the diaphragm being relaxed and the air driven through the mouth. In *sneezing*, on the contrary, the cavity of the mouth being shut off from the pharynx by the approxima-

tion of the soft palate and the base of the tongue, the air
is forced through the nasal passages.

112. Residual, Supplemental, and Tidal Air. — It thus
appears that the thorax, the lungs, and the trachea, constitute a sort of bellows without a valve, in which the thorax
and the lungs represent the body of the bellows, while the

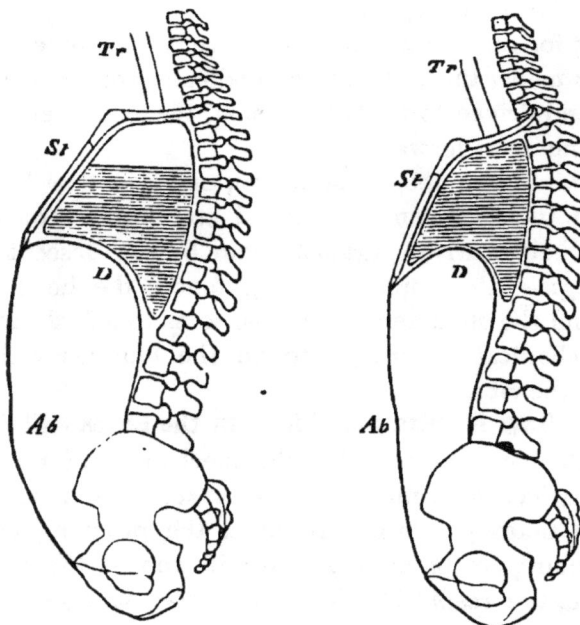

FIG. 30. FIG. 81.

DIAGRAMMATIC SECTIONS OF THE BODY IN

Fig. 30, inspiration; Fig. 31, expiration. *Tr.*, trachea; *St.*, sternum; *D.*, diaphragm;
Ab., abdominal walls. The shading roughly indicates the stationary air.

trachea is the pipe; and the effect of the respiratory movements is just the same as that of the approximation and
separation of the handles of the bellows, which drive out
and draw in the air through the pipe. There is, however,
one difference between the bellows and the respiratory apparatus, of great importance in the theory of respiration,

though frequently overlooked; and that is, that the sides
of the bellows can be brought close together so as to force
out all, or nearly all, the air which they contain; while the
walls of the chest, when approximated as much as possible,
still inclose a very considerable cavity (Fig. 31); so that,
even after the most violent expiratory effort, a very large
quantity of air is left in the lungs.

The amount of this air which cannot be got rid of, and
is called *Residual air*, is, on the average, from seventy-five
to one hundred cubic inches.

About as much more in addition to this remains in the
chest after an ordinary expiration, and is called *Supplemental air*.

In ordinary breathing, twenty to thirty cubic inches
of what is conveniently called *Tidal air* pass in and out.
It follows that, after an ordinary inspiration, 100 + 100 +
30 = 230 cubic inches may be contained in the lungs.
By taking the deepest possible inspiration, another one
hundred cubic inches, called *Complemental air*, may be
added.

113. Office of the Stationary Air.—It results from these
data that the lungs, after an ordinary inspiration, contain
about two hundred and thirty cubic inches of air, and that
only about one-seventh to one-eighth of this amount is
breathed out and taken in again at the next inspiration.
Apart from the circumstance, then, that the fresh air inspired has to fill the cavities of the hinder part of the
mouth, and the trachea, and the bronchi, if the lungs were
mere bags fixed to the ends of the bronchi, the inspired air
would descend as far only as to occupy that one-fourteenth
to one-sixteenth part of each bag which was nearest to the
bronchi, whence it would be driven out again at the next
expiration. But, as the bronchi branch out into a prodigious number of bronchial tubes, the inspired air can
only penetrate for a certain distance along these, and can
never reach the air-cells at all.

Thus the residual and supplemental air taken together are, under ordinary circumstances, *stationary*—that is to say, the air comprehended under these names merely shifts its outer limit in the bronchial tubes, as the chest dilates and contracts, without leaving the lungs; the *tidal* air, alone, being that which leaves the lungs and is renewed in ordinary respiration.

It is obvious, therefore, that the business of respiration is essentially transacted by the stationary air, which plays the part of a middleman between the two parties—the blood and the fresh tidal air—who desire to exchange their commodities, carbonic acid for oxygen, and oxygen for carbonic acid.

Now, there is nothing interposed between the fresh tidal air and the stationary air; they are aëriform fluids, in complete contact and continuity, and hence the exchange between them must take place according to the ordinary laws of gaseous diffusion.

114. Composition of the Stationary Air.—Thus, the stationary air in the air-cells gives up oxygen to the blood, and takes carbonic acid from it, though the exact mode in which the change is effected is not thoroughly understood. By this process it becomes loaded with carbonic acid, and deficient in oxygen, though to what precise extent is not known.   But there must be a very much greater excess of the one, and deficiency of the other, than is exhibited by inspired air, seeing that the latter acquires its composition by diffusion in the short space of time (four to five seconds) during which it is in contact with the stationary air.

In accordance with these facts, it is found that the air expired during the first half of an expiration contains less carbonic acid than that expired during the second half. Further, when the frequency of respiration is increased without altering the volume of each inspiration, though the percentage of carbonic acid in each inspiration is diminished, it is not diminished in the same ratio as that in which the number of inspirations increases; and hence more carbonic acid is got rid of in a given time.

Thus, if the number of inspirations per minute is increased from fifteen to thirty, the percentage of carbonic acid evolved in the second case remains more than half of what it was in the first case, and hence the total evolution is greater.

115. The Nervous System controls Respiration.—Of the various mechanical aids to the respiratory process, the nature and workings of which have now been described, one, the elasticity of the lungs, is of the nature of a dead, constant force. The action of the rest of the apparatus is under the control of the nervous system, and varies from time to time.

As the nasal passages cannot be closed by their own action, air has always free access to the pharynx; but the glottis, or entrance to the windpipe, is completely under the control of the nervous system—the smallest irritation about the mucous membrane in its neighborhood being conveyed, by its nerves, to that part of the cerebro-spinal axis which is called the *medulla oblongata* (*see* 328). The medulla oblongata, thus stimulated, gives rise, by a process which will be explained hereafter, termed *reflex action*, to the contraction of the muscles which close the glottis, and commonly, at the same time, to a violent contraction of the expiratory muscles, producing a cough (*see* 111).

The muscular fibres of the smaller bronchial tubes, no less than the respiratory pump itself, formed by the walls and floor of the thorax, are under the complete control of the nerves which supply the muscles, and which are brought into action in consequence of impressions conveyed to that part of the brain which is called the medulla oblongata, by the pneumogastric and other nerves.

116. Respiration and Circulation compared. — From what has been said, it is obvious that there are many analogies between the circulatory and the respiratory apparatus. Each consists, essentially, of a kind of pump which distributes a fluid (aëriform in the one case, liquid in the other) through a series of ramified distributing-tubes to a system of cavities (capillaries or air-cells), the volume of the contents of which is greater than that of the tubes.

In each, the pump is the cause of the motion of the fluid, though that motion may be regulated, locally, by the contraction, or relaxation, of the muscular fibres contained in the walls of the distributing-tubes. But, while the rhythmic movement of the heart chiefly depends upon a nervous apparatus placed within itself, that of the respiratory apparatus results mainly from the operation of a nervous centre lodged in the medulla oblongata.

SECTION V.—*Effects of Respiration.*

117. Secondary Phenomena.—As there are certain secondary phenomena which accompany, and are explained by, the action of the heart, so there are secondary phenomena which are similarly related to the working of the respiratory apparatus. These are— (*a*) the respiratory sounds, and (*b*) the effect of the inspiratory and expiratory movements upon the circulation.

118. The Respiratory Murmurs.—The *respiratory sounds* or *murmurs* are audible when the ear is applied to any part of the chest which covers one or other of the lungs. They accompany inspiration and expiration, and very much resemble the sounds produced by breathing through the mouth, when the lips are so applied together as to leave a small interval. Over the bronchi the sounds are louder than over the general surface. It would appear that these sounds are produced by the motion of the air along the air-passages.

119. Inspiration assists the Circulation.—In consequence of the elasticity of the lungs, a certain force must be expended in distending them, and this force is found experimentally to become greater and greater the more the lung is distended ; just as, in stretching a piece of India-rubber, more force is required to stretch it a good deal than is needed to stretch it only a little. Hence, when inspiration takes place, and the lungs are distended with air, the heart and the great vessels in the chest are subjected to a less pressure than are the blood-vessels of the rest of the body.

For the pressure of the air contained in the lungs is exactly the same as that exerted by the atmosphere upon the surface of the body ; that is to say, fifteen pounds on the square inch. But a certain amount of this pressure exerted by the air in the lungs is counterbalanced by the elasticity of the distended lungs. Say that in a given condition of inspiration a pound pressure on the square inch is needed to overcome this elasticity, then there will be only fourteen pounds pressure on every square inch of the heart and great vessels. And hence the pressure on the blood in these vessels will be one pound per square inch less than that on the veins and arteries of the rest of the body. If there were no aortic, or pulmonary, valves, and if the composition of the vessels, and the pressure upon the blood in them, were everywhere the same, the result of this excess of pressure on the surface would be, to drive all the blood from the arteries and veins of the rest of the body into the heart and great vessels contained in the thorax. And thus the diminution of the pressure upon the thoracic blood-cavities produced by inspiration would, practically, suck the blood from all parts of the body towards the thorax. But the suction thus exerted, while it hastened the flow of blood to the heart in the veins, would equally oppose the flow from the heart to the arteries, and the two effects would balance one another.

120. Unequal Pressures facilitate the Circulation.—As a matter of fact, however, we know—

(1.) That the blood in the great arteries is constantly under a very considerable pressure, exerted by their elastic walls ; while that of the veins is under little pressure.

(2.) That the walls of the arteries are strong and resisting, while those of the veins are weak and flabby.

(3.) That the veins have valves opening towards the
heart; and that, during the diastole, there is no resistance
of any moment to the free passage of blood into the heart;
while, on the other hand, the cavity of the arteries is shut
off from that of the ventricle during the diastole, by the
closure of the semilunar valves.

Hence it follows that equal pressures applied to the
surface of the veins and to that of the arteries must produce very different effects. In the veins the pressure is
something which did not exist before; and, partly from
the presence of valves, partly from the absence of resistance in the heart, partly from the presence of resistance in
the capillaries, it all tends to accelerate the flow of blood
towards the heart. In the arteries, on the other hand, the
pressure is only a fractional addition to that which existed
before; so that, during the systole, it only makes a comparatively small addition to the resistance which has to be
overcome by the ventricle; and, during the diastole, it
superadds itself to the elasticity of the arterial walls in
driving the blood onwards towards the capillaries, inasmuch as all progress in the opposite direction is stopped
by the semilunar valves.

It is, therefore, clear that the inspiratory movement, on
the whole, helps the heart, inasmuch as its general result
is to drive the blood the way that the heart propels it.

121. Effect of Expiration on the Circulation.—In expiration, the difference between the pressure of the atmosphere on the surface, and that which it exerts on the contents of the thorax through the lungs, becomes less and
less in proportion to the completeness of the expiration.
Whenever, by the ascent of the diaphragm and the descent
of the ribs, the cavity of the thorax is so far diminished
that pressure is exerted on the great vessels, the veins,
owing to the thinness of their walls, are especially affected,

and a check is given to the flow of blood in them, which may become visible as a *venous pulse* in the great vessels of the neck. In its effect on the arterial trunks, expiration, like inspiration, is, on the whole, favorable to the circulation ; the increased resistance to the opening of the valves during the ventricular systole being more than balanced by the advantage gained in the addition of the expiratory pressure to the elastic reaction of the arterial walls during the diastole.

When the skull of a living animal is laid open and the brain exposed, the cerebral substance is seen to rise and fall synchronously with ·the respiratory movements ; the rise corresponding with expiration, and being caused by the obstruction thereby offered to the flow of the blood in the veins of the head and neck.

122. Stoppage of the Heart by Distention of the Lungs. —Hitherto, I have supposed the air-passages to be freely open during the inspiratory and expiratory movements. But, if, the lungs being distended, the mouth and nose are closed, and a strong expiratory effort is then made, the heart's action may be stopped altogether.[1] And the same result occurs if, the lungs being partially emptied, and the nose and mouth closed, a strong inspiratory effort is made. In the latter case the excessive distention of the right side of the heart, in consequence of the flow of blood into it, may be the cause of the arrest of the heart's action ; but, in the former, the reason of the stoppage is not very clear.

123. Circumstances modifying Respiration.—The activity of the respiratory process is greatly modified by the circumstances in which the body is placed. Thus, cold greatly increases the quantity of air which is breathed, the quantity of oxygen absorbed, and of carbonic acid expelled ; exercise and the taking of food have a corresponding effect.

In proportion to the weight of the body, the activity

---

[1] There is danger in attempting this experiment.

of the respiratory process is far greatest in children, and diminishes gradually with age. The excretion of carbonic acid is greatest during the day, and gradually sinks at night, attaining its minimum about midnight, or a little after.

Recent observations appear to show that the rule, that the quantity of oxygen taken in by respiration is, approximately, equal to that given out by expiration, only holds good for the total result of twenty-four hours' respiration. Much more oxygen appears to be given out during the daytime (in combination with carbon as carbonic acid) than is absorbed; while, at night, much more oxygen is absorbed than is excreted as carbonic acid during the same period. And it is very probable that the deficiency of oxygen towards the end of the waking hours, which is thus produced, is one cause of the sense of fatigue which comes on at that time. This difference between day and night is, however, not constant, and appears to depend a good deal on the time when food is taken.

The quantity of oxygen which disappears, in proportion to the carbonic acid given out, is greatest in carnivorous, least in herbivorous animals—greater in a man living on a flesh diet, than when the same man is feeding on vegetable matters.

124. Asphyxia.—When a man is strangled, drowned, or choked, or is, in any other way, prevented from inspiring or expiring sufficiently pure atmospheric air, what is called *asphyxia* comes on. He grows "black in the face;" the veins become turgid; insensibility, not unfrequently accompanied by convulsive movements, sets in, and he is dead in a few minutes.

But, in this asphyxiating process, two deadly influences of a distinct nature are coöperating; one is the *deprivation of oxygen*, the other is the *excessive accumulation of carbonic acid* in the blood. Oxygen starvation and carbonic-acid poisoning, each of which may be fatal in itself, are at work together.

The effects of oxygen starvation may be studied separately, by placing a small animal under the receiver of an air-pump and exhausting the air; or by replacing the air by a stream of hydrogen or nitrogen gas. In these cases no accumulation of carbonic acid is permitted, but, on the other hand, the supply of oxygen soon becomes insufficient, and the animal quickly dies. And if the experiment be made in another way, by placing a small mammal, or bird, in air from which the carbonic acid is removed as soon as it is formed, the animal will nevertheless die as soon as the amount of oxygen is reduced to ten per cent. or thereabouts.

The directly poisonous effect of carbonic acid, on the other hand, has been very much exaggerated. A very large quantity of pure carbonic acid (ten to fifteen or twenty per cent.) may be contained in air, without producing any very serious immediate effect, if the quantity of oxygen be simultaneously increased. And it is possible that what appear to be the directly poisonous effects of carbonic acid may really arise from its taking up the room that ought to be occupied by oxygen. If this be the case, carbonic acid is a negative rather than a positive poison.

125. How it destroys Life. —Whichever may be the more potent agency, the effect of the two, as combined in asphyxia, is to produce an obstruction, firstly, in the pulmonary circulation, and, secondly, in the veins of the body generally. The lungs and the right side of the heart, consequently, become gorged with blood, while the arteries and left side of the heart gradually empty themselves of the small supply of dark and unaërated blood which they receive. The heart becomes paralyzed, partly by reason of the distention of its right side, but chiefly from being supplied with venous blood; and all the organs of the body gradually cease to act.

126. Poisoning by Sulphuretted Hydrogen and Carbonic Oxide.—Sulphuretted hydrogen, so well known by its offensive smell, has long had the repute of being a positive poison. But its evil effects appear to arise chiefly, if not wholly, from the circumstance that its hydrogen combines with the oxygen carried by the blood-corpuscles, and thus gives rise, indirectly, to a form of oxygen starvation.

Carbonic-oxide gas has a much more serious effect, as it turns out the oxygen from the blood-corpuscles, and forms a combination of its own with the hæmoglobin. The compound thus formed is only very gradually decomposed by fresh oxygen, so that if any large proportion of the blood-corpuscles be thus rendered useless, the animal dies before restoration can be effected.

Badly-made common gas sometimes contains twenty to thirty per cent. of carbonic oxide; and, under these circumstances, a leakage of the pipes in a house may be extremely perilous to life.

127. Slow Asphyxiation.—It is not necessary, however, absolutely to strangle, or drown, a man, in order to asphyxiate him. As, other things being alike, the rapidity of diffusion between two gaseous mixtures depends on the difference of the proportions in which their constituents are mixed, it follows that the more nearly the composition of the tidal air approaches that of the stationary air, the slower will be the diffusion of carbonic acid outwards and of oxygen inwards, and the more charged with carbonic acid and defective in oxygen will the air in the air-cells become. And, on diminishing the proportion of oxygen or increasing the proportion of carbonic acid in the tidal air, a point will at length be reached when the change effected in the stationary air is too slight to enable it to relieve the pulmonary blood of its carbonic acid, and to supply it with oxygen to the extent required for its arterialization. In this case the blood, which passes into the aorta, and is thence distributed to the heart and the body generally, being venous, all the symptoms of insensibility, loss of muscular power, and the like, which have been enumerated above us the results of supplying the brain and muscles with venous blood, will follow, and a stage of suffocation, or asphyxia, will supervene.

Asphyxia takes place whenever the proportion of carbonic acid in tidal air reaches ten per cent. (the oxygen being diminished in like proportion). And it makes no difference whether this condition of the tidal air is brought about by shutting out fresh air, or by augmenting the number of persons who are consuming the same air; or by suffering combustion, in any shape, to carry off oxygen from the air.

128. Vital Necessity of Ventilation.—But the deprivation of oxygen, and the accumulation of carbonic acid, cause injury long before the asphyxiating point is reached. Uneasiness and headache arise when less than one per cent. of the oxygen of the air is replaced by other matters; while the persistent breathing of such air tends to lower all kinds of vital energy, and predisposes to disease.

Hence the necessity of sufficient air, and of ventilation for every human being. To be supplied with respiratory air in a fair state of purity, every man ought to have at least eight hundred cubic feet of space [1] to himself, and that space ought to be freely accessible, by direct or indirect channels, to the atmosphere.

CHAPTER V.

THE SOURCES OF LOSS AND OF GAIN TO THE BLOOD.

SECTION I.—*Sources of Loss to the Blood.*

129. Distribution of Arterial Blood.—The blood which has been aërated, or arterialized, by the process described

---

[1] A cubical room nine feet high, wide, and long, contains only seven hundred and twenty-nine cubic feet of air.

in the preceding chapter, is carried from the lungs by the pulmonary veins to the left auricle, and is then forced by the auricle into the ventricle, and by the ventricle into the aorta. As that great vessel traverses the thorax, it gives off several large arteries, by means of which blood is distributed to the head, the arms, and the walls of the body. Passing through the diaphragm (Fig. 29), the aortic trunk enters the cavity of the abdomen, and becomes what is called the *abdominal aorta*, from which vessels are given off to the viscera of the abdomen. Finally, the main stream of blood flows into the *iliac* arteries, whence the viscera of the pelvis and the legs are supplied.

Having traversed the ultimate ramifications of the arteries, the blood, as we have seen, enters the capillaries. Here the products of the waste of the tissues constantly pour into it; and, as the blood is everywhere full of corpuscles, which, like all other living things, decay and die, the results of their decomposition everywhere accumulate in it. It follows that, if the blood is to be kept pure, the waste matters thus incessantly poured into, or generated in it, must be as constantly got rid of, or excreted.

130. The Various Drains upon the Blood. — Three distinct sets of organs are especially charged with this office of continually excreting carbonic acid, water, and urea. They are the *lungs*, the *kidneys*, and the *skin* (*see* 28). These three great organs may therefore be regarded as so many drains from the blood—as so many channels by which it is constantly losing substance.

Further, the blood, as it passes through the capillaries, is constantly losing matter by exudation into the surrounding tissues.

Another kind of loss takes place from the surface of the body generally, and from the interior of the air-passages and lungs. Heat is constantly being given off from the former by radiation, evaporation, and conduction : from the latter, chiefly by evaporation.

131. Loss by the Liver and Lungs. — The blood which enters the liver is constantly losing material to that organ; but the loss is only temporary, as almost all the matter lost, converted into sugar and into bile, reënters the current of the circulation in the liver itself, or elsewhere.

Again, the loss of matter by the lungs in expiration is partially made good by the no less constant gain which results from the quantity of oxygen absorbed at each inspiration: while the combustion which is carried on in the tissues, by means of this oxygen, is the source not only of the heat which is given off through the lungs, but also of that which is carried away from the general surface of the body. And the loss by exudation from the capillaries is, in some degree, compensated by the gain from the lymphatics and ductless glands.

132. Other Losses and Gains. — In the instances just mentioned the loss and gain are constant, and go on while life and health last. But there are certain other operations which cause either loss or gain to the blood, and which are not continuous, but take place at intervals.

These are, on the side of loss, the actions of the many *secretory glands*, which separate certain substances from the blood at recurrent periods, in the intervals of which they are quiescent.

On the side of gain are the contractions of the *muscles*, which, during their activity, cause a great quantity of waste materials to appear in the blood; and the operations of the *alimentary canal*, which, for a certain period after food has been taken, pour new materials into the blood.

Under some circumstances, the skin, by absorbing fluids, may become a source of gain.

133. Table of Sources of Loss and Gain. — The sources of loss and gain to the blood may be conveniently arranged in the following tabular form :

A. Incessantly Active Sources of Loss or Gain to
the Blood.[1]

   a. Sources of loss.

      I. *Loss of Matter.*

         1. The lungs (carbonic acid, water).

         2. The kidneys (urea, water, salines).

         3. The skin (water, carbonic acid).

         4. The liver (bile, glycogen).

         5. The tissues generally (constructive material).

      II. *Loss of heat.*

         1. The free surfaces of the body.

   b. Sources of gain.

      I. *Gain of matter.*

         1. The lungs (oxygen).

         2. The liver (sugar, etc.).

         3. The lymphatics (corpuscles, lymph).

         4. The tissues generally (waste matters).

         5. The spleen and other ductless glands.

      II. *Gain of heat.*

         1. The blood itself and the tissues generally.

B. Intermittently Active Sources of Loss or Gain
to the Blood.

   a. Sources of loss.

         1. Many secreting glands (secretions).

   b. Sources of gain.

         1. The muscles (waste matters).

         2. The alimentary canal (food).

         The skin (absorption of liquids occasionally).

134. Constant Loss by the Kidneys.—In the preceding
chapter I have described the operation by which the lungs

---

[1] The learner must be careful not to confound the losses and gains of the *blood*
with the losses and gains of the *body* as a whole. The two differ in much the same
way as the internal commerce of a country differs from its export and import trade.

withdraw from the blood much carbonic acid and water, and supply oxygen to the blood; I now proceed to the second source of continual loss, the KIDNEYS.

Of these organs, there are two, placed at the back of the abdominal cavity, one on each side of the lumbar region of the spine. Each, though somewhat larger than the kidney of a sheep, has a similar shape. The depressed, or concave, side of the kidney is turned inwards, or towards the spine; and its convex side is directed outwards (Fig. 32). From the middle of the concave side (called the *hilus*) of each kidney, a long tube with a small bore, the *Ureter* (*Ur.*), proceeds to the Bladder (*Bl.*).

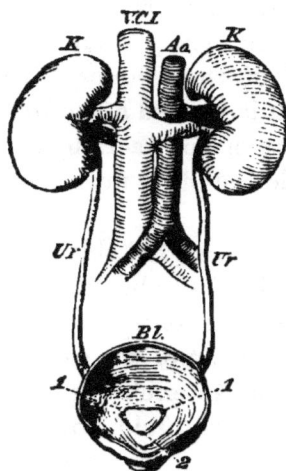

FIG. 32.

The kidneys (*K.*); ureters (*Ur.*); with the aorta (*Ao.*), and vena cava inferior (*V. C.I.*); and the renal arteries and veins. *Bl.* is the bladder, the top of which is cut off so as to show the openings of the ureters (1, 1), and that of the urethra (2).

The latter, situated in the pelvis, is an oval bag, the walls of which contain abundant unstriped muscular fibre, while it is lined, internally, by mucous membrane, and coated externally by a layer of the peritoneum, or double bag of serous membrane which has exactly the same relations to the cavity of the abdomen and the viscera con-

tained in them as the pleura have to the thoracic cavity
and the lungs. The ureters open side by side, but at some
little distance from one another, on the posterior and inferior wall of the bladder (Fig. 32, 1, 1). In front of them
is a single aperture which leads into the canal called the
Urethra (Fig. 32, 2), by which the cavity of the bladder is
placed in communication with the exterior of the body.
The openings of the ureters enter the walls of the bladder
obliquely, so that it is much more easy for the fluid to pass
from the ureters into the bladder than for it to get the
other way, from the bladder into the ureters.

Mechanically speaking, there is little obstacle to the
free flow of fluid from the ureters into the bladder, and
from the bladder into the urethra, and so outwards; but
certain muscular fibres arranged circularly around the part
called the " neck " of the bladder, where it joins the urethra, constitute what is termed a *sphincter*, and are usually,
during life, in a state of contraction, so as to close the exit
of the bladder, while the other muscular fibres of the organ
are relaxed.

It is only at intervals that this state of matters is reversed ; and the walls of the bladder contracting, while its
sphincter relaxes, its contents, the *urine*, are discharged.
But, though the expulsion of the secretion of the kidneys
from the body is thus intermittent, the excretion itself is
constant, and the urinary fluid flows, drop by drop, from
the opening of the ureters into the bladder. Here it accumulates, until its quantity is sufficient to give rise to the
uneasy sensations which compel its expulsion.

135. Composition of Renal Excretion.—The renal excretion has naturally an acid reaction, and consists chiefly of
urea with some *uric acid*, sundry other animal products
of less importance, including certain coloring-matters, and
saline and gaseous substances, all held in solution by a
large quantity of water.

The quantity and composition of the urine vary greatly

according to the time of day; the temperature and moisture of the air; the fasting or replete condition of the alimentary canal; and the nature of the food.

Urea and uric acid are both composed of the elements carbon, hydrogen, oxygen, and nitrogen; but the urea is by far the more soluble in water, and greatly exceeds the uric acid in quantity.

An average healthy man excretes by the kidneys about fifty ounces, or twenty-four thousand grains of water a day. In this are dissolved five hundred grains of urea, but not more than ten to twelve grains of uric acid.

The amount of other animal matters, and of saline substances, varies from one-third as much to nearly the same amount as the urea. The saline matters consist chiefly of common salt, phosphates and sulphates of potash, soda, lime, and magnesia. The gases are the same as those in the blood—namely, carbonic acid, oxygen, and nitrogen. But the quantity is, proportionally, less than one-third as great; and the carbonic acid is in very large, while the oxygen is in very small, amount.

The average specific gravity does not differ very widely from that of blood-serum, being 1.020.

136. Kidneys and Lungs compared.—The excretion of nitrogenous waste and water, with a little carbonic acid, by the kidneys, is thus strictly comparable to that of carbonic acid and water, by the lungs, in the air-cells of which carbonic acid and watery vapors are incessantly accumulating, to be periodically expelled by the act of expiration. But the operation of the renal apparatus differs from that of the respiratory organs, in the far longer intervals between the expulsory acts; and still more in the circumstance that, while the substance which the lungs take into the body is as important as those which they give out, the kidneys take in nothing.

137. The Structure of the Kidney.—It will be observed that all the chief constituents of the urine are already con-

tained in the blood, and indeed, it might almost be said to
be the blood devoid of its corpuscles, fibrin, and albumen.
Speaking broadly, it is such a fluid as might be separated
from the blood by the help of any kind of filter which had
the property of retaining these constituents, and letting
the rest flow off.   The filter required is found in the kidney, with the minute structure of which it is now necessary to become acquainted.

When a longitudinal section of a kidney is made (Fig.
33), the upper end of the ureter (*U*) seems to widen out

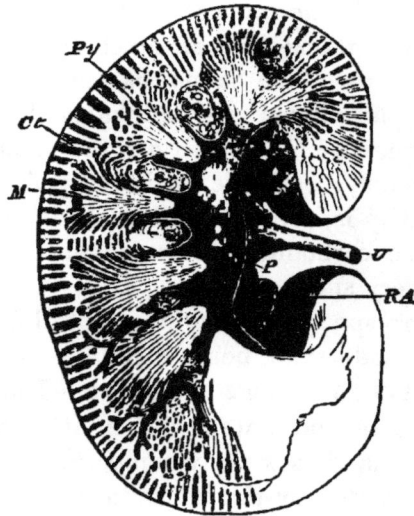

FIG. 33.

LONGITUDINAL SECTION OF THE HUMAN KIDNEY.

Ct., the cortical substance; *M.*, the medullary substance; *P.*, the pelvis of the kidney; *U.*, the ureter; *R.A.*, the renal artery.

into a basin-like cavity (*P*), which is called the *pelvis* of
the kidney.   Into this, sundry conical elevations, called the
pyramids (*Py*) project; and their summits present multitudes of minute openings—the final terminations of the
tubuli, of which the thickness of the kidney is chiefly

made up. If the tubules be traced from their openings towards the outer surface, they are found, at first, to lie parallel with one another in bundles, which radiate towards the surface, and subdivide as they go; but at length they spread about irregularly, and become interlaced. From this circumstance, the middle, or *medullary*, part (marrow, *medulla*) of the kidney looks different from the superficial,

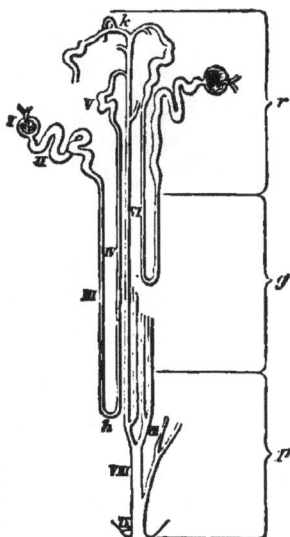

Fig. 84.

Diagrammatic View of the Course of the Tubules in the Kidney.

r, cortical portion answering to *Ct.* in Fig. 33, *k* being close to the surface of the kidneys; *g, p*, medullary portion, *p* reaching to the summit of the pyramid. *IX*, opening of tubule on the pyramid; *VIII, VII, VI*, the straight portion of the tubules; *V—II*, the twisted portion of the tubules; *I*, the Malpighian capsule.

or *cortical*, part (bark, *cortex*); but, in addition, the cortical part is more abundantly supplied with vessels than the medullary, and hence has a darker aspect. The great majority of the tubules, after a very devious course, ultimately terminate in dilatations (Fig. 35), which are called *Malpighian capsules*. Into the summit of each capsule a small vessel (Figs. 35 and 36, *va*), one of the ultimate

branches of the *renal artery* (Fig. 33, *RA*), enters (driving
the thin wall of the capsule before it), and immediately
breaks up into a bunch of looped capillaries, called a *glomerulus* (Fig. 35, *gl*), which nearly fills the cavity of the

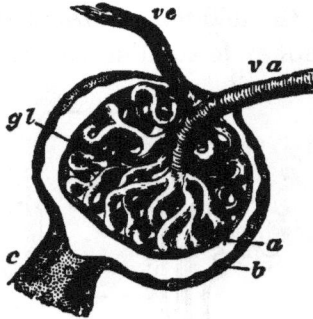

FIG. 35.

A MALPIGHIAN CAPSULE HIGHLY MAGNIFIED.

va, small branch of renal artery entering the capsule, breaking up into the glomerulus, *gl*, and finally joining again to form the vein, *ve*. *c*, the tubule; *a*, the epithelium
over the glomerulus; *b*, the epithelium lining the capsule.

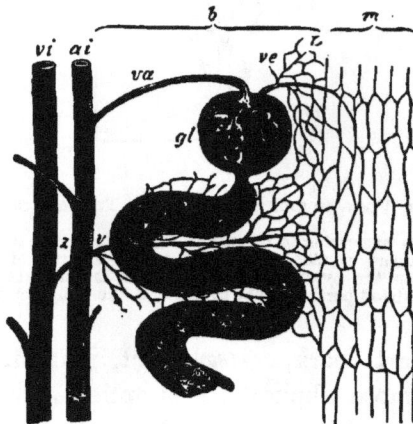

FIG. 36.

CIRCULATION IN THE KIDNEY.

ai, small branch of renal artery giving off the branch *va*, which enters glomerulus,
issues as *ve*, and then breaks up into capillaries, which, after surrounding the tubule,
find their way by *v* into *vi*, branch of the renal vein; *m*, capillaries around tubules in
parts of the cortical substance where there are no glomeruli.

capsule. The blood is carried away from this *glomerulus* by a small vein (*ve*), which does not, at once, join with other veins into a larger venous trunk, but opens into the net-work of capillaries (Fig. 36) which surrounds the tubule, thus repeating the portal circulation on a small scale.

The tubule has an epithelial lining (Fig. 35, *c*, and Fig. 37, *a*), continuous with that of the pelvis of the kidney, and the urinary passages generally. The epithelium is thick and plain enough in the tubule, but it becomes very delicate, or even disappears, in the capsule and on the glomerulus (Fig. 35, *a*, *b*).

138. The Filtering Mechanism.—It is obvious, from this description, that the surface of the glomerulus is, practically, free, or in direct communication with the exterior by means of the cavity of the tubule ; and further, that, in each vessel of the glomerulus, a thin stream of blood constantly flows, only separated from the cavity of the tubule by the very delicate membrane of which the

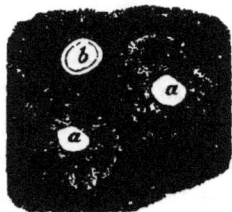

FIG. 87.

TRANSVERSE SECTION OF TWO TUBULES.

a a, canals of tubules surrounded by their epithelium. *b*, a blood-vessel cut across.

wall of the vessel is composed. The Malpighian capsule may, in fact, be regarded as a funnel, and the membranous walls of the glomerulus as a piece of very delicate filtering-paper, into which the blood is poured.

139. Changes of the Blood while passing through the Kidneys.—The blood which supplies the kidneys is brought directly from the aorta by the renal arteries, so that it has but shortly left the heart. The venous blood which enters the heart, and is propelled to the lungs, charged with the nitrogenous, as well as with the other products of waste, loses only an inappreciable quantity of the former in its course through the lungs ; so that the arterial blood which fills the aorta is pure only as regards carbonaceous waste, while it is impure as regards urea and uric acid.

In the healthy condition, the walls of the minute renal arteries and veins are relaxed, so that the passage of the blood is very free ; and but little waste, arising from muscular contraction in the walls of these vessels, is thrown into the renal blood. And, as the urine which is separated from the renal blood contains proportionately less oxygen and more carbonic acid than the blood itself, any gain of carbonic acid from this source is probably at once counterbalanced. Hence, so long as the kidney is performing its functions properly, the blood which leaves the organ by the renal vein is as bright scarlet as that which enters it by the renal artery. Strictly speaking, it is the purest blood in the body, careful analysis having shown that it contains a sensibly smaller quantity of urea and of water than that of the left side of the heart. This difference is, of course, a necessary result of the excretion of the urinary fluid from the blood as it travels through the kidney.

As the renal veins pour their contents directly into the inferior vena cava (*see* Fig. 32), it follows that the blood in the upper part of this vein is so much the less impure, or venous, than that contained in the inferior vena cava, below the renal veins.

140. The Nervous System controls the Renal Excretion. —Irritation of the nerves which supply the walls of the vessels of the kidney has the immediate effect of stopping the excretion of urine, and rendering the renal blood dark and venous. The first effect would appear to be explicable by the diminution of the pressure exerted upon the blood in the Malpighian tufts, in consequence of the diminution in the size of the channels—the small arteries—by which the blood reaches them. And the second effect is probably, in part, a secondary result of the first—the excretion of carbonic acid by the urine ceasing with the suppression of that fluid; while, to a large extent, it is also the result of a pouring in of carbonic acid into the renal blood, in consequence of the work of the muscles of the small vessels, and the waste which results therefrom.

141. The Loss by the Skin.—That the *skin* is a source of continual loss to the blood may be proved in various ways. If the whole body of a man, or one of his limbs, be inclosed in a caoutchouc bag, full of air, it will be found that this air undergoes changes which are similar in kind to those which take place in the air which is inspired into the lungs. That is to say, the air loses oxygen and gains carbonic acid; it also receives a great quantity of watery vapor, which condenses upon the sides of the bag, and may be drawn off by a properly-disposed pipe.

Under ordinary circumstances no liquid water appears upon the surface of the integument, and the whole process receives the name of the *insensible perspiration*. But, when violent exercise is taken, or under some kinds of mental emotion, or when the body is exposed to a hot and moist atmosphere, the perspiration becomes *sensible*; that is, appears in the form of scattered drops upon the surface.

142. Quantity of the Cutaneous Excretions.—The quantity of *sweat*, or sensible perspiration, and also the total amount of both sensible and insensible perspiration, vary immensely, according to the temperature and other conditions of the air, and according to the state of the blood and of the nervous system. It is estimated that, as a general rule, the quantity of water excreted by the skin is about double that given out by the lungs in the same time. The quantity of carbonic acid is not above $\frac{1}{30}$th or $\frac{1}{40}$th of that excreted by the lungs; and it is not certain that in health any *appreciable* quantity of urea is given off.

In its normal state the sweat is acid, and contains fatty matters, even when obtained free from the fatty products of the *sebaceous glands.* Ordinarily, perspiration, as it collects upon the skin, is mixed with the fatty secretion of these glands; and, in addition, contains scales of the external layers of the epidermis, which are constantly being shed.

143. Perspiration by Simple Transudation.—In analyzing the process by which the perspiration is eliminated from the body, it must be recollected, in the first place, that the skin, even if there were no glandular structures connected with it, would be in the position of a moderately thick, permeable membrane, interposed between a hot fluid, the blood, and the atmosphere. Even in hot climates the air is, usually, far from being completely saturated with watery vapor, and in temperate climates it ceases to be so saturated the moment it comes into contact with the skin, the temperature of which is, ordinarily, twenty or thirty degrees above its own.

A bladder exhibits no sensible pores, but, if filled with water and suspended in the air, the water will gradually ooze through the walls of the bladder, and disappear by evaporation. Now, in its relation to the blood, the skin is such a bladder full of hot fluid.

Thus, perspiration to a certain amount must always be going on through the substance of the integument; but what the amount of this perspiration may be cannot be accurately ascertained, because a second and very important source of the perspiration is to be found in what are called the *sweat-glands.*

144. The Sweat-Glands.—All over the body the integument presents minute apertures, the ends of channels excavated in the epidermis or scarf-skin, and each continuing the direction of a minute tube, usually about $\frac{1}{300}$th of an inch in diameter, and a quarter of an inch long, which is embedded in the dermis. Each tube is lined with an epithelium continuous with the epidermis (Fig. 40, *e*). The tube sometimes divides, but, whether single or branched, its inner end or ends are blind, and coiled up into a sort of knot, interlaced with a mesh-work of capillaries (Fig 38, *g*, and Fig. 41).

The blood in these capillaries is therefore separated from the cavity of the sweat-gland only by the thin walls of the capillaries, that of the glandular tube, and its epithelium, which, taken together, constitute but a very thin pellicle; and the arrangement, though different in detail,

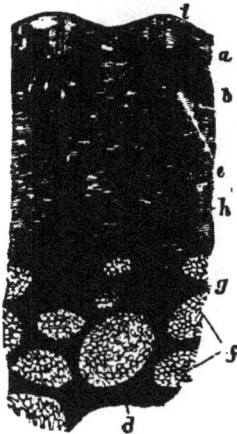 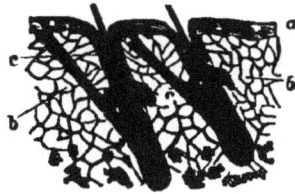

Fig. 38.   Fig. 39.

Fig. 38.—Section of the skin showing the sweat-glands. *a*, the epidermis; *b*, its deeper layer, the *rete Malpighii; c, d,* the dermis or true skin; *f,* fat-cells; *g,* the coiled end of a sweat-gland; *h,* its duct; *i,* its opening on the surface of the epidermis.

Fig. 39.—A section of the skin showing the roots of the hairs and the sebaceous glands. *b,* muscle of *c,* the hair-sheath, on the left hand.

is similar in principle to that which obtains in the kidney. In the latter, the vessel makes a coil within the Malpighian capsule, which ends a tubule. Here the perspiratory tubule coils about and among the vessels. In both cases the same result is arrived at—namely, the exposure of the blood to a large, relatively free, surface, on to which certain of its contents transude.

The number of these glands varies in different parts of
the body. They are fewest in the back and neck, where
their number is not much more than four hundred to a
square inch. They are more numerous on the skin of the
palm and sole, where their apertures follow the ridges
visible on the skin, and amount to between two and three

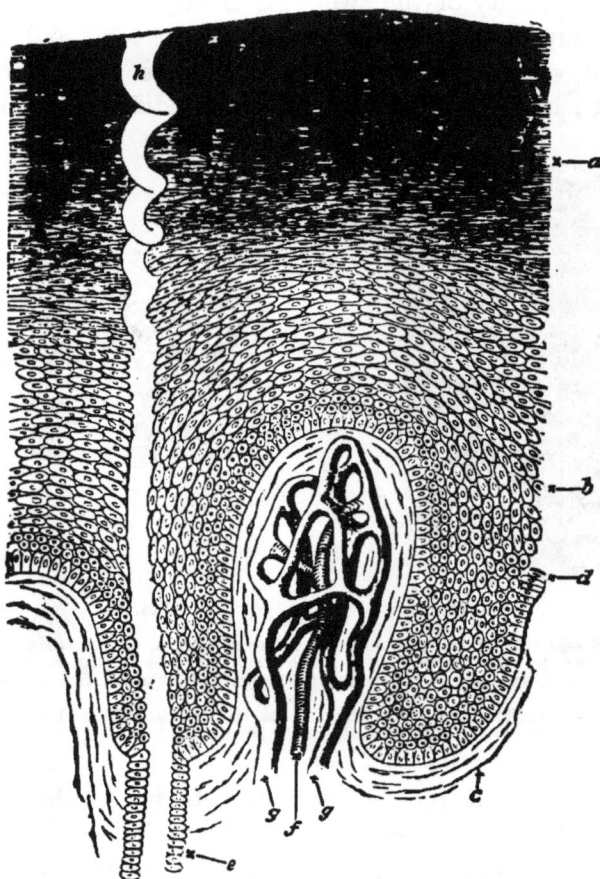

FIG. 40.

Portion of Fig. 39, more highly magnified—somewhat diagrammatic. *a,* horny
epidermis; *b,* softer layer, *rete Malpighii; c,* dermis; *d,* lowermost vertical layer of
epidermic cells; *e,* cells lining the sweat-duct continuous with epidermic cells; *h,*
corkscrew canal of sweat-duct. To the right of the sweat-duct the dermis is raised
into a papilla, in which the small artery, *f,* breaks up into capillaries, ultimately forming the veins, *g.*

thousand on the square inch. At a rough estimate, the whole integument probably possesses not fewer than from two millions and a quarter to two millions and a half of these tubules, which therefore must possess a very great aggregate secreting power.

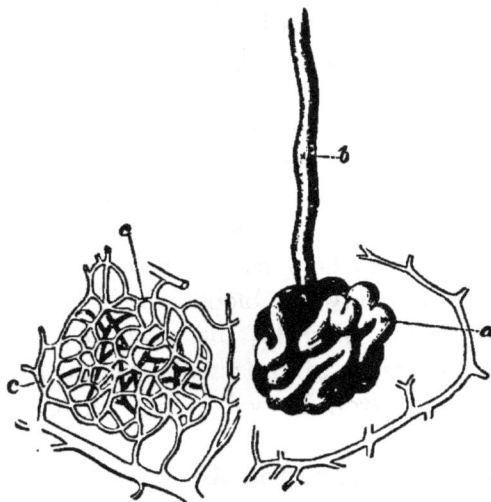

FIG. 41.

Coiled end of a sweat-gland (Fig. 38, *g*), epithelium not shown. *a*, the coil; *b*, the duct; *c*, net-work of capillaries, inside which the duct-gland lies.

145. These Glands are controlled by the Nervous System.—The sweat-glands are greatly under the influence of the nervous system. This is proved, not merely by the well-known effects of mental emotion in sometimes suppressing the perspiration and sometimes causing it to be poured forth in immense abundance, but has been made a matter of direct experiment. There are some animals, such as the horse, which perspire very freely. If the sympathetic nerve of one side, in the neck of a horse, be cut, the same side of the head becomes injected with blood, and its temperature rises (67); and, simultaneously, sweat is poured out abundantly over the whole surface thus affected. On irritating that end of the cut nerve which is in connection with the vessels, the muscular walls of the latter, to which the nerve is distributed, contract, the congestion ceases, and with it the perspiration.

146. Variations in the Perspiratory Losses.—The amount of matter which may be lost by perspiration, under certain circumstances, is very remarkable. Heat and severe labor, combined, may reduce the weight of a man two or three pounds in an hour, by means of the cutaneous perspiration alone; and, as there is some reason to believe that the quantity of solid matter carried off from the blood does not diminish with the increase of the amount of the perspiration, the total amount of solids which are eliminated by profuse sweating may be considerable.

The difference between blood which is coming from, and that which is going to, the skin, can only be concluded from the nature of the substances given out in the perspiration; but arterial blood is not rendered venous in the skin.

147. The Lungs, Skin, and Kidneys, compared.—It will now be instructive to compare together, in more detail than has been done in the first chapter (28), the three great organs—lungs, kidneys, and skin—which have been described.

In ultimate anatomical analysis, each of these organs consists of a moist animal membrane separating the blood from the atmosphere.

Water, carbonic acid, and solid matter, pass out from the blood through the animal membrane in each organ, and constitute its secretion or excretion; but the three organs differ in the absolute and relative amounts of the constituents the escape of which they permit.

Taken by weight, water is the predominant excretion in all three: most solid matter is given off by the kidneys; most gaseous matter by the lungs.

The skin partakes of the nature of both lungs and kid-

neys, seeing that it absorbs oxygen and exhales carbonic
acid and water, like the former, while it excretes organic
and saline matter in solution, like the latter; but the skin
is more closely related to the kidneys than to the lungs.
Hence, when the free action of the skin is interrupted, its
work is usually thrown upon the kidneys, and *vice versa.*
In hot weather, when the excretion by the skin increases,
that of the kidneys diminishes, and the reverse is observed
in cold weather.

This power of mutual substitution, however, only goes
a little way; for, if the kidneys be extirpated, or their
functions much interfered with, death ensues, however active the skin may be. And, on the other hand, if the skin
be covered with an impenetrable varnish, the temperature
of the body rapidly falls, and death takes place, though the
lungs and kidneys remain active.

SECTION II.—*Losses and Gains by the Liver.*

148. Structure and Connections of the Liver.—The *liver*
is a constant source both of loss, and, in a sense, of gain,
to the blood which passes through it. It gives rise to
loss, because it separates a peculiar fluid, the *bile,* from the
blood, and throws that fluid into the intestine. It is also
in another way a source of loss because it elaborates from
the blood passing through it a substance called *glycogen,*
which is stored up sometimes in large, sometimes in small,
quantities in the cells of the liver. This latter loss, however, is only temporary, and may be sooner or later converted into a gain, for this glycogen very readily passes
into sugar, and either in that form or in some other way is
carried off by the blood. In this respect, therefore, there
is a gain to the blood of kind or quality, though not of
quantity, of material. Finally, it is very probable that
the liver is one source of the colorless corpuscles of the
blood.

The liver is the largest glandular organ in the body,

ordinarily weighing about fifty or sixty ounces. It is a
broad, dark, red-colored organ, which lies on the right side
of the body, immediately below the diaphragm, with which
its upper surface is in contact, while its lower surface
touches the intestines and the right kidney.

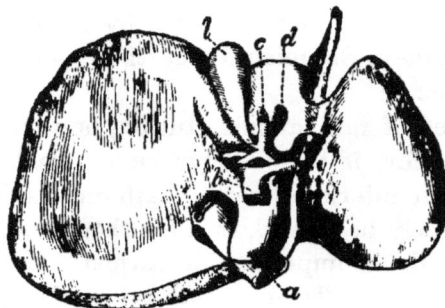

FIG. 42.

THE LIVER TURNED UP AND VIEWED FROM BELOW.

a, vena cava; *b*, vena portæ; *c*, bile-duct; *d*, hepatic artery; *l*, gall-bladder. The
termination of the hepatic vein in the vena cava is not seen, being covered by the
piece of the vena cava.

The liver is invested by a coat of peritoneum, which
keeps it in place. It is flattened from above downwards,
and convex and smooth above, where it fits into the concavity of the lower surface of the diaphragm. Flat and
irregular below (Fig. 42), it is thick behind, but ends in a
thin edge in front.

Viewed from below, as in Fig. 42, the *inferior vena
cava*, *a*, is seen to traverse a notch in the hinder edge of
the liver as it passes from the abdomen to the thorax. At
b the trunk of the *vena portæ* is observed dividing into the
chief branches which enter into, and ramify through, the
substance of the organ. At *d*, the *hepatic artery*, coming
almost directly from the aorta, similarly divides, enters the
liver, and ramifies through it; while at *c* is the single
trunk of the duct, called the *hepatic duct*, which conveys
away the bile brought to it by its right and left branches

from the liver. Opening into the hepatic duct is seen the duct of a large oval sac, *l*, the *gall-bladder*. The duct is smaller than the artery, and the artery than the portal vein.

If the branches of the artery, the portal vein, and the bile-duct, be traced into the substance of the liver, they will be found to accompany one another, and to branch out and subdivide, becoming smaller and smaller. At length

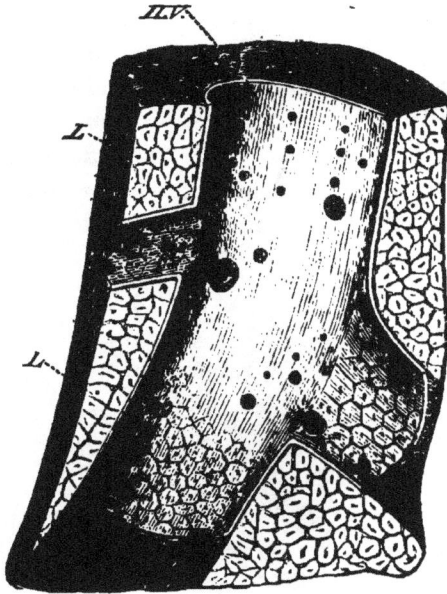

Fig. 43.

A section of part of the liver to show *H.V.*, a branch of the hepatic vein, with *L.*, the lobules or acini of the liver, seated upon its walls, and sending their intralobular veins into it.

the portal vein and hepatic artery (Fig. 45, *V.P.*) will be found to end in the capillaries, which traverse, like a network, the substance of the smallest obvious subdivisions of the liver-substance—polygonal masses of one-tenth of an inch in diameter, or less, which are termed the *lobules*. Every *lobule* is seated by its base upon one of the ramifications of a great vein—the *hepatic vein*—and the blood of the capillaries of the lobule is poured into that vein by a minute veinlet, called *intralobular* (Fig. 45, *H. V.*), which traverses the centre of the lobule, and pierces its base. Thus the venous blood of the portal vein and the arterial blood of the hepatic artery reach the surfaces of the lobules by the ultimate ramifications of that vein and artery, become mixed in the capillaries of each lobule, and are carried off by its *intralobular* veinlet, which pours its contents into one of the ramifications of the hepatic vein. These ramifications, joining together, form larger and larger trunks, which at length reach the hinder margin of the liver, and finally open into the *vena cava inferior*, where it passes upwards in contact with that part of the organ.

Thus the blood with which the liver is supplied is a mixture of arterial and venous blood; the former brought

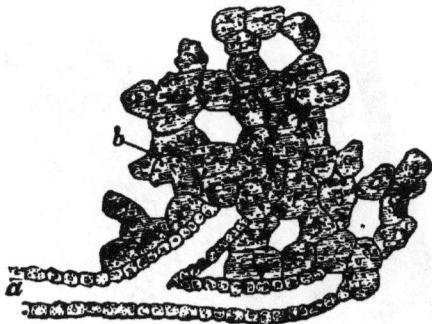

Fig. 44.

a, ultimate branches of the hepatic duct; *b*, liver-cells.

by the hepatic artery directly from the aorta, the latter by the portal vein from the capillaries of the stomach, intestines, pancreas, and spleen.

What ultimately becomes of the ramifications of the hepatic duct is not certainly known. Lined by an epithelium, which is continuous with that of the main duct, and thence with that of the intestines, into which the main

duct opens, they may be traced to the very surface of the
lobules.   Their ultimate ramifications are not yet thor-

FIG. 45.

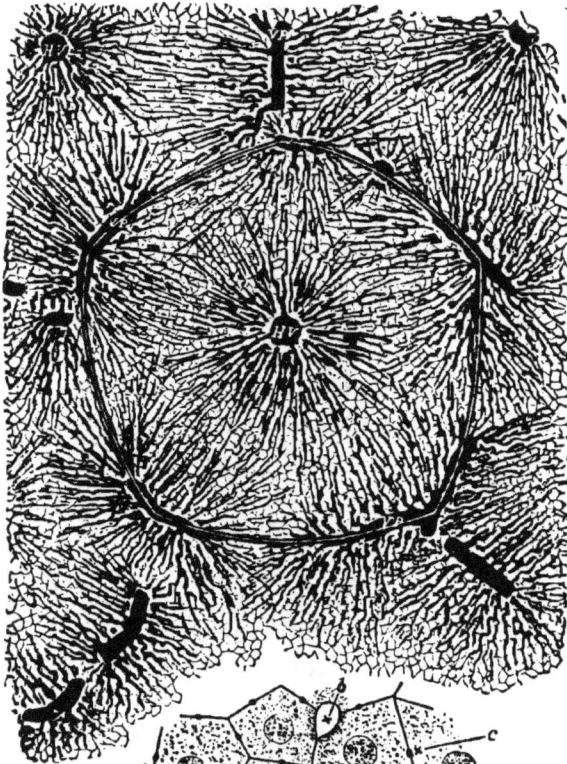

FIG. 46.

Fig. 45.—Section of partially-injected liver magnified. The artificial white line is
introduced to mark the limits of a lobule.   *V.P.*, branches of portal vein breaking up
into capillaries, which run towards the centre of the lobule, and join *H.V.*, the intralobular branch of the hepatic vein. The outlines of the liver-cells are seen as a fine
net-work of lines throughout the whole lobule.

Fig. 46.—Portion of lobule very highly magnified. *a*, liver-cell with *n*, nucleus (two
are often present); *b*, capillaries cut across; *c*, minute biliary passages between the
cells, injected with coloring-matter.

oughly determined: but recent investigations tend to show
that they communicate with minute passages left between
the hepatic cells, and traversing the lobule in the intervals
left by the capillaries (Fig. 46). However this may be,
any fluid separated from the blood by the lobules must
really find its way into them.

In the lobules themselves all the meshes of the blood-
vessels are occupied by the liver-cells. These are many-
sided, minute bodies, each about $\frac{1}{1000}$th of an inch in
diameter, possessing a nucleus in its interior, and frequently having larger and smaller granules of fatty matter
distributed through its substance (Fig. 46, a). It is in
the liver-cells that the active powers of the liver are supposed to reside.

149. The Active Powers of the Liver-Cells.—The nature
of these active powers, so far as the liver is a source of loss
to the blood which traverses it, is determined by ascertain-
ing—

a. The character of that fluid, the bile, which incessantly flows down the biliary duct, and which, if digestion
is not going on, and the passage into the intestine is
closed, flows back into and fills the gall-bladder.

b. The difference between the blood which enters the
liver and that which leaves it.

150. The Bile—its Quantity and Composition.—a. The total quantity of bile secreted in the twenty-four hours varies,
but probably amounts to not less than from two to three
pounds. It is a golden-yellow, slightly alkaline fluid, of
extremely bitter taste, consisting of water with from seventeen per cent. to half that quantity of solid matter in
solution. The solids consist, in the first place, of a somewhat complex substance which may be separated by crystallization, and has been called *bilin*. It is in reality a
mixture of two acids, in combination with soda, one called
glycocholic, and consisting of carbon, hydrogen, nitrogen,
and oxygen, the other *taurocholic*, and containing in addi-

tion to the other elements a considerable quantity of sulphur. Besides the taurocholate and glycocholate of soda, or bile-salts as they are sometimes called, the bile contains a remarkable crystalline substance, very fatty-looking, but not really of a fatty nature, called *cholesterin*, one or more peculiar coloring-matters probably related to the hæmatin of the blood, and certain saline matters.

b. Of these constituents of the bile, the water, the cholesterin, and the saline matters, alone, are discoverable in the blood; and, though doubtless some difference obtains between the blood which enters the liver and that which leaves it, in respect of the proportional quantity of these constituents, great practical difficulties lie in the way of the precise ascertainment of the amount of that difference. The blood of the hepatic vein, however, is certainly poorer in water than that of the portal vein.

151. Bile is formed in the Liver-Cells.—As the essential constituents of bile, the bile-acids and the coloring-matter are not discoverable in the blood which enters the liver; they must be formed at the expense of the tissue of that organ itself, or of some constituent of the blood passing through it.

SECTION III.—*Sources of Gain to the Blood.*

152. The Skin as an Organ of Respiration.—We must next consider the chief sources of constant gain to the blood; and, in the first place, *the sources* of *gain of matter.*

The lungs and skin are, as has been seen, two of the principal channels by which the body loses liquid and gaseous matter, but they are also the sole means by which one of the most important of all substances for the maintenance of life, *oxygen*, is introduced into the blood. It has already been pointed out that the volume of the oxygen taken into the blood by the lungs is rather greater than that of the carbonic acid given out. The absolute

7

weight of oxygen thus absorbed may be estimated at ten
thousand grains (*see* 165).

How much is taken in by the skin of man is not certainly known, but in some of the lower animals, such as
the frog, the skin plays a very important part in the performance of the respiratory function.

153. Reaction of the Liver upon the Blood.—The blood
leaving the liver by the hepatic vein not only contains proportionally less water and fibrin, but proportionally more
corpuscles, especially colorless corpuscles, and, what is
still more important, under certain circumstances at least,
a larger quantity of liver-sugar, or *glucose*, than that
brought to it by the portal veins and hepatic artery.

That the blood leaving the liver should contain proportionally less water and more corpuscles than that entering
it, is no more than might be expected from the fact that the
formation of the bile, which is separated from this blood,
necessarily involves a loss of water and of some solid matters, while it does not abstract any of the corpuscles.

We do not know why less fibrin separates from the
blood of the hepatic vein than from the blood brought to
the liver.   But the reason why there is always more sugar
in the blood leaving the liver than in that entering it, and
why, in fact, there may be plenty of sugar in the blood of
the hepatic vein even when none whatever is brought to it
by the hepatic artery, or portal vein, has been made out by
careful and ingenious experimental research.

154. Sugar-forming Function of the Liver.—If an animal be fed upon purely animal food, the blood of the portal vein will contain no sugar, none having been absorbed
by the walls of the alimentary canal, nor will that of the
hepatic artery contain any, or, at any rate, more than the
merest trace.   Nevertheless, plenty will be found, at the
same time, in the blood of the hepatic vein and in that of
the vena cava, from the point at which it is joined by the
hepatic vein, as far as the heart.

Secondly, if, from an animal so fed, the liver be extracted, and a current of cold water forced into the *vena portæ*, it will flow out by the hepatic vein, carrying with it all the blood of the organ, and will, after a time, come out colorless, and devoid of sugar. Nevertheless, if the organ be left to itself at a moderate temperature, sugar will soon again become abundant in it.

Thirdly, from the liver, washed as above described, a substance may be extracted, by appropriate methods, which resembles starch or dextrine, in chemical composition, consisting as it does of carbon united with hydrogen and oxygen, the latter being in the same proportions as in water. This "amyloid" substance is the *glycogen* spoken of in 148. It may be dried and kept for long periods without undergoing any change.

But, like the vegetable starch and dextrine, this animal amyloid, which must be formed in the liver, since it is certainly not contained either in the blood of the portal vein, or in that of the hepatic artery, is very readily changed, by contact with certain matters, which act as ferments, into sugar.

Fourthly, it may be demonstrated that a ferment, competent to change the "amyloid" glycogen into saccharine "*glucose*," exists under ordinary circumstances in the liver.

Putting all these circumstances together, the following explanation of the riddle of the appearance of sugar in the blood of the hepatic vein and vena cava, when neither it, nor any compound out of which it is easily formed, exists in the blood brought to the liver, appears to have much probability; though it may possibly require modification, in some respects, hereafter.

The liver forms glycogen out of the blood with which it is supplied. The same blood supplies the ferment which, at the temperature of the body, very speedily converts the comparatively little soluble glycogen into very soluble sugar; and this sugar is dissolved and carried away by each intralobular vein to the hepatic vein, and thence to the vena cava.

Though after death a very considerable quantity of sugar accumulates in the hepatic vein, the amount which, *at any given moment*, can be detected during life is extremely small. This has led some physiologists to suppose that, in health, glycogen is not converted into sugar, but undergoes some other change. A very small quantity of sugar, however, so small as to almost escape detection, thrown into the hepatic vein every instant, would amount to a considerable quantity in the twenty-four hours.

This formation of glycogen in the liver goes on in the total absence of starch or sugar from the food. It must, therefore, in such cases be formed at the expense of proteid material (*see* 176). It appears, however, that the presence of starch or sugar in the food, though not essential, is very favorable to the production of glycogen in the liver.

155. Gain by the Lymphatics.—The *lymphatic system* has been already mentioned as a feeder of the blood with a fluid which, in general, appears to be merely the superfluous drainage, as it were, of the blood-vessels; though at intervals, as we shall see, the lacteals make substantial additions of new matter. It is very probable that the multitudinous *lymphatic glands* may effect some change in the fluid which traverses them, or may add to the number of corpuscles in the lymph.

Nothing *certain* is known of the functions of certain bodies which are sometimes called ductless glands, but have quite a different structure from ordinary secreting glands; and indeed do not resemble each other in structure. These are, the *thyroid* gland, which lies in the part of the throat below the larynx, and is that organ which, when enlarged by disease, gives rise to "Derbyshire neck" or "goître;" the *thymus* gland, situated at the base of the heart, largest in infants, and gradually disappearing in

adult, or old, persons; and the *supra-renal* capsules, which
lie above the kidneys.

156. The Spleen—its Functions unknown.—We are as
much in the dark respecting the office of the large viscus
called the *spleen*, which lies upon the left side of the
stomach in the abdominal cavity (Fig. 47).   It is an elongated flattened red body, abundantly supplied with blood
by an artery called the *splenic artery*, which proceeds almost directly from the aorta.   The blood which has trav-

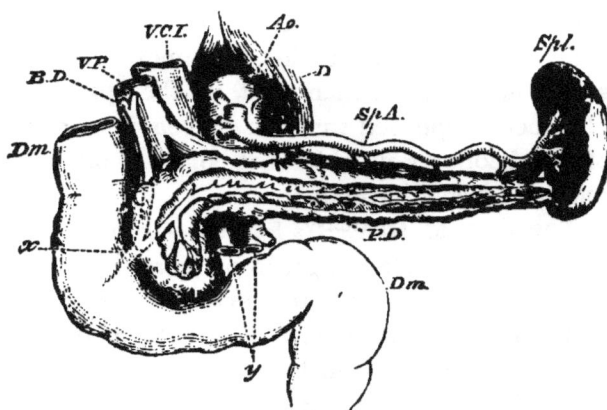

Fig. 47.

The spleen (*Spl.*) with the splenic artery (*SpA.*).   Below this is seen the splenic
vein running to help to form the vena portæ (*V.P.*).   *Ao.*, the aorta; *D.*, a pillar of
the diaphragm; *P.D.*, the pancreatic duct exposed by dissection in the substance of
the pancreas; *Dm.*, the duodenum; *B.D.*, the biliary duct uniting with the pancreatic
duct into the common duct, *x*; *y*, the intestinal vessels.

ersed the spleen is collected by the *splenic vein*, and is
carried by it to the *vena portæ*, and so to the liver.

A section of the spleen shows a dark-red spongy mass
dotted over with minute whitish spots.   Each of these last
is the section of one of the spheroidal bodies called *corpuscles of the spleen*, which are scattered through its substance, and consist of a solid aggregation of minute bodies,
like the white corpuscles of the blood, traversed by a capillary net-work, which is fed by a small twig of the splenic

artery. The dark-red part of the spleen, in which these corpuscles are embedded, is composed of fibrous and elastic tissue supporting a very spongy vascular net-work.

The elasticity of the splenic tissue allows the organ to be readily distended, and enables it to return to its former size after distention. It appears to change its dimensions with the state of the abdominal viscera, attaining its largest size about six hours after a full meal, and falling to its minimum bulk six or seven hours later, if no further supply of food be taken.

The blood of the splenic vein is found to contain proportionally fewer red corpuscles, but more colorless corpuscles and more fibrin, than that in the splenic artery; and it has been supposed that the spleen is one of those parts of the economy in which the colorless corpuscles of the blood are especially produced.

157. The Gain of Heat—its Source.—It has been seen that *heat* is being constantly given off from the integument and from the air-passages; and every thing that passes from the body carries away with it, in like manner, a certain quantity of heat. Furthermore, the surface of the body is much more exposed to cold than its interior. Nevertheless, the temperature of the body is maintained very evenly, at all times and in all parts, within the range of two degrees on either side of 99° Fahr.

This is the result of three conditions: The first, that heat is constantly being generated in the body; the second, that it is as constantly being distributed through the body; the third, that it is subject to incessant regulation.

Heat is generated whenever oxidation takes place; and hence, whenever proteid substances (*see* 167) or fats, or amyloidal matters, are being converted into the more highly-oxidated waste products—urea, carbonic acid, and water—heat is necessarily evolved. But these processes are taking place in all parts of the body by which vital activity is manifested; and hence every capillary vessel and every extra-vascular islet of tissue is really a small fire-place in which heat is being evolved, in proportion to the activity of the chemical changes which are going on.

158. Distribution of Heat by the Blood-Current.—But, as the vital activities of different parts of the body, and of the whole body, at different times, are very different, and as some parts of the body are so situated as to lose their heat by radiation and conduction much more easily than others, the temperature of the body would be very unequal in its different parts, and at different times, were it not for the arrangements by which the heat is distributed and regulated.

Whatever oxidation occurs in any part, raises the temperature of the blood which is in that part at the time to a proportional extent. But this blood is swiftly hurried away into other regions of the body, and rapidly gives up its increased temperature to them. On the other hand, the blood which by being carried to the vessels in the skin on the surface of the body begins to have its temperature lowered by evaporation, etc., is hurried away, before it has time to get thoroughly cooled, into the deeper organs; and in them it becomes warm by contact, as well as by the oxidating processes in which it takes a part. Thus the blood-vessels and their contents might be compared to a system of hot-water pipes, through which the warm water is kept constantly circulating by a pump; while it is heated, not by a great central boiler as usual, but by a multitude of minute gas-jets, disposed beneath the pipes, not evenly, but more here and fewer there. It is obvious that, however much greater might be the heat applied to one part of the system of pipes than to another, the general temperature of the water would be even throughout, if it were kept moving with sufficient quickness by the pump.

159. Evaporation regulates Temperature. — If such a system were entirely composed of closed pipes, the temperature of the water might be raised to any extent by the gas-jets.   On the other hand, it might be kept down to any required degree by causing a larger, or smaller, portion of the pipes to be wetted with water, which should be able to evaporate freely—as, for example, by wrapping them in wet cloths.   And the greater the quantity of water thus evaporated, the lower would be the temperature of the whole apparatus.

Now, the regulation of the temperature of the human body is effected on this principle.   The vessels are closed pipes, but a great number of them are inclosed in the skin and in the mucous membrane of the air-passages, which are, in a physical sense, wet cloths freely exposed to the air.   It is the evaporation from these which exercises a more important influence than any other condition upon the regulation of the temperature of the blood, and, consequently, of the body.

160. Regulative Agency of the Nervous System.—But, as a further nicety of adjustment, the wetness of the regulator is itself determined by the state of the small vessels, inasmuch as exudation from these takes place more readily when the walls of the veins and arteries are relaxed, and the blood distends them and the capillaries.   But the condition of the walls of the vessels depends upon the nerves by which they are supplied; and it so happens that cold affects these nerves in such a manner as to give rise to contraction of the small vessels, while moderate warmth has the reverse effect.

Thus the supply of blood to the surface is lessened, and loss of heat is thereby checked, when the external temperature is low; while, when the external temperature is high, the supply of blood to the surface is increased, the fluid exuded from the vessels pours out by the sweat-glands, and the evaporation of this fluid checks the rise in the temperature of the superficial blood.

Hence it is that, so long as the surface of the body perspires freely, and the air-passages are abundantly moist, a man may remain with impunity, for a considerable time, in an oven in which meat is being cooked. The heat of the air is expended in converting this superabundant perspiration into vapor, and the temperature of the man's blood is hardly raised.

161. Intermittent Action of the Glands.—The chief *intermittently active sources of loss* to the blood are found among the glands proper, all of which are, in principle, narrow pouches of the mucous membranes, or of the integument of the body, lined by a continuation of the epithelium, or of the epidermis. In the *glands of Lieberkühn,* which exist in immense numbers in the walls of the small intestines, each gland is nothing more than a simple blind sac of the mucous membrane, shaped like a small test-tube, with its closed end outwards, and its open end on the inner surface of the intestine (Fig. 48, 1). The sweat-glands of the skin, as we have already seen, are equally simple, blind, tube-like involutions of the integument, the ends of which become coiled up. The *sebaceous glands*, usually connected with the hair-sacs, are shorter, and their blind ends are somewhat subdivided, so that the gland is divided into a narrow neck and a more dilated and sacculated end (Fig. 48, 5).

The neck by which the gland communicates with the free surface is called its *duct.* More complicated glands are produced by the elongation of the duct into a long tube, and the division and subdivision of the blind end into multitudes of similar tubes, each of which ends in a dilatation (Fig. 48, 6). These dilatations, attached to their branched ducts, somewhat resemble a bunch of grapes. Glands of this kind are called *racemose.* The *salivary glands* and the *pancreas* are such glands.

Now, many of these glands, such as the salivary, and the pancreas (with the perspiratory, or sudoriparous glands, which it has been convenient to consider already), are only active when certain impressions on the nervous system

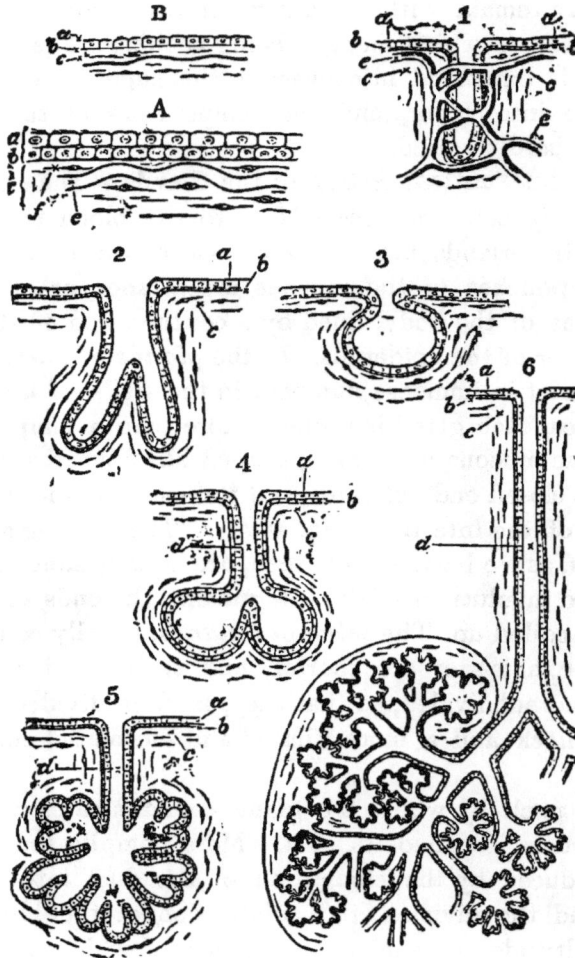

FIG. 48.

A DIAGRAM TO ILLUSTRATE THE STRUCTURE OF GLANDS.

A. Typical structure of the mucous membrane. *a*, an upper, and *b*, a lower, layer of epithelium cells; *c*, the dermis with *e*, a blood-vessel, and *f*, connective-tissue corpuscles.

B. The same, with only one layer of cells, *a* and *b*, the so-called basement membrane between the epithelium, *a*, and dermis, *c*.

1. Simple tubular gland.
2. Tubular gland bifid at its base. In this and succeeding figures the blood-vessels are omitted.
3. Simple saccular gland.
4. Divided saccular gland, with a duct, *d*.
5. Similar gland still more divided.
6. Racemose gland, part only being drawn.

give rise to a particular condition of the gland, or of its vessels, or of both.

162. Action of the Salivary Glands.—Thus the sight or smell, or even the thought of food, will cause a flow of saliva into the mouth; the previously quiescent gland suddenly pouring out its fluid secretion, as a result of a change in the condition of the nervous system.   And, in animals, the salivary glands can be made to secrete abundantly, by irritating a nerve which supplies the gland and its vessels. How far this effect is the result of the mechanical influence of the nerve on the state of the circulation, by widening the small arteries (*see* 65) and so supplying the gland with more blood, and how far it is the result of a more direct influence of the nerve upon the state of the tissue of the gland itself, making the *cells secrete*, just as a nerve, when stimulated makes a muscle contract, is not at present finally determined.

The liquids poured out by the intermittent glands are always very poor in solid constituents, and consist chiefly of water.   Those poured on to the surface of the body are lost, but those which are received by the alimentary canal are doubtless in a great measure reabsorbed.

163. Gain of Waste Products from the Muscles.—The great *intermittent sources of gain of waste products* to the blood are the muscles, every contraction of which is accompanied by a pouring of certain products into the blood. That much of this waste is carbonic acid is certain from the facts (*a*) that the blood which leaves a contracting muscle is always highly venous, far more so than that which leaves a quiescent muscle; (*b*) that muscular exertion at once immensely increases the quantity of carbonic acid expired; but whether the amount of nitrogenous waste is increased under these circumstances, or not, is a point yet under discussion.

CHAPTER VI.

THE FUNCTION OF ALIMENTATION.

SECTION I.—*Properties of Food-Stuffs.*

164. The Alimentary Canal the Chief Source of Gain. —The great source of gain to the blood, and, except the lungs, the only channel by which altogether new material is introduced into that fluid, putting aside the altogether exceptional case of absorption by the skin, is the *aliment- ary canal*, the totality of the operations of which consti- tutes the function of *alimentation*. It will be useful to consider the general nature and results of the performance of this function before studying its details.

165. Quantity of Dry, Solid, and Gaseous Aliment daily taken.—A man daily takes into his mouth, and thereby in- troduces into his alimentary canal, a certain quantity of solid and liquid food, in the shape of meat, bread, butter, water, and the like. The amount of chemically dry, solid matter, which must thus be taken into the body, if a man of average size and activity is neither to lose, nor to gain, in weight, has been found to be about 8,000 grains. In ad- dition to this, his blood absorbs by the lungs about 10,000 grains of oxygen gas, making a grand total of 18,000 grains (or nearly two pounds and three-quarters avoirdu- pois) of daily gain of dry, solid, and gaseous matter.

166. Daily Loss of Dry Solids.—The weight of dry solid matter passed out from the alimentary canal does not, on the average, amount to more than one-tenth of that which is taken into it, or 800 grains. Now, the alimentary canal is the only channel by which any appreciable amount of solid matter leaves the body in an undissolved condition. It follows, therefore, that, in addition to the 10,000 grains of oxygen, 7,200 grains of dry, solid matter must pass out of the body by the lungs, skin, or kidneys, either in the form of gas, or dissolved in the liquid excretions of those organs. Further, as the general composition of the body remains constant, it follows either that the elementary constituents of the solids taken into the body must be identical with those of the body itself: or that, in the course of the vital processes, the food alone is destroyed, the substance of the body remaining unchanged: or, finally, that both these alternatives hold good, and that food is, partly, identical with the wasting substance of the body, and replaces it; and, partly, differs from the wasting substance, and is consumed without replacing it.

167. Classification of Aliments.—As a matter of fact, all the substances which are used as food come under one of four heads. They are either what may be termed *Proteids*, or they are *Fats*, or they are *Amyloids*, or they are *Minerals*.

Proteids are composed of the four elements—carbon, hydrogen, oxygen, and nitrogen, sometimes united with sulphur and phosphorus.

Under this head come the *Gluten* of flour; the *Albumen* of white of egg, and blood-serum; the *Fibrin* of the blood; the *Syntonin*, which is the chief constituent of muscle and flesh, and *Casein*, one of the chief constituents of cheese, and many other similar but less common bodies; while *Gelatin*, which is obtained, by boiling, from connective tissue, and *Chondrin*, which may be produced in the same way from cartilage, may be considered to be outlying members of the same group.

Fats are composed of carbon, hydrogen, and oxygen only, and contain more hydrogen than is enough to form water if united with the oxygen which they possess.

All vegetable and animal fatty matters and oils come under this division.

Amyloids are substances which also consist of carbon,

hydrogen, and oxygen only. But they contain no more hydrogen than is just sufficient to produce water with their oxygen. These are the matters known as *Starch*, *Dextrine*, *Sugar*, and *Gum*.

It is the peculiarity of the three groups of food-stuffs just mentioned that they can only be obtained (at any rate, at present) by the activity of living beings, whether animals or plants, so that they may be conveniently termed *vital food-stuffs*.

Food-stuffs of the fourth class, on the other hand, or *Minerals*, are to be procured as well from the not-living, as the living world. They are *water*, and *salts* of sundry alkalies, earths, and metals. To these, in strictness, *oxygen* ought to be added, though, as it is not taken in by the alimentary canal, it hardly comes within the ordinary acceptation of the word food.

168. Ultimate Composition of Aliments. — In ultimate analysis, then, it appears that *vital food-stuffs* contain either three or four of the elements: carbon, hydrogen, oxygen, and nitrogen; and that *mineral food-stuffs* are water and salts. But the human body, in ultimate analysis, also proves to be composed of the same four elements, *plus* water, and the same saline matters as are found in food.

More than this, no substance can serve permanently for food—that is to say, can prevent loss of weight and change in the general composition of the body—unless it contains a certain amount of proteid matter in the shape of albumen, fibrin, syntonin, casein, etc.; while, on the other hand, any substance which contains proteid matter, in a readily assimilable shape, is competent to act as a permanent vital food-stuff.

The human body, as we have seen, contains a large quantity of proteid matter in one or other of the forms which have been enumerated; and, therefore, it turns out to be an indispensable condition that every substance,

which is to serve permanently as food, must contain a sufficient quantity of the most important and complex component of the body ready made. It must also contain a
sufficient quantity of the mineral ingredients which are required. Whether it contains either fats or amyloids, or
both, its essential power of supporting the life and maintaining the weight and composition of the body remains
unchanged.

169. No Absolute Necessity for Other Food-Stuffs.—The
necessity of constantly renewing the supply of proteid
matter arises from the circumstance that the secretion of
urea from the body (and consequently the loss of nitrogen)
goes on continually, whether the body is fed or not : while
there is only one form in which nitrogen (at any rate, in
any considerable quantity) can be taken into the blood,
and that is in the form of a solution of proteid matter. If
proteid matter be not supplied, therefore, the body must
needs waste, because there is nothing in the food competent to make good the loss of nitrogen.

On the other hand, if proteid matter be supplied, there
can be no *absolute* necessity for any other but the mineral
food - stuffs, because proteid matter contains carbon and
hydrogen in abundance, and hence is competent to give
origin to the other great products of waste, carbonic acid
and water.

In fact, the final results of the oxidation of proteid
matters are carbonic acid, water, and ammonia; and these,
as we have seen, are the final shapes of the waste products
of the human economy.

170. Nitrogen Starvation.—From what has been said,
it becomes readily intelligible that, whether an animal be
herbivorous or carnivorous, it begins to starve from the
moment its vital food-stuffs consist of pure amyloids, or
fats, or any mixture of them. It suffers from what may be
called *nitrogen starvation*, and, sooner or later, will die.

In this case, and still more in that of an animal deprived of vital food altogether, the organism, so long as it continues to live, feeds upon itself. In the former case, those excretions which contain nitrogen, in the latter, all its waste products, are necessarily formed at the expense of its own body; whence it has been rightly enough observed that a starving sheep is as much a carnivore as a lion.

171. Disadvantages of a Purely Nitrogenous Diet.—But though proteid matter is the essential element of food, and under certain circumstances may suffice, by itself, to maintain the body, it is a very disadvantageous and uneconomical food.

Albumen, which may be taken as the type of the proteids, contains about 53 parts of carbon and 15 of nitrogen in 100 parts. If a man were to be fed on white of egg, therefore, he would take in, speaking roughly, 3½ parts of carbon for every part of nitrogen.

But it is proved experimentally, that a healthy, full-grown man, keeping up his weight and heat, and taking a fair amount of exercise, eliminates 4,000 grains of carbon to only 300 grains of nitrogen, or, roughly, only needs one-thirteenth as much nitrogen as carbon. However, if he is to get his 4,000 grains of carbon out of albumen, he must eat 7,547 grains of that substance. But 7,547 grains of albumen contain 1,132 grains of nitrogen, or nearly four times as much as he wants.

To put the case in another way, it takes about four pounds of fatless meat (which generally contains about one-fourth its weight of dry solid proteids) to yield 4,000 grains of carbon, whereas one pound will furnish 300 grains of nitrogen.

Thus a man, confined to a purely proteid diet, must eat a prodigious quantity of it. This not only involves a great amount of physiological labor in comminuting the food, and a great expenditure of power and time in dissolving and absorbing it, but throws a great quantity of wholly

profitless labor upon those excretory organs, which have
to get rid of the nitrogenous matter, three-fourths of which,
as we have seen, is superfluous.

172. Economy of Physiological Power.—Unproductive
labor is as much to be avoided in physiological, as in
political, economy; and it is quite possible that an animal
fed with perfectly nutritious, proteid matter should die of
starvation: the loss of power in various operations required for its assimilation overbalancing the gain; or the
time occupied in their performance being too great to
check waste with sufficient rapidity. The body, under
these circumstances, falls into the condition of a merchant
who has abundant assets, but who cannot get in his debts
in time to meet his creditors.

173. Economy of a Mixed Diet.—These considerations
lead us to the physiological justification of the universal
practice of mankind in adopting a mixed diet, in which
proteids are mixed either with fats, or with amyloids, or
with both.

Fats may be taken to contain about 80 per cent. of
carbon, and amyloids about 40 per cent. Now, it has been
seen that there is enough nitrogen to supply the waste of
that substance per diem, in a healthy man, in a pound of
fatless meat; which also contains 1,000 grains of carbon,
leaving a deficit of 3,000 grains of carbon. Rather more
than half a pound of fat, or a pound of sugar, will supply
this quantity of carbon. The former, if properly subdivided, the latter, by reason of its solubility, passes with
great ease into the economy, the digestive labor of which
is consequently reduced to a minimum.

174. Advantages of a Mixed Diet.—Several apparently
simple articles of food constitute a mixed diet in themselves. Thus butcher's meat commonly contains from 30 to
50 per cent. of fat. Bread, on the other hand, contains the
proteid, gluten, and the amyloids, starch and sugar, with
minute quantities of fat. But, from the proportion in

which these proteid and other constituents exist in these substances, they are neither, taken alone, such physiologically economical foods as they are when combined in the proportion of about 200 to 75; or two pounds of bread to three-quarters of a pound of meat per diem.

175. Intermediate Changes of the Food. — It is quite certain that nine-tenths of the dry, solid food which is taken into the body sooner or later leaves it in the shape of carbonic acid, water, and urea (or uric acid); and it is also certain that the compounds which leave the body not only are more highly oxidized than those which enter it, but in them is carried away out of the body all the oxygen taken into the blood by the lungs.

The intermediate stages of this conversion are, however, by no means so clear. It is highly probable that the amyloids and fats are very frequently oxidized in the blood, without, properly speaking, ever forming an integral part of the substance of the body; but whether the proteids may undergo the same changes in the blood, or whether it is necessary for them first to be incorporated with the living tissue, is not positively known.

So, again, it is certain that, in becoming oxidized, the elements of the food must give off heat, and it is probable that this heat is sufficient to account for all that is given off by the body; but it is possible, and indeed probable, that there may be other minor sources of heat.

176. Objections to the Common Classification. — Food-stuffs have been divided into *heat-producers* and *tissue-formers*—the amyloids and fats constituting the former division, the proteids the latter. But this is a very misleading classification, inasmuch as it implies, on the one hand, that the oxidation of the proteids does not develop heat; and, on the other, that the amyloids and fats, as they oxidize, subserve only the production of heat.

Proteids are *tissue-formers*, inasmuch as no tissue can be produced without them; but they are also *heat-pro-*

ducers, not only directly, but because, as we have seen (153, 154), they are competent to give rise to amyloids by chemical metamorphosis within the body.

If it is worth while to make a special classification of the vital food-stuffs at all, it appears desirable to distinguish the *essential* food-stuffs, or proteids, from the *accessory* food-stuffs, or fats and amyloids—the former alone being, in the nature of things, necessary to life, while the latter, however important, are not absolutely necessary.

177. Purpose of the Alimentary Mechanism.—All food-stuffs being thus proteids, fats, amyloids, or mineral matters, pure or mixed up with other substances, the whole purpose of the alimentary apparatus is to separate these proteids, etc., from the innutritious residue, if there be any; and to reduce them into a condition either of solution or of excessively fine subdivision, in order that they may make their way through the delicate structures which form the walls of the vessels of the alimentary canal. To these ends food is taken into the mouth and masticated, is mixed with saliva, is swallowed, undergoes gastric digestion, passes into the intestine, and is subjected to the action of the secretions of the glands attached to that viscus; and, finally, after the more or less complete extraction of the nutritive constituents, the residue, mixed up with certain secretions of the intestines, leaves the body as the *fæces.*

SECTION II.—*Preliminaries of Digestion.*

178. The Mouth and Pharynx.—The cavity of the mouth is a chamber with a fixed roof, formed by the hard *palate* (Fig. 49, *l*), and with a movable floor, constituted by the lower jaw, and the tongue (*k*), which fills up the space between the two branches of the jaw. Arching round the margins of the upper and the lower jaws are the thirty-two teeth, sixteen above and sixteen below, and external to these, the closure of the cavity of the mouth is completed by the cheeks at the sides, and by the lips in front.

When the mouth is shut, the back of the tongue comes
into close contact with the palate; and, where the hard
palate ends, the communication between the mouth and
the back of the throat is still further impeded by a sort of
fleshy curtain—the soft *palate* or *velum*—the middle of
which is produced into a prolongation, the *uvula* (*f*),
while its sides, skirting the sides of the passage, or *fauces*,
form double muscular pillars, which are termed the *pillars
of the fauces*. Between these the *tonsils* are situated, one
on each side.

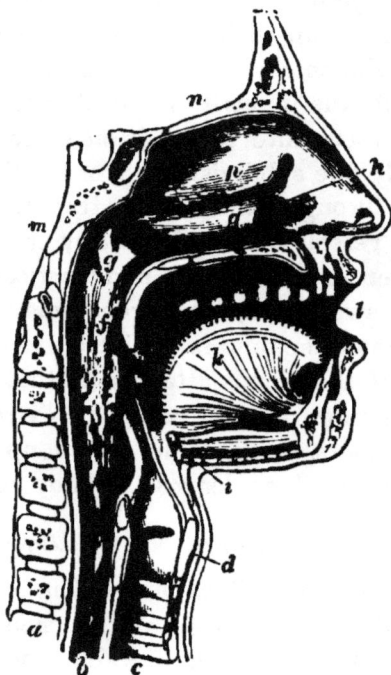

FIG. 49.

A SECTION OF THE MOUTH AND NOSE TAKEN VERTICALLY, A LITTLE TO THE LEFT OF
THE MIDDLE LINE.

a, the vertebral column; *b*, the gullet; *c*, the windpipe; *d*, the thyroid cartilage
of the larynx; *e*, the epiglottis; *f*, the uvula; *g*, the opening of the left Eustachian
tube; *h*, the opening of the left lachrymal duct; *i*, the hyoid bone; *k*, the tongue; *l*,
the hard palate; *m*, *n*, the base of the skull; *o*, *p*, *q*, the superior, middle, and inferior
turbinal bones. The letters *g*, *f*, *e*, are placed in the pharynx.

The velum with its uvula comes into contact below with the upper part of the back of the tongue, and with a sort of gristly, lid-like process connected with its base, the *epiglottis* (*e*).

Behind the partition thus formed lies the cavity of the *pharynx*, which may be described as a funnel-shaped bag with muscular walls, the upper margins of the slanting, wide end of which are attached to the base of the skull, while the lateral margins are continuous with the sides, and the lower with the floor, of the mouth. The narrow end of the pharyngeal bag passes into the gullet or œsophagus (*b*), a muscular tube, which affords a passage into the stomach.

There are no fewer than six distinct openings into the front part of the pharynx—four in pairs, and two single ones in the middle line. The two pairs are, in front, the hinder openings of the nasal cavities; and at the sides, close to these, the apertures of the *Eustachian tubes* (*g*). The two single apertures are, the hinder opening of the mouth between the soft palate and the epiglottis; and, behind the epiglottis, the upper aperture of the respiratory passage, or the *glottis*.

179. The Salivary Glands. — The mucous membrane which lines the mouth and the pharynx is beset with minute glands, the *buccal glands;* but the great glands from which the cavity of the mouth receives its chief secretion are the three pairs which, as has been already mentioned, are called *parotid, submaxillary, sublingual,* and which secrete the principal part of the saliva (Fig. 50).

Each parotid gland is placed just in front of the ear, and its duct passes forwards along the cheek, until it opens in the interior of the mouth, opposite the second upper grinding tooth.

The submaxillary and sublingual glands lie between the lower jaw and the floor of the mouth, the submaxillary being situated farther back than the sublingual. Their

ducts open in the floor of the mouth below the tip of the
tongue. The secretion of these salivary glands, mixed
with that of the small glands of the mouth, constitutes the
saliva—a fluid which, though thin and watery, contains a
small quantity of animal matter, called *Ptyalin*, which has
certain very peculiar properties. It does not act upon proteid food-stuffs, nor upon fats ; but, if mixed with starch,
and kept at a moderate warm temperature, it turns that
starch into grape-sugar. The importance of this operation

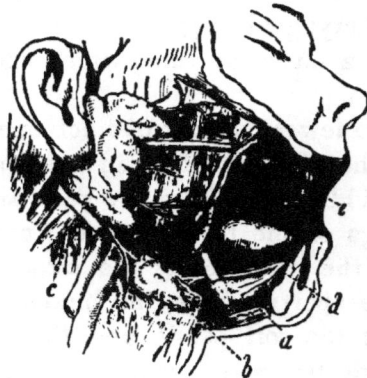

FIG. 50.

A dissection of the right side of the face, showing *a*, the sublingual ; *b*, the submaxillary glands, with their ducts opening beside the tongue in the floor of the mouth
at *d ; c*, the parotid gland and its duct, which opens on the side of the cheek at *e*.

becomes apparent when one reflects that starch is insoluble, and therefore, as such, useless as nutriment, while
sugar is highly soluble, and readily oxidizable.

180. The Teeth.—Each of the thirty-two teeth which
have been mentioned consists of a *crown* which projects
above the gum, and of one or more *fangs*, which are embedded in sockets, or what are called *alveoli*, in the jaws.

The eight teeth on opposite sides of the same jaw are
constructed upon exactly similar patterns, while the eight
teeth, which are opposite to one another, and bite against
one another above and below, though similar in kind, differ
somewhat in the details of their patterns.

The two teeth in each eight which are nearest the middle line in the front of the jaw, have wide but sharp and chisel-like edges. Hence they are called *incisors*, or cutting teeth. The tooth which comes next is a tooth with a more conical and pointed crown. It answers to the great tearing and holding tooth of the dog, and is called the *canine* or eye-tooth. The next two teeth have broader crowns, with two cusps, or points, on each crown, one on the inside and one on the outside, whence they are termed *bicuspid* teeth, and sometimes false grinders. All these teeth have usually one fang each, except the bicuspid, the fangs of which may be more or less completely divided into two. The remaining teeth have two or three fangs each, and their crowns are much broader. As they crush and grind the matters which pass·between them, they are called *molars*, or true grinders. In the upper jaw their crowns present four points at the four corners, and a diagonal ridge connecting two of them. In the lower jaw the complete pattern is five-pointed, there being two cusps on the inner side and three on the outer.

181. Working of the Jaw.—The muscles of the parts which have been described have such a disposition that the lower jaw can be depressed, so as to open the mouth and separate the teeth; or raised, in such a manner as to bring the teeth together; or move obliquely from side to side, so as to cause the face of the grinding teeth and the edges of the cutting teeth to slide over one another. And the muscles which perform the elevating and sliding movements are of great strength, and confer a corresponding force upon the grinding and cutting actions of the teeth. In correspondence with the pressure they have to resist, the superficial substance of the crown of the teeth is of great hardness, being formed of *enamel*, which is the hardest substance in the body, so dense and hard, indeed, that it will strike fire with steel (*see* 352). But, notwithstanding its extreme hardness, it becomes worn down in old persons, and, at an earlier age, in savages who live on coarse food.

182. Masticating and Swallowing.—When solid food is taken into the mouth, it is cut and ground by the teeth, the fragments which ooze out upon the outer side of their crowns being pushed beneath them again by the muscular contractions of the cheeks and lips; while those which escape on the inner side are thrust back by the tongue, until the whole is thoroughly rubbed down.

While mastication is proceeding, the salivary glands pour out their secretion in great abundance, and the saliva mixes with the food, which thus becomes interpenetrated not only with the salivary fluid, but with the air which is entangled in the bubbles of the saliva.

When the food is sufficiently ground it is collected, enveloped in saliva, into a mass or bolus, which rests upon the back of the tongue, and is carried backwards to the aperture which leads into the pharynx. Through this it is thrust, the soft palate being lifted and its pillars being brought together, while the backward movement of the tongue at once propels the mass and causes the epiglottis to incline backwards and downwards over the glottis, and so to form a bridge by which the bolus can travel over the opening of the air-passage without any risk of tumbling into it. While the epiglottis directs the course of the mass of food below, and prevents it from passing into the trachea, the soft palate guides it above, keeps it out of the nasal chamber, and directs it downwards and backwards towards the lower part of the muscular pharyngeal funnel. By this the bolus is immediately seized and tightly held, and the muscular fibres contracting above it, while they are comparatively lax below, it is rapidly thrust into the œsophagus. By the muscular walls of this tube it is grasped and propelled onwards, in a similar fashion, until it reaches the stomach.

183. Drinking.—Drink is taken in exactly the same way.

It does not fall down the pharynx and gullet, but each gulp
is grasped and passed down. Hence it is that jugglers are
able to drink standing upon their heads, and that a horse,
or ox, drinks with its throat lower than its stomach, feats
which would be impossible if fluid simply fell down the
gullet into the gastric cavity.

During these processes of mastication, insalivation, and
deglutition, what happens to the food is, first, that it is
reduced to a coarser or finer pulp; secondly, that any matters it carries in solution are still more diluted by the water
of the saliva; thirdly, that any starch it may contain begins
to be changed into sugar by the peculiar constituent (ptyalin) of the saliva.

Section III.—*Stomach-Digestion.*

184. The Stomach and the Gastric Juice.—The stomach,
like the gullet, consists of a tube with muscular walls composed of smooth muscular fibres, and lined by an epithelium; but it differs from the gullet in several circumstances.
In the first place, its cavity is greatly larger, and its left
end is produced into an enlargement which, because it is
on the heart-side of the body, is called the *cardiac* dilatation (Fig. 51, *b*). The opening of the gullet into the stomach, termed the *cardiac aperture*, is consequently nearly
in the middle of the whole length of the organ, which presents a long, convex, *greater curvature*, along its front or
under edge, and a short concave, *lesser curvature*, on its
back or upper contour. Towards its right extremity the
stomach narrows, and, where it passes into the intestine,
the muscular fibres are so disposed as to form a sort of
sphincter around the aperture of communication. This is
called the *pylorus* (Fig. 51, *d*).

The mucous membrane lining the wall of the stomach
is very delicate, and multitudes of small glands open upon
its surface. Some of these are simple, but others (Fig. 52)
possess a somewhat more complicated structure, their blind

8

ends being subdivided. It is these glands, and more especially the more complicated ones, the so-called *peptic glands*, which, when food passes into the stomach, throw out a thin acid fluid, the *gastric juice*.

When the stomach is empty, its mucous membrane is pale and hardly more than moist. Its small arteries are then in a state of contraction, and comparatively little blood is sent through it. On the entrance of food, a nervous action is set up, which causes these small arteries to dilate; the mucous membrane consequently receives a much larger quantity of blood, it becomes very red, little

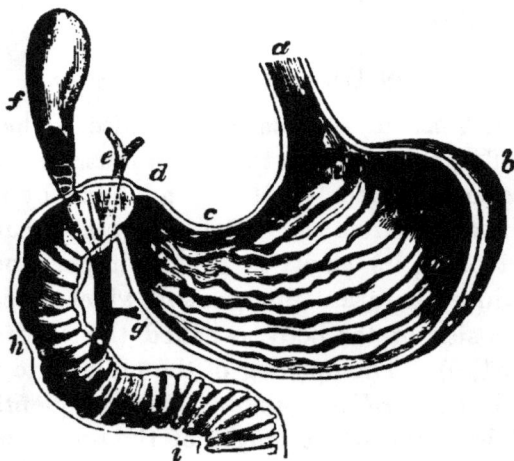

FIG. 51.

THE STOMACH LAID OPEN BEHIND.

a, the œsophagus; *b*, the cardiac dilatation; *c*, the lesser curvature; *d*, the pylorus; *e*, the biliary duct; *f*, the gall-bladder; *g*, the pancreatic duct, opening in common with the cystic duct opposite *h*; *h, i*, the duodenum.

drops of fluid gather at the mouth of the glands, and finally run down as gastric juice. The process is very similar to the combined blushing and sweating which takes place when the sympathetic in the neck is divided.

Pure gastric juice appears to consist of little more than water, containing a few saline matters in solution, and its acidity is due to the presence of free hydrochloric acid; it possesses, however, in addition a small quantity of a peculiar substance called *pepsin*, which seems to be not altogether dissimilar in chemical composition to, though very different in its effects from, *ptyalin* (179).

Thus, when the food passes into the stomach, the contractions of that organ roll it about and mix it thoroughly with the gastric juice.

185. Artificial Digestion.—It is easy to ascertain the properties of gastric juice experimentally, by putting a small portion of that part of the mucous membrane which contains the peptic glands into acidulated water containing small pieces of meat, hard-boiled egg, or other proteids, and keeping the mixture at a temperature of about 100°. After a few hours it will be found that the white of egg, if not in too great quantity, has become dissolved; while all that remains of the meat is a pulp, consisting chiefly of the connective tissue and fatty matters which it contained. This is *artificial digestion*, and it has been proved by experiment that precisely the same operation takes place when food undergoes natural digestion within the stomach of a living animal.

The proteid solution thus effected is called a *peptone*, and has pretty much the same characters, whatever the nature of the proteid which has been digested.

186. Osmosis.—Peptone differs from all other proteids in its extreme solubility, and in the readiness with which it passes through animal membranes. Many proteids, as fibrin, are naturally insoluble in water, and others, such as white of egg, though apparently soluble, are not completely so, and can be rendered quite solid or coagulated by being simply heated, as when an egg is boiled. A solution of peptone, however, is perfectly fluid, does not become solid, and is not at all coagulated by boiling. Again, if a quantity of white of egg be tied up in a bladder, and the bladder immersed in water, very little of the proteid will pass

through the bladder into the water, provided that there are
no holes. If, however, peptone be used instead of albumen,
a very large quantity will speedily pass through into the
water, and a quantity of water will pass from the outside
into the bladder, causing it to swell up. This process is
called *osmosis*, and is evidently of great importance in the
economy; and the purpose of the conversion of the various
proteids by digestion into peptone seems to be, in part at

FIG. 52.

One of the Glands, which secrete the Gastric Juice, magnified about three hundred and
fifty diameters.

least, to enable this class of food-stuff to pass readily into
the blood through the thin partition formed by the walls
of the mucous membrane of the intestine and the coats of
the capillaries.

Similarly, starch, even when boiled, and so partially

dissolved, will not pass through membranes, whereas sugar does so with the greatest ease. Hence the reason of the

Fig. 53.

THE VISCERA OF A RABBIT AS SEEN UPON SIMPLY OPENING THE CAVITIES OF THE THORAX AND ABDOMEN WITHOUT ANY FURTHER DISSECTION.

A, cavity of the thorax, pleural cavity on either side; *B*, diaphragm; *C*, ventricles of the heart; *D*, auricles; *E*, pulmonary artery; *F*, aorta; *G*, lungs, collapsed, and occupying only back part of chest; *H*, lateral portions of pleural membranes; *I*, cartilage at the end of sternum (ensiform cartilage); *K*, a portion of the wall of the body left between thorax and abdomen; *a*, cut ends of the ribs; *L*, the liver, in this case lying more to the left than the right of the body; *M*, the stomach, a large part of the greater curvature being shown; *N*, duodenum; *O*, small intestine; *P*, the cæcum, so largely developed in this and other herbivorous animals; *Q*, the large intestine.

conversion of starch, by digestion, into sugar. It takes a very long time (some days) for the dilute acid alone to dissolve proteid matters, and hence the solvent power of gastric juice must be chiefly attributed to the pepsin.

As far as we know, gastric juice has no direct action on fats; by breaking up, however, the proteid framework in which animal and vegetable fats are embedded, it sets these free, and so helps their digestion by exposing them to the action of other agents. It appears, too, that gastric juice has no direct action on amyloids; on the contrary, the conversion of the starch into sugar, begun in the mouth, appears to be wholly or partially arrested by the acidity of the contents of the stomach, ptyalin being active only in an alkaline or neutral mixture.

187. Absorption from the Stomach.—By continual rolling about, with constant additions of gastric juice, the food becomes reduced to the consistence of pea-soup, and is called *chyme*. In this state it is, in part, allowed to escape through the pylorus and to enter the duodenum; but a great deal of the fluid (consisting of peptone, together with any saccharine fluids resulting from the partial conversion of starch, or otherwise), is at once absorbed, making its way, by imbibition, through the walls of the delicate and numerous vessels of the stomach into the current of the blood, which is rushing through the gastric veins to the *vena portæ*.

Section IV.—*Intestinal Digestion.*

188. The Large and Small Intestines. — The *intestines* form one long tube, with mucous and muscular coats, like the stomach; and, like it, they are enveloped in peritoneum. They are divided into two portions—the *small intestines* and the *large intestines;* the latter having a much greater diameter than the former. The small intestines again are subdivided into the *duodenum*, the *jejunum*, and the *ileum*, but there is no natural line of demarcation between these. The *duodenum*, however, is distinguishable as that part of the small intestine which immediately succeeds the stomach, and is bent upon itself and fastened by the peritoneum against the back wall of the abdomen, in the loop shown in Fig. 51. It is in this loop that the head of the pancreas lies (Fig. 47).

The ileum (Fig. 54, *a*), is no wider than the jejunum or duodenum, so that the transition from the small intestine to the large (*e*) is quite sudden. The opening of the small intestine into the large is provided with prominent lips

Fig. 54.

The termination of the ileum. *a*, in the cæcum, and the continuation of the latter into the colon, *c ; d*, the ileo-cæcal valve ; *e*, the aperture of the *appendix vermiformis* (*b*) into the cæcum.

which project into the cavity of the latter, and oppose the passage of matters from it into the small intestine, while they readily allow of a passage the other way. This is the *ileo-cœcal* valve (Fig. 54, *d*).

The large intestine forms a blind dilatation beyond the ileo-cæcal valve, which is called the *cœcum ;* and from this an elongated, blind process is given off, which, from its shape, is called the *vermiform appendix* of the cæcum (Fig. 54, *b*).

The cæcum lies in the lower part of the right side of the abdominal cavity. The *colon*, or first part of the large intestine, passes upwards from it as the *ascending colon ;* then making a sudden turn at a right angle, it passes across to the left side of the body, being called the *transverse colon* in this part of its course ; and next, suddenly bending backwards along the left side of the abdomen, it be-

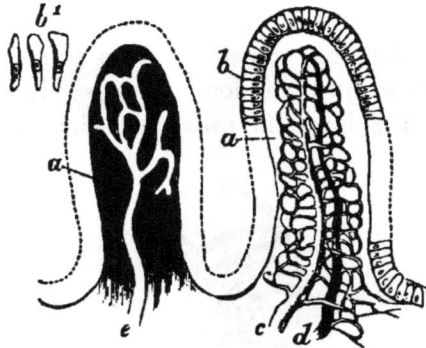

FIG. 55.

SEMI-DIAGRAMMATIC VIEW OF TWO VILLI OF THE SMALL INTESTINES.
(Magnified about fifty diameters.)

a, substance of the villus ; *b*, its epithelium, of which some cells are seen detached at *b*[1] ; *c, d,* the artery and vein, with their connecting capillary net-work, which envelops and hides *e*, the lacteal radicle which occupies the centre of the villus and opens into a net-work of lacteal vessels at its base.

comes the *descending colon.*   This reaches the middle line and becomes the *rectum*, which is that part of the large intestine which opens externally.

189. Their Parts and Actions.—The mucous membrane of the whole intestine is provided with numerous small and simple glands (named after Lieberkühn), which pour into it a secretion, the *intestinal juice*, the precise functions of which are unknown, though it appears in some creatures at least to possess the power of converting starch into sugar, and proteids into peptone.   At the commencement of the duodenum are certain racemose glands, called the glands of Brunner, whose function is wholly unknown.

Structures peculiar to the small intestine are the *valvulæ conniventes*, transverse folds of the mucous membrane, which increase the surface ; and the *villi*, which are minute thread-like processes of the mucous membrane on the *valvulæ conniventes* and elsewhere, set side by side, like the pile of velvet. Each villus is coated by epithelium, and contains in its interior the radicle, or commencement, of a lacteal vessel (44), between which and the epithelium lies a capillary net-work with its afferent artery and efferent vein. The intestines receive their blood almost directly from the aorta. Their veins carry the blood which has traversed the intestinal capillaries to the *vena portæ.*

190. Peristaltic Contraction.—The fibres of the muscular coat of the intestines (which lies between the mucous membrane and the serous, or peritoneal, investment) are disposed longitudinally and circularly; the longitudinal coat being much thinner, and placed outside the circular coat. Now, the circular fibres of any part contract, successively, in such a manner that the lower fibres, or those on the side of the anus, contract after the upper ones, or those on the side of the pylorus. It follows from this so-called *peristaltic contraction,* that the contents of the intestines are constantly being propelled, by successive and progressive narrowing of their calibre, from their upper towards their lower parts.

The large intestine presents noteworthy peculiarities in the arrangement of the longitudinal muscular fibres of the colon into three bands, which are shorter than the walls of the intestine itself, so that the latter is thrown into puckers and pouches; and in the disposition of muscular fibres around the termination of the rectum into a ring-like sphincter muscle, which keeps the aperture firmly closed, except when defecation takes place.

191. Entrance of Bile and Pancreatic Juice.—The only secretions, besides those of the proper intestinal glands, which enter the intestine, are those of the liver and the pancreas—the *bile* and the *pancreatic juice.* The ducts of these organs have a common opening in the middle of the bend of the duodenum; and, since the common duct passes obliquely through the coats of the intestine, its walls serve as a kind of valve, obstructing the flow of the contents of the duodenum into the duct, but readily permitting the passage of bile and pancreatic juice into the duodenum (Figs. 44, 47, 51).

Pancreatic juice is an alkaline fluid not unlike saliva in many respects; it differs, however, in containing a considerable quantity of proteid material. Bile we have already studied.

After gastric digestion has been going on some time, and the semi-digested food begins to pass on into the duodenum, the pancreas comes into activity, its blood-vessels dilate, it becomes red and full of blood, its cells secrete rapidly, and a copious flow of pancreatic juice takes place along its duct into the intestine.

The secretion of bile by the liver is much more continuous than that of the pancreas, and is not so markedly increased by the presence of food in the stomach. There is, however, a store of bile laid up in the gall-bladder; and as the acid chyme passes into the duodenum, and flows over the common aperture of the gall and pancreatic ducts, a quantity of bile from this reservoir in the gall-bladder is ejected into the intestine. The bile and pancreatic juice together here mix with the chyme and convert it into what is called *chyle*.

192. Chyle—Absorption from the Intestines.—Chyle differs from chyme in two respects. In the first place, the alkali of the bile neutralizes the acid of the chyme; in the second place, both the bile and the pancreatic juice appear to exercise an influence over the fatty matters contained in the chyme, which facilitates the subdivision of these fats into very minute separate particles. The chyme, in fact, which results from the digestion of fatty food, is a mere mixture of watery fluid with oily matters, which are ready to separate from it and unite with one another. In the chyle, on the other hand, the fatty matters are suspended in the fluid, just as oil may be evenly diffused through water by gradually rubbing it up with white of egg into what is termed an *emulsion ;* or as the fat (that is, the butter) of milk is naturally held suspended in the watery basis of milk.

The chyle, with these suspended particles, looks white and milky, for the same reason that milk has the same aspect—the multitude of minute suspended fatty particles reflecting a great amount of light.

The conversion of starch into sugar, which seems to be suspended wholly, or partially, so long as the food remains in the stomach, on account of the acidity of the chyme, is resumed as soon as the latter is neutralized, the pancreatic and intestinal juices operating powerfully in this direction.

Recent observations, moreover, have shown that pancreatic juice has a powerful effect on proteid matters, converting them into peptones differing little, if at all, from the peptones resulting from gastric digestion. It would appear, too, that fats are not only minutely divided or emulsionized by the bile and pancreatic juice, i. e., acted upon mechanically, but also to a small extent converted by a chemical change into soaps, and thus rendered more soluble. Hence it appears that, while in the mouth amyloids only, and in the stomach proteids only, are digested, in the intestine all three kinds of food-stuffs, proteids, fats, and amyloids, are either completely dissolved or minutely subdivided, and so prepared for their passage into the vessels.

As the chyle is thrust along the small intestines by the grasping action of the peristaltic contractions, the dissolved matter which it contains is absorbed, in the ordinary way, by osmosis into the vessels of the villi. The minute particles of fatty matter, on the other hand, which, not being dissolved, are incapable of osmosis, pass bodily through the soft substance of the epithelium into that of the villi, and so into the beginning of the lacteal.

The exact manner in which this is effected is at present a matter of dispute. The contents of the intestine are undoubtedly subject to pressure from the peristaltic contractions of the muscular walls; and this may help to squeeze the fat into the villi, just as mercury may be squeezed through the pores of a piece of wash-leather. The process, however, is probably not one of mere pressure only.

As the net-work of capillaries lies outside the lacteal radicle in each villus, it would appear probable that the blood-vessels must carry off the greater part of the more soluble matters of the chyle. It is possible, however, that some of these pass by simple diffusion into the lacteals as well as into the blood-vessels. We are not, in fact, in possession of exact knowledge as to which constituents of the chyle pass into the lacteals, and which into the blood-vessels (or which into both), except on one point; and that is, that the minutely-divided fat passes not into the blood-vessels, but into the lacteals, fills them, and only enters the blood after a roundabout passage through the mesenteric lymphatics and the thoracic duct (43, 44).

193. Digestion in the Large Intestines.—The digested matters, as they are driven along the small intestines, gradually become deprived of their peptones, fats, and soluble amyloids, and are forced through the ileo-cæcal valve into the cæcum and large intestine. Here they acquire an acid reaction and the characteristic fecal odor and color, which become more and more marked as they approach the rectum. It has been supposed that a sort of second digestion occurs in the upper part of the large intestine.

*

CHAPTER VII.

MOTION AND LOCOMOTION.

SECTION I.—*Instruments of Motion.*

194. The Vital Eddy.—In the preceding chapters the
manner in which the incomings of the human body are
converted into its outgoings has been explained. It has
been seen that new matter, in the form of vital and mineral foods, is constantly appropriated by the body, to
make up for the loss of old matter, in the shape, chiefly,
of carbonic acid, urea, and water, which is as constantly
going on.

The vital foods are derived directly, or indirectly, from
the vegetable world : and the products of waste either are
such compounds as abound in the mineral world, or immediately decompose into them. Consequently, the human
body is the centre of a stream of matter which sets incessantly from the vegetable and mineral worlds into the
mineral world again. It may be compared to an eddy in
a river, which may retain its shape for an indefinite length
of time, though no one particle of the water of the stream
remains in it for more than a brief period.

But·there is this peculiarity about the human eddy,
that a large portion of the particles of matter which flow
into it have a much more complex composition than the
particles which flow out of it. To speak in what is not
altogether a metaphor, the atoms which enter the body
are, for the most part, piled up in large heaps, and tumble
down into small heaps before they leave it. The force
which they set free, in thus tumbling down, is the source
of the active powers of the organism.

195. Organs of Motion.—These active powers are chiefly

manifested in the form of motion—movement, that is, either of part of the body, or of the body as a whole, which last is termed *locomotion*.

The organs which produce total or partial movements of the human body are of three kinds: *cells exhibiting amœboid movements, cilia,* and *muscles.*

The *amœboid movements* of the white corpuscles of the blood have been already described, and it is probable that similar movements are performed by many other simple cells of the body in various regions.

The amount of movement which each cell is thus capable of giving rise to may appear perfectly insignificant; nevertheless, there are reasons for thinking that these amœboid movements are of great importance to the economy, and may under certain circumstances be followed by very notable consequences.

196. Action of the Cilia.—*Cilia* are filaments of extremely small size, attached by their bases to, and indeed growing out from, the free surfaces of epithelial cells (*see* 341); there being in most instances very many (thirty, for instance), but, in some cases, only a few cilia on each cell. In some of the lower animals, cells may be found possessing only a single cilium. They are in incessant waving motion, so long as life persists in them. Their most common form of movement is that each cilium is suddenly bent upon itself, becomes sickle-shaped instead of straight, and then more slowly straightens again, both movements, however, being extremely rapid and repeated about ten times every second. These two movements are of course antagonistic; the bending drives the water or fluid in which the cilium is placed in one direction, while the straightening drives it back again. Inasmuch, however, as the bending is much more rapid than the straightening, the force expended on the water in the former movement is greater than in the latter. The total effect of the double movement therefore is to drive the fluid in the direction towards which the cilium is bent; that is, of course, if the cell on which the cilia are placed is fixed. If the cell be floating free, the effect is to drive or row the cell backwards; for their movements may continue even for some time after the epithelial cell, with which they are connected, is detached from the body. And not only do the movements of the cilia thus go on independently of the rest of the body, but they cannot be controlled by the action of the nervous system. Each cilium seems to be composed of *contractile* substance, and the cause of its movement would appear to be the alternate contraction and relaxation of its opposite sides along its whole length or at its base only; but why these alternations take place is unknown.

Although no other part of the body has any control over the cilia, and though, so far as we know, they have no direct communication with one another, yet their action is directed towards a common end—the cilia, which cover extensive surfaces, all working in such a manner as to sweep whatever lies upon that surface in one and the same direction. Thus, the cilia which are developed upon the epithelial cells, which line the greater part of the nasal cavities and the trachea, with its ramifications, tend to drive the mucus in which they work, outwards.

In addition to the air-passages, cilia are found, in the human body, in the ventricles of the brain, and in one or two other localities; but the part which they play in man is insignificant in comparison with their function in the lower animals, among many of which they become the chief organs of locomotion.

197. Muscular Contraction.—*Muscles* (18) are accumulations of fibres, each fibre having a definite structure which is different in the *striated* and *unstriated* kinds (*see* 355). These fibres are bound up by fibrous (or connective) tissue with blood-vessels, etc., into small bundles; and these bundles are again similarly bound up together in various ways so as to form muscles of various shapes and sizes. Every fibre has the power, under certain conditions, of shortening in length, while it increases its other dimensions, so that the absolute volume of the fibre remains unchanged. This power is called *muscular contractility ;* and whenever, in virtue of this power, a muscular fibre *contracts*, it tends to bring its two ends, with whatever may be fastened to them, together.

The condition which ordinarily determines the contraction of a muscular fibre is a change of state in a nerve-fibre, which is in close anatomical connection with the muscular fibre. The nerve-fibre is thence called a *motor* fibre, because, by its influence on a muscle, it becomes the indirect means of producing motion (317).

Muscle is a highly-elastic substance. It contains a large amount of water (about as much as the blood), and during life has a clear and semi-transparent aspect.

198. Rigor Mortis.—When subjected to pressure in the perfectly fresh state, and after due precautions have been taken to remove all the contained blood, *striated* muscle (355) yields a fluid which undergoes spontaneous coagulation at ordinary temperatures. At a longer or shorter time after death this coagulation takes place within the muscles themselves. They become more or less opaque, and, losing their previous elasticity, set into hard, rigid masses, which retain the form which they possess when the coagulation commences. Hence the limbs become fixed in the position in which death found them, and the body passes into the condition of what is termed the "death-stiffening," or *rigor mortis*. After the lapse of a certain time the coagulated matter liquefies, and the muscles pass into a loose and flaccid condition, which marks the commencement of putrefaction.

It has been observed that the sooner *rigor mortis* sets in, the sooner it is over; and, the later it commences the longer it lasts. The greater the amount of muscular exertion, and consequent exhaustion before death, the sooner *rigor mortis* sets in.

199. Composition of Muscle.—*Rigor mortis* evidently presents some analogies with the coagulation of the blood, and the substance which thus coagulates within the fibre (*myosin*, or muscle-clot, as it is sometimes called), is in many respects not unlike fibrin. It forms at least the greater part of the substance which may be extracted from muscle by dilute acids, and is called *syntonin* (*see* 167). Besides myosin, muscle contains other varieties of proteid material about which we at present know little; a variable quantity of fat; certain inorganic saline matters, phosphates and potash being, as is the case in the red blood-corpuscles, in excess; and a large number of substances existing in small quantities, and often classed together as "extractives." Some of these extractives contain nitrogen; the most important of this class is *creatin*, a crystalline body which is supposed to be the chief form in which nitrogenous waste matter leaves the muscle on its way to become urea.

The other class of extractives contains bodies free from nitrogen. Perhaps the most important of these is *lactic acid*, which seems always to be formed when a muscle contracts, or when it enters into *rigor mortis*. For it is a curious fact that a muscle when at rest has a neutral or alkaline reaction, as shown by testing it with litmus, but becomes acid when it has been contracting for some time or become rigid by death.

Most muscles are of a deep-red color; this is due in part to the blood remaining in their vessels; but only in part, for each fibre (into which no capillary enters) has a reddish color of its own, like a blood-corpuscle, but fainter. And this color is probably due to the fibre possessing a small quantity of that same hæmoglobin in which the blood-corpuscles are so rich.

200. Attachment of Muscles. — Muscles may be conveniently divided into two groups, according to the manner in which the ends of their fibres are fastened—into muscles not attached to solid levers, and muscles attached to solid levers.

201. Muscles not attached to Solid Levers.—Under this head come the muscles which are appropriately called *hollow* muscles, inasmuch as they inclose a cavity or surround a space; and their contraction lessens the capacity of that cavity, or the extent of that space.

The muscular fibres of the heart, of the blood-vessels, of the lymphatic vessels, of the alimentary canal, of the urinary bladder, of the ducts of the glands, of the iris of the eye, are so arranged as to form hollow muscles.

In the heart the muscular fibres are of the striated kind, and their disposition is exceedingly complex. The cavities which they inclose are those of the auricles and ventricles; and, as we have seen, the fibres, when they contract, do so suddenly and together.

The iris of the eye is like a curtain, in the middle of which is a circular hole. The muscular fibres are of the smooth or unstriated kind (*see* 355), and they are disposed in two sets: one set radiating from the edges of the hole to the circumference of the curtain; and the other set arranged in circles, concentrically with the aperture. The muscular fibres of each set contract suddenly and together, the radiating fibres necessarily enlarging the hole, the circular fibres diminishing it.

In the alimentary canal the muscular fibres are also of the unstriated kind, and they are disposed in two layers; one set of fibres being arranged parallel with the length of the intestines, while the others are disposed circularly, or at right angles to the former.

As has been stated above (190), the contraction of these muscular fibres is successive; that is to say, all the muscular fibres, in a given length of the intestines, do not contract at once, but those at one end contract first, and the others follow them until the whole series have contracted. As the order of contraction is, naturally, always the same, from the upper towards the lower end, the effect of this peristaltic contraction is, as we have seen, to force any matter, contained in the alimentary canal, from its upper towards its lower extremity. The muscles of the walls of the ducts of the glands have a substantially similar arrangement. In these cases the contraction of each fibre is less sudden, and lasts longer than in the case of the heart.

SECTION II.—*Mechanism of Bodily Movement.*

202. Muscles attached to Definite Levers. — The great majority of the muscles in the body are attached to distinct levers, formed by the bones, the minute structure of which is explained in Chapter XII. In such bones as are ordinarily employed as levers, the osseous tissue is arranged in the form of a *shaft* (Fig. 56, *b*), formed of a very dense and compact osseous matter, but often containing a great central cavity (*b*) which is filled with a very delicate vascular and fibrous tissue loaded with fat called *marrow*. Towards the two ends of the bone, the compact matter of the shaft thins out, and is replaced by a much thicker but looser sponge-work of bony plates and fibres, which is termed the *cancellous* tissue of the bone. The surface even of this part, however, is still formed by a thin sheet of denser bone.

At least one end of each of these bony levers is fashioned into a smooth, articular surface, covered with cartilage, which enables the relatively fixed end of the bone to play upon the corresponding surface of some other bone with which it is said to be *articulated*, or, contrariwise, allows that other bone to move upon it.

It is one or other of these extremities which plays the part of fulcrum when the bone is in use as a lever.

Thus, in the accompanying figure (Fig. 57), of the bones of the upper extremity, with the attachment of the *biceps* muscle to the shoulder-blade and to one of the two bones of the forearm called the *radius*, P indicates the

point of action of the power (the contracting muscle) upon
the radius.

But, to understand the action of the bones, as levers,
properly, it is necessary to possess a knowledge of the

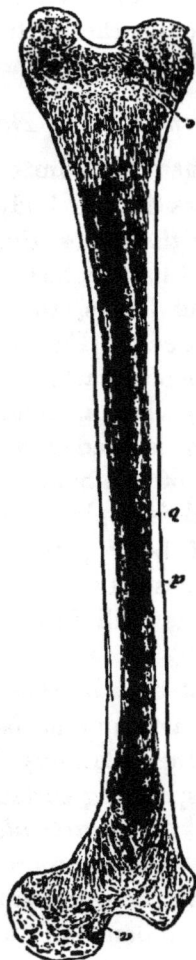

FIG. 56.

LONGITUDINAL SECTION OF THE SHAFT OF A HUMAN FEMUR OR THIGH-BONE.

a, the head, which articulates with the haunch-bone; *b*, the medullary cavity, and
d, the dense bony substance of the shaft; *c*, the part which enters into the knee-joint,
articulating with the shin-bone, or tibia.

different kinds of levers, and be able to refer the various combinations of the bones to their appropriate lever-classes.

A lever is a rigid bar, one part of which is absolutely or relatively fixed, while the rest is free to move. Some one point of the movable part of the lever is set in motion

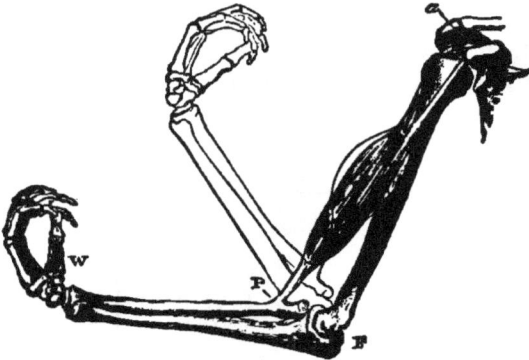

FIG. 57.

THE BONES OF THE UPPER EXTREMITY, WITH THE BICEPS MUSCLE.

The two tendons by which this muscle is attached to the scapula are seen at a; P indicates the attachment of the muscle to the radius, and hence the point of action of the power; F, the fulcrum, the lower end of the humerus on which the upper end of the radius (together with the ulna) moves; W, the weight (of the hand).

by a force, in order to communicate more or less of that motion to another point of the movable part, which presents a resistance to motion in the shape of a weight or other obstacle.

203. Three Orders of Levers. — Three kinds of levers are enumerated by mechanicians, the definition of each kind depending upon the relative positions of the point of support, or *fulcrum;* of the point which bears the *resistance, weight,* or other obstacle to be overcome by the force; and of the point to which the force, or *power* employed to overcome the obstacle, is applied.

If the fulcrum be placed between the power and the weight, so that, when the power sets the lever in motion, the weight and the power describe arcs, the concavities of which are turned towards one another, the lever is said to be of the *first order*. (Fig. 58.)

If the fulcrum be at one end, and the weight be between it and the power, so that weight and power describe concentric arcs, the weight moving through the less space when the lever moves, the lever is said to be of the *second order*. (Fig. 59.)

And if, the fulcrum being still at one end, the power be between the weight and it, so that, as in the former case,

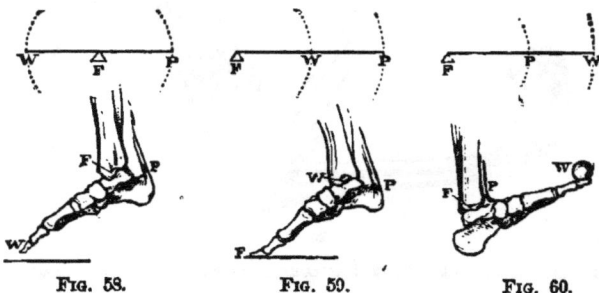

FIG. 58.   FIG. 59.   FIG. 60.

The upper portions of the three figures represent the three kinds of levers; the lower portions, the foot, when it takes the character of each kind. W, weight or resistance; F, fulcrum; P, power.

the power and weight describe concentric arcs, but the power moves through the less space, the lever is of the *third order*. (Fig. 60.)

204. Levers of the First Order.—In the human body, the following parts present examples of levers of the first order.

(*a*) The skull in its movements upon the atlas, as *fulcrum*.

(*b*) The pelvis in its movements upon the heads of the thigh-bones, as *fulcrum*.

(*c*) The foot, when it is raised, and the toe tapped on the ground, the ankle-joint being *fulcrum*. (Fig. 58.)

The positions of the weight and of power are not given in either of these cases, because they are reversed according to circumstances. Thus, when the face is being depressed, the power is applied in front, and the weight to the back part, of the skull; but, when the face is being raised, the power is behind and the weight in front. The like is true of the pelvis, according as the body is bent forward, or backward, upon the legs. Finally, when the toes, in the action of tapping, strike the ground, the power is at the heel, and the resistance in the front of the foot. But, when the toes are raised to repeat the act, the power is in front, and the weight, or resistance, is at the heel, being, in fact, the inertia and elasticity of the muscles and other parts of the back of the leg.

But, in all these cases, the lever remains one of the first class, because the fulcrum, or fixed point on which the lever turns, remains between the power and the weight, or resistance.

205. Levers of the Second Order. — The following are three examples of levers of the second order:

(*a*) The thigh-bone of the leg, which is bent up towards the body and not used, in the action of hopping. .

For, in this case, the fulcrum is at the hip-joint. The power (which may be assumed to be furnished by the thick muscle [1] of the front of the thigh) acts upon the knee-cap; and the position of the weight is represented by that of the centre of gravity of the thigh and leg, which will lie somewhere between the end of the knee and the hip.

(*b*) A rib when depressed by the *rectus* muscle [2] of the abdomen, in expiration.

Here the fulcrum lies where the rib is articulated with the spine; the power is at the sternum—virtually the opposite end of the rib; and the resistance to be overcome lies between the two.

---

[1] This muscle, called *rectus*, is attached above to the haunch-bone and below to the knee-cap (Fig. 4, 2). The latter bone is connected by a strong ligament with the *tibia*.

[2] This muscle lies in the front abdominal wall on each side of the middle line. It is attached to the sternum above and to the front of the pelvis below (Fig. 4, 3).

(*c*) The rising of the body upon the toes, in standing on tiptoe, and in the first stage of making a step forwards. (Fig. 59.)

Here the fulcrum is the ground on which the toes rest; the power is applied by the muscles of the calf to the heel (Fig. 4, I.); the resistance is so much of the weight of the body as is borne by the ankle-joint of the foot, which, of course, lies between the heel and the toes.

206. Levers of the Third Order. — Three examples of levers of the third order are :

(*a*) The spine, head, and pelvis, considered as a rigid bar, which has to be kept erect upon the hip-joints. (Fig. 4.)

Here the fulcrum lies in the hip-joints; the weight is at the centre of gravity of the head and trunk, high above the fulcrum; the power is supplied by the extensor, or flexor, muscles of the thigh, and acts upon points comparatively close to the fulcrum. (Fig. 4, 2 and II.)

(*b*) Flexion of the forearm upon the arm by the *biceps* muscle, when a weight is held in the hand.

In this case, the weight being in the hand and the fulcrum at the elbow-joint, the power is applied at the point of attachment of the tendon of the biceps, close to the latter. (Fig. 57.)

(*c*) Extension of the leg on the thigh at the knee-joint.

Here the fulcrum is the knee-joint; the weight is at the centre of gravity of the leg and foot, somewhere between the knee and the foot; the power is applied by the muscles in front of the thigh (Fig. 4, 2), through the ligament of the knee-cap, or *patella*, to the tibia, close to the knee-joint.

207. Each Kind represented in the Foot.—In studying the mechanism of the body, it is very important to recollect that one and the same part of the body may represent each of the three kinds of levers, according to circumstances. Thus it has been seen that the foot may, under some circumstances, represent a lever of the first, in others, of the second order. But it may become a lever of the third order, as when one dances a weight, resting upon the toes, up and down, by moving only the foot. In this case, the fulcrum is at the ankle-joint, the weight is at the toes, and the power is furnished by the extensor muscles at the front of the leg (Fig. 4, 1), which are inserted between the fulcrum and the weight. (Fig. 59.)

208. Joints.—It is very important that the levers of the body should not slip, or work unevenly, when their movements are extensive, and to this end they are connected together in such a manner as to form strong and definitely-arranged *joints* or *articulations*.

Joints may be classified into imperfect and perfect.

209. Imperfect Joints are those in which the conjoined levers (bones or cartilages) present no smooth surfaces, capable of rotatory motion, to one another, but are connected by continuous cartilages, or ligaments, and have only so much mobility as is permitted by the flexibility of the joining substance.

Examples of such joints as these are to be met with in the vertebral column—the flat surfaces of the bodies of the vertebræ, being connected together by thick plates of very elastic fibro-cartilage, which confer upon the whole column considerable play and springiness, and yet prevent any great amount of motion between the several vertebræ. In the pelvis (*see* Plate, Fig. VI.), the pubic bones are united to each other in front, and the iliac bones to the sacrum behind, by fibrous or cartilaginous tissue, which allows of only a slight play, and so gives the pelvis a little more elasticity than it would have if it were all one bone.

210. Perfect Joints.—In all perfect joints, the opposed bony surfaces which move upon one another are covered with cartilage, and between them is placed a sort of sac, which lines these cartilages, and, to a certain extent, forms the side-walls of the joint; and which, secreting a small

9

quantity of viscid, lubricating fluid—the *synovia*—is called
a *synovial membrane.*

211. Structure and Working of Joints.—The opposed
surfaces of these *articular* cartilages, as they are called,
may be spheroidal, cylindrical, or pulley-shaped; and the
convexities of the one answer, more or less completely, to
the concavities of the other.

Sometimes, the two articular cartilages do not come
directly into contact, but are separated by independent
plates of cartilage, which are termed *inter-articular.* The
opposite faces of these inter-articular cartilages are fitted
to receive the faces of the proper articular cartilages.

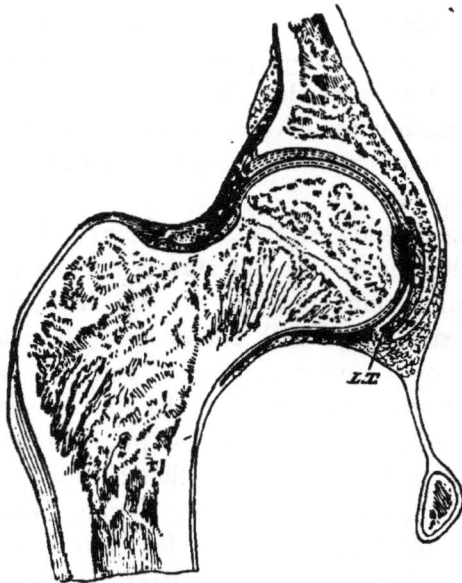

FIG. 61.

A SECTION OF THE HIP-JOINT TAKEN THROUGH THE ACETABULUM OR ARTICULAR
CUP OF THE PELVIS AND THE MIDDLE OF THE HEAD AND NECK OF THE THIGH-
BONE.

L. T., ligamentum teres, or round ligament. The spaces marked with an interrupted line (- - - -) represent the articular cartilages. The cavity of the synovial
membrane is indicated by the dark line between, and, as is shown, extends along the
neck of the femur beyond the limits of the cartilage. The peculiar shape of the pelvis
causes the section to have the remarkable outline shown in the cut. This will be intelligible if compared with Fig. VI. in the Plate.

While these coadapted surfaces and synovial membranes provide for the free mobility of the bones entering into a joint, the nature and extent of their motion are defined, partly by the forms of the articular surfaces, and partly by the disposition of the *ligaments,* or firm, fibrous cords, which pass from one bone to the other.

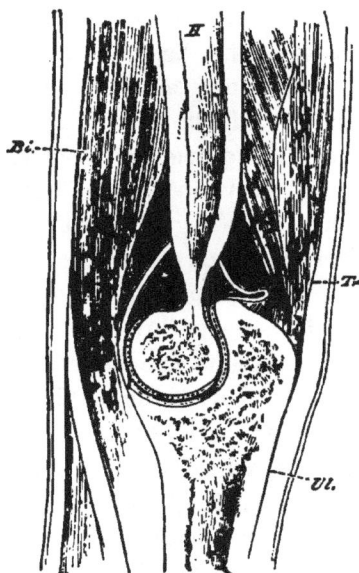

Fig. 62.

LONGITUDINAL AND VERTICAL SECTION THROUGH THE ELBOW-JOINT.
H., humerus; *Ul.,* ulna; *Tr.,* the *triceps* muscle which extends the arm; *Bi.,* the *biceps* muscle which flexes it.

212. Ball-and-Socket Joints.—As respects the nature of the articular surfaces, joints may be what are called *ball-and-socket joints,* when the spheroidal surface furnished by one bone plays in a cup furnished by another. In this case the motion of the former bone may take place in any direction, but the extent of the motion depends upon the shape of the cup—being very great when the cup is shallow, and small in proportion as it is deep. The shoulder is an example of a ball-and-socket joint with a shallow cup; the hip, of such a joint with a deep cup (Fig. 61).

213. **Hinge-Joints** are single or double. In the former case, the nearly cylindrical head of one bone fits into a corresponding socket of the other. In this form of hinge-joint the only motion possible is in the direction of a plane perpendicular to the axis of the cylinder, just as a door can only be made to move round an axis passing through its hinges. The elbow is the best example of this joint in the human body, but the movement here is limited, because the *olecranon,* or part of the ulna which rises up behind the humerus, prevents the arm being carried back behind the straight line; the arm can thus be bent to, or straightened, but not bent back (Fig. 62). The knee and ankle present less perfect specimens of a single hinge-joint.

A double hinge-joint is one in which the articular surface of each bone is concave in one direction, and convex in another, at right angles to the former. A man seated in a saddle is "articulated" with the saddle by such a joint. For the saddle is concave from before backwards, and convex from side to side, while the man presents to it the concavity of his legs astride, from side to side, and the convexity of his seat, from before backwards.

The metacarpal bone of the thumb is articulated with the bone of the wrist, called *trapezium,* by a double hinge-joint.

214. **Pivot-Joints.**—A pivot-joint is one in which one bone furnishes an axis or pivot, on which another turns; or itself turns on its own axis, resting on another bone. A remarkable example of the former arrangement is afforded by the *atlas* and *axis,* or two uppermost vertebræ of the neck (Figs. 63, 64). The axis possesses a vertical peg, the so-called *odontoid* process (*b*), and at the base of the peg are two, obliquely-placed, articular surfaces (*a*). The atlas is a ring-like bone, with a massive thickening on each side. The inner side of the front of the ring plays round the

neck of the odontoid peg, and the under surfaces of the
lateral masses glide over the articular faces on each side
of the base of the peg. A strong ligament passes between
the inner sides of the two lateral masses of the atlas, and
keeps the hinder side of the neck of the odontoid peg
in its place (Fig. 63). By this arrangement, the atlas is
enabled to rotate through a considerable angle either way
upon the axis, without any danger of falling forwards or
backwards—accidents which would immediately destroy
life by crushing the spinal marrow.

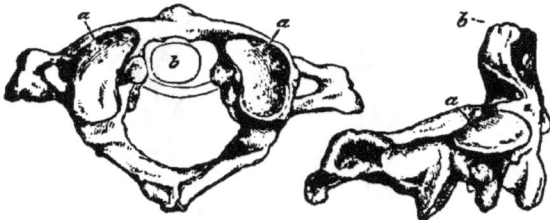

FIG. 63.   FIG. 64.

Fig. 63.—The atlas viewed from above: *a a*, upper articular surfaces of its lateral
masses for the condyles of the skull; *b*, the peg of the axis vertebra.
Fig. 64.—Side view of the axis vertebra: *a*, articular surface for the lateral mass
of the atlas; *b*, peg or odontoid process.

The lateral masses of the atlas have, on their upper
faces, concavities (Fig. 63, *a*) into which the two convex, occipital condyles of the skull fit, and in which they
play upward and downward. Thus the nodding of the
head is effected by the movement of the skull upon the
atlas; while, in turning the head from side to side, the
skull does not move upon the atlas, but the atlas slides
round the odontoid peg of the axis vertebra.

The second kind of pivot-joint is seen in the forearm.
If the elbow and forearm, as far as the wrist, are made to
rest upon a table, and the elbow is kept firmly fixed, the
hand can nevertheless be freely rotated so that either the
palm, or the back, is turned directly upwards. When the

palm is turned upwards, the attitude is called *supination* (Fig. 65); when the back, *pronation* (Fig. 66).

The forearm is composed of two bones; one, the *ulna*, which articulates with the *humerus* at the elbow by the hinge-joint already described, in such a manner that it can move only in flexion and extension (*see* 216), and has no power of rotation. Hence, when the elbow and wrist are rested on a table, this bone remains unmoved.

But the other bone of the forearm, the *radius*, has its

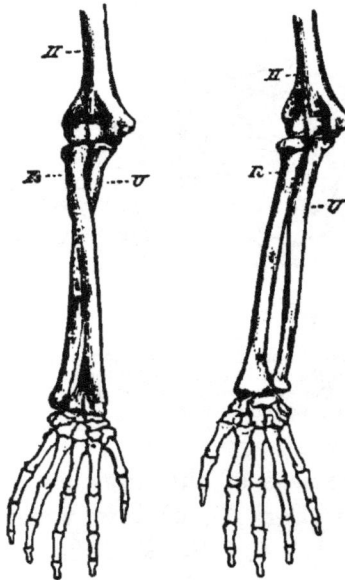

FIG. 66.　　　FIG. 65.

Fig. 65.—The bones of the right forearm in supination.
Fig. 66—in pronation.—*H.*, humerus; *R.*, radius; *U.*, ulna.

small upper end shaped like a very shallow cup with thick edges. The hollow of the cup articulates with a sphe-roidal surface furnished by the humerus; the lip of the cup, with a concave depression on the side of the ulna.

The large lower end of the radius bears the hand, and

has, on the side next the ulna, a concave surface, which articulates with the convex side of the small lower end of that bone.

Thus the upper end of the radius turns on the double surface, furnished to it by the pivot-like ball of the humerus, and the partial cup of the ulna : while the lower end of the radius can rotate round the surface furnished to it by the lower end of the ulna.

In *supination*, the radius lies parallel with the ulna, with its lower end to the outer side of the ulna (Fig. 65). In *pronation*, it is made to turn on its own axis above, and round the ulna below, until its lower half crosses the ulna, and its lower end lies on the inner side of the ulna (Fig. 66).

215. The Ligaments.—The ligaments which keep the mobile surfaces of bones together are, in the case of ball-

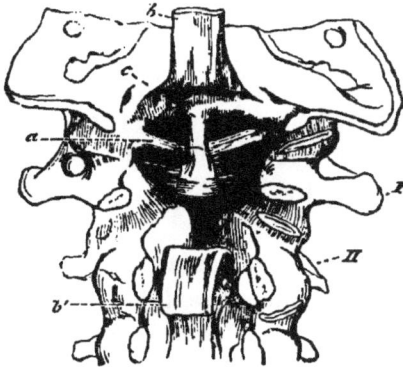

Fɪɢ. 67.

The vertebral column in the upper part of the neck laid open, to show—*a*, the check ligaments of the axis; *b*, the broad ligament which extends from the front margin of the occipital foramen along the hinder faces of the bodies of the vertebræ; it is cut through, and the cut ends turned back to show, *c*, the special ligament which connects the point of the "odontoid" peg with the front margin of the occipital foramen; *I.*, the atlas; *II.*, the axis.

and-socket joints, strong fibrous *capsules* which surround the joint on all sides. In hinge-joints, on the other hand, the ligamentous tissue is chiefly accumulated, in the form of *lateral ligaments*, at the sides of the joints. In some cases ligaments are placed within the joints, as in the knee, where the bundles of fibres which cross obliquely between the femur and the tibia are called *crucial* ligaments ; or, as in the hip, where the *round ligament* passes from the bottom of the socket or acetabulum of the pelvis to the ball furnished by the head of the femur (Fig. 61).

Again, two ligaments pass from the apex of the odontoid peg to either side of the margins of the occipital foramen, i. e., the large hole in the base of the skull, through which the spinal cord passes to join the brain; these, from their function in helping to stop excessive rotation of the skull, are called *check ligaments* (Fig. 67, *a*).

In one joint of the body, the hip, the socket or *acetabulum* (Fig. 61) fits so closely to the head of the femur, and the capsular ligament so completely closes its cavity on all sides, that the pressure of the air must be reckoned among the causes which prevent dislocation. This has been proved experimentally by boring a hole through the floor of the acetabulum, so as to admit air into its cavity, when the thigh-bone at once falls as far as the round and capsular ligaments will permit it to do, showing that it was previously pushed close up by the pressure of the external air.

216. The Various Movements of Joints.—The different kinds of movement which the levers thus connected are capable of performing, are called *flexion* and *extension ;* *abduction* and *adduction ; rotation* and *circumduction*.

A limb is *flexed*, when it is bent; *extended*, when it is straightened out. It is *abducted*, when it is drawn away from the middle line; *adducted*, when it is brought to the middle line. It is *rotated*, when it is made to turn on its own axis; *circumducted*, when it is made to describe a conical surface by rotation round an imaginary axis.

No part of the body is capable of perfect rotation like a wheel, for the simple reason that such motion would necessarily tear all the vessels, nerves, muscles, etc., which unite it with other parts.

217. How these Movements are effected. — Any two bones united by a joint may be moved one upon another in, at fewest, two different directions. In the case of a pure hinge-joint, these directions must be opposite and in the same plane; but, in all other joints, the movements may be in several directions and in various planes.

In the case of a pure hinge-joint, the two practicable movements—viz., flexion and extension—may be effected by means of two muscles, one for either movement, and running from one bone to the other, but on opposite sides of the joint. When either of these muscles contracts, it will pull its attached ends together, and bend or straighten, as the case may be, the joint towards the side on which it is placed. Thus at the elbow joint there is, in front of the joint, the biceps muscle, running from the arm to the forearm (*Bi.*, Fig. 62); when this contracts it pulls its two ends together, and so flexes the forearm on the arm. At the back of the joint there is the triceps (*Tr.*); when this contracts, it straightens or extends the forearm on the arm.

In the other extreme form of articulation—the ball-and-socket joint—movement in any number of planes may be effected, by attaching muscles in corresponding number and direction, on the one hand, to the bone which affords the socket, and, on the other, to that which furnishes the head. Circumduction will be effected by the combined and successive contraction of these muscles.

218. Tendons and their Functions.—It usually happens that the bone to which one end of a muscle is attached is absolutely or relatively stationary, while that to which the other is fixed is movable. In this case, the attachment to the stationary bone is termed the *origin*, that to the movable bone the *insertion*, of the muscle.

The fibres of muscles are sometimes fixed directly into the parts which serve as their origins and insertions : but, more commonly, strong cords or bands of fibrous tissue, called *tendons*, are interposed between the muscle proper and its place of origin or insertion. When the tendons play over hard surfaces, it is usual for them to be separated from these surfaces by sacs containing fluid, which are called *bursœ;* or even to be invested by synovial sheaths, i. e., quite covered for some distance by a synovial bag forming a double sheath very much in the same way that the bag of the pleura covers the lung and the chest-wall.

Usually, the direction of the axis of a muscle is that of a straight line joining its origin and its insertion. But in some muscles, as the *superior oblique muscle* of the eye, the tendon passes over a pulley formed by ligament, and completely changes its direction before reaching its insertion. (*See* 285).

Again, there are muscles which are fleshy at each end, and have a tendon in the middle. Such muscles are called *digastric*, or two-bellied. In the curious muscle which pulls down the lower jaw, and specially receives this name of *digastric*, the middle tendon runs through a pulley connected with the hyoid bone ; and the muscle, which passes downwards and forwards from the skull to this pulley, after traversing it, runs upwards and forwards, to the lower jaw (Fig. 68).

SECTION III.—*Movements of Locomotion.*

219. Walking.—We may now pass from the consideration of the mechanism of mere motion to that of locomotion.

When a man who is standing erect on both feet preceeds to *walk*, beginning with the right leg, the body is inclined so as to throw the centre of gravity forward; and, the right foot being raised, the right leg is advanced for the length of a step, and the foot is put down again. In the mean while, the left heel is raised, but the toes of the

left foot have not left the ground when the right foot has
reached it, so that there is no moment at which both feet
are off the ground. For an instant, the legs form two
sides of an equilateral triangle, and the centre of the body
is consequently lower than it was when the legs were parallel and close together.

The left foot, however, has not been merely dragged
away from its first position, but the muscles of the calf,
having come into play, act upon the foot as a lever of the
second order, and thrust the body, the weight of which

Fɪɢ. 68.

Tʜᴇ Cᴏᴜʀꜱᴇ ᴏꜰ ᴛʜᴇ Dɪɢᴀꜱᴛʀɪᴄ Mᴜꜱᴄʟᴇ.

D, its posterior belly; D', its anterior belly; between the two is the tendon passing
through its pulley connected with *Hy.*, the hyoid bone.

rests largely on the left astragalus, upwards, forwards, and
to the right side. The momentum thus communicated to
the body causes it, with the whole right leg, to describe an
arc over the right astragalus, on which that leg rests below.
The centre of the body consequently rises to its former
height as the right leg becomes vertical, and descends
again as the right leg, in its turn, inclines forward.

When the left foot has left the ground, the body is supported on the right leg, and is well in advance of the left
foot; so that, without any further muscular exertion, the
left foot swings forward like a pendulum, and is carried by
its own momentum beyond the right foot, to the position
in which it completes the second step.

220. Economy of Force in Walking.—When the intervals of the steps are so timed that each swinging leg comes forward into position for a new step without any exertion on the part of the walker, walking is effected with the greatest possible economy of force. And, as the swinging leg is a true pendulum—the time of vibration of which depends, other things being alike, upon its length (short pendulums vibrating more quickly than long ones)—it follows that, on the average, the natural step of short-legged people is quicker than that of long-legged ones.

221. Running and Jumping.— In *running*, there is a period when both legs are off the ground. The legs are advanced by muscular contraction, and the lever action of each foot is swift and violent. Indeed, the action of each leg resembles, in violent running, that which, when both legs act together, constitutes a *jump*, the sudden extension of the legs adding to the impetus, which, in slow walking, is given only by the feet.

SECTION IV.— *Vocal Movements.*

222. Conditions of the Production of Voice. — Perhaps the most singular motor apparatus in the body is the *larynx*, by the agency of which *voice* is produced.

The essential conditions of the production of the human voice are:

a. The existence of the so-called *vocal chords.*

b. The parallelism of the edges of these chords, without which they will not vibrate in such a manner as to give out sound.

c. A certain degree of tightness of the vocal chords, without which they will not vibrate quickly enough to produce sound.

d. The passage of a current of air between the parallel edges of the vocal chords of sufficient power to set the chords vibrating.

223. The Larynx.—The larynx is a short tubular bo::

opening above into the bottom of the pharynx, and below into the top of the trachea. Its framework is supplied by certain cartilages more or less movable on each other, and these are connected together by joints, membranes, and muscles. Across the middle of the larynx is a transverse partition, formed by two folds of the lining mucous membrane, stretching from either side, but not quite meeting in the middle line. They thus leave, in the middle line, a

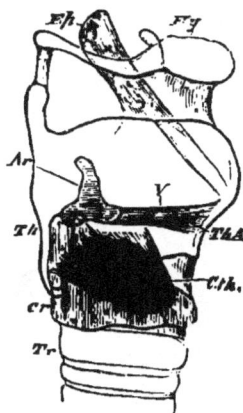

FIG. 69.

Diagram of the larynx, the thyroid cartilage (*Th*) being supposed to be transparent, and allowing the right arytenoid cartilage (*Ar.*), vocal chords (*V.*), and thyro-arytenoid muscle (*Th.A.*), the upper part of the cricoid cartilage (*Cr.*), and the attachment of the epiglottis (*Ep.*), to be seen; *C.th.*, the right crico-thyroid muscle; *Tr.*, the trachea; *Hy.*, the hyoid bone.

chink or slit, running from the front to the back, called the *glottis*. The two edges of this slit are not round and flabby, but sharp and, so to speak, clean cut; they are also strengthened by a quantity of elastic tissue, the fibres of which are disposed lengthways in them. These sharp free edges of the *glottis* are the so-called *vocal chords* or *vocal ligaments*.

224. The Cartilages of the Larynx.—The *thyroid* cartilage (Fig. 69, *Th.*) is a broad plate of gristle bent upon itself into a V-shape, and so disposed that the point of the

V is turned forwards, and constitutes what is commonly called "Adam's apple." Above, the thyroid cartilage is attached by ligament and membrane to the *hyoid* bone (Fig. 69, *Hy.*). Below and behind, its broad sides are produced into little elongations or horns, which are articulated by ligaments with the outside of a great ring of cartilage, the *cricoid* (Fig. 69, *Cr.*), which forms, as it were, the top of the windpipe.

The *cricoid* ring is much higher behind than in front, and a gap, filled up by membrane only, is left between its

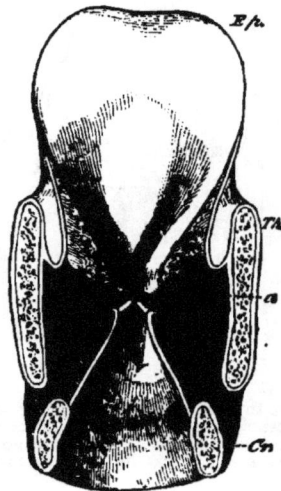

Fig. 70.

A VERTICAL AND TRANSVERSE SECTION THROUGH THE LARYNX, THE HINDER HALF OF WHICH IS REMOVED.

Ep., epiglottis; *Th.*, thyroid cartilage; *a*, cavities called the *ventricles of larynx* above the vocal ligaments (*V.*); × the right thyro-arytenoid muscle cut across: *Cr.*, the cricoid cartilage.

upper edge and the lower edge of the front part of the thyroid, when the latter is horizontal. Consequently, the thyroid cartilage, turning upon the articulations of its horns with the hinder part of the cricoid, as upon hinges, can be moved up and down through the space occupied by this membrane. When it moves downwards, the distance between the front part of the thyroid cartilage and the back of the cricoid is necessarily increased; and, when it moves back again to the horizontal position, diminished. There is, on each side, a large muscle, the *crico-thyroid*, which passes from the outer side of the cricoid cartilage obliquely upwards and backwards to the thyroid, and pulls the latter down (Fig. 69, *C.th.*).

Perched side by side, upon the upper edge of the back part of the cricoid cartilage are two small irregularly-shaped but, roughly speaking, pyramidal cartilages, the *arytenoid* cartilages (Fig. 71, *Ary.*). Each of these is

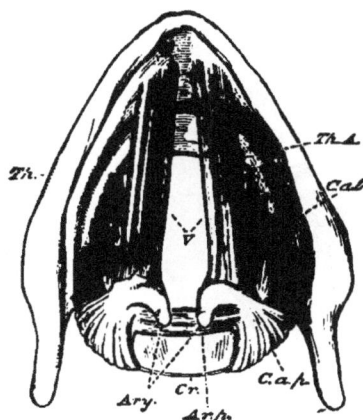

FIG. 71.

THE PARTS SURROUNDING THE GLOTTIS PARTIALLY DISSECTED AND VIEWED FROM ABOVE.

Th., the thyroid cartilage; *Cr.*, the cricoid cartilage; *V.*, the edges of the vocal ligaments bounding the glottis; *Ary.*, the arytenoid cartilages; *Th. A.*, thyro-arytenoid; *C.a.l.*, lateral crico-arytenoid; *C.a.p.*, posterior crico-arytenoid; *Ar.p.*, posterior arytenoid muscles.

articulated by its base with the cricoid cartilage by means of a shallow joint which permits of very varied movements, and especially allows the front portions of the two arytenoid cartilages to approach, or to recede from, each other.

225. Attachment of the Vocal Ligaments.—It is to the fore part of one of these arytenoid cartilages that the hinder end of each of the two vocal ligaments is fastened; and they stretch from these points horizontally across the cavity of the larynx, to be attached, close together, in the reëntering angle of the thyroid cartilage rather lower than half-way between its top and bottom.

226. The Muscles of the Larynx.—Now, when the arytenoid cartilages diverge, as they do when the larynx is in

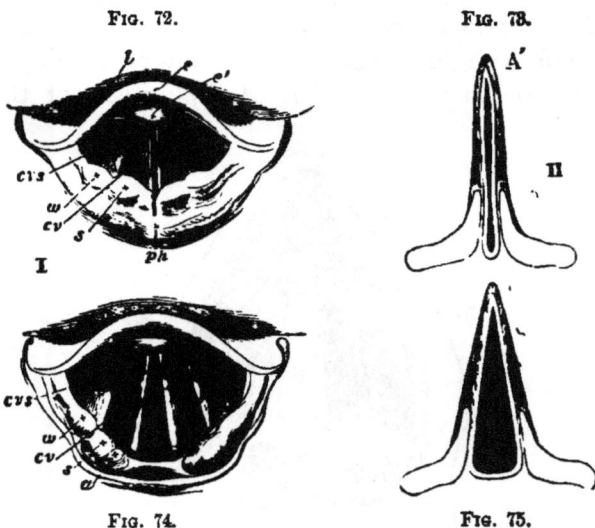

FIG. 72.

FIG. 73.

cvs
w
cv
s
ph
I

A'
II

cvs
w
cv
s
a

FIG. 74.

FIG. 75.

Fig. 72.—View of the human larynx from above as actually seen by the aid of the instrument called the laryngoscope.
Fig. 73.—In the condition when voice is being produced.
Figs. 74, 75.—At rest, when no voice is produced.
e. Epiglottis (foreshortened).
c.v. The vocal chords.
c.v.s. The so-called false vocal chords, folds of mucous membrane lying above the real vocal chords.
a. Elevation caused by the arytenoid cartilages.
s.w. Elevations caused by small cartilages connected with the arytenoids.
l. Root of the tongue.

a state of rest, it is evident that the aperture of the glottis will be V-shaped, the point of the V being forwards, and the base behind.

For, in front, or in the angle of the thyroid, the two vocal ligaments are fastened permanently close together, whereas, behind, their extremities will be separated as far

as the arytenoids, to which they are attached, are separated from each other. Under these circumstances a current of air passing through the glottis produces no sound,
the parallelism of the vocal chords being wanting; whence
it is that, ordinarily, expiration and inspiration take place
quietly. Passing from one arytenoid cartilage to the
other, at their posterior surfaces are certain muscles called
the *posterior arytenoid* (Fig. 71, *Ar.p.*). There are also two
sets of muscles connecting each arytenoid with the cricoid,
and called from their positions respectively the *posterior*
and *lateral crico-arytenoid* (Fig. 71, *C.a.p.*, *C.a.l.*). By
the more or less separate or combined action of these muscles, the arytenoid cartilages and, consequently, the hinder
ends of the vocal chords attached to them, may be made
to approach or recede from each other, and thus the vocal
chords rendered parallel or the reverse.

We have seen that the crico-thyroid muscle pulls the
thyroid cartilage down, and thus increases the distance.
between the front of the thyroid and the back of the
cricoid, on which the arytenoids are seated. This movement, the arytenoids being fixed, must tend to pull out
the vocal chords lengthways, or, in other words, to tighten
them.

Running from the reëntering angle in the front part of
the thyroid, backward, to the arytenoids, alongside the
vocal chords (and indeed embedded in the transverse folds,
of which the chords are the free edges) are two strong
muscles, one on each side (Fig. 71, *Th.A.*), called the
thyro-arytenoid. The effect of the contraction of these
muscles is to pull up the thyroid cartilage after it has been
depressed by the crico-thyroid muscles, and consequently
to slacken the vocal chords.

Thus the parallelism (*b*) of the vocal chords is determined chiefly by the relative distance from each other of
the arytenoid cartilages; the tension (*c*) of the vocal chords
is determined chiefly by the upward or downward move-

ment of the thyroid cartilage; and both these conditions
are dependent on the action of certain muscles.

227. Notes—Range and Quality of Voice.—The current
of air whose passage sets the chords vibrating is supplied
by the movements of expiration, which, when the chords
are sufficiently parallel and tense, produce that musical
note which constitutes the voice, but otherwise give rise
to no audible sound at all.

Other things being alike, the musical note will be low
or high, according as the vocal chords are relaxed or tight-

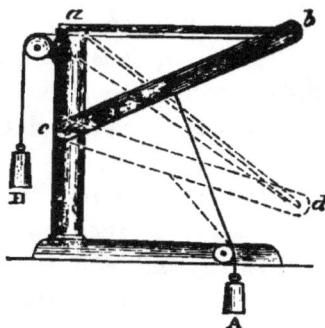

Fig. 76.

Diagram of a model illustrating the action of the levers and muscles of the larynx.
The stand and vertical pillar represent the cricoid and arytenoid cartilages, while the
rod (*b c*), moving on a pivot at *c*, takes the place of the thyroid cartilage; *a b* is an
elastic band representing the vocal ligament. Parallel with this runs a cord fastened
at one end to the rod *b c*, and, at the other, passing over a pulley to the weight B. This
represents the thyro-arytenoid muscle. A cord attached to the middle of *b c*, and passing over a second pulley to the weight A, represents the crico-thyroid muscle. It is
obvious that, when the bar (*b c*) is pulled down to the position of *c d*, the elastic band
(*a b*) is put on the stretch.

ened; and this again depends upon the relative predomi-
nance of the contraction of the crico-thyroid and thyro-
arytenoid muscles. For when the thyro-arytenoid muscles
are fully contracted, the thyroid cartilage will be pulled up
as far as it can go, and the vocal chords will be rendered
relatively lax; while, when the crico-thyroid muscles are
fully contracted, the thyroid cartilage will be depressed as
much as possible, and the vocal chords will be made more
tense.

The *range* of any voice depends upon the difference of tension which can be given to the vocal chords, in these two positions of the thyroid cartilage. *Accuracy* of singing depends upon the precision with which the singer can voluntarily adjust the contractions of the thyro-arytenoid and crico-thyroid muscles—so as to give his vocal chords the exact tension at which their vibration will yield the notes required.

The *quality* of a voice—treble, bass, tenor, etc.—on the other hand, depends upon the make of the particular larynx, the primitive length of its vocal chords, their elasticity, the amount of resonance of the surrounding parts, and so on.

Thus, men have deeper notes than boys and women, because their larynxes are larger and their vocal chords longer—whence, though equally elastic, they vibrate less swiftly.

228. Speech.—*Speech* is voice modulated by the throat, tongue, and lips. Thus, voice may exist without speech; and it is commonly said that speech may exist without voice, as in whispering. This is only true, however, if the title of voice be restricted to the sound produced by the vibration of the vocal chords; for, in whispering, there is a sort of voice produced by the vibration of the muscular walls of the lips which thus replace the vocal chords. A whisper is, in fact, a very low whistle.

229. Vowel and Consonant Sounds.—The *modulation* of the voice into speech is effected by changing the form of the cavity of the mouth and nose, by the action of the muscles which move the walls of those parts.

Thus, if the pure *vowel* sounds—

E (as in *he*),	*A* (as in *hay*),	*A'* (as in *ah*),
O (as in *or*),	*O'* (as in *oh*),	*OO* (as in *cool*),

are pronounced successively, it will be found that they may be all formed out of the sound produced by a con-

tinuous expiration, the mouth being kept open, but the
form of its aperture, and the extent to which the lips are
thrust out or drawn in so as to lengthen or shorten the
distance of the orifice from the larynx, being changed for
each vowel.   It will be narrowest, with the lips most
drawn back, in *E*, widest in *A'*, and roundest, with the
lips most protruded, in *O O*.

Certain *consonants* also may be pronounced without
interrupting the current of expired air, by modification of
the form of the throat and mouth.

Thus the aspirate, H, is the result of a little extra expiratory force—a sort of incipient cough. *S* and *Z, Sh*
and *J* (as in *jugular* = *G* soft, as in *gentry*), *Th, L, R, F,
V,* may likewise all be produced by continuous currents of
air forced through the mouth, the shape of the cavity of
which is peculiarly modified by the tongue and lips.

All the vocal sounds hitherto noted so far resemble one
another, that their production does not involve the stoppage of the current of air which traverses either of the
modulating passages.

But the sounds of *M* and *N* can only be formed by
blocking the current of air which passes through the
mouth, while free passage is left through the nose.   For
M, the mouth is shut by the lips; for *N*, by the application
of the tongue to the palate.

The other consonantal sounds of the English language
are produced by shutting the passage through both nose and
mouth; and, as it were, forcing the expiratory vocal current through the obstacle furnished by the latter, the character of which obstacle gives each consonant its peculiarity. Thus, in producing the consonants *B* and *P*, the
mouth is shut by the lips, which are then forced open in
this *explosive* manner.   In *T* and *D*, the mouth-passage is
suddenly barred by the application of the point of the
tongue to the teeth, or to the front part of the palate;
while in *K* and *G* (hard, as in *go*) the middle and back of

the tongue are similarly forced against the back part of the palate.

230. Speaking-Machines.—An artificial larynx may be constructed by properly adjusting elastic bands, which take the place of the vocal chords ; and, when a current of air is forced through these, due regulation of the tension of the bands will give rise to all the notes of the human voice. As each vowel and consonantal sound is produced by the modification of the length and form of the cavities, which lie over the natural larynx, so, by placing over the artificial larynx chambers to which any requisite shape can be given, the various letters may be sounded. It is by attending to these facts and principles that various speaking-machines have been constructed.

231. Tongueless Speech.—Although the tongue is credited with the responsibility of speech, as the " unruly member," and undoubtedly takes a very important share in its production, it is not absolutely indispensable. Hence, the apparently fabulous stories of people who have been enabled to speak, after their tongues had been cut out by the cruelty of a tyrant, or persecutor, may be quite true.

Some years ago I had the opportunity of examining a person, whom I will call Mr. R——, whose tongue had been removed as completely as a skillful surgeon could perform the operation. When the mouth was widely opened, the truncated face of the stump of the tongue, apparently covered with new mucous membrane, was to be seen, occupying a position as far back as the level of the anterior pillars of the fauces. The dorsum of the tongue was visible with difficulty ; but I believe I could discern some of the circumvallate papillæ upon it. None of these were visible upon the amputated part of the tongue, which had been preserved in spirits ; and which, so far as I could judge, was about two and a half inches long.

When his mouth was open, Mr. R—— could advance his tongue no farther than the position in which I saw it ; but he informed me that, when his mouth was shut, the stump of the tongue could be brought much more forward.

Mr. R——'s conversation was perfectly intelligible; and such words as *think, the, cow, kill*, were well and clearly pronounced. But tin became *fin;* tack, *fack* or *pack;* toll, *pool;* dog, *thog;* dine, *vine;* dew, *thew;* cat, *catf;* mad, *mdf;* goose, *gooth;* big, *pig*, bich, *pich*, with a guttural *ch*.

In fact, only the pronunciation of those letters the formation of which requires the use of the tongue was affected; and, of these, only the two which involve the employment of its tip were absolutely beyond Mr. R——'s power. He converted all *t's*, and *d's*, into *f's*, *p's*, *v's*, or *th's*. *Th* was fairly given in all cases; *s* and *sh, l* and *r*, with more or less of a lisp. Initial *g's* and *k's* were good; but final *g's* were all more or less guttural. In the former case, the imperfect stoppage of the current of air by the root of the tongue was of no moment, as the sound ran on into that of the following vowel; while, when the letter was terminal, the defect at once became apparent.

CHAPTER VIII.

SENSATIONS AND SENSORY ORGANS.

SECTION I.—*Reflex Action— Groups of Sensations.*

232. Efferent and Afferent Nerves.—The agent by which all the motor organs (except the cilia) described in the preceding chapter are set at work, is muscular fibre. But, in the living body, muscular fibre is made to contract only by a change which takes place in the *motor* or *efferent nerve*, which is distributed to it. This change, again, is effected only by the activity of the *central nervous organ*, with which the motor nerve is connected. The central organ is

thrown into activity immediately, or ultimately, only by
the influence of changes which take place in the molecular
condition of nerves, called *sensory* or *afferent*, which are
connected, on the one hand, with the central organ, and,
on the other hand, with some other part of the body.
Finally, the alteration of the afferent nerve is itself produced only by changes in the condition of the part of the
body, with which it is connected; which changes usually
result from external impressions.

233. Conveyance of Molecular Impressions.—Thus the
great majority (if not the whole) of the movements of the
body and of its parts, are the effect of an influence (technically termed a *stimulus* or *irritation*) applied directly, or
indirectly, to the ends of *afferent nerves*, and giving rise to
a molecular change, which is propagated along their substance to the *central nervous organ* with which they are
connected. The molecular activity of the afferent nerve
communicates itself to the central organ, and is then transmitted along the *motor nerves*, which pass from the central
organ to the muscles affected. And, when the disturbance
in the molecular condition of the efferent nerves reaches
their extremities, it is communicated to the muscular
fibres, and causes their particles to take up a new position,
so that each fibre shortens and becomes thicker.

234. Reflex Action. Sensations and Consciousness.—
Such a series of molecular changes as that just described
is called a *reflex action*—the disturbance caused by the
irritation being as it were *reflected* back, along the motor
nerves, to the muscles.

A reflex action, strictly so called, takes place without
our knowing any thing about it, and hundreds of such
actions are going on continually in our bodies without our
being aware of them. But it very frequently happens that
we learn that something is going on, when a stimulus
affects our afferent nerves, by having what we call a *feeling* or *sensation*. We class sensations along with *emotions*,

and *volitions*, and *thoughts*, under the common head of *states of consciousness.* But what consciousness is, we know not; and how it is that any thing so remarkable as a state of consciousness comes about, as the result of irritating nervous tissue, is just as unaccountable as any other ultimate fact of Nature.

235. Subjective Sensations.—Sensations are of very various degrees of definiteness. Some arise within ourselves, we know not how or where, and remain vague and undefinable. Such are the sensations of *uncomfortableness*, or *faintness*, of *fatigue*, or of *restlessness*. We cannot assign any particular place to these sensations, which are very probably the result of affections of the afferent nerves in general brought about by the state of the blood, or that of the tissues in which they are distributed. And however real these sensations may be, and however largely they enter into the sum of our pleasures and pains, they tell us absolutely nothing of the external world. They are not only *diffuse*, but they are also *subjective* sensations.

236. The Muscular Sense.—What is termed the *muscular sense* is less vaguely localized than the preceding, though its place is still incapable of being very accurately defined. This muscular sensation is the feeling of resistance which arises when any kind of obstacle is opposed to the movement of the body, or of any part of it; and it is something quite different from the feeling of contact or even of pressure.

Lay one hand flat on its back upon a table, and rest a disk of card-board a couple of inches in diameter upon the ends of the outstretched fingers; the only result will be a sensation of *contact*—the pressure of so light a body being inappreciable. But put a two-pound weight upon the card-board, and the sensation of *contact* will be accompanied, or even obscured, by the very different feeling of *pressure*. Up to this moment the fingers and arm have rested upon the table; but now let the hand be raised from the table, and another new feeling will make its appearance—that of *resistance to effort.* This feeling comes into existence with the exertion of the muscles which raise the arm, and is the consciousness of that exertion given to us by the muscular sense.

Any one who raises or carries a weight, knows well enough that he has this sensation; but he may be greatly puzzled to say where he has it. Nevertheless, the sense itself is very delicate, and enables us to form tolerably accurate judgments of the relative intensity of resistances. Persons who deal in articles sold by weight are constantly enabled to form very precise estimates of the weight of such articles, by balancing them in their hands; and, in this case, they depend in a great measure upon the muscular sense.

237. The Higher Senses.—In a third group of sensations, each feeling, as it arises, is assigned to a definite part of the body, and is produced by a stimulus applied to that part of the body; but the bodies, or forces, which are competent to act as stimuli, are very various in character. Such are the sensations of *touch,* which is restricted to the integument covering the surface, and to some portions of the membranes lining the internal cavities of the body; and of *taste* and *smell,* which are similarly confined to certain regions of the mucous membrane of the mouth and nasal cavities.

Any portion of the body to which a sensation is thus restricted is called a sensory organ.

And lastly, in a fourth group of sensations, each feeling requires for its production the application of a single kind of stimulus to a very specially-modified part of the integument. The latter serves as an intermediator between the physical agent of the sensation and the sensory nerve, which is to convey to the brain the impulse necessary to awake in it that state of consciousness which we call the

10

sensation. Such are the sensations of *sight* and *hearing*. The physical agents which can alone awaken these sensations (under natural circumstances) are light and sound. The modified parts of the integument, which alone are competent to intermediate between these agents and the nerves of sight and hearing, are the *eye* and the *ear*.

238. General Plan of a Sensory Organ.—In every sensory organ it is necessary to distinguish the terminal expansion of the afferent or sensory nerve, and the structures which intermediate between this expansion and the physical agent which gives rise to the sensation.

And in each group of special sensations there are certain phenomena which arise out of the structure of the organ, and others which result from the operation of the central apparatus of the nervous system upon the materials supplied to it by the sensory organ.

Section II.— *Touch, Taste, and Smell.*

239. The Sense of Touch.—The sense of Touch (including that of heat and cold) is possessed, more or less acutely, by all parts of the free surface of the body, and by the walls of the mouth and nasal passages.

Whatever part possesses this sense consists of a membrane (integumentary or mucous) composed of a deep layer made up of fibrous tissue, containing a capillary network and the ultimate terminations of the sensory nerves; and of a superficial layer consisting of epithelial or epidermic cells, among which are no vessels.

Wherever the sense of touch is delicate, the deep layer is not a mere flat expansion, but is raised up into multitudes of small, close-set, conical elevations (*see* Fig. 40), which are called *papillæ*. In the skin, the coat of epithelial or epidermic cells does not follow the contour of these papillæ, but dips down between them and forms a tolerably even coat over them. Thus, the points of the papillæ are much nearer the surface than the general plane of the

deep layer whence these papillæ proceed. Loops of vessels
enter the papillæ, and the fine ultimate terminations of
the sensory nerve-fibres distributed to the skin terminate in
them, but in what way has not been thoroughly made out.

In certain cases, the delicate fibrous sheath, or *neurilemma*, of the nerve, which enters the papilla, enlarges in
the papilla into an oval swelling, which is called a *tactile
corpuscle* (*see* 357). These corpuscles are found in the
papillæ of those localities which are endowed with a very
delicate sense of touch, as in the tips of the fingers, the
point of the tongue, etc.

240. Functions of Epithelium.—It is obvious, from what
has been said, that no direct contact takes place between
a body which is touched and the sensory nerve—a thicker
or thinner layer of epithelium, or epidermis, being situated
between the two. In fact, if this layer is removed, as
when a surface of the skin has been blistered, contact with
the raw surface gives rise to a sense of pain, not to one of
touch properly so called. Thus, in touch, it is the epidermis, or epithelium, which is the intermediator between the
nerve and the physical agent, the external pressure being
transmitted through the horny cells to the subjacent ends
of the nerves, and the kind of impulse thus transmitted
must be modified by the thickness and character of the
cellular layer, no less than by the forms and number of the
papillæ.

241. Varying Tactile Sensibility.—Certain very curious
phenomena appertaining to the sense of touch are probably due to these varying anatomical arrangements. Not
only is tactile sensibility to a single impression much duller
in some parts than in others—a circumstance which might
be readily accounted for by the different thickness of the
epidermic layer—but the power of distinguishing double
simultaneous impressions is very different. Thus, if the
ends of a pair of compasses (which should be blunted with
pointed pieces of cork) are separated by only one-tenth or

one-twelfth of an inch, they will be distinctly felt as two, if applied to the tips of the fingers; whereas, if applied to the back of the hand in the same way, only one impression will be felt; and, on the arm, they may be separated for a quarter of an inch, and still only one impression will be perceived.

Accurate experiments have been made in different parts of the body, and it has been found that two points can be distinguished by the tongue, if only one-twenty-fourth of an inch apart; by the tips of the fingers if one-twelfth of an inch distant; while they may be one inch distant on the cheek, and even three inches on the back, and still give rise to only one sensation.

242. The Sense of Warmth or Cold. — The feeling of warmth, or cold, is the result of an excitation of sensory nerves distributed to the skin, which are probably distinct from those which give rise to the sense of touch. And it would appear that the heat must be transmitted through the epidermic or epithelial layer, to give rise to this sensation; for, just as touching a naked nerve, or the trunk of a nerve, gives rise only to pain, so heating or cooling an exposed nerve, or the trunk of a nerve, gives rise not to a sensation of heat or cold, but simply to pain.

Again, the sensation of heat, or cold, is relative rather than absolute. Suppose three basins be prepared, one filled with ice-cold water, one with water as hot as can be borne, and the third with a mixture of the two. If the hand be put into the hot-water basin, and then transferred to the mixture, the latter will feel cold; but, if the hand be kept a while in the ice-cold water, and then transferred to the very same mixture, it will feel warm.

Like the sense of touch, the sense of warmth varies in delicacy in different parts of the body.

The cheeks are very sensitive, more so than the lips; the palms of the hands are more sensitive to heat than their backs. Hence a washer-woman holds her flat-iron to her cheek to test the temperature, and one who is cold spreads the palms of his hands to the fire.

243. The Sense of Taste—the Tongue. —The organ of the sense of TASTE is the mucous membrane which covers the tongue, especially its back part, and the hinder part of the palate. Like that of the skin, the deep, or vascular,

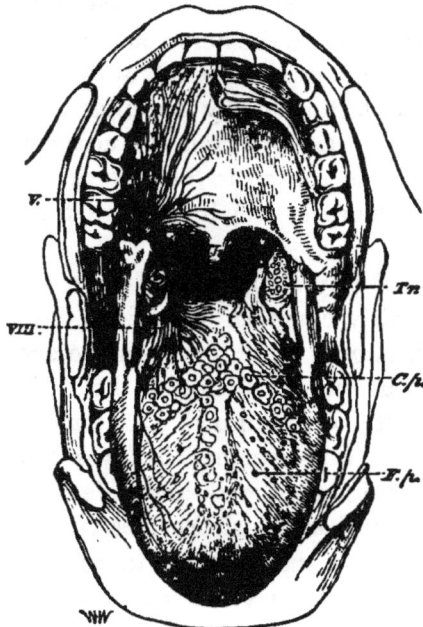

FIG. 77.

THE MOUTH WIDELY OPENED TO SHOW THE TONGUE AND PALATE.

Uv., the uvula; *Tn.*, the tonsil between the anterior and posterior pillars of the fauces; *C.p.*, circumvallate papillæ; *F.p.*, fungiform papillæ. The minute filiform papillæ cover the interspaces between these. On the right side the tongue is partially dissected to show the course of the filaments of the glossopharyngeal nerve, *VIII.*

layer of the mucous membrane of the tongue is raised up into papillæ, but these are large, separate, and have separate coats of epithelium. Towards the tip of the tongue they are for the most part elongated and pointed, and are called *filiform ;* over the rest of the surface of the tongue, these are mixed with other larger papillæ, with broad ends and narrow bases, called *fungiform ;* but, towards its root, there are a number of large papillæ, arranged in the figure of a V, with its point backwards, each of which is like a fungiform papilla surrounded by a wall. These are the circumvallate papillæ (Fig. 77, *C.p.*). The larger of these papillæ have subordinate small ones upon their surfaces. They are very vascular, and they receive nervous filaments from two sources, the one the nerve called *glossopharyngeal,* the other the *gustatory,* which is a branch of the *fifth* nerve. (*See* 330.) The latter chiefly supplies the front of the tongue, the former its back and the adjacent part of the palate; and there is reason to believe that it is the latter region which is more especially the seat of the sense of taste.

The great majority of the sensations we call taste, however, are in reality complex sensations, into which smell and even touch largely enter. When the sense of smell is interfered with, as when the nose is held tightly pinched, it is very difficult to distinguish the taste of various objects. An onion, for instance, the eyes being shut, may then easily be confounded with an apple.

244. Smell—Mechanism of the Nostrils.—The organ of the sense of SMELL is the delicate mucous membrane which lines a part of the nasal cavities, and is distinguished from the rest of the mucous membrane of these cavities—firstly, by possessing no cilia; secondly, by receiving its nervous supply from the olfactory, or first, pair of cerebral nerves, and not, like the rest of the mucous membrane, from the fifth pair.

Each nostril leads into a spacious nasal chamber, separated, in the middle line, from its fellow of the other side, by a partition, or *septum,* formed partly by cartilage and partly by bone, and continuous with that partition which separates the two nostrils one from the other. Below, each nasal chamber is separated from the cavity of the mouth by a floor, the bony palate (Figs. 78, 79, 80); and, when this bony palate comes to an end, the partition is continued down to the root of the tongue by a fleshy curtain, the soft palate, which has been already described. The soft palate and the root of the tongue together constitute, under ordinary circumstances, a movable partition between the mouth and the pharynx, and it will be observed that the opening of the larynx, the *glottis*, lies behind the partition; so that, when the root of the tongue is applied close to the soft palate, no passage of air can take place between the mouth and the pharynx. But in the upper part of the pharynx above the partition are the two hinder openings of the nasal cavities (which are called the *posterior nares*) separated by the termination of the septum; and through these wide openings the air passes, with great readiness, from the nostrils along the lower part of each nasal chamber to the glottis, or in the opposite direction. It is by means of the passages thus freely open to the air, that we breathe, as we ordinarily do, with the mouth shut.

Each nasal chamber rises, as a high vault, far above the level of the arch of the posterior nares—in fact, about as high as the depression of the root of the nose. The uppermost and front part of its roof, between the eyes, is formed by a delicate horizontal plate of bone, perforated, like a sieve, by a great many small holes, and thence called the *cribriform* plate (Fig. 80, *Cr.*). It is this plate (with the membranous structures which line its two faces) alone which, in this region, separates the cavity of the nose from that which contains the brain. The olfactory lobes which are directly connected with, and form indeed a part of, the brain, enlarge at their ends, and their broad extremities rest upon the upper side of the cribriform plate: sending immense numbers of delicate filaments, the olfactory nerves, through it to the olfactory mucous membrane (Fig. 79).

On each wall of the septum this mucous membrane

forms a flat expansion, but on the side walls of each nasal
cavity it follows the elevations and depressions of the
inner surfaces of what are called the upper and middle

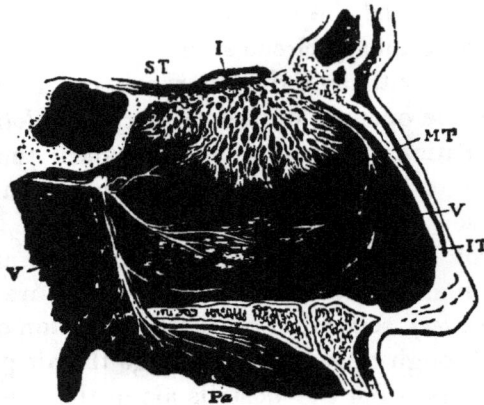

FIG. 78.

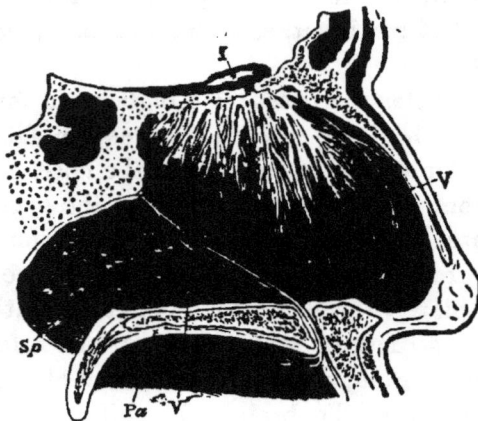

FIG. 79.

VERTICAL LONGITUDINAL SECTIONS OF THE NASAL CAVITY.

Fig. 78 represents the outer wall of the left nasal cavity.
Fig. 79 represents the right side of the middle partition, or septum (*Sp.*), of the
nose, which forms the inner wall of the right nasal cavity. *I*, the olfactory nerve and
its branches; *V*, branches of the fifth nerve; *Pa.*, the palate, which separates the
nasal cavity from that of the mouth; *S.T.*, the superior turbinal bone; *M.T.*, the middle turbinal; *I.T.*, the inferior turbinal. The letter *I* is placed in the cerebral cavity;
and the partition on which the olfactory lobe rests, and through which the filaments
of the olfactory nerves pass, is the cribriform plate.

turbinal, or spongy bones. These bones are called spongy because the interior of each is occupied by air cavities separated from each other by very delicate partitions only, and communicating with the nasal cavities. Hence the bones, though massive-looking, are really exceedingly light and delicate, and fully deserve the appellation of spongy (Fig. 80).

There is a third light scroll-like bone distinct from these two, and attached to the maxillary bone, which is called the *inferior* turbinal, as it lies lower than the other two, and imperfectly separates the air passages from the proper olfactory chamber (Fig. 78). It is covered by the ordinary ciliated mucous membrane of the nasal passage, and receives no filaments from the olfactory nerve (Fig. 78).

245. The Reason of " Sniffing."—From the arrangements which have been described, it is clear that, under ordinary circumstances, the gentle inspiratory and expiratory currents will flow along the comparatively wide, direct passages afforded by so much of the nasal chamber as lies below the middle turbinal; and that they will hardly move the air inclosed in the narrow interspace between the septum and the upper and middle spongy bones, which is the proper olfactory chamber.

If the air-currents are laden with particles of odorous matter, they can only reach the olfactory membrane by diffusing themselves into this narrow interspace; and, if there be but few of these particles, they will run the risk of not reaching the olfactory mucous membrane at all, unless the air in contact with it be exchanged for some of the odoriferous air. Hence it is that, when we wish to perceive a faint odor more distinctly, we sniff, or snuff up the air. Each sniff is a sudden inspiration, the effect of which must reach the air in the olfactory chamber at the same time as, or even before, it affects that at the nostrils; and thus must tend to draw a little air out of that chamber from behind. At the same time, or immediately afterwards, the air sucked in at the nostrils entering with a sudden vertical rush, part of it must tend to flow directly into the olfactory chamber, and replace that thus drawn out.

The loss of smell which takes place in the course of a severe cold may, in part, be due to the swollen state of

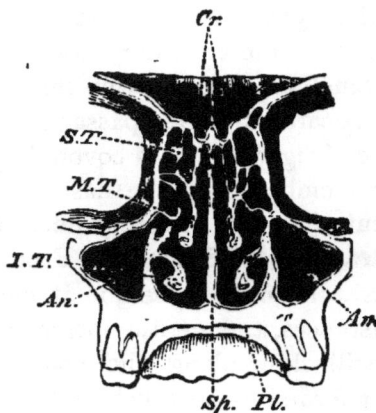

Fig. 80.

A TRANSVERSE AND VERTICAL SECTION OF THE OSSEOUS WALLS OF THE NASAL CAVITY TAKEN NEARLY THROUGH THE LETTER *I* IN THE FOREGOING FIGURE.

Cr., the cribriform plate; *S.T.*, *M.T.*, the chambered superior and middle turbinal bones on which and on the septum (*Sp.*) the filaments of the olfactory nerve are distributed; *I.T.*, the inferior turbinal bone; *Pl.*, the palate; *An.*, the *Antrum* or chamber which occupies the greater part of the maxillary bone and opens into the nasal cavity.

the mucous membrane which covers the inferior turbinal bones, which thus impedes the passage of odoriferous air to the olfactory chamber.

SECTION III.—*The Mechanism of Hearing.*

246. Structure of the Ear.—The EAR, or organ of the sense of Hearing, is very much more complex than either of the sensory organs yet described. It will be useful to distinguish the *essential* parts of this complicated apparatus from certain other parts, which, though of great assist-

ance to the sense, are not absolutely necessary, and therefore may be called *accessory*.

The essential parts, on either side of the head, consist,
substantially, of two peculiarly-formed membranous bags,
called, respectively, the *membranous labyrinth* and the
scala media of the cochlea. Both these bags are lodged
in cavities which they do not completely fill, situated in
the midst of a dense and solid mass of bone (from its
hardness called *petrosal*), which forms a part of the temporal bone, and enters into the base of the skull.

Each bag is filled with a fluid, and is also supported in
a fluid which fills the cavity in which it is lodged. In the
interior of each bag, certain small, mobile, hard bodies
are contained; and the ultimate filaments of the auditory
nerves are so distributed upon the walls of the bags that
their terminations must be knocked by the vibrations of
these small hard bodies, should any thing set them in
motion. It is also quite possible that the vibrations of the
fluid contents of the sacs may themselves suffice to affect
the filaments of the auditory nerve; but, however this
may be, any such effect must be greatly intensified by the
coöperation of the solid particles.

In bathing in a tolerably smooth sea, on a rocky shore,
the movement of the little waves as they run backwards
and forwards is hardly felt by any one lying down; but, in
bathing on a sandy and gravelly beach, the pelting of the
showers of little stones and sand, which are raised and let
fall by each wavelet, makes a very definite impression on
the nerves of the skin.

Now, the membrane on which the ends of the auditory
nerves are spread out is virtually a sensitive beach, and
waves, which by themselves would not be felt, are readily
perceived when they raise and let fall hard particles.

Both these membranous bags are lined by an epithelium.

The auditory nerve, after passing through the dense

bone of the skull, is distributed to certain regions of each
bag, where its ultimate filaments come into peculiar connection with the epithelial lining. The epithelium itself,
too, at these spots becomes specially modified. In certain
parts of the membranous labyrinth, for instance, the epithelium connected with the terminations of the auditory
nerve is produced into long, stiff, slender, hair-like pro-

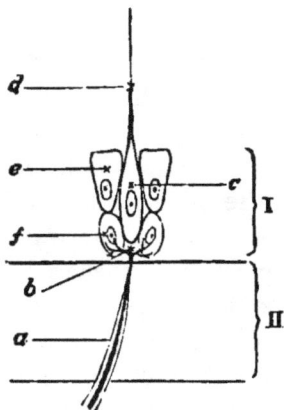

Fig. 81.

DIAGRAM TO ILLUSTRATE THE TERMINATION OF THE AUDITORY NERVE IN AN
AMPULLA.

I. The epithelium of the ampulla. II. The membranous wall of the ampulla on
which the epithelium rests.
   a, a filament of the auditory nerve running through the wall of the ampulla and
breaking up into a fine net-work (b) in the epithelium; c, epithelium cell with long,
stiff, hair-like filament, d (this cell is supposed by some to be directly continuous with
the nerve net-work); e, cells, not bearing filaments, placed by the side of and supporting the filament-bearing cells; f, a deeper layer of smaller cells.

cesses (Fig. 81, d), which project into the fluid filling the
bag, and which therefore are readily affected by any vibration of that fluid, and communicate the impulse to the ends
of the nerve. In certain other parts of the same labyrinth
these hairs are scanty or absent, but their place is supplied
by minute angular particles of calcareous sand (called *otoconia* or *otolithes*), lying free in the fluid of the bag.
These, driven by the vibrations of that fluid, strike the
epithelium and so affect the auditory nerve.

In the scala media of the cochlea, minute, rod-like bodies, called the *fibres of Corti*, and which are peculiarly modified cells of the epithelial lining of the scala, appear to serve the same object.

247. The Vestibule.—For simplicity's sake, the membranous labyrinth and the scala media have hitherto been spoken of as if they were simple bags; but this is not the case, each bag having a very curious and somewhat complicated form. (Figs. 82 and 83.)

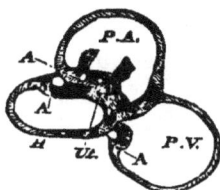

FIG. 82.

THE MEMBRANOUS LABYRINTH, TWICE THE NATURAL SIZE.

Ut., the *Utriculus*, or part of the vestibular sac, into which the semicircular canals open; *A, A, A*, the ampullæ; *P.A.*, anterior vertical semicircular canal; *P. V.*, posterior vertical semicircular canal; *H.*, horizontal semicircular canal. The sacculus is not seen, as in the position in which the labyrinth is drawn the sacculus lies behind the utriculus. The white circles on the ampullæ of the posterior vertical and horizontal canals indicate the cut ends of the branches of the auditory nerve ending in those ampullæ; the branches to the ampulla of the anterior vertical canal are seen in the space embraced by the canal, as is also the branch to the utriculus.

This form is also followed to a certain extent by the bony casing of the cavity in which each is lodged. Thus the membranous labyrinth is surrounded by a *bony labyrinth*, and the scala media is only a part of an intricate structure called the *cochlea*. The bony labyrinth and cochlea, with all the parts inside each, constitute together what is called the *internal ear*.

The *membranous labyrinth* (Fig. 82) has the figure of an oval *vestibular sac*, consisting of two parts, the one called *utriculus*, the other *sacculus hemisphericus*. The hoop-like *semicircular canals* open into the utriculus. They are three in number, and, two being vertical, are called the *anterior* (*P.A.*) and *posterior* (*P. V.*) *vertical semicircular canals ;* while the third, lying outside, and horizontally, is termed the *external horizontal semicircular canal* (*H*). One end of each of these canals is dilated into what is called an *ampulla* (*A*).

It is upon the walls of these ampullæ and those of the vestibular sac that the branches of the auditory nerve are distributed.

In each ampulla the nervous filaments may be traced to a transverse ridge caused by a thickening of the connective tissue which forms the walls of the canal (as well as of all other parts of the membranous labyrinth), and also by a thickening of the epithelium. Some of the epithelium cells are here prolonged into the fine hair-like processes described above. It is probable that these cells are specially connected with the terminations of the nerve-filaments.

In the vestibule are similar but less marked ridges, or patches ; here, however, the hair-like prolongations of the epithelium cells are absent or scanty, but, instead, otolithes are found in the fluid.

The fluid which fills the cavities of the semicircular canals and utriculus is termed *endolymph.* That which separates these delicate structures from the bony chambers in which they are contained is the *perilymph.* Each of these fluids is little more than water.

248. The Cochlea.—In the *scala media* [1] of the cochlea the primitive bag is drawn out into a long tube, which is coiled two and a half times on itself into a conical spiral, and lies in a much wider chamber of corresponding form, excavated in the petrous bone in such a way as to leave a central column of bony matter called the *modiolus.* The scala media has a triangular transverse section (Fig. 83), being bounded above and below by the membranous walls

[1] I employ this term as the equivalent of *canalis cochlearis.* The true nature and connections of these parts have only recently been properly worked out, and the account now given will be found to be somewhat different from that in the first edition of this work. See particularly the explanation of Fig. 84.

which converge internally and diverge externally. At their convergence, the walls are fastened to the edge of a thin plate of bone, the *lamina spiralis* (*L.S.*, Fig. 83), which winds round the modiolus. At their divergence they are fixed to the wall of the containing bony chamber, which thus becomes divided into two passages, communicating at the summit of the spire, but elsewhere separate. These two passages are called respectively the *scala tympani* and *scala vestibuli*, and are filled with perilymph.

The scala media, which thus lies between the other two scalæ, opens below, or at the broad end of the cochlea, by a narrow duct into the sacculus hemisphericus, but at its opposite end terminates blindly.   (Fig. 87.)

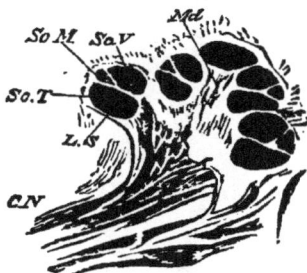

FIG. 83.

A Section through the Axis of the Cochlea, magnified three Diameters.

Sc.M., scala media; *Sc. V.*, scala vestibuli; *Sc.T.*, scala tympani; *L.S.*, lamina spiralis; *Md.*, bony axis, or modiolus, round which the scalæ are wound; *C.N.*, cochlear nerve.

That branch of the auditory nerve which goes to supply the cochlea, enters the broad base of the central column or modiolus, and there divides into branches, which, spreading out in a spiral fashion in channels excavated in the bony tissue, are distributed to the lamina spiralis throughout its whole length. They do not end here; but in any section of the lamina spiralis (Fig. 83, *L.S.*) they may be found running outwards from the central column across the lamina towards the angle of the scala media, in which indeed they become finally lost.

The upper wall of the scala media, that which separates it from the scala vestibuli, is called the *membrane of*

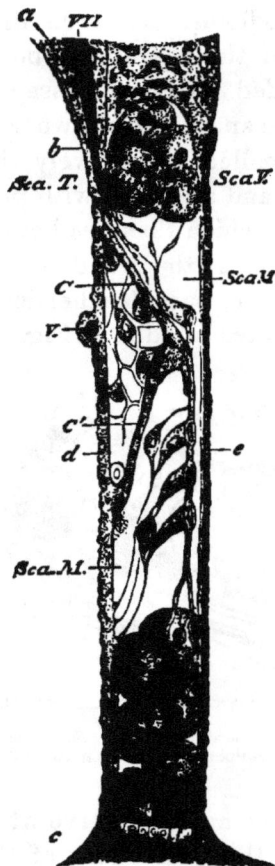

FIG. 84.

A SECTION THROUGH THAT WALL OF THE "SCALA MEDIA" OF THE COCHLEA WHICH LIES NEXT TO THE SCALA TYMPANI.

a, that end of the lamina spiralis which passes into the inner wall, pillar, or modiolus of the bony cochlea; *c,* the outer wall of the bony cochlea; *Sca. T.,* the cavity of the scala tympani; *Sca. M.,* the cavity of the scala media; *d,* the elastic basilar membrane which separates the scala media from the scala tympani; *V.,* a vessel which lies in this, cut through; *e,* the so-called membrane of Corti; *C C,* the fibres of Corti; *VII.,* the filaments of the auditory nerve. It is doubtful whether the membrane of Corti really has the extent and connections given to it in this figure. The membrane of Reissner which separates the scala media from the scala vestibuli is not represented. If it were, the letters *Sca. V.* would be seen to lie in the scala media, and not in the scala vestibuli.

Reissner. The opposite or lower wall, which separates it from the scala tympani, is the *basilar membrane.* The latter is very elastic, and on it rest the *fibres of Corti* (*C C'*, Fig. 84), each of which is composed of two filaments joined at an angle. An immense number of these filaments are set side by side, with great regularity, throughout the whole length of the scala media, so that this organ presents almost the appearance of a key-board, if viewed from either the scala vestibuli or the scala tympani. These fibres of Corti lie among a number of epithelium cells forming the lining of the scala media at this part, and those cells which are close to the fibres of Corti have a peculiarly modified form. The ends of the nerves have not yet been distinctly traced, but they probably come into close relation either with these fibres or with the modified epithelium cells lying close to them, which are capable of being agitated by the slightest impulse.

249. The Bony Labyrinth.—These essential parts of the organ of hearing are, we have seen, lodged in chambers of the petrous part of the temporal bone. Thus the membranous labyrinth is contained in a *bony labyrinth* of corresponding form, of which that part which lodges the sac is termed the *vestibule,* and those portions which contain the semicircular canal, the *bony semicircular canals.* And the scala media is contained in a spirally-coiled chamber, the cochlea, which it divides into two passages. Of these, one, the *scala vestibuli,* is so called because at the broad end or base of the cochlea it opens directly by a wide aperture into the vestibule; by this opening the perilymph which fills the vestibule and bony semicircular canals, and surrounds the membranous labyrinth, is put in free communication with the perilymph which fills the scala vestibuli of the cochlea, and, by means of the communication which exists between the two scalæ at the summit of the spire, with that of the scala tympani also.

In the fresh state, this collection of chambers in the

petrous bone is perfectly closed; but in the dry skull there are two wide openings, termed *fenestræ*, or windows, on its outer wall; i. e., on the side nearest the outside of the skull. Of these fenestræ, one, termed *ovalis* (the oval window), is situated in the wall of the vestibular cavity; the other, *rotunda* (the round window), behind and below this, is the open end of the *scala tympani* at the base of the spire of the cochlea. In the fresh state, each of these windows or fenestræ is closed by a fibrous membrane, continuous with the periosteum of the bone.

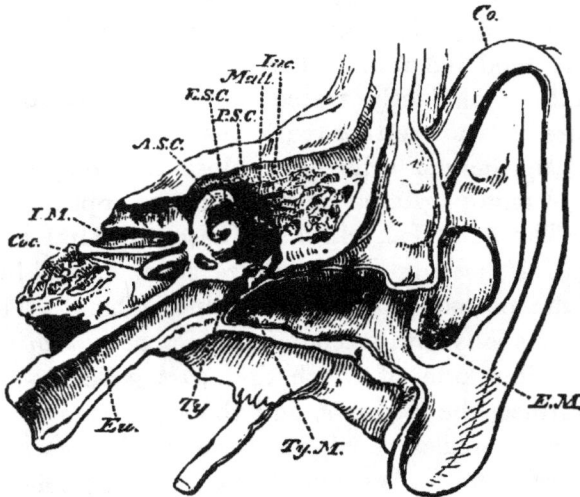

FIG. 85.

TRANSVERSE SECTION THROUGH THE SIDE-WALLS OF THE SKULL TO SHOW THE PARTS OF THE EAR.

Co., concha or external ear; *E.M.*, external auditory meatus; *Ty.M.*, tympanic membrane; *Inc.*, *Mall.*, incus and malleus; *A.S.C.*, *P.S.C.*, *E.S.C.*, anterior, posterior, and external semicircular canals; *Coc.*, cochlea; *Eu.*, Eustachian tube; *I.M.*, internal auditory meatus, through which the auditory nerve passes to the organ of hearing.

The *fenestra rotunda* is closed only by membrane; but fastened to the centre of the membrane of the *fenestra ovalis*, so as to leave only a narrow margin, is an oval plate of bone, part of one of the little bones to be described shortly.

250. Tympanum and Eustachian Tube.—The outer wall of the internal ear is still far away from the exterior of the skull. Between it and the visible opening of the ear, in fact, are placed in a straight line, first, the drum of the ear, or *tympanum;* secondly, the long external passage, or *meatus* (Fig. 85).

The drum of the ear and the external meatus, which together constitute the middle ear, would form one cavity, were it not that a delicate membrane, the tympanic membrane (*Ty.M.*, Fig. 85), is tightly stretched in an oblique direction across the passage, so as to divide the comparatively small cavity of the drum from the meatus.

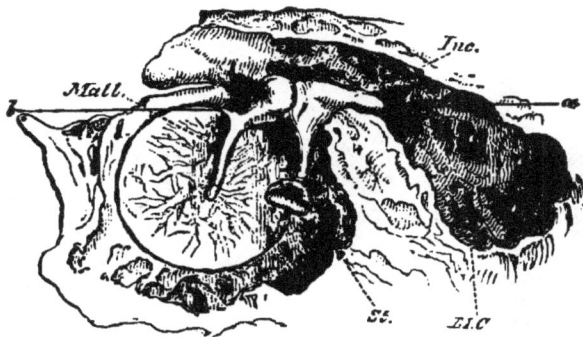

FIG. 86.

THE MEMBRANE OF THE DRUM OF THE EAR SEEN FROM THE INNER SIDE, WITH THE SMALL BONES OF THE EAR; AND THE WALLS OF THE TYMPANUM, WITH THE AIR-CELLS IN THE MASTOID PART OF THE TEMPORAL BONE.

M.C., mastoid cells; *Mall.*, malleus; *Inc.*, incus; *St.*, stapes; *a b*, lines drawn through the horizontal axis on which the malleus and incus turn.

The membrane of the tympanum thus prevents any communication by means of the meatus, between the drum and the external air, but such a communication is provided, though in a roundabout way, by the Eustachian tube (*Eu.*, Fig. 85), which leads directly from the fore part of the drum inwards to the roof of the pharynx, where it opens.

251. The Auditory Ossicles. — Three small bones, the

auditory ossicles, lie in the cavity of the tympanum. One of these is the *stapes*, a small bone shaped like a stirrup. It is the foot-plate of this bone which, as already mentioned, is firmly fastened to the membrane of the *fenestra ovalis*, while its hoop projects outwards into the tympanic cavity (Fig. 86).

Another of these bones is the *malleus* (*Mall.*, Figs. 85, 86, 87), or hammer-bone, a long process of which is similarly fastened to the inner side of the tympanic membrane (Fig. 87), and a very much smaller process, the slender process, is fastened, as is also the body of the malleus, to the bony wall of the tympanum by ligaments. The

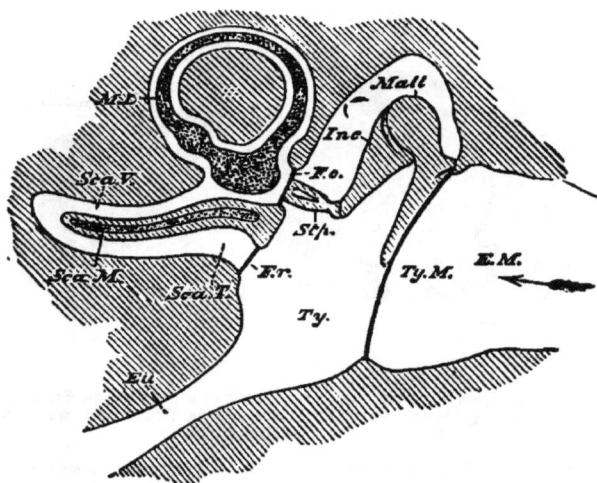

FIG. 87.

A DIAGRAM ILLUSTRATIVE OF THE RELATIVE POSITIONS OF THE VARIOUS PARTS OF THE EAR.

E.M., external auditory meatus; *Ty.M.*, tympanitic membrane; *Ty.*, tympanum; *Mall.*, malleus; *Inc.*, incus; *Stp.*, stapes; *F.o.*, fenestra ovalis; *F.r.*, fenestra rotunda; *Eu.*, Eustachian tube; *M.L.*, membranous labyrinth, only one semicircular canal with its ampulla being represented; *Sca.V.*, *Sca.T.*, *Sca.M.*, the scalæ of the cochlea, which is supposed to be unrolled.

rounded surface of the head of the malleus fits into a corresponding pit in the end of a third bone, the *incus* or anvil-bone, which has two processes—one, horizontal, which rests upon a support afforded to it by the walls of the tympanum; while the other, vertical, descends almost parallel with the long process of the malleus, and articulates with the stapes, or rather unites with a little bone, the *os orbiculare*, which articulates with the stapes (Figs. 86 and 87).

The three bones thus form a chain between the fenestra ovalis and the tympanic membrane; and the whole series turns upon an horizontal axis, the two ends of which, formed by the horizontal process of the incus and the slender process of the malleus, rest in the walls of the tympanum. The general direction of this axis is represented by the line *a b* in Fig. 86, or by a line perpendicular to the plane of the paper, passing through the head of the malleus in Fig. 87. It follows, therefore, that whatever causes the membrane of the drum to vibrate backwards and forwards, must force the handle of the malleus to travel in the same way. This must cause a corresponding motion of the long process of the incus, the end of which must drag the stapes backwards and forwards. And, as this is fastened to the membrane of the fenestra ovalis, which is in contact with the perilymph, it must set this fluid vibrating throughout its whole extent, the thrustings in of the membrane of the fenestra ovalis being compensated by corresponding thrustings out of the membrane of the fenestra rotunda, and *vice versa*.

The vibrations of the perilymph thus produced will affect the endolymph, and this the otolithes, hairs, or fibres; by which, finally, the auditory nerves will be excited.

252. The Muscles of the Tympanum. — The membrane of the fenestra ovalis and the tympanic membrane will necessarily vibrate the more freely the looser they are, and the reverse. But there are two muscles—one, called the *stapedius*, which passes from the floor of the tympanum to the orbicular bone, and the other, the *tensor tympani*, from the front wall of the drum to the malleus. Each of the muscles when it contracts tightens the membranes in question, and restricts their vibrations, or, in other words, tends to check the effect of any cause which sets these membranes vibrating.

253. The Concha.—The outer extremity of the external meatus is surrounded by the *concha* or external ear (*Co.*, Fig. 85), a broad, peculiarly-shaped, and for the most part cartilaginous plate, the general plane of which is at right angles with that of the axis of the auditory opening. The concha can be moved by most animals, and by some human beings, in various directions by means of muscles, which pass to it from the side of the head.

Section IV.— *Working of the Auditory Mechanism.*

254. Nature of Sound.—The manner in which the complex apparatus now described intermediates between the physical agent, which is the condition of the sensation of sound, and the nervous expansion, the affection of which alone can excite that sensation, must next be considered.

All bodies which produce sound are in a state of vibration, and they communicate the vibrations of their own substance to the air with which they are in contact, and thus throw that air into waves, just as a stick waved backwards and forwards in water throws the water into waves.

The aërial waves, produced by the vibrations of sonorous bodies, in part enter the external auditory passage, and in part strike upon the concha of the external ear and the outer surface of the head. It may be that some of the latter impulses are transmitted through the solid structure of the skull to the organ of hearing; but before they reach it they must, under ordinary circumstances, have become so scanty and weak, that they may be left out of consideration. The aërial waves which enter the meatus all impinge upon the membrane of the drum and set it vibrating, stretched membranes taking up vibrations from the air with great readiness.

255. Vibrations of the Tympanum.—The vibrations thus set up in the membrane of the tympanum are communicated, in part, to the air contained in the drum of the ear, and, in part, to the malleus, and thence to the other auditory ossicles.

The vibrations communicated to the air of the drum impinge upon the inner wall of the tympanum, on the greater part of which, from its density, they can produce very little effect. Where this wall is formed by the membrane of the *fenestra rotunda*, however, the communication of motion must necessarily be greater.

The vibrations which are communicated to the malleus and the chain of ossicles may be of two kinds: vibrations of the particles of the bones, and vibrations of the bones as a whole. If a beam of wood, freely suspended, be very gently scratched with a pin, its particles will be thrown into a state of vibration, as will be evidenced by the sound given out, but the beam itself will not be moved. Again, if a strong wind blow against the beam, it will swing visibly, without any vibrations of its particles among themselves. On the other hand, if the beam be sharply struck with a hammer, it will not only give out a sound, showing that its particles are vibrating, but it will also swing from the impulse given to its whole mass.

Under the last mentioned circumstances, a blind man standing near the beam would be conscious of nothing but the sound, the product of molecular vibration, or invisible oscillation of the particles of the beam; while a deaf man, in the same position, would be aware of nothing but the visible oscillation of the beam as a whole.

256. Their Transmission.—Thus, to return to the chain of auditory ossicles, while it seems hardly to be doubted that, when the membrane of the drum vibrates, they may be set vibrating both as a whole and in their particles, it depends upon subsidiary arrangements whether the large vibrations, or the minute ones, shall make themselves obvious to the auditory nerve, which is in the position of our deaf, or blind man.

The evidence at present is in favor of the conclusion, that it is the vibrations of the bones, as a whole, which are the chief agents in transmitting the impulses of the aërial waves.

For, in the first place, the disposition of the bones and the mode of their articulation are very much against the transmission of molecular vibrations through their substance, while, on the other hand, they are extremely favorable to their vibration *en masse*. The long processes of the malleus and incus swing, like a pendulum, upon the axis furnished by the short processes of these bones; while the mode of connection of the incus with the stapes, and of the latter with the edges of the fenestra ovalis, allows that bone free play, inwards and outwards. In the sécond place the total length of the chain of ossicles is very small compared with the length of the waves of audible sounds, and physical considerations teach us that in a like small rod, similarly capable of swinging *en masse*, the minute molecular vibrations would be inappreciable. Thirdly, it is affirmed, as the result of experiments, that the bone called *columella*, which, in birds, takes the place of the chain of ossicles in man, does actually vibrate as a whole, and at the same rate as the membrane of the drum, when aërial vibrations strike upon the latter.

257. The Action of the Auditory Muscles.—Thus, there is reason to believe that when the tympanic membrane is set vibrating, it causes the process of the malleus, which is fixed to it, to swing at the same rate; the head of the malleus consequently turns through a small arc on its pivot, the slender process. But the turning of the head of the malleus involves that of the head of the incus upon its pivot, the short process. In consequence, the long process of the incus swings through an arc which has been estimated as being equal to about two-thirds of that de-

scribed by the handle of the malleus. The extent of the
push is thereby somewhat diminished, but the force of the
push is proportionately increased ; in so confined a space
this change is advantageous. The long process, however,
is so fixed to the stapes that it cannot vibrate without, to
a corresponding extent and at the same rate, pulling this
out of, and pushing it into, the fenestra ovalis. But every
pull and push imparts a corresponding set of shakes to the
perilymph, which fills the bony labyrinth and cochlea, external to the membranous labyrinth and scala media. These
shakes are communicated to the endolymph and fluid of
the scala media, and, by the help of the otolithes and the
fibres of Corti, are finally converted into impulses, which
act as irritants of the ends of the vestibular and cochlear
divisions of the auditory nerve.

**258. Intensity and Quality of Sounds—how discrimi-
nated.** — The difference between the functions of the membranous labyrinth (to which the vestibular nerve is distributed) and those of the cochlea are not quite certainly
made out, but the following views have been suggested :

The membranous labyrinth may be regarded as an apparatus whereby sounds are appreciated and distinguished
according to their intensity or quantity; but which does
not afford any means of discriminating their qualities.
The vestibular nerve tells us that sounds are weak or
loud, but gives us no impression of tone, or melody, or
harmony.

The cochlea, on the other hand, it is supposed, enables
the mind to discriminate the quality rather than the quantity or intensity of sound. It is suggested that the excitement of any single filament of the cochlear nerve gives
rise, in the mind, to a distinct musical impression; and
that every fraction of a tone which a well-trained ear is
capable of distinguishing is represented by its separate
nerve-fibre. Under this view the scala media resembles a
key-board, in function, as well as in appearance, the fibres

11

of Corti being the keys, and the ends of the nerves representing the strings which the keys strike. If it were possible to irritate each of these nerve-fibres experimentally, we should be able to produce any musical tone, at will, in the sensorium of the person experimented upon, just as any note on a piano is produced by striking the appropriate key.

259. Probable Function of the Fibres of Corti. — A tuning-fork may be set vibrating, if its own particular note, or one harmonic with it, be sounded in its neighborhood. In other words, it will vibrate under the influence of a particular set of vibrations, and no others. If the vibrating ends of the tuning-fork were so arranged as to impinge upon a nerve, their repeated minute blows would at once excite this nerve.

Suppose that of a set of tuning-forks, tuned to every note and distinguishing fractions of a note in the scale, one were thus connected with the end of every fibre of the cochlear nerve; then any vibration communicated to the perilymph would affect the tuning-fork which could vibrate with it, while the rest would be absolutely, or relatively, indifferent to that vibration. In other words, the vibration would give rise to the sensation of one particular tone, and no other, and every musical interval would be represented by a distinct impression on the sensorium.

It is suggested that the fibres of Corti are competent to perform the function of such tuning-forks; that each of them is set vibrating to its full strength by a particular kind of wave sent through the perilymph, and by no other; and that each affects a particular fibre of the cochlear nerve only. But it must be remembered that the view here given is a suggestion only which, however probable, has not yet been proved. Indeed, recent inquiries have rather diminished than increased its probability.

The fibres of the cochlear nerve may be excited by internal causes, such as the varying pressure of the blood and the like : and in some persons such internal influences do give rise to veritable musical spectra, sometimes of a very intense character.   But, for the appreciation of music produced external to us, we depend upon the intermediation of the scala media and its Cortian fibres.

260. Function of the Tympanic Muscles and Eustachian Tube.—It has already been explained that the *stapedius* and *tensor tympani* muscles are competent to tighten the membrane of the fenestra ovalis and that of the tympanum, and it is probable that they come into action when the sonorous impulses are too violent, and would produce too extensive vibrations of these membranes. They therefore tend to moderate the effect of intense sound, in much the same way that, as we shall find, the contraction of the circular fibres of the iris tends to moderate the effect of intense light in the eye.

The function of the Eustachian tube is, probably, to keep the air in the tympanum, or on the inner side of the tympanic membrane, of about the same tension as that on the outer side, which could not always be the case if the tympanum were a closed cavity.

CHAPTER IX.

THE ORGAN OF SIGHT.

Section I.—*Structure and Action of the Retina.*

261. General Structure of the Eye.—In studying the organ of the sense of sight, the eye, it is needful to become acquainted, firstly, with the structure and properties of the sensory expansion in which the optic nerve, or nerve of sight, terminates ; secondly, with the physical agent of the sensation ; thirdly, with the intermediate apparatus by

which the physical agent is assisted in acting upon the
nervous expansion.

The ball, or globe, of the eye is a globular body, moving freely in a chamber, the *orbit*, which is furnished to it
by the skull. The optic nerve, the root of which is in the
brain, leaves the skull by a hole at the back of the orbit,
and enters the back of the globe of the eye, not in the
middle, but on the inner, or nasal, side of the centre.
Having pierced the wall of the globe, it spreads out into
a very delicate membrane, varying in thickness from $\frac{1}{80}$th
of an inch to less than half that amount, which lines the
hinder two-thirds of the globe, and is termed the *retina*.
This retina is the only organ connected with sensory nervous fibres which can be affected, by any agent, in such a
manner as to give rise to the sensation of light.

262. The Surface of the Retina. — If the globe of the
eye be cut in two, transversely, so as to divide it into an
anterior and a posterior half, the retina will be seen lining
the whole of the concave wall of the posterior half as a
membrane of great delicacy, and, for the most part, of even
texture and smooth surface. But, exactly opposite the
middle of the posterior wall, it presents a slight circular
depression of a yellowish hue, the *macula lutea*, or yellow
spot (Fig. 90, *m.l.* ; Fig. 94, 8″)—not easily seen, however,
unless the eye be perfectly fresh—and, at some distance
from this, towards the inner, or nasal, side of the ball is
a radiating appearance, produced by the entrance of the
optic nerve and the spreading out of its fibres into the
retina.

263. Microscopic Structure of the Retina.—A very thin
vertical slice of the retina, in any region except the yellow
spot, and the entrance of the optic nerve, may be resolved
into the structures represented separately in Figs. 88, 89.
The one of these (Fig. 88) occupies the whole thickness of
the section, and comprises its essential, or nervous elements. The outer (or posterior) fourth, or rather less, of

the thickness of these consists of a vast multitude of minute, either rod-like or conical, bodies, ranged side by side, perpendicularly to the plane of the retina.   This is the *layer of rods and cones* (*b c*).   From the front ends or bases of the rods and cones very delicate fibres pass, and in each is developed a granule-like body (*b′ c′*), which

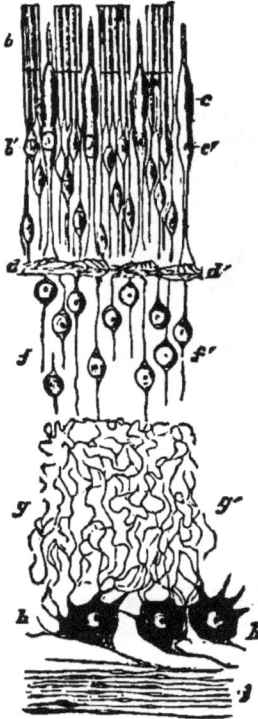 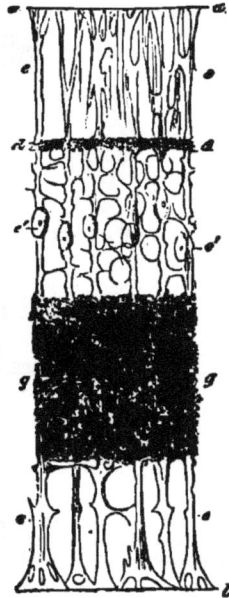

FIG. 88.   FIG. 89.

DIAGRAMMATIC VIEWS OF THE NERVOUS (FIG. 88), AND THE CONNECTIVE (FIG. 89), ELEMENTS OF THE RETINA, SUPPOSED TO BE SEPARATED FROM ONE ANOTHER. (Magnified about two hundred and fifty diameters.)

Fig. 88.—The nervous structures: *b*, the rods; *c*, the cones; *b′ c′*, the granules of the outer layer, with which these are connected; *d d′*, interwoven very delicate nervous fibres, from which fine nervous filaments, bearing the inner granules, *f f′*, proceed towards the front surface; *g g′*, the continuation of these fine nerves, which become convoluted and interwoven with the processes of the ganglionic corpuscles, *h h′*; *i i*, the expansion of the fibres of the optic nerve.

Fig. 89.—The connective tissue: *a a*, external or posterior limiting membrane; *e e*, radial fibres passing to the internal or anterior limiting membrane; *e′ e′*, nuclei; *d d*, the intergranular layer; *g g*, the molecular layer; *l*, the anterior limiting membrane.

forms a part of what has been termed the *outer layer of granules*. It is probable that these fibres next pass into and indeed form the close meshwork of very delicate nervous fibres which is seen at *d d'* (Fig. 88). From the anterior surface of this meshwork other fibres proceed, containing a second set of granules, which forms the *inner granular layer* (*f f'*). In front of this layer is a stratum of convoluted fine nervous fibres (*g g'*), and anterior to this

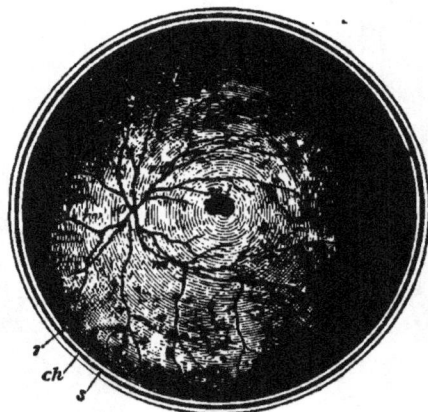

FIG. 90.

THE EYEBALL DIVIDED TRANSVERSELY IN THE MIDDLE LINE, AND VIEWED FROM THE FRONT.

s., sclerotic; *ch.*, choroid, seen in section only; *r.*, the cut edge of the retina; *v.v.*, vessels of the retina, springing from *o.*, the optic nerve or blind spot; *m.l.*, the yellow spot, the darker spot in its middle being the fovea centralis.

again numerous ganglionic corpuscles (*h h'*). Processes of these ganglionic corpuscles extend, on the one hand, into the layer of convoluted nerve-fibres; and, on the other, are probably continuous with the stratum of fibres of the optic nerve (*i*).

These delicate nervous structures are supported by a sort of framework of connective tissue of a peculiar kind (Fig. 89), which extends from an *inner* or *anterior limiting membrane* (*l*), which bounds the retina and is in contact with the vitreous humor, to an *outer* or *posterior lim-*

iting membrane, which lies at the anterior ends, or bases, of the rods and cones near the level of b' c' in Fig. 88. Thus the framework is thinner than the nervous substance of the retina, and the rods and cones lie altogether outside of it, and wholly unsupported by any connective tissue. They are, however, as we shall see, embedded in the layer of pigment on which the retina rests (277).

The fibres of the optic nerve spread out between the limiting membrane (l) and the ganglionic corpuscles (h'), and the vessels which enter along with the optic nerve ramify between the limiting membrane and the inner granules (ff'). Thus, not only the nervous fibres, but the vessels, are placed altogether in front of the rods and cones.

At the entrance of the optic nerve itself, the nervous fibres predominate, and the rods and cones are absent. In the yellow spot, on the contrary, the cones are abundant and close set, becoming at the same time longer and more slender, while rods are scanty, and are found only towards its margin. The layer of fibres of the optic nerve disappears, and all the other layers, except that of the cones, become extremely thin in the centre of the *macula lutea* (Fig. 91).

264. The Sensation of Light.—The most notable property of the retina is its power of converting the vibrations of ether, which constitute the physical basis of light, into a stimulus to the fibres of the optic nerve—which fibres, when excited, have the power of awakening the sensation of light in, or by means of, the brain. The sensation of light, it must be understood, is the work of the brain, not of the retina; for, if an eye be destroyed, pinching, galvanizing, or otherwise irritating the optic nerve, will still excite the sensation of light, because it throws the fibres of the optic nerve into activity; and their activity, however produced, brings about in the brain certain changes which give rise to the sensation of light.

Light, falling directly on the optic nerve, does not ex-

cite it; the fibres of the optic nerve, in themselves, are as
blind as any other part of the body. But just as the delicate filaments of the ampullæ, or the otoconia of the vestibular sac, or the Cortian fibres of the cochlea, are contrivances for converting the delicate vibrations of the

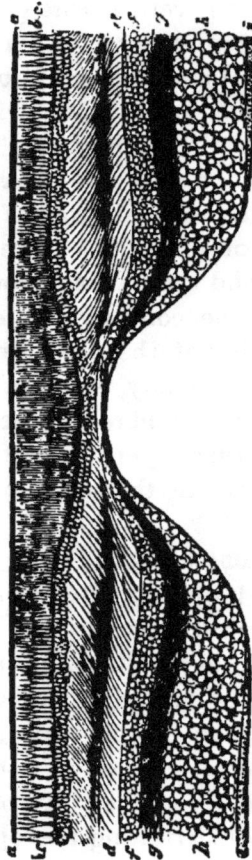

FIG. 91.

A DIAGRAMMATIC SECTION OF THE MACULA LUTEA, OR YELLOW SPOT.
(Magnified about sixty diameters.)

a a, the pigment of the choroid; *b c*, rods and cones; *d d*, outer granular layer;
f f, inner granular layer; *g g*, molecular layer; *h h*, ayer of ganglionic cells; *i i*, fibres
of the optic nerve.

perilymph and endolymph into impulses which can excite the auditory nerves, so the structures in the retina appear to be adapted to convert the infinitely more delicate pulses of the luminiferous ether into stimuli of the fibres of the optic nerve.

265. The "Blind Spot."—The sensibility of the different parts of the retina to light varies very greatly. The point of entrance of the optic nerve is absolutely blind, as may be proved by a very simple experiment. Close the left eye, and look steadily with the right at the cross on the page, held at ten or twelve inches' distance:

✚   ·   ·   ●

The black dot will be seen quite plainly, as well as the cross. Now, move the book slowly towards the eye, which must be kept steadily fixed upon the cross; at a certain point the dot will disappear, but, as the book is brought still closer, it will come into view again. It results from optical principles that, in the first position of the book, the figure of the dot falls between that of the cross (which throughout lies upon the yellow spot) and the entrance of the optic nerve: while in the second position, it falls on the entrance of the optic nerve itself; and, in the third, inside that point. So long as the image of the spot rests upon the entrance of the optic nerve it is not perceived, and hence this region of the retina is called the *blind spot.*

266. Duration of Luminous Impressions.—The impression made by light upon the retina not only remains during the whole period of the direct action of the light, but has a certain duration of its own, however short the time during which the light itself lasts. A flash of lightning is, practically, instantaneous, but the sensation of light produced by that flash endures for an appreciable period. It is found, in fact, that a luminous impression lasts for about one-eighth of a second; whence it follows that, if any two luminous impressions are separated by a less interval, they are not distinguished from one another.

For this reason a "Catherine-wheel," or a lighted stick turned round very rapidly by the hand, appears as a circle of fire; and the spokes of a coach-wheel at speed are not separately visible, but only appear as a sort of opacity, or film, within the tire of the wheel.

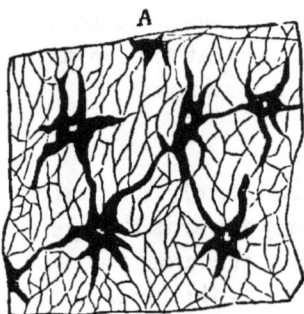
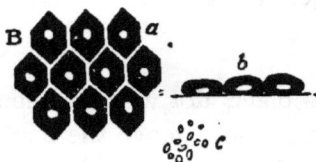

FIG. 92.   FIG. 93.

PIGMENT-CELLS FROM THE CHOROID COAT.

Fig. 92.—Branched pigment-cells from the deep layer.
Fig. 93.—Pigment epithelium. *a*, seen in face; *b*, seen in profile; *c*, pigment granules.

267. Exhaustion of the Retina.—The excitability of the retina is readily exhausted. Thus, looking at a bright light rapidly renders the part of the retina on which the light falls, insensible; and, on looking from the bright light towards a moderately-lighted surface, a dark spot, arising from a temporary blindness of the retina in this part, appears in the field of view. If the bright light be of one color, the part of the retina on which it falls becomes insensible to rays of that color, but not to the other rays of the spectrum. This is the explanation of the appearance of what are called *complementary colors*. For example, if a bright-red wafer be stuck upon a sheet of white paper, and steadily looked at for some time with one eye, when the eye is turned aside to the white paper a greenish spot will appear, of about the size and shape of the wafer. The red image has, in fact, fatigued the part of the retina on which it fell for red light, but has left it sensitive to the remaining colored rays of which white light is composed. But we know that, if from the variously colored rays which make up the spectrum of white light we take away all the red rays, the remaining rays together make up a sort of green. So that, when white light falls upon this part, the red rays in the white light having no effect, the result of the operation of the others is a greenish hue. If the wafer be *green*, the *complementary image*, as it is called, is *red*.

268. Color-Blindness.—In some persons, the retina appears to be affected in one and the same way by rays of light of various colors, or even of all colors. Such *color-blind* persons are unable to distinguish between the leaves of a cherry-tree and its fruit by the color of the two, and see no difference between blue and yellow cloth.

This peculiarity is simply unfortunate for most people, but it may be dangerous if unknowingly possessed by railway guards or sailors. It probably arises either from a defect in the retina, which renders that organ unable to respond to different kinds of luminous vibrations, and consequently insensible to red rays or yellow rays, etc., as the case may be, or it may proceed from some unusual absorptive power of the humors of the eye which prevents particular rays from reaching the retina; or the fault may lie in the brain itself.

269. Luminous Effects of Pressure on the Eye. — The sensation of light may be excited by other causes than the impact of the vibrations of the luminiferous ether upon the retina. Thus, an electric shock sent through the eye, gives rise to the appearance of a flash of light: and pressure on any part of the retina produces a luminous image, which lasts as long as the pressure, and is called a *phosphene*. If the point of the finger be pressed upon the outer side of the ball of the eye, the eyes being shut, a luminous image —which, in my own case, is dark in the centre, with a bright ring at the circumference (or, as Newton described it, like the "eye" in a peacock's tail)—is seen; and this image lasts as long as the pressure is continued. Most persons, again, have experienced the remarkable display of subjective fireworks which follows a heavy blow upon the eyes, produced by a fall from a horse, or by other methods well known to English youth.

It is doubtful, however, whether these effects of pressure, or shock, really arise from the excitation of the retina proper, or whether they are not rather the result of the violence done to the fibres of the optic nerve apart from the retina.

270. Function of the Rods and Cones.—The last paragraph raises a distinction between the "fibres of the optic nerve" and the "retina" which may not have been anticipated, but which is of much importance.

We have seen that the fibres of the optic nerve ramify in the inner or anterior fourth of the thickness of the retina, while the layer of rods and cones forms its outer or posterior fourth. The light, therefore, must fall first upon the fibres of the optic nerve, and, only after traversing them, can it reach the rods and cones. Consequently, if the fibrillæ of the optic nerve themselves are capable of being affected by light, the rods and cones can only be some sort of supplementary optical apparatus. But, in fact, it is the rods and cones which are affected by light, while the fibres of the optic nerve are themselves insensible to it. The evidence on which this statement rests is—

a. The blind spot is full of nervous fibres, but has no cones or rods.

b. The yellow spot, where the most acute vision is situated, is full of close-set cones, but has no nerve-fibres.

c. If you go into a dark room with a single small bright candle, and, looking towards a dark wall, move the light up

and down, close to the outer side of one eye, so as to allow
the light to fall very obliquely into the eye, one of what are
called *Purkinje's figures* is seen.   This is a vision of a series
of diverging, branched, red lines on a dark field, and in
the interspace of two of these lines is a sort of cup-shaped
disk.   The red lines are the retinal blood-vessels, and the
disk is the yellow spot.   As the candle is moved up and
down, the red lines shift their position, as shadows do
when the light which throws them changes its place.

Now, as the light falls on the inner face of the retina,
and the images of the vessels to which it gives rise shift
their position as it moves, whatever perceives these images
must needs lie on the other, or outer, side of the vessels.
But the fibres of the optic nerve lie among the vessels, and
the only retinal structures which lie outside them' are the
granular layers and the rods and cones.

d. Just as, in the skin, there is a limit of distance
within which two points give only one impression, so
there is a minimum distance by which two points of light
falling on the retina must be separated in order to appear
as two.   And this distance corresponds pretty well with
the diameter of the cones.

Thus it would appear that these remarkable structures,
set upon the outer surface of the retina, are like so many
finger-points, endowed with a touch delicate enough to feel
the luminous vibrations.

271. Formation of Visual Ideas.—We, however, are not
only conscious of the general sensation of light, we can
not only appreciate the quantity and color of the light
admitted into the eye, the rods and cones of our retina
are not only capable of converting luminous vibrations
into stimuli of the optic nerve, but they can do this in
such a way that different objects in the external world
give rise to different and distinct processes in the sensory
nerve and the parts of the brain with which it is connected, and so excite different and distinct ideas.   For

instance, the light coming from a tree not only causes luminous sensations of a certain intensity and of certain shades of color, but makes such an impression on our brain as to give rise to the idea of a tree. In other words, we possess the power of distinct vision of objects which are conceived as external.

Now, one of the conditions of distinct vision is, that a sharp, well-defined image of the thing to be seen should be thrown upon the retina, and a great deal of the intermediate apparatus of the eye is concerned with the production of this well-defined image. We often speak of the ideas caused by external objects as images; but it will of course be remembered that the image on the retina, which is a mere physical thing, is altogether different from that mental image which arises in consequence of changes which the affection of the retina causes in the brain, and which is an idea.

Section II.—*The Luminous Agent.*

272. The Convex Lens. — The physical agent which gives rise to vision is *light*, which is now conceived to be a very attenuated fluid, the ether, vibrating in a particular way. The properties of this physical agent, and the principles of optics, must be studied elsewhere. At present it is only necessary to advert to some facts, of which every one can assure himself by simple experiments. An ordinary spectacle-glass is a transparent body denser than the air, and convex on both sides. If this *lens* be held at a certain distance from a screen or wall in a dark room, and a lighted candle be placed on the opposite side of it, it will be easy to adjust the distances of candle, lens, and wall, so that an image of the flame of the candle, upside down, shall be thrown upon the wall.

273. Formation of the Luminous Picture.—The spot on which the image is formed is called a *focus*. If the candle be now brought nearer to the lens, the image on the wall will enlarge, and grow blurred and dim, but may be restored to brightness and definition by moving the lens farther from the wall. But, if, when the new adjustment has taken place, the candle be moved away from the lens, the image will again become confused, and, to restore its clearness, the lens will have to be brought nearer the wall.

Thus a convex lens forms a distinct picture of luminous objects, but only at the focus on the side of the lens opposite to the object; and that focus is nearer when the object is distant, and farther off when it is near.

274. Effect of varying the Convexity.—Suppose, however, that, leaving the candle unmoved, a lens with more convex surfaces is substituted for the first, the image will be blurred, and the lens will have to be moved nearer the wall to give it definition. If, on the other hand, a lens with less convex surfaces is substituted for the first, it must be moved farther from the wall to attain the same end.

In other words, other things being alike, the more convex the lens, the nearer its focus; the less convex, the farther off its focus.

If the lens were elastic, pulling it at the circumference would render it flatter, and thereby lengthen its focus; while, when let go again, it would become more convex, and of shorter focus.

Any material more refractive than the medium in which it is placed, if it have a convex surface, causes the rays of light which pass through the less refractive medium to that surface to converge towards a focus. If a watch-glass be fitted into one side of a box, and the box be then filled with water, a candle may be placed at such a distance outside the watch-glass that an image of its flame shall fall on the opposite wall of the box. If, under these circumstances, a doubly convex lens of glass were introduced into the water in the path of the rays, it would act (though less powerfully than if it were in air) in bringing the rays more quickly to a focus, because glass refracts light more strongly than water does.

A *camera-obscura* is a box, into one side of which a lens is fitted, so as to be able to slide backwards and forwards, and thus throw on the screen at the back of the box distinct images of bodies at various distances off. Hence the arrangement just described might be termed a *water camera.*

Section III.—*The Intermediate Apparatus.*

275. The Visual Mechanism.—The intermediate organs, by means of which the physical agent of vision, light, is enabled to act upon the expansion of the optic nerve, comprise three kinds of apparatus : (*a*) a "water camera," the eyeball; (*b*) muscles for moving the eyeball; (*c*) organs for protecting the eyeball, viz., the eyelids, with their lashes, glands, and muscles; the conjunctiva; and the lachrymal gland and its ducts.

The *eyeball* is composed, in the first place, of a tough, firm, spheroidal case consisting of fibrous or connective tissue, the greater part of which is white and opaque, and is called the *sclerotic* (Fig. 94, 2). In front, however, this fibrous capsule of the eye, though it does not change its essential character, becomes transparent, and receives the name of the *cornea* (Fig. 94, 1). The corneal portion of the case of the eyeball is more convex than the sclerotic portion, so that the whole form of the ball is such as would be produced by cutting off a segment from the front of a spheroid of the diameter of the sclerotic, and replacing this by a segment cut from a smaller, and consequently more convex, spheroid.

276. The Humors and Crystalline Lens.—The corneosclerotic case of the eye is kept in shape by what are termed the *humors*—watery or semi-fluid substances, one of which, the *aqueous* humor (Fig. 94, 7′), which is hardly more than water holding a few organic and saline substances in solution, distends the corneal chamber of the eye, while the other, the *vitreous* (Fig. 94, 13), which is rather a delicate jelly than a regular fluid, keeps the sclerotic chamber full.

The two humors are separated by the very beautiful, transparent, doubly-convex *crystalline lens* (Fig. 94, 12), denser, and capable of refracting light more strongly than either of the humors. The crystalline lens is composed of fibres having a somewhat complex arrangement, and is highly elastic. It is more convex behind than in front,

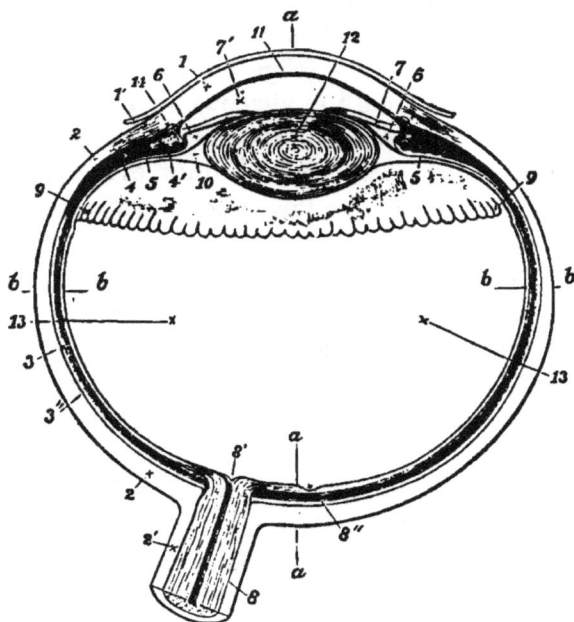

FIG. 94.

HORIZONTAL SECTION OF THE EYEBALL.

1, cornea; 1', conjunctiva; 2, sclerotic; 2', sheath of optic nerve; 3, choroid; 3'', rods and cones of the retina; 4, ciliary muscle; 4', circular portion of ciliary muscle; 5, ciliary process; 6, posterior chamber between 7, the iris, and the suspensory ligament; 7', anterior chamber; 8, artery of retina in the centre of the optic nerve; 8', centre of blind spot; 8'', macula lutea; 9, ora serrata (this is of course not seen in a section such as this, but is introduced to show its position); 10, space behind the suspensory ligament (canal of Petit); 12, crystalline lens; 13, vitreous humor; 14 marks the position of the ciliary ligament; *a*, optic axis (in the actual eye of which this is an exact copy, the yellow spot happened, curiously enough, not to be in the optic axis); *b*, line of equator of the eyeball.

and it is kept in place by a delicate, but at the same time strong and elastic, membranous frame or *suspensory ligament*, which extends from the edges of the lens to what are termed the *ciliary processes* of the choroid coat (Figs. 94, 5, and 95, c). In the ordinary condition of the eye this ligament is kept tense, i. e., is stretched pretty tight, and the front part of the lens is consequently flattened against it.

277. The Choroid and Ciliary Processes.—This *choroid coat* (Fig. 94, 3) is a highly-vascular membrane, in close contact with the sclerotic externally, and lined, internally, by a layer of small polygonal bodies containing much pigmentary matter, called *pigment-cells* (Figs. 92, 93). These pigment-cells are separated from the vitreous humor by the retina only. The rods and cones of the latter are in immediate contact with them. The choroid lines every part of the sclerotic, except just where the optic nerve enters it at a point below, and to the inner side of the centre of the back of the eye; but, when it reaches the front part of the sclerotic, its inner surface becomes raised up into a number of longitudinal ridges, with intervening depressions, like the crimped frills of a lady's dress, terminating within and in front by rounded ends, but passing, externally, into the iris. These ridges, which when viewed from behind seem to radiate on all sides from the lens (Figs. 95, c, and 94, 5), are the above-mentioned ciliary processes.

278. The Iris and Ciliary Muscle. — The *iris* itself (Figs. 94, 7, and 95, a, b) is, as has been already said, a curtain with a round hole in the middle, provided with circular and radiating unstriped muscular fibres, and capable of having its central aperture enlarged or diminished by the action of these fibres, the contraction of which, unlike that of other unstriped muscular fibres, is extremely rapid. The edges of the iris are firmly connected with the capsule of the eye, at the junction of the cornea and sclerotic, by the connective tissue which enters into the composition of the so-called *ciliary ligament.* Unstriped muscular fibres, having the same attachment in front, spread backwards on to the outer surface of the choroid, constituting the *ciliary muscle* (Fig. 94, 4). If these fibres contract, it is obvious that they will pull the choroid forward ; and as the frame, or suspensory ligament of the lens, is connected with the

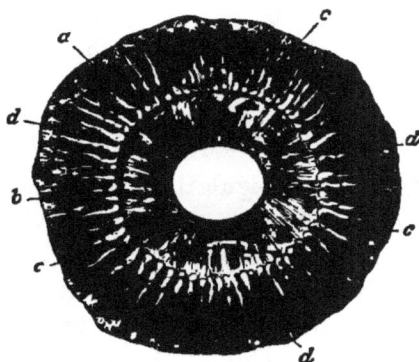

FIG. 95.

VIEW OF FRONT HALF OF EYEBALL SEEN FROM BEHIND.

a, circular fibres; *b,* radiating fibres of the iris; *c,* ciliary processes ; *d,* choroid. The crystalline lens has been removed.

ciliary processes (which simply form the anterior termination of the choroid), this pulling forward of the choroid comes to the same thing as a relaxation of the tension of that suspensory ligament, which, as I have just said, like the lens itself, is highly elastic.

The iris does not hang down perpendicularly into the space between the front face of the crystalline lens and the posterior surface of the cornea, which is filled by the aqueous humor, but applies itself very closely to the anterior face of the lens, so that hardly any interval is left between the two (Figs. 94 and 96).

279. Position of the Retina.—The retina, as we have seen, lines the interior of the eye, being placed between the choroid and vitreous humor, its rods and cones being embedded in the former, and its anterior limiting membrane touching the latter.

About a third of the distance back from the front of the eye the retina seems to end in a wavy border called the *ora serrata* (Fig. 94, 9), and in reality the nervous elements of the retina do end here, having become considerably reduced before this line is reached. Some of the connective-tissue elements, however, pass on as a delicate kind of membrane at the back of the ciliary processes towards the crystalline lens.

Section IV.—*Focal Adjustment.*

280. The Iris a Self-regulating Diaphragm.—The eyeball, the most important constituents of which have now been described, is, in principle, a camera of the kind described above—a water camera. That is to say, the sclerotic answers to the box, the cornea to the watch-glass, the aqueous and vitreous humors to the water filling the box, the crystalline to the glass lens, the introduction of which was imagined. The back of the box corresponds with the retina.

But further, in an ordinary camera obscura, it is found desirable to have what is termed a *diaphragm* (that is, an opaque plate with a hole in its centre) in the path of the rays, for the purpose of moderating the light and cutting off the marginal rays which, owing to certain optical properties of spheroidal surfaces, give rise to defects in the image formed at the focus.

In the eye, the place of this diaphragm is taken by the iris, which has the peculiar advantage of being self-regulating: dilating its aperture, and admitting more light when the light is weak; but contracting its aperture and admitting less light when the illumination is strong.

281. Necessity of Adjustment.—In the water camera, constructed according to the description given above, there is the defect that no provision exists for adjusting the focus to the varying distances of objects. If the box were so made that its back, on which the image is supposed to be thrown, received distinct images of very distant objects, all near ones would be indistinct. And if, on the other hand, it were fitted to receive the image of near objects, at a given distance, those of either nearer, or more distant, bodies would be blurred and indistinct. In the ordinary camera this difficulty is overcome by sliding the lenses in and out, a process which is not compatible with the construction of our water camera. But there is clearly one way, among many, in which this adjustment might be effected—namely, by changing the glass lens; putting in a less convex one when more distant objects had to be pictured, and a more convex one when the images of nearer objects were to be thrown upon the back of the box.

But it would come to the same thing, and be much more convenient, if, without changing the lens, one and the same lens could be made to alter its convexity. This is what actually is done in the adjustment of the eye to distances.

282. Experiment—Adjustment requires Effort. — The simplest way of experimenting on the *adjustment of the eye* is to stick two stout needles upright into a straight piece of wood, not exactly, but nearly in the same straight line, so that, on applying the eye to one end of the piece of wood, one needle (*a*) shall be seen about six inches off, and the other (*b*) just on one side of it at twelve inches' distance.

If the observer look at the needle *b*, he will find that he sees it very distinctly, and without the least sense of effort; but the image of *a* is blurred and more or less double. Now let him try to make this blurred image of the needle *a* distinct. He will find he can do so readily enough, but that the act is accompanied by a sense of effort somewhere in the eye. And, in proportion as *a* becomes distinct, b will become blurred.   Nor will any effort enable him to see a and b distinctly at the same time.

283. The Mechanism of Adjustment explained.—Multitudes of explanations have been given of this remarkable power of adjustment, but it is only within the last few years that the problem has been solved, by the accurate determination of the nature of the changes in the eye which accompany the act.   When the flame of a taper is held near, and a little on one side of, a person's eye, any one, looking into the eye from a proper point of view, will see three images of the flame, two upright and one inverted.   One upright figure is reflected from the front of

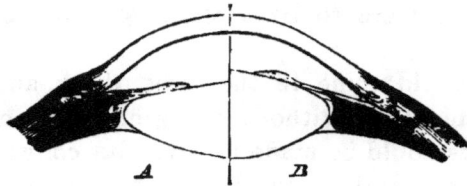

FIG. 96.

Illustrates the change in the form of the lens when adjusted—A to distant, B to near objects.

the cornea, which acts as a convex mirror.   The second proceeds from the front of the crystalline lens, which has the same effect; while the inverted image proceeds from the posterior face of the lens, which, being convex backwards, is, of course, concave forwards, and acts as a concave mirror.

Suppose the eye to be steadily fixed on a distant object, and then adjusted to a near one in the same line of vision, the position of the eyeball remaining unchanged. Then the upright image reflected from the surface of the cornea, and the inverted image from the back of the lens, will remain unchanged, though it is demonstrable that their size or apparent position must change if either the cornea, or the back of the lens, alter either their form or their position. But the second upright image, that reflected by the front face of the lens, does change both its size and its position; it comes forward and grows smaller, proving that the front face of the lens has become more convex. The change of form of the lens is, in fact, that represented in Fig. 96.

These may be regarded as the *facts of adjustment*, with which all explanations of that process must accord. They at once exclude the hypotheses (1) that adjustment is the result of the compression of the ball of the eye by its muscles, which would cause a change in the form of the cornea; (2) that adjustment results from a shifting of the lens bodily, for its hinder face does not move; (3) that it results from the pressure of the iris upon the front face of the lens, for under these circumstances the hinder face of the lens would not remain stationary. This last hypothesis is further negatived by the fact that adjustment takes place equally well when the iris is absent.

One other explanation remains, which is, in all probability, the true one, though not altogether devoid of difficulties. The lens, which is very elastic, is kept habitually in a state of tension by the elasticity of its suspensory ligament, and consequently has a flatter form than it would take if left to itself. If the ciliary muscle contracts, it must, as has been seen, relax that ligament, and thereby diminish its elastic tension upon the lens. The lens, consequently, will become more convex, returning to its former shape when the ciliary muscle ceases to contract, and allows the choroid to return to its ordinary place.

If this be the true explanation of adjustment, the sense of effort we feel must arise from the contraction of the ciliary muscle.

284. Limits of the Power of Adjustment.—Adjustment can take place only within a certain range, which admits of great individual variations. As a rule, no object which is brought within less than about ten inches of the eye can be seen distinctly without effort.

But many persons are born with the surface of the cornea more convex than usual, or with the refractive power of the eye increased in some other way; while, very generally, as age draws on, the cornea flattens. In the former case, objects at ordinary distances are seen indistinctly, because these images fall not on the retina, but in front of it; while, in the latter, the same indistinctness is the result of the rays of light striking upon the retina before they have been brought to a focus. The defect of the former, or short-sighted people, is amended by wearing concave glasses, which cause the rays to diverge; of the latter, or long-sighted people, by wearing convex glasses, which make the rays converge.

In the water camera the image brought to a focus on the screen at the back is *inverted;* the image of a tree, for instance, is seen with the roots upwards and the leaves and branches hanging downwards. The right of the image also corresponds with the left of the object, and *vice versa.* Exactly the same thing takes place in the eye with the image focussed on the retina. It, too, is inverted. (*See* 300.)

Section V.—*Appendages of the Eyeball.*

285. Muscles of the Eyeball.—The *muscles* which move the eyeball are altogether six in number—four straight muscles, or *recti*, and two oblique muscles, the *obliqui* (Fig. 97). The straight muscles are attached to the back of the orbit, round the edges of the hole through which the optic nerve passes, and run straight forward to their insertions into the sclerotic—one, the *superior rectus*, in the middle line above; one, the *inferior*, opposite it below; and one half-way on each side, the *external* and *internal recti*. The eyeball is completely embedded in fat behind and laterally; and these muscles turn it as on a cushion; the superior rectus inclining the axis of the eye upwards, the inferior downwards, the external outwards, the internal inwards.

The two oblique muscles are both attached on the outer side of the ball, and rather behind its centre; and they both pull in a direction from the point of attachment towards the inner side of the orbit—the lower, because it arises here; the upper, because, though it arises along with the

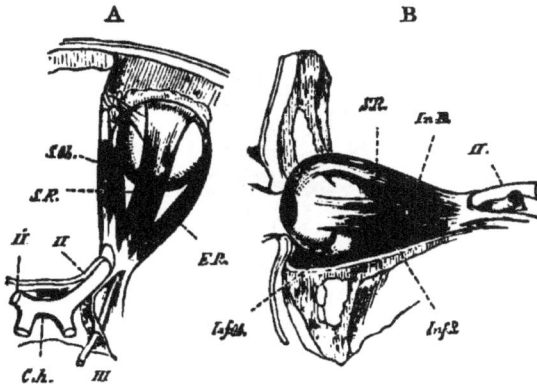

Fig. 97.

A, the muscles of the right eyeball viewed from above, and B of the left eyeball viewed from the outer side; *S.R.*, the superior rectus; *Inf.R.*, the inferior rectus; *E.R.*, *In.R.*, the external rectus; *S.Ob.*, the superior oblique; *Inf.Ob.*, the inferior oblique; *Ch.*, the chiasma of the optic nerves (*II.*); *III.*, the third nerve which supplies all the muscles except the superior oblique and the external rectus.

recti from the back of the orbit, yet, after passing forwards and becoming tendinous at the upper and inner corner of the orbit, it traverses a pulley-like loop of ligament, and then turns downwards and outwards to its insertion. The action of the oblique muscles is somewhat complicated, but their general tendency is to roll the eyeball on its axis, and pull it a little forward and inward.

286. The Eyelids.—The *eyelids* are folds of skin containing thin plates of cartilage, and fringed at their edges with hairs—the *eyelashes*—and with a series of small glands called *Meibomian*. Circularly-disposed fibres of striped

12

muscle lie beneath the integuments of the eyelids, and constitute the *orbicularis* muscle which shuts them.   The
upper eyelid is raised by a special muscle, the *levator* of
the upper lid, which arises at the back of the orbit and
runs forwards to end in the lid.

The lower lid has no special depressor.

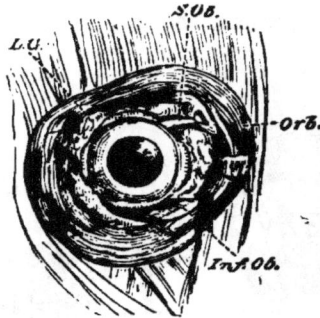

FIG. 98.

The front view of the right eye dissected to show, *Orb.*, the orbicular muscle of the
eyelids ; the pulley and insertion of the superior oblique, *S.Ob.*, and the inferior oblique,
Inf.Ob.; L.G., the lachrymal gland.

287. The Lachrymal Apparatus. — At the edge of the
eyelids the integument becomes continuous with a delicate, vascular, and highly-nervous mucous membrane, the
conjunctiva, which lines the interior of the lids and the
front of the eyeball, its epithelial layer being even continued over the cornea.   The numerous small ducts of a
gland which is lodged in the orbit, on the outer side of the
ball (Fig. 98, *L. G.*), the *lachrymal gland*, constantly pour
its watery secretion into the interspace between the conjunctiva lining the upper eyelid and that covering the
ball.   On the inner side of the eye is a reddish fold, the
caruncula lachrymalis, a sort of rudiment of that third
eyelid which is to be found in many animals.   Above and
below, close to the caruncula, the edge of each eyelid presents a minute aperture (the *punctum lachrymale*), the
opening of a small canal.   The canals from above and be-

low converge and open into the *lachrymal sac ;* the upper blind end of a duct (*L.D.*, Fig. 99), which passes down from the orbit to the nose, opening below the inferior turbinal bone (Fig. 49, *h*). It is through this system of canals

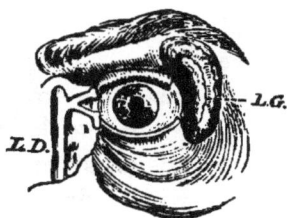

Fig. 99.

A front view of the left eye, with the eyelids partially dissected to show lachrymal gland, *L.G.*, and lachrymal duct, *L.D.*

that the conjunctival mucous membrane is continuous with that of the nose; and it is by them that the secretion of the lachrymal canal is ordinarily carried away as fast as it forms.

But, under certain circumstances, as when the conjunctiva is irritated by pungent vapors, or when painful emotions arise in the mind, the secretion of the lachrymal gland exceeds the drainage-power of the lachrymal duct, and the fluid, accumulating between the lids, at length overflows in the form of tears.

CHAPTER X.

SENSATIONS AND JUDGMENT.

SECTION I.— *Compound Sensations.*

288. Our Sensations mostly Composite.— In explaining the functions of the sensory organs, I have hitherto confined myself to describing the means by which the physical agent of a sensation is enabled to irritate a given sensory nerve; and to giving some account of the simple sensations which are thus evolved.

Simple sensations of this kind are such as might be produced by the irritation of a single nerve-fibre, or of several nerve-fibres by the same agent. Such are the sensations of contact, of warmth, of sweetness, of an odor, of a musical note, of whiteness, or redness.

But very few of our sensations are thus simple. Most of even those which we are in the habit of regarding as simple, are really compounds of different sensations, or of sensations with ideas, or with judgments. For example, in the preceding cases, it is very difficult to separate the sensation of contact from the judgment that something is touching us; of sweetness, from the idea of something in the mouth; of sound or light, from the judgment that something outside us is shining, or sounding.

289. Sensations of Smell the Simplest.—The sensations of smell are those which are least complicated by accessories of this sort. Thus, particles of musk diffuse themselves with great rapidity through the nasal passages, and give rise to the sensation of a powerful odor. But beyond a broad notion that the odor is in the nose, this sensation is unaccompanied by any ideas of locality and direction. Still less does it give rise to any conception of form, or size, or force, or of succession, or contemporaneity. If a man had no other sense than that of smell, and musk were the only odorous body, he could have no sense of *outness* —no power of distinguishing between the external world and himself.

290. Analysis of a Tactile Sensation. — Contrast this with what may seem to be the equally simple sensation obtained by drawing the finger along the table, the eyes being shut. This act gives one the sensation of a flat, hard surface outside one's self, which appears to be just as simple as the odor of musk, but is really a complex state of feeling compounded of:

(*a*) Pure sensations of contact.

(*b*) Pure muscular sensations of two kinds—the one arising from the resistance of the table, the other from the actions of those muscles which draw the finger along.

(*c*) Ideas of the order in which these pure sensations succeed one another.

(*d*) Comparisons of these sensations and their order, with the recollection of like sensations similarly arranged, which have been obtained on previous occasions.

(*e*) Recollections of the impressions of extension, flatness, etc., made on the organ of vision when these previous tactile and muscular sensations were obtained.

Thus, in this case, the only pure sensations are those of contact and muscular action. The greater part of what we call the sensation is a complex mass of present and recollected ideas and judgments.

291. Complexity of the Notion of Roundness. —Should any doubt remain that we do thus mix up our sensations with our judgments into one indistinguishable whole, shut the eyes as before, and, instead of touching the table with the finger, take a round lead-pencil between the fingers, and draw that along the table. The "sensation" of a flat hard surface will be just as clear as before; and yet all that we touch is the round surface of the pencil, and the only pure sensations we owe to the table are those afforded by the muscular sense. In fact, in this case, our "sensation" of a flat hard surface is entirely a judgment based upon what the muscular sense tells us is going on in certain muscles.

A still more striking case of the tenacity with which we adhere to complex judgments, which we conceive to be pure sensations, and are unable to analyze otherwise than by a process of abstract reasoning, is afforded by our sense of roundness.

Any one taking a marble between two fingers will say that he feels it to be a single round body; and he will probably be as much at a loss to answer the question how he knows that it is round, as he would be if he were asked how he knows that a scent is a scent.

Nevertheless, this notion of the roundness of the marble is really a very complex judgment, and that it is so may be shown by a simple experiment. If the index and middle fingers be crossed, and the marble placed between them, so as to be in contact with both, it is utterly impossible to avoid the belief that there are two marbles instead of one. Even looking at the marble, and seeing that there is only one, does not weaken the apparent proof derived from touch that there are two.[1]

The fact is, that our notions of singleness and roundness are, really, highly-complex judgments based upon a few simple sensations; and, when the ordinary conditions of those judgments are reversed, the judgment is also reversed.

With the index and middle fingers in their ordinary position, it is, of course, impossible that the outer sides of each should touch opposite surfaces of one spheroidal body. If, in the natural and usual position of the fingers, their outer surfaces simultaneously give us the impression of a spheroid (which itself is a complex judgment), it is in the nature of things that there must be two spheroids. But, when the fingers are crossed over the marble, the outer side of each finger is really in contact with a spheroid; and the mind, taking no cognizance of the crossing, judges in accordance with its universal experience, that two spheroids, and not one, give rise to the sensations which are perceived.

SECTION II.—*Delusions of Judgment.*

292. There are no "Delusions of the Senses." — Phenomena of this kind are not uncommonly called *delusions*

---

[1] A ludicrous form of this experiment is to apply the crossed fingers to the end of the nose, when it at once appears double; and, in spite of the absurdity of the conviction, the mind cannot expel it, so long as the sensations last.

of the senses; but there is no such thing as a fictitious, or delusive, sensation. A sensation must exist to be a sensation, and, if it exists, it is real and not delusive. But the judgments we form respecting the causes and conditions of the sensations of which we are aware, are very often erroneous and delusive enough; and such judgments may be brought about in the domain of every sense, either by artificial combinations of sensations, or by the influence of unusual conditions of the body itself. The latter give rise to what are called *subjective sensations.*

Mankind would be subject to fewer delusions than they are, if they constantly bore in mind their liability to false judgments due to unusual combinations, either artificial or natural, of true sensations. Men say: " I felt," " I heard," " I saw " such and such a thing, when, in ninety-nine cases out of a hundred, what they really mean is that they judge that certain sensations of touch, hearing, or sight, of which they were conscious, were caused by such and such things.

293. Subjective Sensations. — Among *subjective sensations* within the domain of touch, are the feelings of creeping and prickling of the skin, which are not uncommon in certain states of the circulation. The subjective evil smells and bad tastes which accompany some diseases are very probably due to similar disturbances in the circulation of the sensory organs of smell and taste.

Many persons are liable to what may be called *auditory spectra*—music of various degrees of complexity sounding in their ears, without any external cause, while they are wide awake. I know not if other persons are similarly troubled, but, in reading books written by persons with whom I am acquainted, I am sometimes tormented by hearing the words pronounced in the exact way in which these persons would utter them, any trick or peculiarity of voice, or gesture, being also very accurately reproduced. And I suppose that every one must have been startled, at times, by the extreme distinctness with which his thoughts have embodied themselves in apparent voices.

The most wonderful exemplifications of subjective sensation, however, are afforded by the organ of sight.

Any one who has witnessed the sufferings of a man laboring under *delirium tremens* (a disease produced by excessive drinking), from the marvelous distinctness of his visions, which sometimes take the forms of devils, sometimes of creeping animals, but almost always of something fearful or loathsome, will not doubt the intensity of subjective sensations in the domain of vision.

294. Remarkable Case of Delusive Appearances. — But that illusive visions of great distinctness should appear, it is not necessary for the nervous system to be thus obviously deranged. People in the full possession of their faculties, and of high intelligence, may be subject to such appearances, for which no distinct cause can be assigned. An excellent illustration of this is the famous case of Mrs. A., given by Sir David Brewster in his "Natural Magic:"

"(1) The first illusion to which Mrs. A. was subject, was one which affected only the ear. On the 21st of December, 1830, about half-past four in the afternoon, she was standing near the fire in the hall, and on the point of going up to dress, when she heard, as she supposed, her husband's voice calling her by name: '——, ——, come here! come to me!' She imagined that he was calling at the door to have it opened; but, upon going there and opening the door, she was surprised to find no person there. Upon returning to the fire she again heard the same voice calling out very distinctly and loudly, '——, come, come here!' She then opened two other doors of the same room, and, upon seeing no person, she returned to the fireplace. After a few moments she heard the same voice still calling, 'Come to me, come! come away!' in a loud, plaintive, and somewhat impatient tone; she answered as loudly, 'Where are you? I don't know where you are,' still imagining that he was somewhere in search of her; but, receiving no answer, she shortly went up-stairs. On Mr. A.'s return to the house, about half an hour afterwards, she inquired why he had called her so often, and where he was, and she was of course greatly surprised to learn that he had not been near the house at the time. A similar illusion, which excited no particular notice at the time, occurred to Mrs. A. when residing at Florence, about ten years before, and when she was in perfect health. When she was undressing after a ball, she heard a voice call her repeatedly by name, and she was at that time unable to account for it.

" (2) The next illusion which occurred to Mrs. A. was of a more alarming character. On the 30th of December, about four o'clock in the afternoon, Mrs. A. came downstairs into the drawing-room, which she had quitted only a few minutes before, and, on entering the room, she saw her husband, as she supposed, standing with his back to the fire. As he had gone out to take a walk about half an hour before, she was surprised to see him there, and asked him why he had returned so soon. The figure looked fixedly at her with a serious and thoughtful expression of countenance, but did not speak. Supposing that his mind was absorbed in thought, she sat down in an arm-chair near the fire, and within two feet, at most, of the figure, which she still saw standing before her. As its eyes, however, still continued to be fixed upon her, she said, after a lapse of a few minutes, 'Why don't you speak?' The figure immediately moved off towards the window at the farther end of the room, with its eyes still gazing on her, and it passed so very close to her in doing so, that she was struck with the circumstance of hearing no step or sound, nor feeling her clothes brushed against, nor even any agitation in the air.

" Although she was now convinced that the figure was not her husband, yet she never for a moment supposed that it was any thing supernatural, and was soon convinced that it was a spectral illusion. As soon as this conviction had established itself in her mind, she recollected the experiment which I had suggested of trying to double the object; but, before she was able distinctly to do this, the figure had retreated to the window, where it disappeared. Mrs. A. immediately followed it, shook the curtains, and examined the window, the impression having been so distinct and forcible, that she was unwilling to believe that it was not a reality. Finding, however, that the figure had no natural means of escape, she was convinced that she had seen a spectral apparition like that recorded in Dr. Hibbert's work, and she consequently felt no alarm or agitation. The appearance was seen in bright daylight, and lasted four or five minutes. When the figure stood close to her, it concealed the real objects behind it, and the apparition was fully as vivid as the reality.

" (3) On these two occasions Mrs. A. was alone, but, when the next phantom appeared, her husband was present. This took place on the 4th of January, 1830. About ten o'clock at night, when Mr. and Mrs. A. were sitting in the drawing-room, Mr. A. took up the poker to stir the fire, and, when he was in the act of doing this, Mrs. A. exclaimed, 'Why, there's the cat in the room!' 'Where?' exclaimed Mr. A. 'There—close to you,' she replied. 'Where?' he repeated. 'Why, on the rug, to be sure, between yourself and the coal-scuttle.' Mr. A., who still had the poker in his hand, pushed it in the direction mentioned. 'Take care!' cried Mrs. A., 'take care! you are hitting her with the poker.' Mr. A. again asked her to point out exactly where she saw the cat. She replied, 'Why, sitting up there close to your feet on the rug; she is looking at me. It is Kitty—come here, Kitty!' There were two cats in the house, one of which went by this name, and they were rarely, if ever, in the drawing-room.

" At this time Mrs. A. had no idea that the sight of the

cat was an illusion. When she was asked to touch it, she got up for the purpose, and seemed as if she was pursuing something which moved away. She followed a few steps, and then said, 'It has gone under the chair.' Mr. A. assured her that it was an illusion, but she would not believe it. He then lifted up the chair, and Mrs. A. saw nothing more of it. The room was searched all over, and nothing found in it. There was a dog lying on the hearth, who would have betrayed great uneasiness if a cat had been in the room, but he lay perfectly quiet. In order to be quite certain, Mr. A. rang the bell, and sent for the cats, both of which were found in the house-keeper's room.

"(4) About a month after this occurrence, Mrs. A., who had taken a somewhat fatiguing drive during the day, was preparing to go to bed about eleven o'clock at night, and, sitting before the dressing-glass, was occupied in arranging her hair. She was in a listless and drowsy state of mind, but fully awake. When her fingers were in active motion among the papillotes, she was suddenly startled by seeing in the mirror the figure of a near relative, who was then in Scotland, and in perfect health. The apparition appeared over her left shoulder, and its eyes met hers in the glass. It was enveloped in grave-clothes, closely pinned, as is usual with corpses, round the head and under the chin; and, though the eyes were open, the features were solemn and rigid. The dress was evidently a shroud, as Mrs. A. remarked even the punctured pattern usually worked in a peculiar manner round the edges of that garment. Mrs. A. described herself as, at the time, sensible of a feeling like what we conceive of fascination, compelling her, for the time, to gaze upon this melancholy apparition, which was as distinct and vivid as any reflected reality could be, the light of the candle upon the dressing-table appearing to shine fully upon its face. After a few minutes she turned round to look for the reality of the form over her shoulder, but it was not visible, and it had also disappeared from the glass when she looked again in that direction.

. . . . . .

"(7) On the 17th of March, Mrs. A. was preparing for bed. She had dismissed her maid, and was sitting with her feet in hot water. Having an excellent memory, she had been thinking upon and repeating to herself a striking passage in the *Edinburgh Review*, when, on raising her eyes, she saw seated in a large easy-chair before her the figure of a deceased friend, the sister of Mr. A. The figure was dressed, as had been usual with her, with great neatness, but in a gown of a peculiar kind, such as Mrs. A. had never seen her wear, but exactly such as had been described to her by a common friend as having been worn by Mr. A.'s sister during her last visit to England. Mrs. A. paid particular attention to the dress, air, and appearance of the figure, which sat in an easy attitude in the chair, holding a handkerchief in one hand. Mrs. A. tried to speak to it, but experienced a difficulty in doing so, and in about three minutes the figure disappeared.

"About a minute afterwards, Mr. A. came into the room, and found Mrs. A. slightly nervous, but fully aware of the delusive nature of the apparition. She described it as having all the vivid coloring and apparent reality of life; and for some hours preceding this and other visions, she experienced a peculiar sensation in her eyes, which seemed to be relieved when the vision had ceased.

. . . . . .

"(9) On the 11th of October, when sitting in the drawing-room, on one side of the fireplace, she saw the figure of another deceased friend moving towards her from the window at the farther end of the room. It approached the fireplace, and sat down in the chair opposite. As there were several persons in the room at the time, she describes the idea uppermost in her mind to have been a fear lest they should be alarmed at her staring, in the way she was conscious of doing, at vacancy, and should fancy her intellect disordered. Under the influence of this fear, and recollecting a story of a similar effect in your[1] work on 'Demonology,' which she had lately read, she summoned up the requisite resolution to enable her to cross the space before the fireplace, and seat herself in the same chair with the figure. The apparition remained perfectly distinct till she sat down, as it were, in its lap, when it vanished."

295. Personal Characteristics.—It should be mentioned that Mrs. A. was naturally a person of very vivid imagination, and that, at the time the most notable of these illusions appeared, her health was weak from bronchitis and enfeebled digestion.

It is obvious that nothing but the singular courage and clear intellect of Mrs. A. prevented her from becoming a mine of ghost-stories of the most excellently authenticated kind. And the particular value of her history lies in its showing that the clearest testimony of the most unimpeachable witness may be quite inconclusive as to the objective reality of something which the witness has seen.

296. The Senses not at Fault.—Mrs. A. undoubtedly saw what she said she saw. The evidence of her eyes as to the existence of the apparitions, and of her ears to those of the voices, was, in itself, as perfectly trustworthy as their evidence would have been had the objects really existed. For there can be no doubt that exactly those parts of her retina which would have been affected by the image of a cat, and those parts of her auditory organ which would have been set vibrating by her husband's voice, or the portions of the sensorium with which those organs of sense are connected, were thrown into a corresponding state of activity by some internal cause.

What the senses testify is neither more nor less than the fact of their own affection. As to the cause of that

---

[1] Sir Walter Scott, to whom Sir David Brewster's "Letters on Natural Magic" were addressed.

affection they really say nothing, but leave the mind to form its own judgment on the matter. A hasty or superstitious person in Mrs. A.'s place would have formed a wrong judgment, and would have stood by it on the plea that "she must believe her senses."

297. Ventriloquism.—The delusions of the judgment, produced not by abnormal conditions of the body, but by unusual or artificial combinations of sensations, or by suggestions of ideas, are exceedingly numerous, and occasionally are not a little remarkable.

Some of those which arise out of the sensation of touch have already been noted. I do not know of any produced through smell or taste, but hearing is a fertile source of such errors.

What is called *ventriloquism* (speaking from the belly), and is not uncommonly ascribed to a mysterious power of producing voice somewhere else than in the larynx, depends entirely upon the accuracy with which the performer can simulate sounds of a particular character, and upon the skill with which he can suggest a belief in the existence of the causes of these sounds. Thus if the ventriloquist desire to create the belief that a voice issues from the bowels of the earth, he imitates with great accuracy the tones of such a half-stifled voice, and suggests the existence of some one uttering it by directing his answers and gestures towards the ground. These gestures and tones are such as would be produced by a given cause; and no other cause being apparent, the mind of the bystander insensibly judges the suggested cause to exist.

Section III.— *Visual Sensations and Mental States.*

298. Optical Delusions.—The delusions of the judgment through the sense of sight—*optical delusions*, as they are called—are more numerous than any others, because such a great number of what we think to be simple visual sensations are really very complex aggregates of visual sensations, tactile sensations, judgments, and recollections of former sensations and judgments.

It will be instructive to analyze some of these judgments into their principles, and to explain the delusions by the application of these principles.

299. Externality of Visible Objects.— *When an external body is felt by the touch to be in a given place, the image of that body falls on a point of the retina which lies at one end of a straight line joining the body and the retina, and traversing a particular region of the centre of the eye. This straight line is called the* OPTIC AXIS.

Conversely, when any part of the surface of the retina is excited, the luminous sensation is referred by the mind to some point outside the body, in the direction of the optic axis.

It is for this reason that when a phosphene is created by pressure, say on the outer and lower side of the eyeball, the luminous image appears to lie above, and to the inner side of, the eye. Any external object which could produce the sense of light in the part of the retina pressed upon must, owing to the inversion of the retinal images (284), in fact occupy this position; and hence the mind refers the light seen to an object in that position.

300. The Inversion of the Visual Images.—The same kind of explanation is applicable to the apparent paradox that, while all the pictures of external objects are certainly inverted on the retina by the refracting media of the eye, we nevertheless see them upright. It is difficult to understand this, until one reflects that the retina has, in itself, no means of indicating to the mind which of its parts lies at the top, and which at the bottom; and that the mind learns to call an impression on the retina high or low, right or left, simply on account of the association of such an impression with certain coincident tactile impressions. In other words, when one part of the retina is affected, the object causing the affection is found to be near the right

hand; when another, the left; when another, the hand
has to be raised to reach the object; when yet another, it
has to be depressed to reach it. And thus the several impressions on the retina are called right, left, upper, lower,
quite irrespectively of their real positions, of which the
mind has, and can have, no cognizance.

301. Correspondence of Objects and Images.— *When
an external body is ascertained by touch to be simple, it
forms but one image on the retina of a single eye; and,
when two or more images fall on the retina of a single
eye, they ordinarily proceed from a corresponding number
of bodies which are distinct to the touch.*

*Conversely, the sensation of two or more images is
judged by the mind to proceed from two or more objects.*

If two pin-holes be made in a piece of card-board at a
distance less than the diameter of the pupil, and a small
object like the head of a pin be held pretty close to the
eye, and viewed through these holes, two images of the
head of the pin will be seen. The reason of this is, that
the rays of light from the head of the pin are split by the
card into two minute pencils, which pass into the eye on
either side of its centre, and cannot be united again and
brought to one focus on account of the nearness of the
pin to the eye. Hence they fall on different parts of the
retina, and each pencil of rays, being very small, makes a
tolerably distinct image of its own of the pin's head on
the retina. Each of these images is now referred outward
(299) in the direction of the appropriate optic axis, and
two pins are apparently seen instead of one. A like explanation applies to *multiplying-glasses* and *doubly-refract-
ing* crystals, both of which, in their own ways, split the
pencils of light proceeding from a single object into two
or more separate bundles. These give rise to as many
images, each of which is referred by the mind to a distinct
external object.

302. Judgment of Distance—Perspective.— *Certain vis-*

ual phenomena ordinarily accompany those products of tactile sensation to which we give the name of size, distance, and form.   Thus, other things being alike, the space of the retina covered by the image of a large object is larger than that covered by a small object; while that covered by a near object is larger than that covered by a distant object ; and, other conditions being alike a near object is more brilliant than a distant one.   Furthermore, the shadows of objects differ with the forms of their surfaces, as determined by touch.

Conversely, if these visual sensations can be produced, they inevitably suggest a belief in the existence of objects competent to produce the corresponding tactile sensations.

What is called *perspective*, whether *solid* or *aërial*, in drawing, or painting, depends on the application of these principles.   It is a kind of visual ventriloquism — the painter putting upon his canvas all the conditions requisite for the production of images on the retina, having the size, relative form, and intensity of color of those which would actually be produced by the objects themselves in Nature. And the success of his picture, as an imitation, depends upon the closeness of the resemblance between the images it produces on the retina, and those which would be produced by the objects represented.

303. Magnifying-Glasses.—To most persons the image of a pin, at five or six inches from the eye, appears blurred and indistinct—the eye not being capable of adjustment to so short a focus.   If a small hole be made in a piece of card, the circumferential rays which cause the blur are cut off, and the image becomes distinct.   But at the same time it is magnified, or looks bigger, because the image of the pin, in spite of the loss of the circumferential rays, occupies a much larger extent of the retina when close than when distant.   All convex glasses produce the same effect—while concave lenses diminish the apparent size of an object, because they diminish the size of its image on the retina.

304. Why the Sun and Moon look larger near the Horizon.—The moon, and the sun, when near the horizon, appear very much larger than they are when high in the sky. When in the latter position, in fact, we have nothing to compare them with, and the small extent of the retina which their images occupy suggests small absolute size. But, as they set, we see them passing behind great trees and buildings which we know to be very large and very distant, and yet occupying a larger space on the retina than the latter do. Hence the vague suggestion of their larger size.

305. Judgment of Form by Shadows.—If a convex surface be lighted from one side, the side towards the light is bright—that turned from the light, dark, or in shadow; while a concavity is shaded on the side towards the light, bright on the opposite side.

If a new half-crown, or a medal with a well-raised head upon its face, be lighted sideways by a candle, we at once know the head to be raised (or a *cameo*) by the disposition of the light and shade; and if an *intaglio*, or medal on which the head is hollowed out, be lighted in the same way, its nature is as readily judged by the eye.

But now, if either of the objects thus lighted be viewed with a convex lens, which inverts its position, the light and dark sides will be reversed. With the reversal the judgment of the mind will change, so that the cameo will be regarded as an intaglio, and the intaglio as a cameo; for the light still comes from where it did, but the cameo appears to have the shadows of an intaglio, and *vice versa*. So completely, however, is this interpretation of the facts a matter of judgment, that, if a pin be stuck beside the medal so as to throw a shadow, the pin and its shadow, being reversed by the lens, will suggest that the direction of the light is also reversed, and the medals will seem to be what they really are.

306. Judgment of Changes of Form.— *Whenever an ex-*

ternal object is watched rapidly changing its form, a continuous series of different pictures of the object is impressed upon the same spot of the retina.

Conversely, if a continuous series of different pictures of one object is impressed upon one part of the retina, the mind judges that they are due to a single external object, undergoing changes of form.

This is the principle of the curious toy called the *thaumatrope*, or "zootrope," or "wheel of life," by the help of which, on looking through a hole, one sees images of jugglers throwing up and catching balls, or boys playing at leap-frog over one another's backs. This is managed by painting at intervals, on a disk of card, figures and jugglers in the attitudes of throwing, waiting to catch, and catching; or boys "giving a back," leaping, and coming into position after leaping. The disk is then made to rotate before an opening, so that each image shall be presented for an instant, and follow its predecessor before the impression of the latter has died away. The result is that the succession of different pictures irresistibly suggests one or more objects undergoing successive changes—the juggler seems to throw the balls, and the boys appear to jump over one another's backs.

307. Single Vision with Two Eyes.— *When an external object is ascertained by touch to be single, the centres of its retinal images in the two eyes fall upon the centres of the yellow spots of the two eyes, when both eyes are directed towards it; but, if there be two external objects, the centres of both their images cannot fall, at the same time, upon the centres of the yellow spots.*

Conversely, when the centres of two images, formed simultaneously in the two eyes, fall upon the centres of the yellow spots, the mind judges the images to be caused by a single external object; but if not, by two.

This seems to be the only admissible explanation of the facts, that an object which appears single to the touch and when viewed with one eye, also appears single when it is viewed with both eyes, though two images of it are necessarily formed; and on the other hand, that when the centres of the two images of one object do not fall on the centres of the yellow spots, both images are seen separately, and we have double vision. In squinting, the axes of the two eyes do not converge equally towards the object viewed. In consequence of this, when the centre of the image formed by one eye falls on the centre of the yellow spot, the corresponding part of that formed by the other eye does not, and double vision is the result.

For simplicity's sake we have supposed the images to fall on the centre of the yellow spot. But, though vision is distinct only in the yellow spot, it is not absolutely limited to it; and it is quite possible for an object to be seen as a single object with two eyes, though its images fall on the two retinas outside the yellow spots. All that is necessary is that the two spots of the retinas on which the images fall should be similarly disposed towards the centres of their respective yellow spots. Any two points of the two retinas thus similarly disposed towards their respective yellow spots (or more exactly to the points in which the optic axes end), are spoken of as *corresponding points ;* and any two images covering two corresponding areas are conceived of as coming from a single object. It is obvious that the inner (or nasal) side of one retina *corresponds* to the outer (or cheek) side of the other.

308. The Pseudoscope.—*In single vision with two eyes, the axes of the two eyes, of the movements of which the muscular sense gives an indication, cut one another at a greater angle when the object approaches, at a less angle when it goes farther off.*

Conversely, if, without changing the position of an object, the axes of the two eyes which view it can be made to converge or diverge, the object will seem to approach or go farther off.

In the instrument called the *pseudoscope*, mirrors or prisms are disposed in such a manner that the angle at which rays of light from an object enter the two eyes, can be altered without any change in the object itself; and consequently the axes of these eyes are made to converge or diverge.   In the former case the object seems to approach ; in the latter, to recede.

309. Judgment of Solidity—the Stereoscope.— *When a body of moderate size, ascertained by touch to be solid, is viewed with both eyes, the images of it, formed by the two eyes, are necessarily different (one showing more of its right side, the other of its left side). Nevertheless, they coalesce into a common image, which gives the impression of solidity.*

Conversely, if the two images of the right and left aspects of a solid body be made to fall upon the retinas of the two eyes in such a way as to coalesce into a common image, they are judged by the mind to proceed from the single solid body which alone, under ordinary circumstances, is competent to produce them.

The *stereoscope* is constructed upon this principle. Whatever its form, it is so contrived as to throw the images of two pictures of a solid body, such as would be obtained by the right and left eye of a spectator, on to such parts of the retinas of the person who uses the stereoscope as would receive these images, if they really proceeded from one solid body.   The mind immediately judges them to arise from a single external solid body, and sees such a solid body in place of the two pictures.

The operation of the mind upon the sensations presented to it by the two eyes is exactly comparable to that which takes place when, on holding a marble between the finger and thumb, we at once declare it to be a single sphere (291).   That which is absolutely presented to the mind by the sense of touch in this case is by no means the sensation of one spheroidal body, but two distinct sensations of two convex surfaces. That these two distinct convexities belong to one sphere, is an act of judgment, or process of unconscious reasoning, based upon many particulars of past and present experience, of which we have, at the moment, no distinct consciousness.

CHAPTER XI.

THE NERVOUS SYSTEM AND INNERVATION.

SECTION I.—*The Spinal Cord—Reflex Actions.*

310. The General Nervous System.—The sensory organs are, as we have seen, the channels through which particular physical agents are enabled to excite the sensory nerves with which these organs are connected; and the activity of these nerves is evidenced by that of the central organ of the nervous system, which activity becomes manifest as a state of consciousness—the sensation.

We have also seen that the muscles are instruments by which a motor nerve, excited by the central organ with which it is connected, is able to produce motion.

The sensory nerves, the motor nerves, and the central organ, constitute the greater part of the *nervous system*, which, with its function of *innervation*, we must now study somewhat more closely, and as a whole.

311. The Cerebro-Spinal and Sympathetic Systems.—The nervous apparatus consists of two sets of nerves and nerve-centres, which are intimately connected together and yet may be conveniently studied apart. These are the *cerebro-spinal* system and the *sympathetic* system. The former consists of the *cerebro-spinal axis* (composed of the *brain* and *spinal cord*) and the *cerebral* and *spinal nerves*, which are connected with this axis. The latter comprises the chain of *sympathetic ganglia*, the nerves which they

give off, and the nervous cords by which they are connected with one another and with the cerebro-spinal nerves.

312. Nerve-Fibres and Nerve-Centres.—Nerves are made
up entirely of nerve-fibres, the structure of which is somewhat different in the cerebro-spinal and in the sympathetic
systems. (*See* 356.) Nerve-centres, on the other hand,
are composed of *nerve-cells* or *ganglionic corpuscles*, mingled with nerve-fibres (356). Such cells, or corpuscles, are
found in various parts of the brain and spinal cord, in the
sympathetic ganglia, and also in the ganglia belonging to
spinal nerves as well as in certain sensory organs, such as
the retina and the internal ear.

313. Membrane of the Cerebro-Spinal Axis.—The *cerebro-spinal axis* lies in the cavity of the skull and spinal
column, the bony walls of which cavity are lined by a very
tough fibrous membrane, serving as the periosteum of the
component bones of this region, and called the *dura mater.*
The brain and spinal cord themselves are closely invested
by a very vascular fibrous tissue, called *pia mater.* The
numerous blood-vessels supplying these organs run for
some distance in the pia mater, and, where they pass into
the substance of the brain or cord, the fibrous tissue of the
pia mater accompanies them to a greater or less depth.

The outer surface of the *pia mater* and the inner surface of the *dura mater* pass into a delicate fibrous tissue,
lined by an epithelium, which is called the *arachnoid* membrane. Thus one layer of arachnoid coats the brain and
spinal cord, and another lines the dura mater. As these
layers become continuous with one another at various
points, the arachnoid forms a sort of shut sac, like the *pericardium ;* and, in common with other serous membranes,
it secretes a fluid, the *arachnoid fluid,* into its interior.
The interspace between the internal and external layers
of the arachnoid of the brain is, for the most part, very
small; that between the corresponding layers of the arachnoid of the spinal cord is larger.

314. The Spinal Cord.—The *spinal cord* (Figs. 100, 101) is a column of grayish-white soft substance, extending from the top of the spinal canal, where it is continuous with the brain, to about the second lumbar vertebra, where it tapers off into a filament. A deep fissure, the *anterior fissure* (Fig. 102, 1), divides it in the middle line in front, nearly down to its centre: and a similar cleft, the *posterior fissure* (Fig. 102, 2), also extends nearly to its centre in the middle line behind. The pia mater extends into each of these fissures, and supports the vessels which supply the cord with blood. In consequence of the presence of these fissures, only a narrow bridge of the substance of the cord connects its two halves, and this bridge is traversed throughout its entire length by a minute canal, the centre canal of the cord (Fig. 102, 3).

Each half of the cord is divided longitudinally into three equal parts, the anterior, lateral, and posterior col-

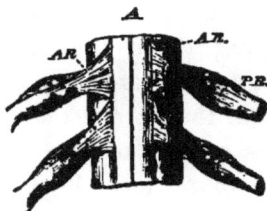 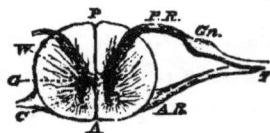

FIG. 100.   FIG. 101.

THE SPINAL CORD.

Fig. 100.—A front view of a portion of the cord. On the right side, the anterior roots, *A. R.*, are entire; on the left side they are cut, to show the posterior roots, *P.R.*

Fig. 101.—A transverse section of the cord. *A*, the anterior fissure; *P*, the posterior fissure; *G*, the central canal; *C*, the gray matter; *W*, the white matter; *A.R.*, the anterior root, *P R.*, the posterior root, *Gn.*, the ganglion, and *T.*, the trunk, of a spinal nerve.

umns (Fig. 102, 6, 7, 8), by the lines of attachment of two parallel series of delicate bundles of nervous filaments, the roots of the spinal nerves. The roots of the nerves which arise along that line which is nearer the posterior surface of the cord are called posterior roots; those which arise along the other line are the anterior roots. A certain number of anterior and posterior roots, on the same level on each side of the cord, converge and form anterior and posterior bundles, and then the two bundles, anterior and posterior, coalesce into the trunk of a spinal nerve; but, before doing so, the posterior bundle presents an enlargement—*the ganglion of the posterior root.*

The trunks of the spinal nerves pass out of the spinal canal by apertures between the vertebræ, called the *intervertebral foramina*, and then divide and subdivide, their ultimate ramifications going for the most part to the muscles and to the skin.

There are thirty-one pairs of these spinal nerves, and, consequently, twice as many sets of roots of spinal nerves given off, in two lateral series, from each half of the cord.

315. Transverse Section of a Cord.—A transverse section of the cord (Figs. 101 and 102) shows that each half contains two substances—a white substance on the outside, and a grayish-red substance in the interior. And this *gray matter*, as it is called, is so disposed that, in a transverse section, it looks something like a crescent, with one end bigger than the other, and with the concave side turned outwards. The two ends of the crescents are called its *horns* or *cornua* (Fig. 102, *e e*), the one directed forwards being the *anterior cornu ;* the one turned backwards the *posterior cornu* (Fig. 102, *a a*). The convex sides of the cornu of the gray matter approach one another, and are joined by the bridge which contains the central canal.

Many of the nerve-fibres of which the anterior roots are composed may be traced into the anterior cornu, while those of the posterior roots enter the posterior cornu.

316. Difference between Gray and White Matter.—There is a fundamental difference in structure between the gray and the white matter. The white matter consists entirely of nerve-fibres supported in a delicate framework of connective tissue, and accompanied by blood-vessels. Most of these fibres run lengthways in the cord, and con-

13

sequently, in a transverse section, the white matter is really composed of a multitude of the cut ends of these fibres.

The gray matter, on the other hand, contains, in addition, a number of nerve-cells or ganglionic corpuscles, some of them of considerable size. These cells are wholly absent in the white matter.

317. Physiological Properties of Nerves. — The physio-

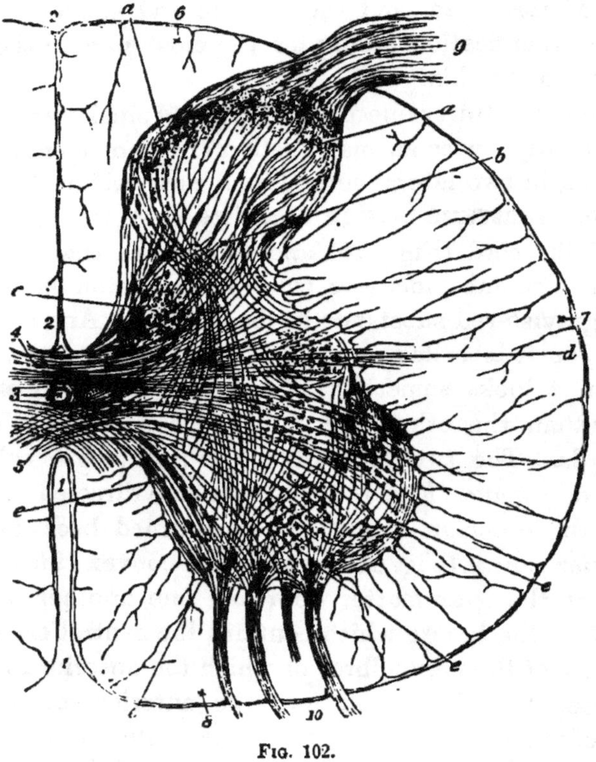

Fig. 102.

Transverse Section of one-half of the Spinal Cord (in the Lumbar Region), magnified.

1, anterior fissure; 2, posterior fissure; 3, central canal; 4 and 5, bridges connecting the two halves (posterior and anterior commissures); 6, posterior column; 7, lateral column; 8, anterior column; 9, posterior root; 10, anterior root of nerve.

a, a, posterior horn of gray matter; e, e, e, anterior horn of gray matter. Through the several columns 6, 7, and 8, each composed of white matter, are seen the prolongations of the pia mater, which carry blood-vessels into the cord from the outside. The pia mater itself is seen over the whole of the cord.

logical properties of the organs now described are very remarkable.

If the *trunk* of a spinal nerve be irritated in any way, as by pinching, cutting, galvanizing, or applying a hot body, two things happen: in the first place, all the muscles to which filaments of this nerve are distributed, contract; in the second, acute pain is felt, and the pain is referred to that part of the skin to which fibres of the nerve are distributed. In other words, the effect of irritating the trunk of a nerve is the same as that of irritating its component fibres at their terminations.

The effects just described will follow upon irritation of part of the *branches* of the nerve: except that, when a branch is irritated, the only muscles directly affected, and the only region of the skin to which pain is referred, will be those to which that branch sends nerve fibres. And these effects will follow upon irritation of any part of a nerve from its smallest branches up to the point of its trunk, at which the anterior and posterior bundles of root-fibres unite.

318. Functions of Anterior and Posterior Roots.—If the anterior bundle of root-fibres be irritated in the same way, only half the previous effects are brought about. That is to say, all the muscles to which the nerve is distributed contract, but no pain is felt.

So again if the posterior, ganglionated bundle be irritated, only half the effects of irritating the whole trunk is produced. But it is the other half; that is to say, none of the muscles to which the nerve is distributed contract, but intense pain is referred to the whole area of skin to which the fibres of the nerve are distributed.

It is clear enough, from these experiments, that all the power of causing muscular contraction which a spinal nerve possesses, is lodged in the fibres which compose its anterior roots; and all the power of giving rise to sensation, in those of its posterior roots. Hence the anterior roots are commonly called *motor*, and the posterior *sensory*.

319. Experiment—Paralysis.—The same truth may be illustrated in other ways. Thus, if, in a living animal, the anterior roots of a spinal nerve be cut, the animal loses all control over the muscles to which that nerve is distributed, though the sensibility of the region of the skin supplied by the nerve is perfect. If the posterior roots be cut, sensation is lost, and voluntary movement remains. But, if both roots be cut, neither voluntary movement nor sensibility is any longer possessed by the part supplied by the nerve. The muscles are said to be paralyzed, and the skin may be cut, or burnt, without any sensation being excited.

If, when both roots are cut, that end of the motor root which remains connected with the trunk of the nerve be irritated, the muscles contract; while, if the other end be so treated, no apparent effect results. On the other hand, if the end of the sensory root connected with the trunk of the nerve be irritated, no apparent effect is produced, while, if the end connected with the cord be thus served, violent pain immediately follows.

When no apparent effect follows upon the irritation of any nerve, it is not probable that the molecules of the nerve remain unchanged. On the contrary, it would appear that the same change occurs in all cases; but a motor nerve is connected with nothing that can make that change apparent save a muscle: and a sensory nerve with nothing that can show an effect but the central nervous system.

320. Molecular Changes in Irritated Nerves.—It will be observed that in all the experiments mentioned there is evidence that, when a nerve is irritated, a something, probably a change in the arrangement of its molecules, is propagated along the nerve-fibres. If a motor or a sensory nerve be irritated at any point, contraction in the muscle, or sensation in the central organ, immediately follows. But, if the nerve be cut, or even tightly tied at any point between the part irritated and the muscle or central organ, the effect at once ceases, just as cutting a telegraph-wire stops the transmission of the electric current or impulse. When a limb, as we say, "goes to sleep," it is because the nerves supplying it have been subjected to pressure sufficient to destroy the nervous [1] continuity of the fibres. We lose voluntary control over, and sensation in, the limb, and these powers are only gradually restored as that nervous continuity returns.

Having arrived at this notion of an impulse traveling along a nerve, we readily pass to the conception of a sensory nerve as a nerve which, when active, brings an impulse to the central organ, or is *afferent ;* and of a motor nerve, as a nerve which carries away an impulse from the organ, or is *efferent.* It is very convenient to use these terms, to denote the two great classes of nerves; for, as we shall find (323), there are afferent nerves which are not sensory in the sense of giving rise to a change of consciousness, or sensation, while there are efferent nerves which are not motor, in the sense of inducing muscular contraction. Such, for example, are the nerves by which the electrical fishes give rise to discharges of electricity from peculiar organs to which those nerves are distributed. The pneumogastric, when it stops the beat of the heart, cannot be called a motor, and yet is then acting as an efferent nerve. It will, of course, be understood, as pointed out above, that the use of these words does not imply that, when a nerve is irritated in the middle of its length, the impulses set up by that irritation travel only away from the central organ if the nerve be efferent, and towards if it be afferent. On the contrary, we have evidence that in

---

[1] Their "nervous continuity "—because their physical continuity is not interrupted as a whole, but only that of the substance which acts as a conductor of the nervous influence ; or, it may be that only the conducting power of a part of that substance is interfered with. Imagine a telegraph-cable, made of delicate caoutchouc tubes, filled with mercury—a squeeze would interrupt the "electrical continuity" of the cable, without destroying its physical continuity. This analogy may not be exact, but it helps to make the nervous phenomena intelligible.

both cases the impulses travel both ways. All that is meant is this, that the afferent nerve, from the disposition of its two ends, in the skin, etc., and in the central organ, is of use only when impulses are traveling along it towards the central organ, and similarly the efferent nerve is of use only when impulses are traveling along it, away from the central organ.

321. Similarity of Afferent and Efferent Nerves.—There is no difference in structure, in chemical or in physical character, between afferent and efferent nerves. The impulse which travels along them requires a certain time for its propagation, and is vastly slower than many other forces—even slower than sound.

322. Properties of the Spinal Cord.—Up to this point our experiments have been confined to the nerves. We may now test the properties of the spinal cord in a similar way. If the cord be cut across (say in the middle of the back), the legs and all the parts supplied by nerves which come off below the section, will be insensible, and no effort of the will can make them move; while all the parts above the section will retain their ordinary powers. When a man hurts his back by an accident, the cord is not unfrequently so damaged as to be virtually cut in two, and then paralysis and insensibility of the lower part of the body ensue.

If, when the cord is cut across in an animal, the cut end of the portion below the division, or away from the brain, be irritated, violent movements of all the muscles supplied by nerves given off from the lower part of the cord take place, but there is no sensation. On the other hand, if that part of the cord, which is still connected with the brain, or better, if any afferent nerve connected with that part of the cord be irritated, great pain ensues, as is shown by the movements of the animal, but in these movements the muscles supplied by nerves coming from the spinal cord below the cut take no part; they remain perfectly quiet.

323. Reflex Action through the Spinal Cord.—Thus, it may be said that, in relation to the brain, the cord is a great mixed motor and sensory nerve. But it is also much more. For, if the trunk of a spinal nerve be cut through, so as to sever its connection with the cord, an irritation of the skin to which the sensory fibres of that nerve are distributed, produces neither motor nor sensory effect.

But, if the cord be cut through anywhere so as to sever its connection with the brain, irritation applied to the skin of the parts supplied with sensory nerves from the part of the cord below the section, though it gives rise to no sensation, may produce violent motion of the parts supplied with motor nerves from the same part of the cord.

Thus, in the case supposed above, of a man whose legs are paralyzed and insensible from spinal injury, tickling the soles of the feet will cause the legs to kick out convulsively. And as a broad fact, it may be said that, so long as both roots of the spinal nerves remain connected with the cord, irritation of any afferent nerve is competent to give rise to excitement of some, or the whole, of the efferent nerves so connected.

If the cord be cut across a second time at any distance below the first section, the efferent nerves below the second cut will no longer be affected by irritation of the afferent nerves above it—but only of those below the second section. Or, in other words, in order that an afferent impulse may be converted into an efferent one by the spinal cord, the afferent nerve must be in uninterrupted material communication with the efferent nerve, by means of the substance of the spinal cord.

This peculiar power of the cord, by which it is competent to convert afferent into efferent impulses, is that which distinguishes it physiologically, as a central organ, from a nerve, and is called *reflex action*. It is a power possessed by the gray matter, and not by the white substance of the cord.

324. Distribution of Reflex Effects.—The number of the efferent nerves which may be excited by the reflex action of the cord is not regulated alone by the number of the afferent nerves which are stimulated by the irritation which gives rise to the reflex action. Nor does a simple excitation of the afferent nerve by any means necessarily imply a corresponding simplicity in the arrangement and succession of the reflected motor impulses. Tickling the sole of the foot is a very simple excitation of the afferent fibres of its nerves; but, in order to produce the muscular actions by which the legs are drawn up, a great multitude of efferent fibres must act in regulated combination. In fact, in a multitude of cases, a reflex action is to be regarded rather as an order given by an afferent nerve to the cord, and executed by it, than as a mere rebound of the afferent impulse into the first efferent channels open to it.

The various characters of these reflex actions may be very conveniently studied in the frog. If a frog be decapitated, or, better still, if the spinal cord be divided close to the head and the brain be destroyed by passing a blunt wire into the cavity of the skull, the animal is thus deprived (by an operation which, being almost instantaneous, can give rise to very little pain) of all consciousness and volition, and yet the spinal cord is left intact. At first the animal is quite flaccid and apparently dead, no movement of any part of the body (except the beating of the heart) being visible. This condition, however, being the result merely of the so-called shock of the operation, very soon passes off, and then the following facts may be observed:

So long as the animal is untouched, so long as no stimulus is brought to bear upon it, no movement of any kind takes place—volition is wholly absent.

If, however, one of the toes be gently pinched, the leg is immediately drawn up close to the body.

If the skin between the thighs around the anus be

pinched, the legs arc suddenly drawn up and thrust out again violently.

If the flank be very gently stroked, there is simply a twitching movement of the muscles underneath; if it be more roughly touched, or pinched, these twitching movements become more general along the whole side of the creature, and extend to the other side, to the hind-legs, and even to the front-legs.

If the digits of the front-limbs be touched, these will bo drawn close under the body as in the act of clasping.

If a drop of vinegar or any acid be placed on the top of one thigh, rapid and active movements will take place in the leg. The foot will bo seen distinctly trying to rub off the drop of acid from the thigh. And, what is still more striking, if the leg be held tight and so prevented from moving, the other leg will begin to rub off the acid. Sometimes, if the drop be too large or too strong, both legs begin at once, and then frequently the movements spread from the legs all over the body, and the whole animal is thrown into convulsions.

Now, all these various movements, even the feeblest and simplest, require a certain combination of muscles, and some of them, such as the act of rubbing off the acids, arc in the highest degree complex. In all of them, too, a certain purpose or end is evident, which is generally either to remove the body or part of the body from the stimulus, from the cause of irritation, or to thrust away the offending object from the body: in the more complex movements such a purpose is strikingly apparent.

It seems, in fact, that in the frog's spinal cord there are sets of nervous machinery destined to be used for a variety of movements, and that a stimulus passing along a sensory nerve to the cord sets one or the other of these pieces of machinery at work.

325. The Spinal Cord as a Conductor.—Thus the spinal cord is, in part, merely a transmitter of impulses to and from the brain; but, in part, it is an independent nervous centre, capable of originating combined movements upon the reception of the impulse of an afferent nerve.

Regarding it merely as a conductor, the question arises, Do all parts of it conduct all kinds of impulses indifferently? or, are certain kinds of impulses communicated only through particular parts of the cord?

The following experiments furnish a partial reply to these questions:

If the anterior half of the white matter of the dorsal part of the cord be cut through, the will is no longer capable of exerting any influence on the muscles which are supplied with nerves from the lower segment of the cord. A similar section, carried through the posterior half of the white matter in this region, has no effect on the transmission of voluntary impulses. It is obvious, therefore, that, in the dorsal part of the cord, nervous impulses *from* the brain are sent through the anterior part of the white matter.

326. Conduction of the Gray Matter. — The posterior half of the white matter may be cut through at one point, and the anterior half at a point a little higher up, so that all the white fibres shall be divided transversely by the one cut or the other, without any interference with the material continuity of the cord, or damage to the gray matter.

When this has been done, irritation of those sensory nerves which are connected with parts below the section excites the sensation of pain as strongly as ever. Hence it follows that the afferent impulses, which excite pain when they reach the brain, pass through, and are conveyed by, the gray matter. And it has been found, by experiment, that, so long as even a small portion of the gray matter remains entire, these afferent impulses are efficiently transmitted. Singularly enough, however, irritation of the gray matter itself is said not to cause pain.[1]

---

[1] This is why, in the experiment described at end of Chapter II., it is better, for testing the presence of sensations, to irritate afferent nerves connected with the cord rather than the cut end of the cord itself.

If one-half of the cord, say the right, be cut through, transversely, down to its very middle, so as to interrupt all continuity of both white and gray matter between its upper and lower parts, irritation of the skin of the right side of the body, below the line of section, will give rise to as much pain as before, but all voluntary power will be lost in those muscles of that side, which are supplied by nerves coming off from the lower portion of the cord. Hence it follows, that the channels by which the afferent impulses are conveyed must cross over from the side of the cord which they enter to the opposite side; while the efferent impulses, sent down from the brain, must travel along that side of the cord by which they pass out.

If this be true, it is clear that a longitudinal section, taken through the exact middle of the cord, will greatly impair, if not destroy, the sensibility of both sides of the body below the section, but will leave the muscles under the control of the will. And it is found experimentally that such is very largely the case.

Section II.—*The Brain.*

327. The Vaso-motor Centres.—Such are the functions of the spinal cord, taken as a whole. The *spinal* nerves are, as we have said, chiefly distributed to the muscles and to the skin. The nerves of the blood-vessels, for instance, the so-called *vaso-motor* nerves (65), belong not to the spinal, but to the *sympathetic* system. Along the spinal column, however, the spinal nerves give off branches which run in and join the sympathetic system. And it appears that many at least of the fibres which run along in the sympathetic nerves going to blood-vessels, do really spring from the spinal cord, finding their way into the sympathetic system through these communicating or commissural branches.

Experiments, moreover, go to show that the nervous influence which keeps up the tone of the blood-vessels, that

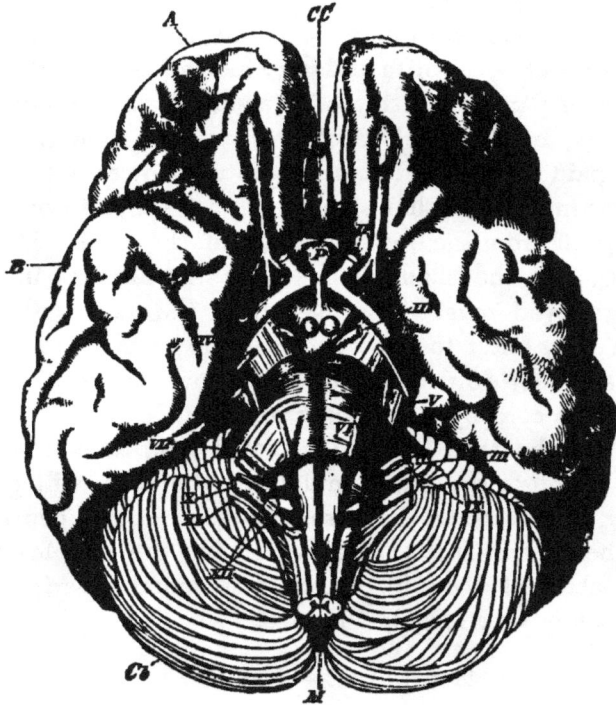

Fig. 108.

THE BASE OF THE BRAIN.

A, frontal lobe; *B*, temporal lobe of the cerebral hemispheres; *Cb*, cerebellum; *I.*, the olfactory nerve; *II.*, the optic nerve; *III.*, *IV.*, *VI.*, the nerves of the muscles of the eye; *V.*, the trigeminal nerve; *VII.*, the portio dura; *VIII.*, the auditory nerve *IX.*, the glossopharyngeal; *X.*, the pneumogastric: *XI.*, the spinal accessory; *XII.*, the hypoglossal, or motor nerve of the tongue. The number *VI.* is placed upon the *pons Varolii.* The *crura cerebri* are the broad bundles of fibres which lie between the third and the fourth nerves on each side. The medulla oblongata (*M*) is seen to be really a continuation of the spinal cord; on the lower end are seen the two crescents of gray matter; the section, in fact, has been carried through the spinal cord, a little below the proper medulla oblongata. From the sides of the medulla oblongata are seen coming off the *X.*, *XI.*, and *XII.* nerves; and just where the medulla is covered, so to speak, by the transversely disposed *pons Varolii*, are seen coming off the *VII.* nerve, and more towards the middle line the *VI.* Out of the substance of the *pons* springs the *V.* nerve. In front of that is seen the well-defined anterior border of the *pons;* and coming forward in front of that line, between the *IV.* and *III.* nerves, on either side, are seen the crura cerebri. The two round bodies in the angle between the diverging crura are the so-called *corpora albicantia*, and in front of them is *P*, the pituitary body. This rests on the chiasma, or junction, of the optic nerves; the continuation of each nerve is seen sweeping round the crura cerebri on either side. Immediately in front, between the separated frontal lobes of the cerebral hemispheres, is seen the corpus callosum, *CC*. The fissure of Sylvius, about on a level with *I.* on the left and *II.* on the right side, marks the division between frontal and temporal lobes.

is, which keeps them in the usual condition of moderate contraction, proceeds from the spinal cord.

The cord is, therefore, spoken of as containing *centres* for the vaso-motor nerves, or, more shortly, *vaso-motor centres.*

For example, the muscular walls of the blood-vessels supplying the ear and the skin of the head generally, are made to contract, as has been already mentioned, by nervous fibres derived immediately from the sympathetic. These fibres, however, do not arise from the sympathetic ganglia, but simply pass through them on their way from the spinal cord to the upper dorsal region of which they can all be traced. At least, this is the conclusion drawn from the facts, that irritation of this region of the cord produces the same effect as irritation of the vaso-motor nerves themselves, and that destruction of this part of the cord paralyzes them.

Recent researches, however, have shown that the nervous influence does not originate here, but proceeds from higher up, from the medulla oblongata in fact, and simply passes down through this part of the spinal cord on its way to join the sympathetic ganglia.

328. Outlines of Anatomy of the Brain. — The brain (Fig. 103) is a complex organ, consisting of several parts, the hindermost of which, termed *medulla oblongata*, passes insensibly into, and in its lower part has the same structure as, the spinal cord.

Above, however, it widens out, and the central canal, spreading with it, becomes a broad cavity, which (leaving certain anatomical minutiæ aside) may be said to be widely open above. This cavity is termed the *fourth ventricle.* Overhanging the fourth ventricle is a great laminated mass, the *cerebellum* (*Cb.*, Figs. 103, 104, 105). On each side, this organ sends down several layers of transverse fibres, which sweep across the brain and meet in the middle line of its base, forming a kind of bridge (called *pons Varolii*, Fig.

103), in front of the medulla oblongata. The longitudinal nerve-fibres of the medulla oblongata pass forwards, among, and between these layers of transverse fibres, and become visible, in front of the pons, as two broad diverging bundles, called *crura cerebri* (Fig. 103). Above the crura cere-

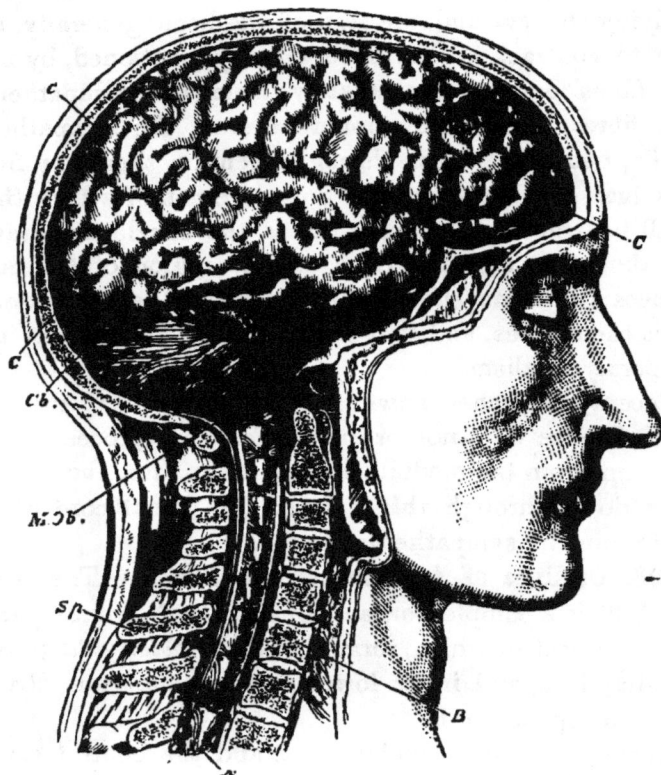

FIG. 104.

A side-view of the brain and upper part of the spinal cord in place—the parts which cover the cerebro-spinal centres being removed. *C. C.*, the convoluted surface of the right cerebral hemisphere; *Cb.*, the cerebellum; *M. Ob.*, the medulla oblongata; *B.*, the bodies of the cervical vertebræ; *Sp.*, their spines; *N.*, the spinal cord with the spinal nerves.

bri lies a mass of nervous matter raised up into four hemispherical elevations, called *corpora quadrigemina* (C.Q., Fig. 105). Between these and the crura cerebri is a narrow passage, which leads from the fourth ventricle into what is termed the *third ventricle* of the brain. The third ventricle is a narrow cavity lodged between two great masses of nervous matter, called *optic thalami*, into which the crura cerebri pass. The roof of the third ventricle is merely membranous; and a peculiar body of unknown function, the *pineal body*, is connected with it. The floor of the third ventricle is produced into a sort of funnel, which ends in another anomalous organ, the *pituitary body* (*Pt.*, Fig. 105; *P.*, Fig. 103).

The third ventricle is closed, in front, by a thin layer of nervous matter; but, beyond this, on each side, there is an aperture in the boundary wall of the third ventricle which leads into a large cavity. The latter occupies the centre of the *cerebral hemisphere*, and is called the *lateral ventricle*. Each hemisphere is enlarged backwards, downwards, and forwards, into as many *lobes ;* and the lateral ventricle presents corresponding prolongations, or *cornua*.

The floor of the lateral ventricle is formed by a mass of nervous matter called the *corpus striatum*, into which the fibres that have traversed the optic thalamus enter (Fig. 105, *C.S.*).

The hemispheres are so large that they overlap all the other parts of the brain, and, in the upper view, hide them.

Their applied faces are separated by a medium fissure for the greater part of their extent; but, inferiorly, are joined by a thick mass of transverse fibres, the *corpus callosum* (Fig. 103, *C.C.*).

The outer surfaces of the hemispheres are marked out into *convolutions*, or *gyri*, by numerous deep *fissures* (or *sulci*), into which the pia mater enters. One large and deep fissure, which separates the anterior from the middle division of the hemisphere is called the *fissure of Sylvius* (Fig. 103).

329. Arrangement of the White and Gray Matter.—In the *medulla oblongata* the arrangement of the white and gray matter is substantially similar to that which obtains in the spinal cord; that is to say, the white matter is external and the gray internal. But, in the *cerebellum* and *cerebral hemispheres,* the gray matter is external and the white internal; while, in the optic *thalami* and *corpora striata,* gray matter and white matter are variously intermixed.

SECTION III.—*The Cerebral Nerves.*

330. Their Distribution. — Nerves are given off from the brain in pairs, which succeed one another from before backwards, to the number of twelve (Fig. 105).

The *first pair,* counting from before backwards, are the *olfactory nerves,* and the *second* are the *optic* nerves. The functions of these have already been described.

The *third pair* are called *motores oculi* (movers of the eye), because they are distributed to all the muscles of the eye except two.

The nerves of the *fourth pair* and of the *sixth pair* supply each one of the muscles of the eye, on each side; the fourth going to the superior oblique muscle, and the sixth to the external rectus. Thus the muscles of the eye, small and close together as they are, receive their nervous stimulus by three distinct nerves.

Each nerve of the *fifth pair* is very large. It has two roots, a motor and a sensory, and further resembles a spinal nerve in having a ganglion on its sensory root. It is the nerve which supplies the skin of the face and the muscles of the jaws, and, having three chief divisions, is often called *trigeminal.* One branch, containing sensory fibres, supplies the front of the tongue, and is often spoken of as the *gustatory.*

The *seventh pair* furnish with motor nerves the muscles of the face, and some other muscles, and are called *facial.*

The *eighth pair* are the *auditory* nerves. As the seventh and eighth pairs of nerves leave the cavity of the skull together, they are often, and especially by English

writers on anatomy, reckoned as one, divided into *portio
dura*, or hard part (the facial); and *portio mollis*, or soft
part (the auditory) of the "seventh" pair.

The *ninth pair* in order, the *glossopharyngeal*, are
mixed nerves; each being, partly, a nerve of taste, and
supplying the back of the tongue, and, partly, a motor
nerve for the pharyngeal muscles.

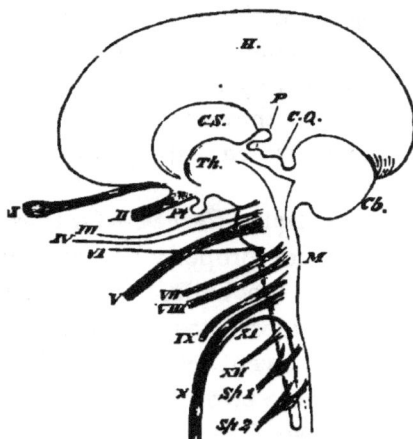

FIG. 105.

A DIAGRAM ILLUSTRATING THE ARRANGEMENT OF THE PARTS OF THE BRAIN AND
THE ORIGIN OF THE NERVES.

H., the cerebral hemispheres; *C.S.*, corpus striatum; *Th.*, optic thalamus; *P.*,
pineal body; *Pt.*, pituitary body; *C.Q.*, corpora quadrigemina; *Cb.*, cerebellum; *M.*,
medulla oblongata; *I.—XII.*, the pairs of cerebral nerves; *Sp.* 1, *Sp.* 2, the first and
second pairs of spinal nerves.

The *tenth pair* is formed by the two *pneumogastric*
nerves, often called the *par vagum*. These very important nerves, and the next pair, are the only cerebral nerves
which are distributed to regions of the body remote from
the head. The pneumogastric supplies the larynx, the
lungs, the liver, and the stomach, and branches of it are
connected with the heart.

The *eleventh pair*, again, called *spinal accessory*, differ
widely from all the rest, in arising from the sides of the

spinal marrow, between the anterior and posterior roots of
the dorsal nerves. They run up, gathering fibres as they
go, to the medulla oblongata, and then leave the skull by
the same aperture as the pneumogastric and glossopharyngeal. They are purely motor nerves, supplying certain
muscles of the neck, while the pneumogastric is mainly
sensory, or at least afferent. As, on each side, the glossopharyngeal, pneumogastric, and spinal accessory nerves,
leave the skull together, they are frequently reckoned as
one pair, which is then counted as the *eighth.*

The last two nerves, by this method of counting, become the *ninth* pair, but they are really the *twelfth.* They
are the motor nerves which supply the muscles of the
tongue.

331. Olfactory and Optic Nerves.—Of these nerves, the
two foremost pair do not properly deserve that name, but
are really processes of the brain. The olfactory pair are
prolongations of the cerebral hemispheres; the optic pair,
of the walls of the third ventricle; and it is worthy of remark, that it is only these two pair of what may be called
false nerves which arise from any part of the brain but
the medulla oblongata—all the other *true nerves* being
indirectly, or directly, traceable to that part of the brain,
while the olfactory and optic nerves are not so traceable.

332. Effects of Injuries to the Medulla Oblongata.—As
might be expected from this circumstance alone, the medulla oblongata is an extremely important part of the
cerebro-spinal axis, injury to it giving rise to immediate
evil consequences of the most serious kind.

Simple puncture of one side of the floor of the fourth
ventricle produces for a while an increase of the quantity
of sugar in the blood, beyond that which can be destroyed
in the organism. The sugar passes off by the kidneys,
and thus this slight injury to the medulla produces a
temporary disorder closely resembling the disease called
diabetes.

More extensive injury arrests the respiratory processes, the medulla oblongata being the nervous centre which gives rise to the contractions of the respiratory muscles and keeps the respiratory pump at work.

The motor nerves engaged in ordinary respiration are certain spinal nerves, viz., the intercostal nerves supplying the intercostal muscles, and the *phrenic* nerve supplying the diaphragm. These motor nerves are undoubtedly brought into action by impulses proceeding at intervals from the medulla oblongata. But how these rhythmic impulses originate in the medulla oblongata is not very clear. There are reasons for thinking that the presence of venous blood in the lungs acts as a stimulus to the endings of the pneumogastric nerves, and sets going impulses which, traveling up along those nerves to the medulla oblongata, there produce respiratory movements by reflex action. But this is not all, for respiration, though profoundly modified, is not arrested by division or destruction of the pneumogastric nerves. Probably the medulla oblongata contains a nervous mechanism which acts as an independent centre in a manner somewhat similar to the ganglia of the heart; and so goes on of itself, though extremely sensitive to, and thus continually influenced by, the condition of the blood not only in the lungs but all over the body.

If the injuries to the medulla oblongata be of such a kind as to irritate the roots of the pneumogastric nerve violently, death supervenes by the stoppage of the heart's action in the manner already described. (*See* 69.)

333. Crossing of Impulses in the Medulla.—The afferent impulses, which are transmitted through the cord to the brain and awake sensation there, cross, as we have seen, from one half of the cord to the other, immediately after they enter it by the posterior roots of the spinal nerves; while the efferent, or volitional, impulses from the brain remain, throughout the cord, in that half of it from which they will eventually pass by the anterior roots. But, at the lower and front part of the medulla oblongata, these also cross over; and the white fibres which convey them are seen passing obliquely from left to right and from right to left in what is called the *decussation of the anterior pyramids* (Fig. 103). Hence, any injury, at a point higher up than the decussation, to the nerve-fibres which convey motor impulses from the brain, paralyzes the muscles of the body and limbs of the opposite side.

Division, therefore, of one of the *crura cerebri*, say the right, gives rise to paralysis of the left side of the body and limbs, and the animal operated upon falls over to the left side, because the limbs of that side are no longer able to support the weight.

But, as the motor nerves given off from the brain itself and arising from the medulla above the decussation of the pyramids do not cross over in this way, it follows, that disease or injury at a given point, on one side of the medulla oblongata, involving at once the course of the volitional motor channels to the spinal marrow, and the origins of the cranial motor nerves, will affect the same side of the head as that of the injury, but the opposite side of the body.

If the origin of the left facial nerve, for example, be injured, and the volitional motor fibres going to the cord destroyed, in the upper part of the medulla oblongata, the muscles of the face of the left side will be paralyzed, and the features will be drawn over to the opposite side, the muscles of the right side having nothing to counteract their action. But it is the right arm, and the right leg and side of the body, which will be powerless.

SECTION IV.— *Unconscious Cerebration.*

334. Seat of Intelligence and Will.—The functions of most of the parts of the brain which lie in front of the medulla oblongata are, at present, very ill understood; but it is certain that extensive injury, or removal, of the cerebral hemispheres puts an end to intelligence and voluntary movement, and leaves the animal in the condition of a machine, working by the reflex action of the remainder of the cerebro-spinal axis.

We have seen that in the frog the movements of the body which the spinal cord alone, in the absence of the whole of the brain including the medulla oblongata, is capable of executing, are of themselves strikingly complex and varied. But none of these movements are voluntary or spontaneous; they never occur unless the animal be stimulated. Removal of the cerebral hemispheres is alone sufficient to deprive the frog of all spontaneous or voluntary movements; but the presence of the medulla oblongata and other parts of the brain (such as the corpora quadrigemina, or what corresponds to them in the frog, and the cerebellum) renders the animal master of movements of a far higher nature than when the spinal cord only is left. In the latter case the animal does not breathe when left to itself, lies flat on the table with its fore-limbs beneath it in an unnatural position; when irritated kicks out its legs, and may be thrown into actual convulsions, but never jumps from place to place; when thrown into a basin of water falls to the bottom like a lump of lead, and when placed on its back will remain so, without making any effort to turn over. In the former case the animal sits on the table, resting on its front-limbs, in the position natural to a frog; breathes quite naturally; when pricked behind jumps away, often getting over quite a considerable distance; when thrown into water begins at once to swim, and continues swimming until it finds some object on which it can rest; and when placed on its back immediately turns over and resumes its natural position. Not only so, but the following very striking experiment may be performed with it: Placed on a small board it remains perfectly motionless so long as the board is horizontal; if, however, the board be gradually tilted up so as to raise the animal's head, directly the board becomes inclined at such an angle as to throw the frog's centre of gravity too much backwards, the creature begins slowly to creep up the board, and, if the board continues to be inclined, will at last reach the edge, upon which when the board becomes vertical he will seat himself with apparent great content. Nevertheless, though his movements when they do occur are extremely well combined and apparently identical with those of a frog possessing the whole of his brain, he never moves spontaneously, and never stirs unless irritated.

There can be no doubt that the cerebral hemispheres are the seat of powers essential to the production of those phenomena which we term intelligence and will; but there is no satisfactory proof, at present, that the manifestation of any particular kind of mental faculty is especially allotted to, or connected with, the activity of any particular region of the cerebral hemispheres.

335. Reflex Action of the Brain.—Even while the cerebral hemispheres are entire, and in full possession of their powers, the brain gives rise to actions which are as completely reflex as those of the spinal cord.

When the eyelids wink at a flash of light, or a threatened blow, a reflex action takes place, in which the afferent nerves are the optic, the efferent the facial. When a bad smell causes a grimace, there is a reflex action through the same motor nerve, while the olfactory nerves constitute the afferent channels. In these cases, therefore, reflex action must be effected through the brain, all the nerves involved being cerebral.

When the whole body starts at a loud noise, the afferent auditory nerve gives rise to an impulse which passes to the medulla oblongata, and thence affects the great majority of the motor nerves of the body.

336. Reflex Actions in reading aloud.—It may be said

that these are mere mechanical actions, and have nothing
to do with the operations which we associate with intelligence. But let us consider what takes place in such an
act as reading aloud. In this case, the whole attention of
the mind is, or ought to be, bent upon the subject-matter
of the book; while a multitude of most delicate muscular
actions are going on, of which the reader is not in the
slightest degree aware. Thus the book is held in the
hand, at the right distance from the eyes; the eyes are
moved from side to side, over the lines and up and down
the pages. Further, the most delicately-adjusted and
rapid movements of the muscles of the lips, tongue, and
throat, of the laryngeal and respiratory muscles, are involved in the production of speech. Perhaps the reader
is standing up and accompanying the lecture with appropriate gestures. And yet every one of these muscular acts
may be performed with utter unconsciousness, on his part,
of any thing but the sense of the words in the book. In
other words, they are reflex acts.

337. Artificial Reflex Actions—Education. — The reflex
actions proper to the spinal cord itself are *natural*, and are
involved in the structure of the cord and the properties of
its constituents. By the help of the brain we may acquire
an infinity of *artificial* reflex actions; that is to say, an action may require all our attention and all our volition for
its first, or second, or third performance, but by frequent
repetition it becomes, in a manner, part of our organization, and is performed without volition, or even consciousness.

As every one knows, it takes a soldier a long time to
learn his drill—for instance, to put himself into the attitude
of "attention" at the instant the word of command is
heard. But, after a time, the sound of the word gives rise
to the act, whether the soldier be thinking of it or not.
There is a story, which is credible enough, though it may
not be true, of a practical joker, who, seeing a discharged

veteran carrying home his dinner, suddenly called out " Attention !" whereupon the man instantly brought his hands down, and lost his mutton and potatoes in the gutter. The drill had been thorough, and its effects had become embodied in the man's nervous structure.

The possibility of all education (of which military drill is only one particular form) is based upon the existence of this power which the nervous system possesses, of organizing conscious actions into more or less unconscious, or reflex, operations. It may be laid down as a rule that, if any two mental states be called up together, or in succession, with due frequency and vividness, the subsequent production of the one of them will suffice to call up the other, and that whether we desire it or not.

The object of intellectual education is to create such indissoluble associations of our ideas of things, in the order and relation in which they occur in Nature; that of a moral education is to unite as fixedly, the ideas of evil deeds with those of pain and degradation, and of good actions with those of pleasure and nobleness.

338. The Sympathetic System. — The *sympathetic system* consists chiefly of a double chain of ganglia, lying at the sides and in front of the spinal column, and connected with one another, and with the spinal nerves, by commissural cords. From these ganglia, nerves are given off which for the most part follow the distribution of the vessels, but which, in the thorax and abdomen, form great net-works, or *plexuses*, upon the heart and about the stomach. It is probable that a great proportion of the fibres of the sympathetic system is derived from the spinal cord; but others also, in all probability, originate in the ganglia of the sympathetic itself. The sympathetic nerves influence the muscles of the vessels generally, and those of the heart, of the intestines, and of some other viscera: and it is probable that their ganglia are centres of reflex action to afferent nerves from these organs. But many of the motor nerves of the vessels are, as we have seen, under the influence of particular parts of the spinal cord, though they pass through sympathetic ganglia.

CHAPTER XII.

HISTOLOGY; OR, THE MINUTE STRUCTURE OF THE TISSUES.

SECTION I.—*Dermal Tissues.*

339. The Microscopical Analysis of the Body. — The various organs and parts of the body, the working of which has now been described, are not merely separable by the eye and the knife of the anatomist into membranes, nerves, muscles, bones, cartilages, and so forth; but each of them is, by the help of the microscope, susceptible of a finer analysis, into certain minute constituents which, for the present, may be considered the ultimate structural elements of the body.

340. Nuclei and Cells.—There is a time when the human body, or rather its rudiment, is of one structure throughout, consisting of a more or less transparent *matrix*, very similar in nature to the substance of which the white blood-corpuscles are composed, and often called *protoplasm*, through which are scattered minute rounded particles of a different optical aspect. These particles are called *nuclei ;* and as the matrix, or matter in which these nuclei are embedded, readily breaks up into spheroidal masses, one for each nucleus, and these investing masses easily take on the form of vesicles or *cells*, this primitive structure is called *cellular*, and each cell is said to be *nucleated.*

The material of the body when in this stage of growth is often spoken of as *indifferent tissue.* A very fair idea of its nature may be formed by supposing a multitude of

14

white blood-corpuscles to be collected together into a soft
but yet semi-solid mass.

In the present use of the term any distinct mass cf protoplasm or living material may be called a *cell.* In the
vast majority of cases, however, the cell contains a *nucleus,*
distinguished, as has just been said, from the *cell-substance*
in which it lies. Very frequently, but by no means always,
the outer layer of the cell-substance is hardened into a distinct casing or envelope, the *cell-wall,* the cell then becoming an undeniable vesicle, and the cell-substance being often
spoken of as the *cell-contents.* The cell-substance may remain as soft semi-solid protoplasm, or may be hardened in
various ways, or may be wholly or partially liquefied; in
the latter case a cell-wall is naturally always present.

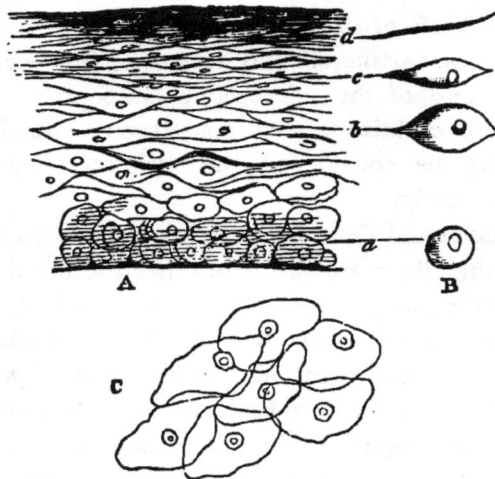

FIG. 106.

A, vertical section of a layer of epidermis, or epithelium, from its free to its deep
surface.   B, lateral views of the cells of which this layer is composed at different
heights; *a*, cell in the deepest layer, and therefore most recently formed and least
altered; *b*, cell higher up, and therefore somewhat changed; *c, d,* cells still more
changed, and much flattened. C, scales such as *d* viewed from their flat side. (Magnified about two hundred and fifty diameters.)

As development goes on, the nuclei simply increase in
number by division and subdivision, without undergoing

any marked change;[1] but the substance in which they are embedded becomes very variously modified, both chemically and structurally, and gives rise to those peculiarities by which completely formed tissues are distinguished from one another.

341. Epidermis and Epithelium.—In the adult body the simplest forms of tissue, i. e., those in which the matrix has been least changed, are perhaps the various kinds of *epithelium* (including the *epidermis*).

These are distinctly *cellular* in nature—that is, the portion of the matrix belonging to each nucleus can, with a little pains, be recognized as distinct from the portions belonging to the other nuclei. In fact, they differ from white blood-corpuscles chiefly in two points: firstly, the matrix of each cell becomes more or less chemically changed so as to lose its soft protoplasmic nature (and, at the same time, its power of executing amœboid movements); and, secondly, takes on a rigid definite form, which may or may not be globular. These epithelial tissues are constantly growing in their deepest parts, and are, as constantly, being shed at their surfaces.

The deep part consists of a layer of such globular, nucleated cells as have been mentioned, the number of which is constantly increasing by the spontaneous division of the nuclei and cells. The increase in number thus effected causes a thrusting of the excess of cell-population towards the surface; on their way to which they become flattened, and their walls acquire a horny texture. Arrived at the surface, they are mere dead horny scales, and are thrown off (Fig. 106).

Epithelium of the kind just described is called *squamous*. It is found in the mouth, and its scales may always be obtained in abundance by scraping the inside of the lip.

---

[1] Each nucleus divides into two, and each half soon grows up into the size of the parent nucleus. While this is going on, the matrix round the nuclei also divides, each new nucleus having a quantity of matrix allotted to it, so as to form a new cell exactly like the old one, from which it sprang.

Epidermis consists of exactly similar cells, except that the conversion of the topmost cells into horny scales is still more complete. The nucleus, too, is eventually lost. The deep layers of epidermis, consisting of softer cells not yet flattened or made horny, often form quite a distinct part, and these are often spoken of as the *rete mucosum.* (*See* Fig. 40, *b ;* Fig. 110, *d*).

In other parts of the alimentary tract, as in the intestines, the full-grown epithelial cells are placed side by side

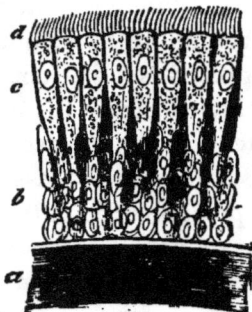

FIG. 107.

CILIATED EPITHELIUM.

a, the submucous vascular tissue; *b*, the deep layer of young epithelium-cells; *c*, the cylindrical full-grown cells, with (*d*) the cilia. (Magnified about three hundred and fifty diameters.)

with one another, and perpendicular to the surface of the membrane. Such epithelium is called *cylindrical* (Fig. 55, *b, b'*), or *columnar.*

In some places, such as in the gastric glands, in some parts of the kidney, in the ureters and elsewhere, the epithelial cells remain *globular* or *spheroidal.*

Squamous epithelium generally consists of many layers of cells, one over the other; in other forms of epithelium there are few, in some cases apparently only two, layers.

Ciliated epithelium is usually of the cylindrical kind, and differs from other epithelium only in the circumstance that one or more incessantly vibrating filaments are developed from the free surface of each cell. (*See* 196.)

342. Nails.—In certain regions of the integument, the epidermis becomes metamorphosed into *nails* and *hairs*.

Underneath each nail the deep or *dermic* layer of the integument is peculiarly modified to form the *bed of the*

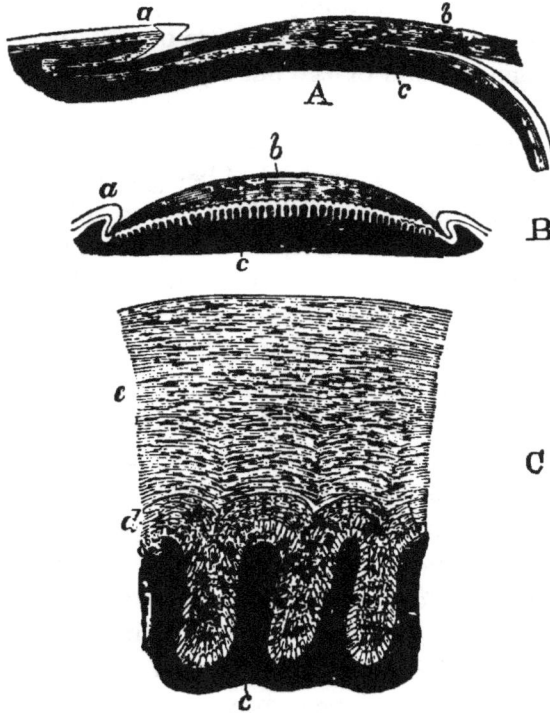

Fɪɢ. 110.

Fig. 108.—A longitudinal and vertical section of a nail: *a*, the fold at the base of the nail; *b*, the nail; *c*, the bed of the nail.

Fig. 109 is a transverse section of the same: *a*, a small lateral fold of the integument; *b*, nail; *c*, bed of the nail, with its ridges.

Fig. 110 is a highly-magnified view of a part of the foregoing: *c*, the ridges; *d*, the deep layers of epidermis; *e*, the horny scales coalesced into nail-substance.

(Figs. 108 and 109 magnified about four diameters; Fig. 110 magnified about two hundred diameters.)

nail. It is very vascular, and raised up into numerous parallel ridges, like elongated papillæ (Figs. 109, 110). The surfaces of all these are covered with growing epidermic cells, which, as they flatten and become converted into

horn, coalesce into a solid continuous plate, the nail. At
the hinder part of the bed of the nail, the integument forms
a deep fold, from the bottom of which, in like manner, new
epidermic cells are added to the base of the nail, which is
thus constrained to move forward.

The nail, thus constantly receiving additions from below and from behind, slides forwards over its bed, and projects beyond the end of the finger, where it is worn away,
or cut off.

343. Hairs.—A *hair*, like a nail, is composed of coalesced horny cells; but, instead of being only partially sunk
in a fold of the integument, it is at first wholly inclosed in
a kind of bag, the *hair-sac*, from the bottom of which a
papilla (Fig. 111, *i*), which answers to a single ridge of the
nail, arises. The hair is developed by the conversion into
horn, and coalescence into a *shaft*, of the superficial epidermic cells coating the papilla. These coalesced and
cornified cells being continually replaced by new growths
from below, which undergo the same metamorphosis, the
shaft of the hair is thrust out until it attains the full length
natural to it. Its base then ceases to grow, and the old
papilla and sac die away, but not before a new sac and papilla have been formed by budding from the sides of the
old one. These give rise to a new hair. The shaft of a
hair of the head consists of a central pith, or *medullary*
matter, of a loose and open texture, which sometimes contains air; of a *cortical* substance surrounding this, made
up of coalesced elongated horny cells; and of an outer
cuticle, composed of flat horny plates, arranged transversely
round the shaft, so as to overlap one another by their outer
edges, like closely-packed tiles. The superficial epidermic
cells of the hair-sac also coalesce by their edges, and become converted into *root-sheaths*, which embrace the root
of the hair, and usually come away with it, when it is
plucked out.

Two sebaceous glands commonly open into the hair-sac

near its opening, and supply the hair with a kind of natural pomatum; and delicate unstriped muscular fibres are so connected with the hair-sac as to cause it to pass from its ordinary oblique position into one perpendicular to the skin, when they contract (Fig. 39).

They are made to contract by the influence of cold and

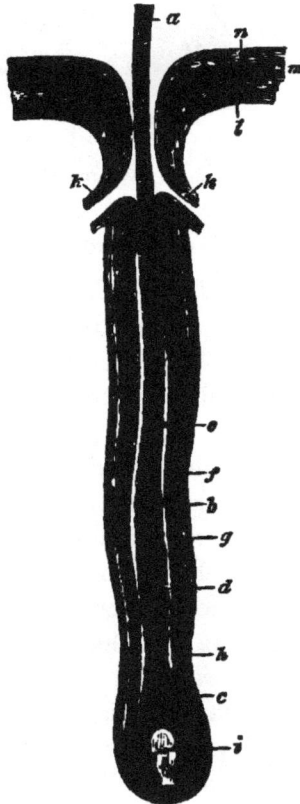

FIG. 111.

A HAIR IN ITS HAIR-SAC.

a, shaft of hair above the skin; *b*, cortical substance of the shaft, the medulla not being visible; *c*, newest portion of hair growing on the papilla (*i*); *d*, cuticle of hair; *e*, cavity of hair-sac; *f*, epidermis (and root-sheaths) of the hair-sac corresponding to that of the integument (*m*); *g*, division between dermis and epidermis; *h*, dermis of hair-sac corresponding to dermis of integument (*l*); *k*, mouths of sebaceous glands; *n*, horny epidermis of integument.

terror, which thus give rise to "horripilation," or "goose-skin," and the "standing of the hair on end."

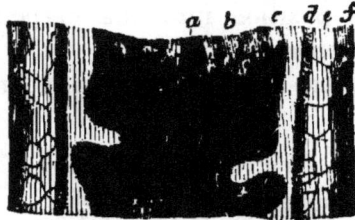

FIG. 112.

Part of the shaft of a hair inclosed within its root-sheaths and treated with caustic soda, which has caused the shaft to become distorted : *a*, medulla ; *b*, cortical substance ; *c*, cuticle of the shaft ; from *d* to *f*, the root-sheaths, in section. (Magnified about two hundred diameters.)

SECTION II. —*Interior Tissues.*

344. The Crystalline Lens.—The *crystalline lens* is composed of fibres, which are the modified cells of the epidermis of that inverted portion of the integument from which the whole anterior chamber of the eye and the lens are primitively formed.

345. Cartilage.—While *epithelium* and *epidermis* are found only on the free surfaces of the organs, gristle, or cartilage, is a deep-seated structure (*see* 210, 211). Like them it is essentially cellular in nature, but differs from them widely in appearance on account of the development of a large quantity of the so-called *intercellular* substance. That is to say, the several cells do not lie closely packed together and touching each other, but are separated from each other by a quantity of material of a different nature from themselves. Just as in indifferent tissue each nucleus is embedded in a matrix of protoplasm, so in cartilage, each cell, i. e., *each nucleus with its allotted quantity of protoplasm*, is embedded in a matrix of *intercellular substance.*

Inasmuch as during the growth of cartilage the cells remain soft and protoplasmic, while the intercellular substance is converted into a solid semi-transparent hard matter, it comes to pass that the soft nucleated cells appear to lie in cavities in the harder intercellular substance or matrix.

In epithelium it is only the deepest-lying cells which undergo division, and so carry on the growth of the tissue. In cartilage, cell-division is much more general; a cell lying in its cavity divides first into two, then into four, and so on, the intercellular substance meanwhile growing in between the young cells and thrusting them apart. It is by means of the repeated divisions of the cells in this way, and subsequent development of intercellular matrix in between the young cells, that cartilage grows. Conse-

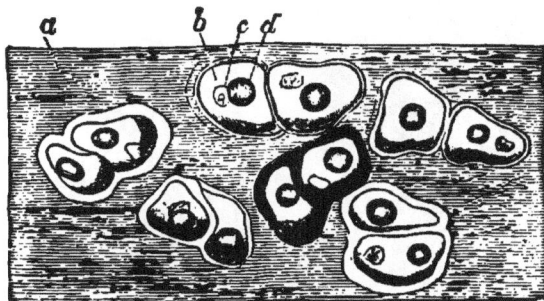

FIG. 113.

A section of cartilage, showing the matrix (*a*), with the groups of cells (*b*) containing nuclei (*c*) and fat-globules (*d*). (Magnified about three hundred and fifty diameters.)

quently, the cells are frequently seen arranged in groups with more or less matrix between, according to their age.

The cells remain during life soft and protoplasmic, but often contain a number of large oil-globules. It is to the hard matrix which yields, on boiling, the substance *chondrine*, that the physical features of cartilage, its solidity and elasticity, are due. Cartilage contains no vessels, or only such as extend a little way into it from adjacent parts.

346. Connective Tissue.— *Connective tissue* (also called *fibrous*, or *areolar*, or sometimes *cellular* tissue), the most extensively diffused of all in the body, at first sight seems to differ wholly from the preceding tissues. Viewed under the microscope, it is seen to consist of bands or cords, or sheets of whitish substance, having a wavy, fibrous appearance, and capable of being split up mechanically into innumerable fine filaments or *fibrillæ*. The addition of acetic acid causes it to swell up and become transparent, entirely

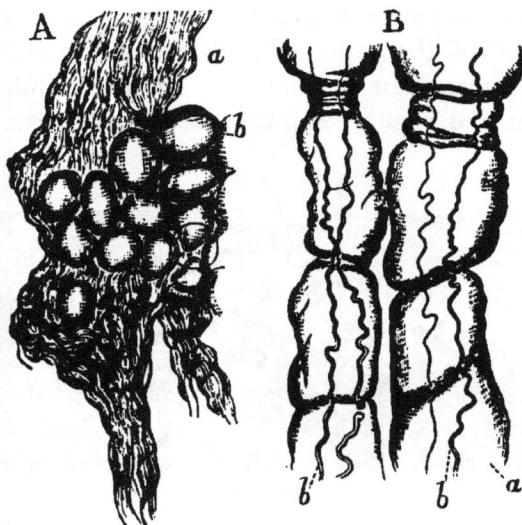

FIG. 114.

CONNECTIVE TISSUE.

A, unchanged: *a*, connective tissue; *b*, fat-cells. B, acted upon by acetic acid. and showing (*a*) the swollen and transparent gelatine-yielding matter, and (*b*) the elastic fibres. (Magnified about three hundred diameters.)

losing its fibrous aspect; and, further, reveals the presence of two elements which acetic acid does not affect, viz., nuclei and certain sharply-defined fibres of different degrees of fineness, which are called elastic fibres. If the acid be now very carefully neutralized by a weak alkali, the connective tissue assumes its former partial opacity and fibrillated aspect. The nuclei thus brought to light by acetic acid are worthy of attention, because careful examination shows that they belong to certain cells which exist in all connective tissue in greater or less number, though never in abundance. These cells, generally called *connective-tissue corpuscles*, consist of a nucleus and protoplasmic cell-substance, and in fact are not unlike cartilage-cells except that they are very often very irregular in form, and as a general rule very small. Indeed, we may very justly compare connective tissue with cartilage, much as they seem to differ in general appearance. The connective-tissue corpuscles

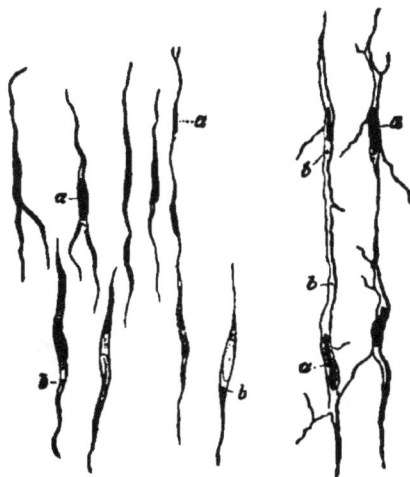

Fig. 115.

Connective-tissue corpuscles (*a*, nucleus, *b*, cell-substances), of various shapes, those to the right hand branching, and the branches joining.

correspond to the cartilage-cells; both are embedded in a matrix which, in the case of cartilage, remains structureless, but becomes solid and dense, while it, in the case of connective tissue, is altered or metamorphosed, as it is said, into a substance composed of excessively fine filaments, mingled with which are elastic fibres.

The fine fibrillated substance is not very elastic, and when boiled swells up and yields *gelatine*. The elastic fibres do not yield gelatine, and, as their name indicates, are highly elastic. The proportion of elastic fibre to the gelatine-yielding constituents of connective tissue varies in different parts of the body. Sometimes it is so great that elasticity is the most marked character of the resulting tissue.

347. Ligaments and Tendons.—*Ligaments* and *tendons* are simply cords, or bands, while *fasciæ* are sheets of very dense connective tissue. In some parts of the body, the connective tissue is more or less mixed with, or passes into, cartilage, and such tissues are called *fibro-cartilages* (*see* Chapter VII.), or, in other words, the matrix of the cartilage becomes more or less fibrillated, thus indicating the analogies of the two tissues.

The name *cellular* applied to this tissue is apt to lead to confusion. When first used it referred to the cavities left in the meshes of the net-work of fibres; it has nothing whatever to do with *cells* technically so called.

348. Fat-Cells.—*Fat-cells* are scattered through the

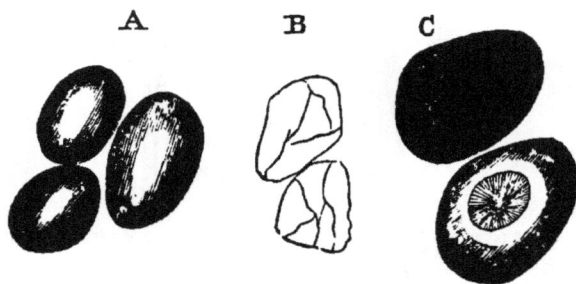

Fig. 116.
FAT-CELLS.

A, having their natural aspect. B, collapsed, the fat being exhausted. C, with fatty crystals. The nuclei are not seen in this case. (Magnified about three hundred and fifty diameters.)

connective tissue, in which they sometimes accumulate in great quantities. They are spheroidal sacs, composed of a delicate membrane, on one side of which is a nucleus, and distended by fatty matter, from which the more solid fats sometimes crystallize out after death. Ether will dissolve out the fat, and leave the sacs empty and collapsed (B, Fig. 116).

They are, in fact, cells with a distinct cell-wall, the cell-contents or cell-substance of which have been wholly, or all but wholly, converted into fat.

Considerable aggregations of fat-cells are constantly present in some parts of the body, as in the orbit, and

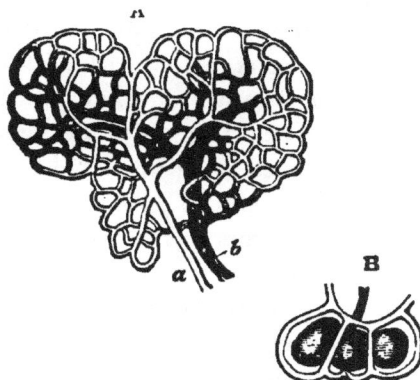

FIG. 117.

CAPILLARIES OF FAT.

A, net-work round a group of fat-cells: *a*, the artery; *b*, the vein. B, the loops of capillaries round three individual fat-cells.

about the kidneys and heart; but elsewhere their presence, in any quantity, depends very much on the state of nutrition. Indeed, they may be regarded simply as a reserve, formed from the nutriment which has been taken into the body in excess of its average consumption.

349. Pigment-Cells.—*Pigment-cells* are either epidermic or epithelial cells, in which colored granules are deposited, or they are connective-tissue corpuscles of the deeper parts of the body, in which a like deposit occurs. Thus the color of the choroid arises partly from the presence of a layer of epithelial cells (*see* Fig. 93), placed close to the retina, containing pigment-granules, and partly from a large number of irregularly-shaped, connective-tissue corpuscles crammed with pigment, which belong to the deeper connective-tissue layer of the choroid. The pigment-cells of the frog's web are essentially connective-tissue corpuscles.

SECTION III.—*Osseous Tissues.*

350. Structure of Bone.—*Bone* is essentially composed of an animal basis impregnated with salts of carbonate and phosphate of lime, through the substance of which are scattered minute cavities — the *lacunæ*, which send out multitudinous ramifications, called *canaliculi*. The canaliculi of different lacunæ unite together, and thus establish a communication between the different lacunæ. If the earthy matter be extracted by dilute acids, a nucleus may be found in each lacuna ; and, if young, fresh bone be carefully examined, a certain amount of cell-substance will be found filling up the lacuna round the nucleus ; and, not unfrequently, the intermediate substance appears minutely fibrillated. In fact bone, if we lay on one side the earthy matters, presents very close analogies in its fundamental structure with both cartilage and connective tissue. The corpuscles lodged in the lacunæ correspond to the corpuscles of connective tissue and to the cells of cartilage, while the matrix in which the earthy matter is deposited corresponds to the matrix of cartilage, and to the fibrillated material of connective tissue. (These three tissues, indeed, are often classed together as " the connective-tissue group.") In a dry bone the lacunæ are usually filled with air. When a thin section of such a bone is, as usual, covered with water and a thin glass, and placed under the microscope, the air in the lacunæ refracts the light which passes through them in such a manner as to prevent its reaching the eye, and they appear black. Hence the lacunæ were, at one time, supposed to be solid bodies, containing the lime-salts of the bone, and were called *bone-corpuscles* (Fig. 118, C).

All bones, except the smallest, are traversed by small canals, converted by side-branches into a net-work, and containing vessels supported by more or less connective tissue and fatty matter. These are called *Haversian canals* (Fig. 118, A, B). They always open, in the long-run, upon the surface of the bone, and there the vessels which they contain become connected with those of a sheet of tough connective tissue, which invests the bone, and is called *periosteum*.

In many long bones, such as the thigh-bone, the centre of the bone is hollowed out into a considerable cavity, containing great quantities of fat, supported by a delicate connective tissue, rich in blood-vessels, and called the *marrow*, or *medulla*. The inner ends of the Haversian canals communicate with this cavity, and their vessels are continuous with those of the marrow.

When a section of a bone containing Haversian canals is made, it is found that the lacunæ are dispersed in concentric zones around each Haversian canal, so that the substance of the bone appears laminated ; and, where a medullary cavity exists, more or fewer of these concentric lamellæ of osseous substance surround it.

351. How Bones grow.—This structure arises from the mode of growth of bones. In the place of every bone there exists, at first, either cartilage, or connective tissue hardly altered from its primitive condition of indifferent tissue. When *ossification* commences, the vessels from the adjacent parts extend into the ossifying tissue, and the calcareous salts are thrown down around them. These calcareous salts invade all the ossifying tissue, except the immediate neighborhood of its nuclei, around each of which a space, the *lacuna*, is left. The lacunæ and canaliculi are thus, substantially, gaps left in the ossific matter around each nucleus, whence it is that nuclei are found in the lacunæ of fully-formed bone.[1]

---

[1] For the sake of simplicity I purposely omit all mention of the complex secondary processes in the ossification of cartilage.

Bone, once formed, does not remain during life, but is constantly disappearing and being replaced in all its parts.

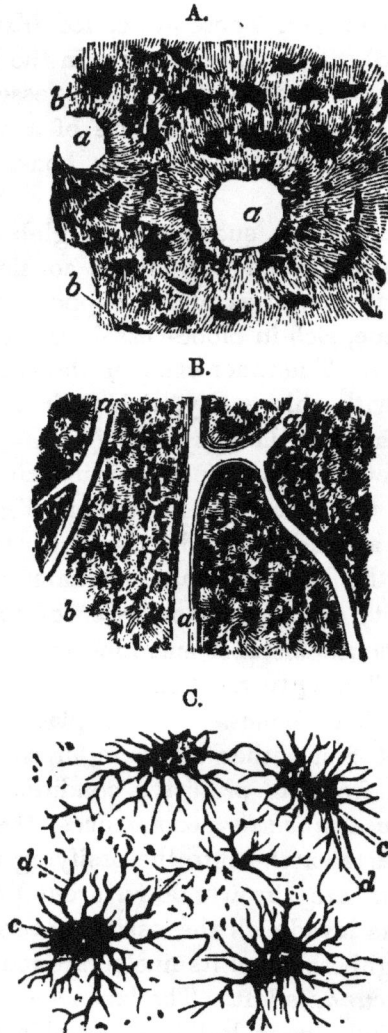

FIG. 118.

A.—A transverse section of bone in the neighborhood of two Haversian canals, *a, a*; *b*, lacunæ. (Magnified about two hundred and fifty diameters.)

B.—A longitudinal section of bone with Haversian canals, *a, a*, and lacunæ, *b*. (Magnified about one hundred diameters.)

C.—Lacunæ, *c*, and canaliculi, *d*. (Magnified about six hundred diameters.)

Nevertheless, the growth of a bone, as a general rule, takes place only by addition to its free ends and surfaces. Thus the bones of the skull grow in thickness, on their surfaces, and in breadth at their edges, where they unite by *sutures ;* and, when the sutures are once closed, they cease to increase in breadth.

The bones of the limbs, which are preceded by complete small cartilaginous models, grow in two ways. The cartilage of which they consist grows and enlarges at its extremities until the bones have attained their full size, and remains to the end of life as *articular cartilage.* But, in the middle, or shaft, of the bone, the cartilage does not grow with the increase in the dimensions of the bone, but the small primary bone which results from the ossification of the cartilaginous model becomes coated by successive layers of bone, produced by the ossification of that part of the periosteum which lies nearest to it, and which really consists of indifferent tissue—that is, of nuclei embedded in a matrix. The shaft of the bone thus formed is gradually hollowed out in its interior to form the medullary cavity, so that, at last, the primitive cartilage totally disappears.

When ossification sets in, the salts of lime are not diffused uniformly through the whole mass of the preëxisting cartilage, or connective tissue, but begin to be deposited at particular points called *centres of ossification,* and spread from them through the bone. Thus, a long bone has usually, at fewest, three centres of ossification—one for the middle, or shaft, and one for each end; and it is only in adult life that the three bony masses thus formed unite into one bone.

352. Structure of the Teeth. — *Teeth* partake more of the nature of bones than of any other organ, and are, in fact, partially composed of true bony matter, here called *cement ;* but their chief constituents are two other tissues, called *dentine* and *enamel.*

Each tooth presents a crown, which is exposed to wear, and one or more fangs, which are buried in a socket furnished by the jaw-bone and the dense mucous membrane of the mouth, which constitutes the *gum*. The line of junction between the crown and the fang is the *neck* of the tooth. In the interior of the tooth is a cavity, which communicates with the exterior by canals, which traverse the fangs and open at their points. This cavity is the *pulp cavity*. It is occupied by a highly-vascular and nervous tissue, the *dental pulp*, which is continuous below, through the openings of the fangs, with the mucous membrane of the gum.

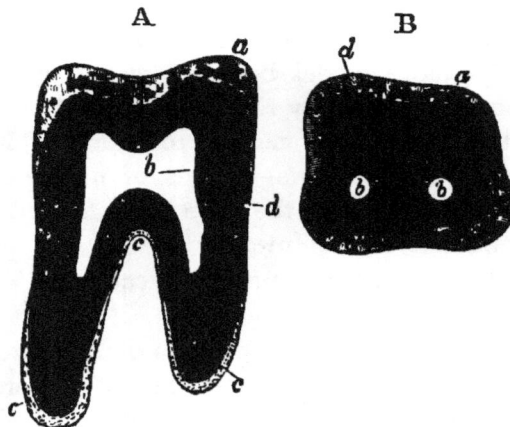

FIG. 119.

A, vertical, B, horizontal section of a tooth: *a*, enamel of the crown; *b*, pulp cavity; *c*, cement of the fangs, *d*, dentine. (Magnified about three diameters.)

The chief constituent of a tooth is *dentine*—a dense calcified substance containing less animal matter than bone, and further differing from it in possessing no lacunæ, or proper canaliculi. Instead of these it presents innumerable, minute, parallel, wavy, tubules, which give off lateral branches. The wider ends of these tubules open into the pulp cavity, while the narrower ultimate terminations ramify at the surface of the dentine, and may even extend into the enamel or cement (Fig. 120, C).

The *enamel* consists of very small six sided fibres, set closely, side by side, nearly at right angles to the surface of the dentine, and covering the crown of the tooth as far as the neck, towards which the enamel thins off and joins the cement (Fig. 120, A, B).

Enamel is the hardest tissue of the body, and contains not more than two per cent. of animal matter.

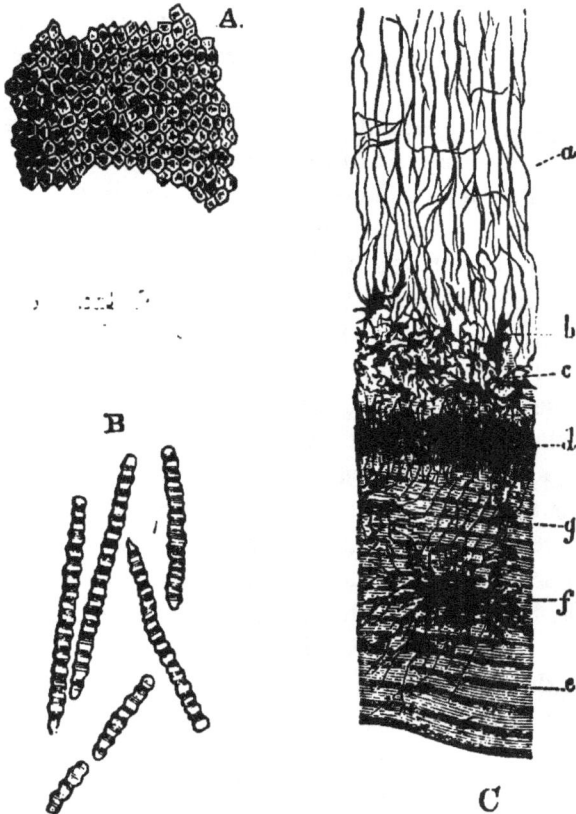

Fig. 120.

A.—Enamel fibres viewed in transverse section.
B.—Enamel fibres separated and viewed laterally.
C.—A section of a tooth at the junction of the dentine (*a*) with the cement (*e*); *b, c,* irregular cavities in which the tubules of the dentine end; *d,* fine tubules continued from them; *f, g,* lacunæ and canaliculi of the cement. (Magnified about four hundred diameters.)

The *cement* coats the fangs, and has the structure of true bone; but, as it exists only in a thin layer, it is devoid of Haversian canals (Fig. 120, C).

353. How Teeth are developed.—The development of the teeth commences long before birth. A groove appears in the gum of each side of each jaw; and, at the bottom of this groove of the gum, five vascular and nervous *papillæ* arise, making twenty in all. The walls of the groove grow together, between and over each of the papillæ, and thus these become inclosed in what are called the *dental sacs*.

Each papilla gradually assumes the form of the future tooth. Next, a deposit of calcific matter takes place at the summit of the papillæ, and extends thence downwards towards its base. In the crown the deposit takes on the form of enamel and dentine; in the root, of dentine and cement. As it increases it encroaches upon the substance of the papilla, which remains as the tooth pulp. The fully-formed teeth press upon the upper walls of the sacs in which they are inclosed, and, causing a more or less complete absorption of these walls, force their way through. The teeth are then, as it is called, *cut*.

The cutting of this first set of teeth, called *deciduous*, or *milk-teeth*, commences at about six months, and ends with the second year. They are altogether twenty in number, eight being cutting teeth, or *incisors ;* four, eye-teeth, or *canines ;* and eight, grinders, or *molars*.

Each dental sac of the milk-teeth, as it is formed, gives off a little prolongation, which becomes lodged in the jaw, enlarges, and develops a papilla from which a new tooth is formed. As the latter increases in size, it presses upon the root of the milk-tooth which preceded it, and thereby causes the absorption of the root and the final falling out, or shedding of the milk-tooth, whose place it takes. Thus, every milk-tooth is replaced by a tooth of what is termed the *permanent dentition*. The permanent *incisors* and *ca-*

nines are larger than the milk-teeth of the same name, but otherwise differ little from them. The permanent *molars*, which replace the milk-molars, are small, and their crowns have only two points, whence they are called *bicuspid.* They never have more than two fangs.

354. The Permanent Molars.—We have thus accounted for twenty of the teeth of the adult. But there are thirty-two teeth in the complete adult dentition, twelve grinders being added to the twenty teeth which correspond with, and replace, those of the milk-set. When the fifth, or hindermost, dental sac of the milk-teeth is formed, the part of the groove which lies behind it also becomes covered over, extends into the back part of the jaw, and becomes divided into three dental sacs. In these, papillæ are formed and give rise to the great permanent back grinders, or *molars*, which have four, or five, points upon their square crowns, and, in the upper jaw, commonly possess three fangs.

The first of these teeth, the anterior molar of each side, is the earliest cut of all the permanent set, and appears at six years of age. The last, or hindermost, molar is the last of all to be cut, usually not appearing till twenty-one or twenty-two years of age. Hence it goes by the name of the " wisdom-tooth."

SECTION IV.—*Muscular and Nervous Tissues.*

355. Muscle, Striated and Smooth. — *Muscle* is of two kinds, *striated*, or *striped*, and *smooth*, *plain*, or *unstriated.* *Striated muscle*, of which all the ordinary muscles of the trunk and limbs consist, is composed of a number of long parallel cylindrical fibres, called *elementary* or *ultimate muscular fibres*, which are bound together by connective tissue into small bundles. These small bundles again are united into larger bundles, and these into one aggregate, by connective tissue, which supports the vessels and nerves of the muscle, and usually forms at one or both ends of the muscle a tendon (*see* 218), and sometimes gives rise to a dense sheath or *fascia* on its exterior.

Into the *ultimate muscular fibre* neither vessels, nor connective tissue, enter. Each fibre is, however, enveloped in a sheath formed by a tough, elastic, transparent structureless membrane, the *sarcolemma* (Fig. 121, D, *b*).

The sarcolemma is not contractile, but its elasticity al-

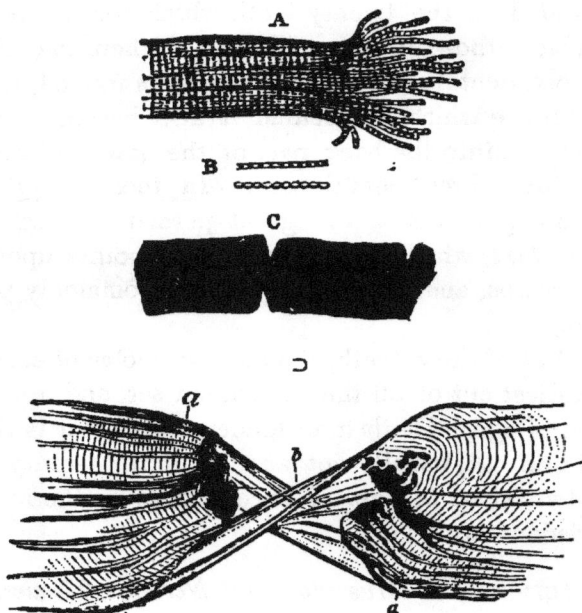

Fig. 121.

A, a muscular fibre, devoid of sarcolemma, and breaking up at one end into its *fibrillæ;* B, separate fibrillæ; C, a muscular fibre breaking up into disks; D, a muscular fibre, the contractile substance of which (*a*) is torn, while the sarcolemma (*b*) has not given way. (Magnified about three hundred and fifty diameters.)

lows it to adjust itself, pretty accurately, to the changes of form of the contractile substance which it contains.

This contractile substance, when uninjured, presents a very strongly-marked transverse striation, its substance appearing to be composed of extremely minute disks of a partially opaque substance, embedded at regular intervals in a more transparent matter. A more faint striation, separating these disks into longitudinal series, is also observable. When the sarcolemma is torn, the contractile substance of dead muscle may, under some circumstances, be divided into disks (Fig. 121, C), but it may be more readily broken up into minute *fibrillæ* (Fig. 121, A, B), each of which, viewed by transmitted light, presents dark and light parts, which alternate at intervals corresponding with the

B.   A.

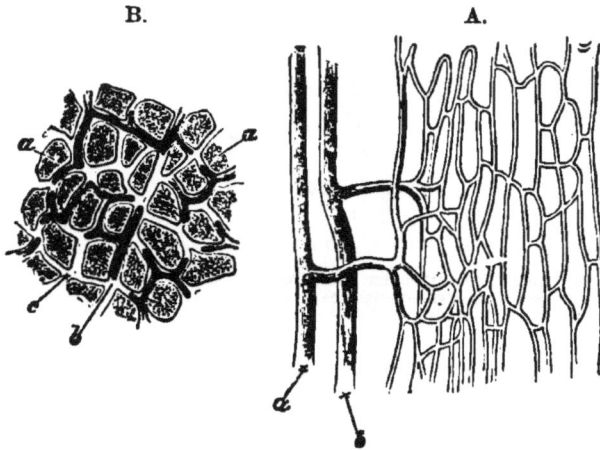

FIG. 122.

CAPILLARIES OF STRIATED MUSCLE.

A.—Seen longitudinally. The width of the meshes corresponds to that of an ultimate fibre. *a*, small artery; *b*, small vein.

B.—Transverse section of striated muscle. *a*, the cut ends of the ultimate fibres; *b*, capillaries filled with injection material; *c*, parts where the capillaries are absent or not filled.

distances of the transverse striæ in the entire fibre. Nuclei are observed here and there in the contractile substance within the sarcolemma.

In the heart, the muscular fibres are striated, and have the same essential structure as that just described, but they possess no sarcolemma.

Smooth muscle consists of elongated band-like fibres, devoid of striation, each of which bears a rod-like nucleus.

These fibres do not break up into fibrillæ, and have no sarcolemma (Fig. 123).

Smooth or non-striated muscular fibres from the middle coat of a small artery; the middle one, having been treated with acetic acid, shows more distinctly the nucleus, *a.* (Magnified about three hundred and fifty diameters.)

356. Nervous Tissue.—*Nervous tissue* contains two elements, *nerve-fibres* and *ganglionic corpuscles.* Ordinary nerve-fibres, such as constitute the essential constituents of all the cerebro-spinal nerves except the olfactory, are during life, or when perfectly fresh, subcylindrical filaments of a clear, somewhat oily, look. But, shortly after death, a sort of coagulation sets up within the fibre, and it is then found to be composed of a very delicate, structureless, outer membrane (which is not to be confounded with the *neurilemma*), forming a tube, through the centre of which runs the *axis-cylinder*, which is probably composed of an aggregation of very fine filaments. Between the axis-cylinder and the tube is a fluid, rich in fatty matters, from which a solid strongly-refracting substance has been thrown down and lines the tube.

Such is the structure of all the larger nerve-fibres which lie, side by side, in the trunks of the nerves, bound together

by delicate connective tissue, and inclosed in a sheath of
the same substance, called the *neurilemma*.   In the trunks
of the nerves, the fibres remain perfectly distinct from one
another, and rarely, if ever, divide.   But, when the nerves
enter the central organs, and when they approach their
peripheral terminations, the nerve-fibres frequently divide
into branches.   In any case they become gradually finer
and finer, until, at length, axis-cylinder, sheath, and contents, are no longer separable, and the nerve-fibre is reduced

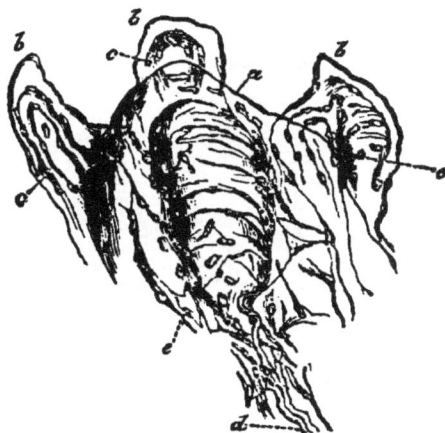

FIG. 124.

PAPILLÆ OF THE SKIN OF THE FINGER.

a, a large papilla containing a tactile corpuscle (*e*) with its nerve (*d*); *b*, other papillæ, without corpuscles, but containing loops of vessels, *c*. (Magnified about three
hundred diameters.)

to a delicate filament, the ultimate termination of which,
in the sensory organs and in the muscles, is not yet thoroughly made out.

357. Tactile Corpuscles.—In Chapter VIII. (239), mention is made of peculiar bodies called *tactile corpuscles,*
which are oval masses of specially modified connective
tissue in relation with the ends of the nerves in the papillæ of the skin.   In Fig. 124 four such papillæ, which
have been rendered transparent and stripped of their epi-

15

dermis, are seen, and the largest contains a tactile corpuscle (*e*). The mode in which nerves, not connected with tactile corpuscles, end in the skin, is not definitely known.

In muscles, the nerve-fibre seems to pierce the sarcolemma, and to end inside the ultimate muscular fibre in a peculiar knob or plate.

In the brain and spinal cord, on the other hand, it is certain that, in many cases, the ends of the nerve-fibres are continued into the processes of the ganglionic corpuscles.

358. The Olfactory Nerves.—The *olfactory nerves* are composed of pale, flat fibres without any distinction into axis-cylinder and contents, but with nuclei set at intervals along their length.

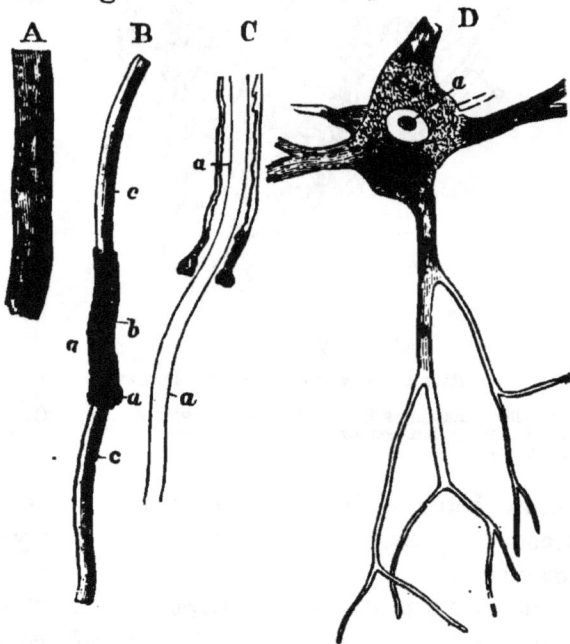

FIG. 125. FIG. 126. FIG. 127.   FIG. 128.

Fig. 125.—A nerve-fibre in its fresh and unaltered condition.
Fig. 126.—A nerve-fibre in which the greater part of the sheath and coagulated contents (*a b*) have been stripped off from the axis-cylinder (*c c*).
Fig. 127.—A nerve-fibre, the upper part of which retains its sheath and coagulated contents, while the axis-cylinder (*a a*) projects.
Fig. 128.—A ganglionic corpuscle—*a*, its nucleus and nucleolus. (Magnified about 350 diameters.)

Similar fibres are found in the sympathetic nerves, mingled with fibres of the same structure as those of the spinal nerves.

359. Ganglionic Corpuscles.— *Ganglionic corpuscles* are chiefly found in the cerebro-spinal axis ; in the ganglia of the posterior nerve-roots, and in those of the sympathetic ; but they occur also elsewhere, notably in some of the sensory organs (*see* Chapter IX.).

They are spheroidal bodies, consisting of a soft semi-solid cell-substance, in the midst of which is a large clear and transparent area usually termed the *nucleus*. Within the nucleus again is generally a smaller body commonly termed the *nucleolus* (Fig. 128, *a*). Each ganglionic corpuscle sends off one, two, or more prolongations, which may divide and subdivide ; and which, in some cases, unite with the prolongations of other ganglionic corpuscles, while, in others, they are continued into nerve-fibres.

CHAPTER XIII.

ANATOMICAL AND PHYSIOLOGICAL CONSTANTS.

360. General Statistics.—The weight of the body of a full-grown man may be taken at 154 pounds.

Such a body would be made up of—

	Pounds.
Muscles and their appurtenances . . .	68
Skeleton	24
Skin	10¼
Fat	28
Brain	3
Thoracic viscera	2½
Abdominal viscera	11
	147 [1]

[1] The addition of 7 pounds of blood, the quantity which will readily drain away from the body, will bring the total to 154 pounds. A considerable quantity of blood

Or of—

	Pounds.
Water	88
Solid matters	66

The solids would consist of the elements oxygen, hydrogen, carbon, nitrogen, phosphorus, sulphur, silicon, chlorine, fluorine, potassium, sodium, calcium (lithium), magnesium, iron (manganese, copper, lead), and may be arranged under the heads of—

Proteids. Amyloids. Fats. Minerals.

Such a body would lose in 24 hours—of water, about 40,000 grains, or 6 pounds; of other matters about 14,500 grains, or over two pounds; among which of carbon 4,000 grains; of nitrogen 300 grains; of mineral matters 400 grains; and would part, per diem, with as much heat as would raise 8,700 pounds of water 0° to 1° Fahr., which is equivalent to 3,000 foot-tons.[1] Such a body ought to do as much work as is equal to 450 foot-tons.

The losses would occur through various organs, thus—by

	WATER. Grains.	OTHER MATTER. Grains.	N. Grains.	C. Grains.
Lungs	5,000	12,000	....	3,300
Kidneys	23,000	1,000	250	140
Skin	10,000	700	10	100
Fæces	2,000	800	40	460
Total	40,000	14,500	300	4,000

The *gains* and *losses* of the body would be as follows:

	Grains.
Creditor—Solid dry food	8,000
Oxygen	10,000
Water	36,500
Total	54,500

will, however, always remain in the capillaries and small blood-vessels, and must be reckoned with the various tissues. The total quantity of blood in the body is now calculated at about 1-13th of the body weight, i. e., about 12 pounds.

[1] A foot-ton is the equivalent of the work required to lift one ton one foot high.

	Grains.
Debtor—Water	40,000
Other matters	14,500
Total	54,500

361. Digestion.—Such a body would require for daily food, carbon 4,000 grains, nitrogen 300 grains; which, with the other necessary elements, would be most conveniently disposed in—

	Grains.
Proteids	2,000
Amyloids	4,400
Fats	1,200
Minerals	400
Water	36,500
Total	44,500

which, in turn, might be obtained, for instance, by means of—

	Grains.
Lean beefsteaks	5,000
Bread	6,000
Milk	7,000
Potatoes	3,000
Butter, dripping, etc.	600
Water	22,900
Total	44,500

The fæces passed, per diem, would amount to about 2,800 grains, containing solid matter 800 grains.

362. Circulation.—In such a body the heart would beat 75 times a minute, and probably drive out, at each stroke from each ventricle, from 5 to 6 cubic inches, or about 1,500 grains of blood.

The blood would probably move in the great arteries at a rate of about 12 inches in a second, in the capillaries at 1 to 1½ inch in a minute; and the time taken up in performing the entire circuit would probably be about 30 seconds.

The left ventricle would probably exert a pressure on the aorta equal to the pressure on the square inch of a column of blood about 9 feet in height; or of a column of mercury about $9\frac{1}{2}$ inches in height; and would do in 24 hours an amount of work equivalent to about 90 foot-tons; the work of the whole heart being about 120 foot-tons.

363. Respiration.—Such a body would breathe 15 times a minute.

The lungs would contain of residual air about 100 cubic inches, of supplemental or reserve air about 100 cubic inches, of tidal air 20 to 30 cubic inches, and of complemental air 100 cubic inches.

The vital capacity of the chest—that is, the greatest quantity of air which could be inspired or expired—would be about 230 cubic inches.

There would pass through the lungs, per diem, about 350 cubic feet of air.

In passing through the lungs, the air would lose from 4 to 6 per cent. of its volume of oxygen, and gain 4 to 5 per cent. of carbonic acid.

During 24 hours there would be consumed about 10,000 grains oxygen; and produced about 12,000 grains carbonic acid, corresponding to 3,300 grains carbon. During the same time about 5,000 grains or 9 ounces of water would be exhaled by the lungs.

In 24 hours such a body would vitiate 1,750 cubic feet of pure air to the extent of 1 per cent., or 17,500 cubic feet of pure air to the extent of 1 per 1,000. Taking the amount of carbonic acid in the atmosphere at 3 parts, and in expired air at 470 parts in 10,000, such a body would require a supply per diem of more than 23,000 cubic feet of ordinary air, in order that the surrounding atmosphere might not contain more than 1 per 1,000 of carbonic acid (when air is vitiated from animal sources with carbonic acid to more than 1 per 1,000, the concomitant impurities become appreciable to the nose). A man of the weight mentioned

(11 stone) ought, therefore, to have at least 800 cubic feet of well-ventilated space.

364. Cutaneous Excretion.—Such a body would throw off by the *skin*—of water about 18 ounces, or 10,000 grains; of solid matters about 300 grains; of carbonic acid about 400 grains, in 24 hours.

365. Renal Excretion.—Such a body would pass by the *kidneys*—of water about 50 ounces; of urea about 500 grains; of other solid matters about 500 grains, in 24 hours.

366. Nervous Action.—In the frog a nervous impulse travels at the rate of about 80 feet in a second.

In a man a nervous (sensory) impulse has been variously calculated to travel 100, 200, or 300 feet in a second.

367. Histology.—Red corpuscles of the blood are about $\frac{1}{3200}$th of an inch in breadth; white corpuscles $\frac{1}{2500}$th.

Striated muscular fibres are about $\frac{1}{400}$th of an inch in breadth; plain $\frac{1}{4000}$th.

Nerve-fibres vary between $\frac{1}{1600}$th and $\frac{1}{12000}$th of an inch in breadth.

Connective-tissue fibrils are about $\frac{1}{4000}$th of an inch in breadth.

Epithelium scales (of the skin) are about $\frac{1}{500}$th of an inch in breadth.

Capillary blood-vessels are from $\frac{1}{3500}$th to $\frac{1}{2000}$th of an inch in breadth.

Cilia (from the windpipe) are about $\frac{1}{3000}$th of an inch in length.

The cones in the " yellow spot " of the retina are about $\frac{1}{10000}$th of an inch in breadth.

PART II.

ELEMENTARY HYGIENE.

CHAPTER XIV.

SCOPE AND AIMS OF HYGIENE.

368. Applied Physiology. — Thus far the student has been occupied in getting an understanding of the truths of physiological science, or of the actions of the living system in normal conditions. This knowledge has two great practical applications: the first to *Hygiene*, or the art of preserving health; and the second to *Medicine*, or the art of restoring it. When the vital machine has once become seriously deranged, profound knowledge and great skill and experience may be required to set it right again, and this is the work of the physician, who has to devote his life to professional study. But, happily, it requires less knowledge to keep what we already have than to recover it when lost. How to take care of the health, or to avoid many causes of disease, may be learned by all. That general acquaintance with the mechanism and working of the living system, which all persons, even moderately educated, should possess, is not only valuable to guard it against injury, but also to improve its various powers and capabilitics. If life and its opportunities be valuable, what knowledge can compare in importance with that which teaches how it is to be prolonged, and its various capacities augmented ?

369. False Conceptions of Disease. — In early ages it was the custom to explain all effects in Nature by supposing personalities like our own which produce them. The air, the earth, the forest, the streams, the sea, were peopled with imaginary beings, who were believed to be the agents by which all the operations of Nature were carried on. The regular actions of the living system were thought to be due to spirits which inhabited it, and its disorders to the agency of evil spirits. Though these superstitions long since passed away, the ideas which replaced them involved errors of a kindred nature. Diseases were no longer considered as personal agencies to be driven out by exorcism, but there still lingered the idea that they were things, independent existences or entities, which were in some mysterious way thrust into the system, and "expelled" from it by the action of medicines. Vague notions of this kind still widely prevail, and great numbers regard diseases as things that come arbitrarily, or are "sent" by Divine Providence as judgments or punishments for sins.

Views of this kind are unfavorable to hygienic efforts. We can easily understand that minds fully possessed by them will tend to a passive acquiescence in what is felt to be unavoidable, and the propitiation of Divine favor, by fasting, humiliations, and prayers, will take the place of intelligent, vigilant, and systematic measures for the prevention of disease. In past times, indeed, such notions have operated as powerful hinderances to hygienic precautions. When quarantine regulations were first instituted to prevent the spread of contagion by ships from port to port, and when vaccination was proposed as a preventive of small-pox, religious ideas were aroused into antagonism, and these beneficent measures were denounced as impiously contravening the Divine designs which employed plagues as scourges to punish the transgressions of mankind. In this way false theories of the nature and causes of disease acted as an obstruction to hygienic improvement.

370. The True Idea of Health and Disease. — Modern physiology has brought us to a better understanding of the subject. As we have seen, throughout the foregoing pages, physiology is the science of vital power. Power is the accompaniment of material change, and the manifestation of all animal functions is dependent upon vital transformations. Not only is the living body in constant visible movement, but in all its minutest parts and tissues there is an incessant metamorphosis—a rapid escape and renewal of the constituent atoms, and it is in this that life essentially consists. That active and unimpeded metamorphosis and prompt elimination of waste products which give rise to the highest and most vigorous life constitute HEALTH; while the obstruction, depression, or perversion of these vital changes constitutes DISEASE. We thus escape from the mischievous error that maladies are foreign intrusions —substantive existences which get mysterious lodgment in the living organism, and find that they are simply disturbed physiological actions. A disease may consist in the loss of power to remove or excrete normal but injurious products; or perverted transformations may give rise to wrong products, and these may create still further disturbance, but in all cases the essence of disease is to be regarded as abnormal activity.

Gout, for example, is a malady in which bad habits pervert the nutritive changes and originate morbid products; its chief peculiarity being the deposition of urate of soda in and about the joints. In health there is scarcely a trace of this salt to be found in the blood, and even this small proportion is being constantly thrown off. Certain conditions of living, however, such as the habitual use of wines or malt liquors, and high feeding upon animal substances, attended with but little exercise, are known greatly to increase its quantity and seriously to interfere with its excretion. It is then deposited as a foreign, or morbid, ingredient in the joints. Careful avoidance of the causes which give rise to this condition of the blood secures complete freedom from attack, even in those who may have inherited a strong predisposition to the disease.

371 Control over the Causes of Disease.—We have seen how directly the great functions of the system depend upon various conditions, such as diet, air, water, clothing, and exercise, by which the healthy changes of life are carried forward. These agencies, in their right action, are causes of health; but, when altered in their influence, they become causes of disease. The gases, liquids, and solids, which maintain the transformations of life, if deficient in quantity or deteriorated in quality, speedily produce bodily derangement; while just in proportion to the importance of these normal actions is the evil which results from their perversion. By the power which intelligence confers over these conditions, man may in great measure control the causes of disturbed health. Diseases may baffle the physician's penetration and defy his remedial skill; but, what is of far more importance, hygienic knowledge enables us to *avoid* them. The efficiency of prevention is proverbial, and we have examples of the value of sanitary knowledge and precautions on the most impressive scale.

372. Examples of the Application of Hygienic Principles. —*Cholera* may be taken as an illustration. In former times, when sanitary questions were but little understood, the approach of this terrible disease was viewed with a horrible dread; and, paralyzed with fear, the people did nothing to stay its advance. When it appeared, medicines were the only remaining resource, and, in spite of their use, the pestilence swept away multitudes of the population of the principal towns. But the connection between the disease and certain conditions, as filth, bad air, over-crowding, and irregularities of living, so common in cities, began at length to be perceived, and steps taken to remove the causes. The adequacy of these measures has been fully vindicated, and, with the knowledge that its conditions are controllable, the predisposing alarms have ceased, the ravages of the epidemic have been greatly circumscribed, and there is the amplest experience to show that thorough, yet simple, measures of purification are sufficient for its complete prevention.

Scurvy is another case in point. This disease, which, until recently, has been the scourge of the sailor and sol-dier, and for centuries was regarded as wholly beyond the power of remedies, also turns out to be fully preventable. "There is no more interesting fact in the history of medi-cine than that this condition, which has been looked upon at various times as plague, as a mysterious infliction of Di-vine justice, against which man could only strive in vain, or as a disease inseparable from long voyages, should have been proved by evidence of a most satisfactory character to arise from causes in the power of man to prevent, and to be curable by means which every habitable country af-fords." Instead of inquiring into the conditions of its origin, and seeking means of prevention, the medical pro-fession, for hundreds of years, was engaged in ransacking Nature, with the hope of finding something that might prove an effectual remedy. The search was fruitless until attention was turned to the cause of the disorder, which proved to be a lack of vegetable food, and the simple pre-caution of furnishing this has been the signal for the almost total disappearance of the disease. Many other illustra-tions might be given of the efficiency of hygienic resources to arrest and prevent the spread of dangerous maladies, but they are needless.

373. Remedial Influence of Hygienic Agencies.—Another important consideration deserves to be stated in this place:

it is that hygienic measures have a most important remedial value. If the conditions of health, when modified or
perverted, become causes of disease, to whatever extent
restorative medicines may be desirable, it is certain that
the first dictate of wisdom is to rectify these wrongly-acting
conditions. Medical treatment, thus, has its hygienic resources, which, with the enlargement of rational experience,
are coming into greater and greater prominence. All, who
have watched the progress of the healing art in recent
times, will note that among the most enlightened prac-
titioners there has been a steadily diminishing confidence
in medication, and an increasing reliance upon the sanitary influence of Nature. It is notorious that in proportion to people's ignorance of their own constitutions and
the true causes of disease, is their credulous confidence
in pills, potions, and quackish absurdities, and, while this
ignorance continues, there will of course be plenty of doc-
tors who will pander to it. And, not the least of the benefits likely to follow the better diffusion of physiological and
sanitary information will be, the protection of the community from the numberless impostures of charlatanism,
and a better discrimination of the qualifications of competent physicians.

374. The Sources of Ill-Health.—The more important material agencies and conditions, closely related to the processes
of life, are air, water, food, clothing, exercise, climate, soil,
and occupation. Some of these, such as air and food, are
indispensable; others, like clothing and exercise, are required to make existence tolerable, and all, when rightly
adjusted, are favorable to health. But all are liable to
changes of character that make them dangerous to bodily
well-being; and, the extent of the danger in the case of
each, when thus depraved, is fairly measured by the importance of the part it plays in healthy physiological action. Life cannot go on, for example, without air and
food, and we accordingly find that both air and food, in

their vitiated states, are among the most common sources of disease. Clothing is not only a requisite of civilization, but has come to have an important share in the regulation of certain physiological operations; and, when not wisely adapted, it too acts as a disturber of the bodily peace. To inquire into the manner in which these various agencies suffer deterioration, and thus become converted into sources of disease, and to point out the methods to be pursued, in order to avoid their ill-effects, are the objects of the following chapters.

CHAPTER XV.

AIR AND HEALTH.

SECTION I.—*Composition and Office of the Air.*

375. Its Chief Constituents.—The chief constituents of the atmosphere are a pair of elements, oxygen and nitrogen, and a pair of compounds, carbonic acid and watery vapor. The student will remember that, in treating of respiration (Chapter IV.), it was stated that oxygen forms twenty-one per cent. and nitrogen seventy-nine per cent., very nearly, of the bulk of the air. Oxygen is the life-sustaining element, and requires to be kept up to this standard for healthy respiration. Nitrogen is the negative or diluting element of the air. The proportion of these constituents is tolerably constant, wherever the air is free from contaminating influences; but the quantity of oxygen is always notably diminished in the air of towns. The amount of carbonic acid ranges from three to six parts in ten thousand. Its proportion is greater in the air of the highest mountains than in the air of plains, and in the air of towns than in country air. Saussure has also shown that air contains more carbonic acid at night than in the daytime, more in summer than in winter, and more in dry than in rainy weather. The quantity of aqueous vapor is highly variable, and is mainly determined by temperature. When, at a given temperature, the air has all it can hold, it is said to be *saturated*. From fifty to seventy-five per cent. of the amount required for complete saturation is usually present, though the quantity frequently ranges both above and below these limits, and then the air becomes unpleasantly moist, or dry, as the case may be.

376. Its Minor Constituents. — Along with the above, natural air contains minute quantities of ammonia, mostly in combination with carbonic acid, sulphur, or chlorine. The proportion rarely exceeds one part in a million of air; ozone (regarded as an allotropic form of oxygen) is also reckoned a normal constituent. Spectrum analysis has shown that the salts of sodium are everywhere present in small amount, and traces of organic matter, either living or dead, are also generally found. Other substances, in minute quantities, are often present in the air of particular localities, but the foregoing constituents, in the proportions named, form the external atmosphere, or what is commonly known as *pure* air.

377. Office of Air in Respiration. — Air performs a double work in the respiratory process. We have learned that one of the essential conditions of life is waste of tissue, and this requires the presence of oxygen in every part of the organism. The oxygen thus employed is furnished by the air, through the medium of the lungs and blood. But, as the work of oxidation goes on within the system, it is necessary that the resulting waste be speedily removed. And here, again, the air comes into play, receiving in the lungs, in the place of the oxygen yielded to the blood, a certain proportion of effete matter in the shape of carbonic acid and watery vapor, which it carries forth into the external atmosphere.

378. Its Action on Noxious Products. — Air performs a

scarcely less important service for the health of man, in the external world. Gaseous and vaporous emanations of all degrees of virulence are constantly pouring into it from numberless sources, and, if these were suffered to accumulate, the earth would soon become unfit for habitation. But, in the air itself, we have a purifying agency that is continually at work on the grandest scale. By means of winds and currents these dangerous contaminations are effectually dispersed, and thus brought in contact with oxygen are rapidly destroyed or rendered innocuous, by oxidation. It not only acts as a purifier of the living body, but, when left to itself, air is a cleanser of foul places everywhere. It is only when man, heedless of Nature's methods, hinders her processes of purification by artificial barriers, that this otherwise beneficent element becomes a source of danger and disease.

Section II.—*Impurities of the Air.*

379. Sources of its Impurities.—Air is rendered impure or unfit for respiratory purposes both by disturbance in the proportion of its normal constituents, and by many substances in the shape of gases, vapors, and solid particles, which are thrown into it from a variety of sources. Those arising from the habitations and works of men are of the most importance, in a hygienic point of view, both because we are constantly exposed to their influence, and because they are most completely subject to control.

380. Their Relation to the Senses.—Many of these impurities can be detected neither by taste nor smell, and are inhaled without any knowledge of their presence. Others are recognized at first; but, as the nerves soon lose their delicate sensibility of discrimination, the senses are unreliable monitors. Hence, injurious influences, that do not result in immediate and painful disease, are generally apt to be neglected. There is, besides, a false logic in the case, it being inferred that, because the senses lose their susceptibility to morbific influences, the system therefore becomes accustomed and adapted to them, when they cease to be detrimental.   But no error could be more pernicious, as it leads to carelessness and indifference with respect to those insidious agencies which slowly and silently sap the foundations of health.   Common instinct is sufficient to guard against palpable causes of injury; intelligence alone can protect us from the latent and deeper agencies of physiological mischief.

381. Carbonic Acid as an Impurity.—Carbonic acid is thrown into the atmosphere by breathing, by combustion, and by the oxidation or decay of organic matter.   A cubic foot of air, of average purity, contains a little less than a cubic inch of carbonic acid.   A cubic foot of air, as it comes from the lungs, contains upwards of seventy cubic inches of carbonic acid.   About three hundred and fifty cubic feet of air pass through the lungs of an adult man in twenty-four hours, losing some seventeen cubic feet of oxygen to the blood, and gaining therefrom a nearly equal quantity of carbonic acid.   The breathing of each adult thus adds about one per cent. of carbonic acid to seventy-three cubic feet of air per hour, which would vitiate to this extent more than one foot per minute, while the effect is much increased by the surface exhalations.

The quantity poured into the air by combustion is enormous; fifteen thousand tons, according to the calculation of Dr. Angus Smith, are daily thrown into the air from this source in the city of Manchester alone.   But the products of firing pass into the outer air, and, if gaseous, are rapidly diffused; but those of lighting, like those of breathing, are often suffered to accumulate in living apartments. The combustion of one cubic foot of coal-gas consumes the oxygen of ten cubic feet of air, and produces two cubic feet of carbonic acid.   The combustion of a pound of oil consumes the oxygen of one hundred and thirty feet of air, and produces about twenty-one cubic feet of carbonic acid.

These facts show the rapidity with which the breathing medium of inhabited apartments tends to become deteriorated.

It is difficult to estimate the amount of carbonic acid arising from the decay of organic matter; but, as such decay, under favorable conditions of temperature, is everywhere going on, the daily aggregate must be very great. The increased quantity of carbonic acid found in the air of towns is doubtless partly derived from this source.

As carbonic acid is constantly generated within the body, we may regard the presence of a certain small amount of it as quite compatible with health. But, when not promptly eliminated, its action becomes quickly injurious. Two volumes in a thousand of air cause headache and vertigo in many persons. Air containing one per cent. of it is soporific and depressing. From five to eight per cent. renders it dangerous to breathe, while ten to twelve per cent. makes it speedily destructive to life.

The presence of an excess of carbonic acid in the air denotes in nearly every case a lessened proportion of oxygen, and, if the air has been contaminated by breathing, a decided increase in the amount of organic matter. These conditions make it dangerous to breathe; but, whether this danger is due to the extra quantity of carbonic acid and organic matter, or to the absence of oxygen, or partly to the one and partly to the other condition, is not yet clearly settled. It is sufficient for all practical purposes, however, to know that the three conditions are commonly associated in air contaminated by respiration.

382. Watery Vapor as an Impurity.—When air enters the lungs its temperature is raised to nearly or quite that of the blood; its capacity for moisture is thereby greatly increased, and when breathed out again it is always completely saturated. Air in this condition, no matter what the source of its moisture, acts injuriously upon the system, as it is unable to further relieve the skin and lungs of the watery vapor that is constantly seeking a means of escape. There follows the feeling of oppression and languor which even the most robust often feel in close and sultry days. By this obstruction of insensible perspiration, not only are the waste matters generated in the system unduly retained, but miasmas introduced through the lungs by respiration are prevented from escaping. This would lead us to expect a greater prevalence of epidemic diseases in moist than in dry districts, a fact observed in the case of cholera, which follows the banks of rivers, and revels in damp, low situations. Moisture, joined with warmth, has a relaxing and weakening influence upon the body. The debilitating effect of the *sirocco* upon the system, and its lowering and dispiriting influence upon the mind, are due to a heated atmosphere surcharged with moisture. Air, cold and damp, has a peculiarly chilling and penetrating effect, as illustrated by the east winds of spring in New England.

383. Organic Matter.—This is a common impurity of the atmosphere, and is often present in dangerous proportions. It exists in the form of vapors and suspended matters, and is found most abundantly diffused in the air of dwellings, hospitals, etc., and in the vicinity of decaying organic substances. In health it is thrown off through the lungs by the process of respiration, and also by exhalation from the skin. The quantity has been estimated all the way from ten to two hundred and forty grains per diem for each adult. It varies, however, with the circumstances, the body excreting a much greater amount during a state of activity than when it is inactive, and more during disease than in a state of health. That coming from the lungs consists of an organic vapor, holding in suspension epithelium-cells that have become detached from the mucous surfaces of the air-passages, pharynx, mouth, etc. By the skin more is given out. Twice as much moisture leaves the body by this route as by the lungs, and it carries with it into the atmosphere fatty matters, epidermic *débris*, and also small quantities of urea.

This organic matter, when drawn through sulphuric acid, darkens it; through permanganate of potash, decolorizes it; and through pure water, renders it offensive. It is probably in a state of combination with water, as the most hygroscopic substances, such as wool, feathers, and damp walls, absorb it in largest quantities. It has a peculiar, fetid smell, and on decomposition yields ammonia, being therefore nitrogenous. It is oxidized slowly, and is supposed to float through the air in clouds instead of undergoing rapid diffusion. The fetid odor of a bedroom in the morning, after it has been occupied during the night, well attests the presence of these organic vapors.

In the air of sick-rooms and hospitals organic matters accumulate in large quantities unless there is the most thorough ventilation. In addition to the amount contributed by respiration, which is often much larger in sickness than in health, the exhalations from the skin are greatly increased, and large quantities of effluvia also escape from the evacuations. Moscatti, who condensed the watery vapor of a hospital ward at Milan, describes it as being "slimy, and having a marshy smell." The dust of a ward in St.-Louis Hospital, in Paris, was discovered by Chalvert to contain, in one experiment, thirty-six per cent., and, in another, forty-six per cent. of organic matter, which consisted chiefly of epithelium, and when burned gave an odor of horn. An equal quantity was found in the plaster walls of the same ward. Pus-cells have been discovered in the air of an ophthalmic ward, and epithelium-cells are found in that of all ill-ventilated rooms. It is very likely that the specific poison of small-pox, scarlet fever, measles, diphtheria, etc., consists of molecular organic matter thrown off from the skin and mucous surfaces. If not rapidly oxidized, it no doubt retains its poisonous properties, and through the medium of the atmosphere conveys the disease. It is equally probable that the effluvia from cholera evacuations, through the medium of an impure atmosphere, propagate cholera.

One part of carbonic acid in a thousand parts of respired air, indicates the presence of an amount of organic matter which, according to Dr. Parkes, is perceptible to the senses and positively injurious to health. Smith, Wilson, and other equally competent observers, corroborate this view.

384. Suspended Matters.—As shown by Tyndall, suspended matters in great variety are widely diffused. In the air of dwellings, starch-cells, hairs, fibres of cotton, wool, etc., are very common. In the air of towns, particles of iron, stone-dust, and animal droppings, are also abundant, while the atmosphere generally contains spores, seeds, pollen, and broken-down vegetable tissue, together with the germs of vibriones, bacteriæ, and other low forms of animal life. Many trades yield deleterious substances to the air in injurious quantities. These will be noticed in connection with the diseases which they commonly excite.

385. Contamination from Sewers and Cesspools.— Noxious gases, entering the air from sewers and cesspools, consist mainly of carbonic acid, sulphuretted hydrogen, light carburetted hydrogen, sulphide of ammonium, and organic matter. They arise from the decomposition of organic matter, and are yielded in large quantities, and at a rapid rate, when the temperature is high and the sewage concentrated. They are undoubted sources of disease, and are also believed to be capable of conveying infectious matters, thus becoming, from their peculiar liability to enter houses, dangerous aids to the spread of epidemics. When distributed upon the land, unless greatly diluted, sewage gives off a disagreeable odor, and is the occasional cause of diarrhœa and dysentery.

386. Marsh Miasms.—Carbonic acid, light carburetted

hydrogen, sulphuretted hydrogen, and organic effluvia, contaminate the air of marshes, which also abounds in vegetable matter and minute animal forms. Whatever the nature of the so-called miasm of marshes, we know that the air of these places frequently contains a something capable of producing the various forms of periodic disease. Exposure to marsh air also gives rise to diarrhœa, dysentery, and other forms of gastric disorder. Marsh diseases often follow the irrigation of meadows, draining of lakes, digging of canals, and excavation of railway-cuttings, and they are then ascribed to vitiation of the air from the decomposition of vegetable matter thus brought to the surface.

387. The Cellar a Reservoir of Bad Air.—Confined air, without access of sunlight, soon becomes dank and unwholesome. In the cellars of dwellings this is a common condition during a large part of the year; the confined air is loaded with decomposing organic matter, given off from the masses of decaying vegetables with which cellars are stored. This foul air reaches the inhabitants of upper apartments in such small quantities as not usually to produce any marked manifestation of disease, yet dangerous fevers have often arisen from neglect of cleanliness in this particular.

Section III.—*Morbid Effects of Impure Air.*

388. Its General Effects.—Besides the various diseases directly traceable to the influence of impure air, its effects are seen in a general depression of the tone of the system. Persons habitually occupying badly-ventilated apartments show this in pallor of countenance, depraved appetites, feeble digestion, and general weakness of body, and such are proverbially subject to attacks of acute disease. Dwellers in low situations, and in the vicinity of marshes, as well as those exposed to the poisonous emanations of sewers, and of decomposing organic matter, suffer in a similar way, and this general impairment of the powers of the body is, doubtless, often the signal for the development of inherited taints that, under more favorable conditions, might lie dormant throughout a long and vigorous life. The incompleteness of nutrition gives strength to the lurking predisposition. Instances are constantly recurring in which consumptive tendencies are developed to a fatal issue through various bad conditions, impure air being the most common. And physicians are aware that the constant presence of a pure atmosphere, with other means for healthy nutrition, will hold the predisposition in check, and maintain the system above the plane of its influence.

389. Consumption.—That breathing air already vitiated by respiration is a powerful aid in the production of consumption is acknowledged by all observers, and some go so far as to affirm that this is its principal cause. The fact has been repeatedly noted that soldiers living in badly-ventilated barracks furnish a much larger percentage of consumptive cases than others who, in this respect, are comfortably housed. The same is true of sailors; and the medical histories of operatives in close and overcrowded work-rooms, both here and in foreign countries, abound with evidence of similar import. We have seen that respired air is deficient in oxygen, and contains an excess of carbonic acid, watery vapor, and organic matter. If it is breathed again, the blood immediately suffers both from lack of oxygen and from the accumulation of effete material. This condition of the blood necessarily hinders the healthy waste and repair of the tissues, and must contribute to the formation of those depraved products which are everywhere characteristic of consumption. The tubercles which in this disease make their appearance in the pulmonary organs consist of crude, coagulated, half-organized masses of albumen, the abortive products of incomplete nutrition. And it seems but natural to expect that the organs with which the foreign ingredients of the atmosphere come more immediately into contact, and the blood-vessels which they must enter on their passage into the system, should feel in a distinctive manner their noxious influence.

Besides acting as a cause of consumption, impure air is a source of much suffering to those already diseased. The reason is obvious. The capacity of the lungs is more or less reduced, hence less air can be conveyed to the blood, and, if this is deficient in oxygen and contains impurities, the malady is directly aggravated.

390. Scrofula.—That imperfect and perverted state of the nutritive functions known as *scrofula* is the common attendant of life in a vitiated atmosphere. Baudoloque, an eminent French physician, declares that "the repeated respiration of the same atmosphere is a primary and efficient cause of scrofula," and that "if there be entirely pure air, there may be bad food, bad clothing, and want of personal cleanliness, but that scrofulous diseases cannot exist. . . . Invariably it will be found on examination that a truly scrofulous disease is caused by a vitiated air, and it is not always necessary that there should have been a prolonged stay in such an atmosphere. Often a few hours each day is sufficient, and it is thus that persons may live in the most healthy country, pass the greater part of the day in the open air, and yet become scrofulous, because of sleeping in a confined place where the air has not been renewed."

In 1832, at Norwood School, in England, where there were six hundred pupils, scrofula broke out extensively among the children and carried off great numbers. This was ascribed to bad and insufficient food. Dr. Arnott was employed to investigate the matter, and immediately decided that the food "was most abundant and good," assigning "defective ventilation and consequent atmospheric impurity" as the true cause.

391. Its Effects in Various Trades.—The most palpable examples of the injurious effects of breathing contaminated air are furnished by the circumstances of certain industrial occupations. As a class the miners of England break down prematurely from bronchitis and pneumonia, caused by the atmosphere in which they live. The colliers of Durham and Northumberland, however, where the mines are well ventilated, do not appear to suffer from an excess of pulmonary disease.

In the various trades, involving the inhalation of much dust by the workmen, bronchitis and its attendant disease, emphysema, are very common. In the pottery-trade, this malady occurs so frequently as to be known as the "potter's asthma." Indeed, nearly all the flat-pressers and scourers, according to Dr. Grenhow, eventually become asthmatical. Steel-grinders suffer terribly from inhaling the dust of their trade. The average duration of life, according to the statistics of Dr. Hall, of dry-grinders of forks is but twenty-nine years; razors, thirty-one years; scissors, thirty-two years; edge-tools, thirty-two years; files, thirty-five years; saws and sickles, thirty-eight years. By the introduction of fans and wet-grinding, however, the danger has been materially reduced. Pearl-button makers are extremely liable to pulmonary disease. Workers in flax, and cotton-weavers, are equally exposed. Dr. Grenhow states that, of one hundred and seven flax-factory operatives, whose cases were taken indiscriminately, seventy-nine were suffering from bronchial irritation, and in nineteen of these there had been hæmoptysis. Among twenty-seven hacklers, twenty-three were diseased. The suspended particles are drawn into the air-passages at each inhalation, and there find lodgment upon the delicate mucous surfaces with which they come in contact. The irritation thus set up disturbs the working of the lungs, and, if maintained, eventually ends in organic disease.

Brass-founders, coppersmiths, plumbers, house-painters, white-lead manufacturers, match-makers, workers in mercury, are all subject to peculiar forms of disease produced

16

by inhaling the fumes with which their business contaminates the air. These fumes gain access to the blood, and, through this, to the whole system, producing severe local disturbance in many cases, and always affecting the general health.

392. Diseases arising from Organic Impurities. — The effects of inhaling air vitiated by organic impurities are scarcely less apparent. Dr. Parkes says that he has known cases " in which the inhalation of such an atmosphere for three or four hours produced in men decided febrile symptoms, increased temperature, quickened pulse, furred tongue, loss of appetite, and thirst, for even twenty-four or forty-eight hours subsequently." Sewer-gas, the effluvia arising from decomposing animal matter, the emanations from manure-manufactories and bone-boiling establishments, all contain organic matter, and are all prolific sources of disease. Diarrhœa and dysentery are the most common affections which spring from these causes; but enteric, or typhoid fever, is held by Dr. Murchison to be produced in a similar way, sewer-air being especially dangerous. Much uncertainty prevails as to the real cause of this disease, but modern investigators incline to the belief that it is infectious, and that it is propagated by the distribution of organic matter in water and air. "I readily admit," says Dr. Murchison, " that we cannot succeed in tracing every case of enteric fever to organic impurities; but, if the disease can be traced to such causes in a few undoubted instances, it is reasonable to infer that its causes are similar in all cases where it has a spontaneous origin. As already stated, the actual poison may, like the miasmata which give rise to ague, be inappreciable to the senses, or by chemical research. During the last four years, however, I have met with few examples of enteric fever which, on investigation, I could not trace to defective drainage, the existence of which was occasionally unknown to the inhabitants of the infected locality."

That the spread of cholera is also due to some specific organic poison is rendered probable by the fact that, where water and air are kept free from organic impurities, the disease is unable to gain a foothold.

393. Effects of Impure Air on the Course of Disease.— Foul air increases the severity of disease, rendering a fatal result much more probable, and, even if this is avoided, greatly prolongs the period of convalescence. It also predisposes to complications, and renders recovery more likely to be followed by subsequent trouble. This appears to hold true of all diseases, but especially of the febrile. It is known that, in the treatment of typhus and typhoid fevers, the freest ventilation, even to the extent of placing the patient in the open air, reduces the mortality more than half, and greatly shortens the time of recovery. A like provision in the treatment of scarlet fever, measles, small-pox, diphtheria, etc., not only renders them much less severe, but does away in a great degree with the necessity for medication, and also markedly diminishes the liability to those distressing sequelæ which, in less favorable conditions, so often supervene.

394. Effects of the Air of Sick-Rooms.— The impurities of a sick-room atmosphere consist largely of organic matter, which not unfrequently bears the specific poison of the disease. This is the case with the exanthemata, as well as with other contagious febrile affections. On uncovering a scarlet-fever patient in the direct rays of the sun, a cloud of fine dust may be seen to rise from the body—contagious dust, that in unventilated localities is but slowly dispersed or destroyed, and that may for days retain its poisonous qualities. Diseases of this character are undoubtedly propagated in other ways, but a confined atmosphere probably does more than all other causes put together towards aiding their diffusion. The spread of erysipelas and gangrene in the surgical wards of hospitals, and the propagation of purulent ophthalmia, observed in some of the London charity schools, take place through the medium of the atmosphere, which becomes highly charged with the emanations from the sick. Besides bearing the specific poison, an atmosphere of this character is exceedingly depressing to those brought within the range of its influence, and, by thus lessening the resisting power of the system, renders the otherwise healthy liable to attack.

395. Morbid Mental Effects of Bad Air.—Breathing an impure atmosphere injures the mind as well as the body. If the blood which is sent from the lungs to the rest of the system is imperfectly aërated, no organ feels it more than the brain. Its immediate effect is to cloud the mind and depress its energy; sharpness of attention, clearness of apprehension, and readiness of memory, are all impaired. "The health of the mental and bodily functions, the spirit, temper, disposition, the correctness of the judgment, and brilliancy of the imagination, depend directly upon pure air."

Dr. Ray remarks: "In a school, or hospital, or other considerable assemblage of people, the purity of the air may be pretty accurately measured by the amount of cheerfulness, activity, and lively interest, which pervades it; and yet so little do people think or care about this subject, that, under existing arrangements, there are very few who do not every day of their lives inspire more or less highly-vitiated air. The listlessness and stupidity of students, and especially of children confined in the school-room, are often due to the bad state of the air they breathe. Using the brain in a vitiated atmosphere is like working with a blunted instrument, and the effect, of course, must be aggravated where the inexperienced are first learning the use of the instrument.

SECTION IV.—*Purification of the Air.*

396. Nature's Resources.—The purification of the general atmosphere is maintained by various agencies. By the law of diffusion all gases intermingle, so that where impurities are set free at any point they tend to exhale, or diffuse away, and thus become weakened and lost in the great body of the atmosphere. The mixture of large masses of air and the dispersion and dilution of local impurities are also effected by the winds. Gaseous exhalations are washed out and absorbed from the atmosphere by the fall of rains. The earth's vegetation destroys carbonic acid, while the oxygen slowly burns up the numberless combustible vapors and contaminations which are thrown into the air. By these means the earth's atmosphere is constantly maintained respirable and pure.

397. Ventilation.—Taking the fresh external air as the standard of purity required for health, the object of ventilation is to conduct it through dwellings, hospitals, workshops, and places of similar character, in a manner that, without inconvenience to the inmates, shall accomplish the rapid and thorough dilution and removal of whatever impurities their atmosphere may contain. To do this effectually, and without risk to the health and comfort of the persons present, the ventilation must conform to certain indispensable conditions:

(1.) *The air which enters must itself be pure.* This may generally be secured by taking it from almost any exposed situation, unless there be some special source of impurity in close proximity. It is desirable, if possible, particularly in cities, to introduce the air from a level a few feet above the surface, as there are more or less exhalations constantly floating in air next the ground.

(2.) *It must be in sufficient quantity.* We find Nature's standard of purity in the external atmosphere, and, other things equal, the nearer we approach this in our dwellings, the healthier will be their inmates. The earlier authorities on ventilation varied greatly in their estimates of the quantity necessary, some placing it as low as sixty cubic feet per head per hour, while others considered five hundred cubic feet as not too much. More thorough investigations have since been made, and it is found that even the highest of these estimates is quite insufficient. Dr. Parkes says: "From a number of experiments in which the outflow of air was measured, and the carbonic acid simultaneously determined, I have found at least two thousand cubic feet per hour must be given to keep the carbonic acid at five or six per one thousand volumes, and to entirely remove the fetid smell of organic matter." Nothing less than this can be tolerated without risk to health, and it is found that a much larger allowance is productive of the best results. It has been stated, from extensive observations, that in mines, if it be wished to keep up the greatest energy of the men, no less than one hundred cubic feet per man per minute (= six thousand cubic feet per hour) must be given. If the quantity is reduced to one-third, or even one-half, there is a decided diminution in the amount of work performed. ·

If possible, the supply for the sick should be unlimited. In some diseases, so much organic matter is thrown off, that scarcely any ventilation is sufficient to remove the odor. Such diseases as pyæmia, typhus and typhoid fevers, small-pox, and the like, are best treated in the open air. This is found of the utmost value, more important even than diet and medicines. Grassi mentions that the air in a ward in the Hôpital Necker, in Paris, was perceptibly tainted by emanations from a cancerous ulcer, although the ventilation at the time was thirty-five hundred cubic feet per head per hour.

(3.) *Its movement must be imperceptible.* Air may move at the rate of one hundred feet per minute without violating this requirement; but this is a much greater velocity than is needed for ventilating purposes—that is to say, after the air has once entered the apartment. In the flues, the rate of movement is of little consequence, except that it be sufficiently rapid to afford the required supply. If there is little or no interference from outside currents, the air within the building may readily be made to move in a body from above downwards, and the rapidity of its movement can be easily regulated. It may be objected to this downward movement that the impurities naturally tend upwards, with the course of the warmer air, and that, by being made to take a downward direction, they are brought back again to be reinhaled. If it were true that the impurities, as such, immediately rose to the ceiling and escaped from the apartment, the objection would hold; but this is not the case. On the contrary, it is known that the carbonic acid and other gaseous impurities are equally diffused, and the weight of the organic substances and other suspended matters leads to the inference that they would gravitate towards the floor, particularly when rising currents of warm air are excluded, as they should be, by introducing it at the top of the room. In no other way can so steady and equable a movement be obtained as by introducing the warm air at the top and removing it below; and, apart from any theoretical considerations, it is found to yield excellent practical results.

(4.) *Its temperature must be suitably regulated.* In this climate, cooling the air is rarely necessary, but in the colder months of the year the incoming air requires to be warmed sufficiently for comfort, and in such manner as not to disturb the normal proportions of its constituents. The great danger is that of overheating it, whereby its capacity for moisture is greatly increased and ventilation becomes converted into a kiln-drying process scarcely less injurious than impure air. The policy should be to introduce large quantities of air raised only to a proper breathing temperature (60° to 70° Fahr.), the temperature to be maintained by a steady and rapid change, so directed as to remove the cooler air of the apartment, and replace it with that freshly warmed. It may be said that this involves a much greater loss of heat than the opposite course, viz., raising to a high temperature smaller quantities of air. Even if this were true, which is not the case, waste of heat would be far preferable to the loss of health, which the latter process involves, both by the increased drying power it gives the air, and by insufficient ventilation.

The heat imparted to the air in this process becomes a means of promoting its movement. With this as a motive power, by the aid of flues and ventilating shafts, very thorough purification may be obtained.

398. Artificial Purification—Disinfectants. — In certain special cases where the air is being rapidly contaminated by foul or poisonous exhalations, and where, either from confinement or other cause, the purifying agencies of Nature are unable to work with sufficient rapidity and vigor, recourse is had to various artificial means of purification, with a view to the immediate destruction of such emanations. The more common and useful of these are heat, charcoal, chlorine, carbolic, nitrous, and sulphurous acids, sulphate of iron (copperas), Condy's fluid, and chloralum.

Heat is highly commended as a means of destroying animal and vegetable germs, and infectious matters. It is especially valuable for the disinfection of clothing, bedding, and the like, where it can be confined, but is not so readily applicable for cleansing the air. To be effective, a heat of at least 140° Fahr. is required; 160° or 180° Fahr. is even more certain, and may be applied without risk to the fabric.

Charcoal presents an immense absorbent surface to the air, a cubic inch of beechwood-coal equaling in surface one hundred square feet (Liebig). It is therefore a powerful oxidizer of organic matter, catching and holding the particles in contact with oxygen, already within it, until their destruction is accomplished. Its effects are especially marked with sewage-gases, and with the organic emanations in disease. Of the different kinds, animal charcoal is regarded as best for disinfecting purposes.

Chlorine decomposes sulphuretted hydrogen and sulphide of ammonium, and also destroys organic odors. It is an energetic aërial disinfectant, but, owing to its irritating effect on the lungs, requires to be used in small quantities, or in uninhabited rooms. It may be easily obtained by mixing one part of powdered binoxide of manganese with four parts of common salt and four of dilute sulphuric acid. A gentle heat will aid the evolution of the gas. Various compounds of chlorine are often employed for disinfecting purposes, but all owe their value to the presence of this element. Chlorides of lime and soda yield it in small quantities when moistened with water. Chloralum is a compound of chlorine and aluminium, but thus combined the chlorine is not volatile; the preparation is, therefore, of little value for purifying the air. Applied to decomposing organic matter, however, it acts as an excellent deodorant, arrests putrefactive change, and at once puts a stop to the development of animalculæ. In solution it is very useful for washing infected clothing, and for cleansing the walls and wood-work of sick-rooms.

Carbolic acid is a powerful antiseptic and disinfectant. It arrests all kinds of putrefactive change, and quickly destroys animal and vegetable germs, and the low forms of life. Being also an excellent deodorant, it is used extensively for disinfecting the vessels of sick-rooms, urinals, stables, manure-heaps, and cesspools. The commercial form is a dark-brown tarry liquid, with the pungent odor of creosote. It is highly poisonous, and hence requires to be used with care.

Nitrous acid may be evolved by placing nitre in sulphuric acid, or by dropping a bit of copper into dilute nitric acid. It is a very efficient disinfecting agent, but irritating to the air-passages and lungs. The ease with which it yields up a portion of its oxygen makes it a powerful oxidizer, which acts rapidly upon organic emanations.

Sulphurous acid is given off when sulphur is burned.

It decomposes sulphuretted hydrogen, and acts with energy upon organic substances.

Sulphate of iron is chiefly valuable for disinfecting sewage, privy-vaults, manure-heaps, and cesspools, where it is desired to arrest decomposition, and the generation of foul odors.

Permanganate of potash, or soda (Condy's fluid), gives off oxygen, and rapidly destroys organic matter. Ammoniacal compounds are at once decomposed. Permanganate of soda, taken into the mouth, quickly destroys the odor of tobacco (Hoffman).

CHAPTER XVI.

WATER AND HEALTH.

SECTION I.—*Physiological Offices of Water.*

399. Amount in the Body.—The student is aware that water is a very large constituent of all parts of the body. The bones contain 130 parts of it in 1,000; muscle, 750; brain, 789; blood, 795; and it forms nearly three-fourths the entire weight of the body.

400. It is the Instrument of Change.—Water gives fullness and flexibility to the softer tissues, and is the great agent of movement within the system. It performs the same office of transportation and exchange in the vital economy that it does by oceans, rivers, and canals, in the commerce of the world. Nutritive substances cannot enter the system, nor the *débris* of the tissues leave it, except in a state of solution; it is the office of water to bring them into this condition, and convey them to their various places of destination.

401. Its Solvent Power.—Water performs these duties by virtue of its remarkable powers as a solvent. Perfectly neutral itself, it becomes sweet, sour, salt, astringent, bitter, or poisonous, accordingly as the bodies it dissolves possess these properties. It readily takes up either gaseous, liquid, or solid substances, and thus becomes a means for their rapid and wide-spread diffusion.

402. Quantity daily taken.—Water is taken not only in the form of drink, but it is a large constituent of the various food-stuffs; hence any estimate of the quantity passing into the system, to be reliable, must include both these sources of supply. It has been found that a healthy adult man ordinarily takes from seventy to ninety ounces in twenty-four hours. The amount, however, varies greatly in different circumstances, sometimes, from individual peculiarities, falling much below, and at other times considerably exceeding this figure.

403. Its Excretion.—Water is constantly escaping from the system, either in a fluid or vaporized form, and carries with it the various substances resulting from the wear and tear of the tissues. Of all that is expelled, about forty-eight per cent. is discharged with the urine and fæces, and about fifty-two per cent. by the lungs and skin. Of the latter, the skin discharges nearly twice as much as the lungs.

SECTION II.—*Different Kinds of Water.*

404. Its Foreign Ingredients.—Owing to its extraordinary solvent power, water, in a natural condition, is never found free from foreign ingredients, which modify its character according to the quantity present, and their own peculiar properties. This gives rise to the several varieties that we know as soft water, hard water, mineral water, and sea-water.

405. Soft Water.—This is water that gives a feeling of softness in washing, from the absence of certain mineral substances, which render it rough or hard. Rain-water may be taken as a fair example, for, when caught in the open country, it is the purest water that Nature provides.

It is not entirely free from foreign matters, however, for, as it falls through the air, it absorbs oxygen, nitrogen, carbonic acid, ammonia, and organic substances, and also washes out any impurities which the atmosphere may happen to contain. Thus, in the vicinity of the ocean the air contains traces of common salt; in the neighborhood of cities, various saline, organic, and gaseous impurities, while dust is raised from the ground and scattered through it by winds. These are all rinsed out by rain. In passing through the air water becomes highly aërated; that is, acquires an atmosphere of its own, which contains from ten to fifteen per cent. more oxygen than ordinary air. This gives to water its agreeable taste.

Soft water, which is free from dissolved mineral matters, makes its way into organized tissues with much greater readiness than hard water. It also exerts a more powerful solvent or extractive action, and is thus a better vehicle for conveying alimentary substances into the living system. In culinary operations, where the object is to soften the texture of animal and vegetable substances, or to extract from them and present in a liquid form some of their valuable parts, as in making soups, broths, stews, or infusions, as tea and coffee, soft water is much to be preferred.

In consequence of its aëration, rain-water is both healthy and pleasant as a beverage. The greatest benefits have resulted in many cases from its use, where the spring and well waters were largely impregnated with earthy salts.

406. Hard Water. — Rain-water, as it penetrates the ground, absorbs a large proportion of carbonic acid from the air in the interstices of the soil, which is two hundred and fifty times richer in this gas than the air above. The presence of this absorbed carbonic acid greatly increases the solvent power of water upon mineral substances. Passing more or less deeply into the earth, it dissolves many substances which it meets; hence the difference between spring and well waters, which are generally hard, and rain-water, which has not come in contact with the ground. The life and sparkle of spring and well water are due to the presence of carbonic acid thus taken up, and, when this is found in a considerable degree, it is safe to infer the additional presence of large quantities of saline matter. The usual ingredients of well and spring water are lime, magnesia, soda, and oxide of iron, combined with carbonic and sulphuric acids, which form carbonates and sulphates. Common salt is also often present. The most usual ingredients, however, are carbonate and sulphate of lime. Carbonate of lime, or limestone, is not soluble in pure water, but dissolves in water containing free carbonic acid.

The amount of mineral matter found in water varies greatly. The water of the river Loka, in Sweden, which flows over insoluble granite, contains only $\frac{1}{25}$th of a grain of mineral matter in an imperial gallon. Common well and spring waters contain from five to seventy grains per gallon. Sea-water contains twenty-six hundred grains to the gallon; and that from some parts of the Dead Sea, or the Great Salt Lake of Utah, as much as twenty thousand grains to the gallon.

Mineral waters are usually those of springs which are highly charged with one or more mineral ingredients. Those abounding in salts of iron are called *chalybeate* waters. If the waters are brisk and sparkling, carbonic acid is present, and they are termed *carbonated*, or *acidulous*.

Limestone-waters are also clear, sparkling, and agreeable to the taste. They differ from the water of chalk districts, in containing more sulphate of lime and less carbonate, and in dolomitic districts much sulphate and carbonate of magnesia. They contain little organic matter, but are very hard, soften little on boiling, and are generally unwholesome.

Sand and gravel waters vary in character in different regions. Some are very pure, containing less than five grains of mineral matter in a gallon, and less than one grain of organic matter. Others again, particularly such as flow over soft sand-rock, are liable to be very impure, containing much chloride of sodium, carbonate of soda, iron, and a little lime and magnesia, amounting altogether to from thirty to eighty grains per gallon. The organic matter may also be in large amount, from four to ten grains per gallon, or even more.

Alluvial waters, as a rule, are highly charged with carbonate of lime, sulphate of lime, sulphate of magnesia, chloride of sodium, carbonate of soda, iron, silica, and often with organic matter. The amount of solids per gallon ranges from twenty to one hundred and twenty grains.

Surface and subsoil water is often very impure. Cultivated lands, with rich, manured soils, furnish a water often containing both organic matter and salts in large quantity. In towns, and among the habitations of men, the surface and shallow well water frequently contains large quantities of nitrites and nitrates, sulphates and phosphates of lime, and soda and chloride of sodium. Organic matter, also, exists often in large amount.

Marsh-water is always impure from the presence of much organic matter, which is chiefly of vegetable origin, and varies in quantity from ten to fifty grains in the gallon. The proportion of mineral ingredients is usually small, unless the marsh be salt, when the mineral constituents of sea-water are present.

River-water varies much in the number and quantity of its constituents. Coming from various sources, it is even more complex in constitution than spring or well water. Oftentimes it is greatly contaminated by the sewage of towns, and the refuse of manufacturing operations, which are carried on along its banks, and it is also likely to contain a large amount of organic matter.

Sea- Water.—The solid constituents of sea-water amount to about three and a half per cent. of its weight, or nearly half an ounce to the pound. It is unfit for use unless distilled. It then answers well for cooking purposes, and, if thoroughly aërated, is palatable. Any organic matter remaining after distillation may be removed, by passing the water through a charcoal filter, or by letting it stand for a few days. Care should be taken that no lead finds its way into distilled water, as it is rapidly taken up. Many cases of lead-poisoning have occurred on board ships, partly from the use of minium in the apparatus, and partly from the use of zinc pipes, with lead in their composition.

407. Purity of Water.—Perfectly pure water can only be obtained by the most careful processes of distillation, and is never found as such in a natural state. Hence the difficulty of defining what are properly impurities, particularly when we remember that water containing considerable quantities of foreign matter may be used for long periods together, without producing any recognizably injurious results. Experience has shown, however, that certain conditions are necessary to health, and cannot be neglected with impunity. The water should be transparent and colorless, free from odor, and without taste. It should also be well aërated, and afford no deposit on standing; above all, it should be free from organic matter. Probably the less it contains of saline ingredients the better. The Sanitary Congress held at Brussels, in 1853, decided that the total amount ought not to exceed eighty-five grains per gallon. But this furnishes no reliable criterion, as a far less quantity of sulphate of lime, or magnesia, is known to be injurious, while the proportion of carbonate of lime, or soda, may considerably exceed this, and produce no manifestly bad effects.

408. Organic Impurities in Water.—These vary exceedingly in character and amount, and may be either mechanically suspended, or dissolved in the water. If suspended, and of vegetable origin, their presence will often be indicated by a peculiar yellowish or brownish tinge, such as

most are familiar with in the water of marshes or peat bogs.
If of animal origin, they may impart no tinge, and are more
likely to be dissolved. They are derived from numberless
sources, but those of most importance, hygienically, are
furnished by the habitations and trades of men. Rain-
water carries down from the air floating organic impurities, and it may also become contaminated by decaying
leaves that have accumulated on the roofs of houses. Cisterns are also liable to receive impurities from the leaking
of sinks or waste-pipes, or by the washing in of leaves from
the roof. Shallow wells are extremely apt to become contaminated by floods carrying in organic surface impurities.
Deep wells frequently drain large areas about them, and
are very often, particularly in towns, rendered impure and
even offensive by collecting the drainage from cesspools,
vaults, etc. In epidemics of typhus and typhoid fever and
cholera, cases have occurred where it was known that the
specific poison of the disease found its way into the system
by this means. Springs and streams oftentimes receive
the discharges from large manufactories; and, although
the water *appears* pure, an examination reveals the presence of organic matter. The effects of this contamination
may be shown by taking a little of the sediment that has
accumulated at the bottom of a cistern, and placing it in a
bottle of perfectly pure distilled water, when, in a short
time, if the weather be warm, it will smell offensively.
Thus, at ordinary summer temperatures, this organic matter is liable to undergo putrefactive change, and it is then
that it exerts its most baneful effects upon the system.
This, no doubt, is one of the causes of the greater prevalence of diarrhœas and dysenteries during the warmer portions of the year.

409. Action of Water on Lead. — Water is known to
possess the power of corroding lead, and forming compounds with it which, if dissolved, render the water highly
poisonous. All waters act upon it more or less, but it is

only when the lead is *dissolved* that the water containing
it becomes dangerous. When ordinary water is placed in
contact with lead, the free oxygen it contains combines
with the metal, forming oxide of lead, with which the
water immediately unites, producing hydrated oxide of
lead, which is nearly insoluble. There is also more or less
carbonic acid existing in all natural waters; this combines
with the oxide of lead, forming carbonate of lead, which
is also highly insoluble. But, if there be in the water
much carbonic acid, a bicarbonate of lead is formed, which
is very soluble, and therefore remains dissolved in the
water. Hence, waters which abound in free carbonic acid,
as also those which contain bicarbonates of lime, magnesia,
and potash, are most liable to become poisoned by lead.
Water containing common salt acts upon the metal, forming a soluble poisonous chloride of lead. The presence
of organic matter, nitrites and nitrates, imparts to the
water a powerfully-corrosive action. If the water contains
vegetable or fatty acids of any kind, or sour milk, or cider,
its action on lead is greatly increased, and it is more likely to dissolve the compounds formed. On the other hand,
waters containing sulphates and phosphates are little injured, these salts exerting a protective influence on the
lead.

The lead itself is more easily acted upon if other metals,
such as iron, zinc, or tin, are in contact with it. Galvanic
action is set up, which greatly facilitates corrosion.

Dr. Hassal says that, " while very soft water cannot be
stored for a lengthened period, with impunity, in leaden
vessels, the danger of the storage of hard water, under the
same circumstances, is in most cases much greater. This
danger, however, is to be estimated neither by the qualities
of hardness or softness, but altogether depends upon the
chemical constitution of each different kind of water. Thus,
if this be ever so soft, and contain free carbonic acid, its
action on lead will be great; whereas, if it be hard from

the presence of sulphates and phosphates principally, and contain but few bicarbonates, little or no solution of the lead will result."

SECTION III.—*Morbid Effects of Impure Water.*

410. Dyspepsia.—Water containing sulphate of lime, chloride of calcium, and the magnesia salts, has a decided tendency to produce stomachic and intestinal derangements. Dr. Sutherland found that the hard water of the sandstone rocks, which was formerly much used in Liverpool, exerted a marked effect in producing constipation, lessening the secretions, and causing visceral obstructions; and, in Glasgow, the substitution of soft for hard water, according to Dr. Leech, lessened the prevalence of dyspeptic complaints. The exact amount capable of producing these symptoms has not been determined. In a well-water which was found so injurious that men would not drink it, there were present nineteen grains of carbonate of lime, eleven grains of sulphate of lime, and thirteen grains of chloride of sodium per gallon. The total solids were fifty grains per gallon. Iron, in quantities sufficient to give the water a slightly-ferruginous taste, often produces dyspepsia, headache, and general uneasiness.

411. Diarrhœa.—That this disease often originates in the use of bad water, there is no doubt. Great numbers of instances are on record where it was traced directly to this cause, and where a change of water was followed by a disappearance of the disease.

Mineral matters, either dissolved or suspended, will give rise to it if present in considerable quantity. The water of many rivers holds in suspension fine particles of clay or marl in great abundance, particularly at certain seasons, and, if drunk for any length of time, will produce diarrhœa. The use of waters containing dissolved mineral substances, particularly sulphates, will also cause diarrhœa. " Parent Duchatelet noticed the constant excess of patients furnished by the prison of St.-Lazare, in consequence of diarrhœa, and he traced this to the water, which 'contained a very large proportion of sulphate of lime and other purgative salts'" (Parkes). Waters impregnated with nitrate of lime will produce diarrhœa. Brackish water acts in the same way, probably from the large quantity of chloride of sodium it contains.

Dissolved or suspended organic matter, whether of vegetable or animal origin, will cause diarrhœa. In the recent war, great numbers of cases occurred from the use of marsh or ditch water; the sickness ceased when wells were sunk. Water containing fecal matter, sulphuretted hydrogen, or other sewage products, often occasions the worst forms of diarrhœa, attended sometimes with marked choleraic symptoms — such as purging, vomiting, and cramps—even when the senses give no indication of these impurities.

The effects of sulphuretted hydrogen are well shown by a case that occurred in the late war in Mexico. The French troops suffered greatly at Orizaba, from the use of water taken from sulphurous and alkaline springs. This produced dyspepsia and diarrhœa, attended with enormous eructations after meals, the eructed gas having a strong smell of sulphuretted hydrogen. Sewage-gases, setting back through untrapped overflow-pipes into tanks and cisterns, often contaminate the water very rapidly.

412. Dysentery.—This also frequently results from the use of impure water. The impurities which produce it appear to be of the same kind as those which cause diarrhœa. The drainage from graveyards contains large quantities of organic matter and nitrates, and its use is very liable to produce this disease. Water contaminated by the discharges of dysenteric patients is known to produce dysentery in others, and thus the disease oftentimes becomes epidemic.

413. Cholera.—Symptoms of this malady often follow

the use of water containing sewage or decomposing organic matter. Many believe that such water is capable of producing the disease, but this point is still unsettled. There is any amount of evidence, however, that the disease is frequently conveyed in drinking-waters which have been tainted with cholera-evacuations. It is also quite certain that the use of impure water of any kind predisposes to cholera. It probably acts by keeping up a constant irritation in the alimentary canal, thus causing diarrhœa, which in cholera epidemics usually precedes the outbreak of the graver disease.

414. Enteric Fever.—The spread of this disease has of late years been frequently traced to the agency of drinking-waters contaminated either with decomposing organic matter, or the discharges of fever-patients. The most usual condition of its outbreak is the use of water from wells or reservoirs that receive the soakage from defective drains, from privy-vaults, or from some other contiguous source of filth. The instances of its originating in this way are too numerous, and have been too clearly traced, to admit of a doubt of the fact, nor does mere dilution of the poison remove the danger, as the following will show: A recent outbreak in an English town was traced to the milk with which numerous families were served, and it was conclusively proved that this milk was poisoned by being stored in cans that had been washed with water contaminated with sewage from an imperfect drain.

415. Malarious Fevers. — There is strong evidence in support of the belief that these are often produced by drinking marsh or ditch water. They are supposed to be caused by some specific poison generated in marshy regions; and that this may find its way into the blood through the agency of water, as well as of air, there is no reason to doubt. Mr. Blower, of Bedford, England, mentions a case in which, in the parish of Houghton, almost the only family which escaped ague at one time was that of a farmer who used well-water, while all the other inhabitants drank ditch-water.

In yellow fever, like dysentery, typhoid fever, and cholera, the alimentary mucous membrane is primarily affected. Hence, there is strong probability that the cause is also swallowed in this case, and enters with the drinking-water.

416. Goitre, or enlargement of the thyroid gland, is most common in limestone regions, and is held by some to be caused by drinking water highly impregnated with lime and magnesia salts. Johnston states that in the jail at Durham, England, when the water contained seventy-seven grains per gallon of lime and magnesia salts, all the prisoners had swellings of the neck. These disappeared when a purer water, containing eighteen grains per gallon, was obtained.

417. Entozoa, or those parasitical creatures which infest other animals, may find their way into the body by means of the drinking-water. While some enter with the food, others (in the embryo state) are known to exist in great numbers in river-water, and doubtless are often swallowed when such water is used for drinking purposes.

SECTION IV.—*Purification of Water.*

418. Examination by the Senses.—If water is examined by the unaided senses, the information obtained is very limited and should not be relied upon. They will only indicate extreme conditions, and are very liable to overlook the most characteristic impurities. Taste, for instance, even though it be extremely delicate, is wholly untrustworthy. Organic matter, when dissolved, is often quite tasteless; 55 grains of carbonate of soda and 70 of chloride of sodium per gallon are imperceptible; 16 grains of carbonate of lime give no taste, and 25 grains of sulphate of lime very little. If, from its effects, a given water is suspected of impurity, and its use cannot be avoided, examination of it should be intrusted to some competent person.

419. Distillation.—Water may be most thoroughly purified by distillation, but this is impracticable when considerable quantities are required, and, besides, the water is not fit to drink until aërated. To render it perfectly pure, it must be redistilled at low temperatures, in silver vessels.

420. Boiling and Freezing.—Boiling kills most animal and vegetable organisms that water may contain, expels gases, and precipitates carbonate of lime. It is the latter that constitutes the fur or crust often seen lining tea-kettles and boilers.

Freezing renders water much purer, by expelling a large proportion of its saline contents. Carbonate and sulphate of lime may be thus got rid of. But, like boiling and distillation, freezing expels the air and thus renders the water insipid. In all these cases the water regains its palatability on standing.

421. Purification by Chemical Means.—The addition of two or three grains of alum to the quart cleanses muddy or turbid water, but often renders it harder than before. When alum is added, the water should not be used under twenty-four hours. Permanganate of potash destroys organic matter and ammoniacal compounds by rapid oxidation, and may be used with advantage for this purpose.

422. Filtration.—This is the most effective and practicable method of purification, and is within the reach of every one. Many substances will answer as filters, such as crushed charcoal, sand, or porous sandstone, flannel, wool, sponges, or any other porous media. Of all these, charcoal is the best. It will remove eighty-eight per cent. of organic matter, and twenty-eight per cent. of mineral matters. If the water is moderately good, one pound of charcoal will purify six hundred pounds, or sixty gallons. Animal charcoal is better than vegetable, though both lose their purifying power sooner or later. It is quickly restored, however, by exposure to air and slight heat. Filters of charcoal should be made of considerable thickness, and the coal finely crushed and well pressed together. The effect of the charcoal is supposed to be chiefly chemical, as it brings the large quantity of oxygen which it holds into the closest contact with any oxidizable matters in the water.

Sand is much used, and answers well for a time, but requires to be often renewed.

CHAPTER XVII.

FOOD AND HEALTH.

SECTION I.—*The Alimentary Principles of Food.*

423. The Four Groups.—It was stated in Chapter VI., Section I., that all substances used as foods may be classed under four heads, either as Proteids, Fats, Amyloids, or Minerals. It is desirable to recapitulate and somewhat extend the observations there made.

424. The Proteids.—This group of alimentary principles includes Gluten, Fibrin, Albumen, Syntonin, Casein, and Gelatin, which are characterized by the presence in their composition of a large amount of nitrogen.

Gluten is the adhesive principle of grain, and is a grayish, tough, elastic substance, left when the starch is thoroughly washed away from flour. From its resemblance to the fibrous part of meat, it is known as vegetable fibrin. *Animal fibrin* exists dissolved in the blood, and solidifies into a fine net-work as the blood coagulates. It constitutes the bulk of lean meat. *Casein* is the curdy principle of milk, which is separated by coagulation, and forms the chief ingredient of cheese. It exists in large quantity (twenty to twenty-eight per cent.) in beans and peas, and is known as vegetable casein. *Albumen* is a transparent, glairy, coagulable fluid, familiar to all as white of egg. It is a large constituent of animal fluid and tissues, and occurs in the seeds and juices of plants. *Syntonin* is the chief constituent of muscle or flesh. It closely resembles albumen in composition, but, unlike it, is not a product of the vegetable kingdom. *Gelatin* is an animal product, chiefly obtained from bones and tendons. It is not found in the vegetable kingdom, and is used for food, principally in the form of jellies and soups.

All the foregoing substances, except gelatin, have a remarkable similarity of composition. They present varieties of aspect and physical properties, and differ in consistency, solubility, and behavior with heat: but they serve a common purpose in the animal economy—that of furnishing material for the formation of the tissues—and on this account have a high nutritive value, and are to a great extent mutually replaceable.

425. The Fats.—These occur in both plants and animals, and, whatever their source, have a great similarity of composition. Like the proteids, they differ in physical properties, but are capable of replacing each other as articles of diet. They are essential to the formation of both muscular and nervous tissue, and, from their large amount of hydrogen and carbon, are the most energetic supporters of the heat-producing function.

426. The Amyloids.—This group comprises the starches, sugars, and gums—principally vegetable products, which in one form or another constitute a large proportion of our ordinary food. Starch is abundant in grain, peas, beans, and potatoes. The different preparations known as sago, tapioca, arrow-root, and the like, consist almost entirely of *starch* extracted from different species of plants. Starch is capable of conversion into sugar, and is thus changed by the juices of the alimentary canal. *Sugar* is produced by both plants and animals, but our supply comes chiefly from the vegetable kingdom, where it occurs in great abundance in sap, fruit, and seeds. By the agency of heat, starch may be converted into *gum*, known as dextrine. Gums are vegetable products widely distributed, but not in great abundance. Their composition is similar to that of starch and sugar, and their dietetical function is supposed to be the same.

427. Their Offices.—It has until lately been supposed that as the nitrogenous and non-nitrogenous substances are clearly separated by chemical compositions, they are also sharply divided in their physiological effects. The first were supposed to nourish the tissues, the decomposition of which was believed to be the sole source of animal power, while the fatty and amyloid group served only to maintain animal heat by their oxidation. But, while it is believed that the bodily tissues can only be reproduced from the nitrogenous elements, it is admitted that the decomposition of these tissues must be a source of heat; and recent researches have established that the combustion of the hydro-carbons is a source of power, part of the heat produced being converted into mechanical force.

428. Mineral Aliments.—The inorganic or mineral constituents of food consist of water and various saline substances. Common salt occurs in all forms of food, but in larger proportion in animal than in vegetable tissues. An instinctive craving impels animals to seek for a larger supply of it than is furnished in their food. Chloride of potassium, phosphate of lime, and alkaline carbonates, are indispensable to digestion, and are furnished in combination with the various aliments.

429. Necessity for a Mixed Diet.—The usual forms of food are combinations of these alimentary principles. Milk, for example, is a highly-complex animal product, containing water, casein, butter, sugar, and various mineral salts —representatives of each of the four classes of alimentary principles. By its excess of salts and nitrogenous matter,

17

it is suited to the wants of the infant, or the period of rapid growth, but it is not a complete or properly-balanced diet for the adult. In the majority of cases, no single article of food is thus perfect in composition, there being usually one or more of the essential elements of a suitable diet wanting. This is the case with the various meats, all of which abound in nitrogenous and fatty substances, but are deficient in the amyloid elements. On the other hand, most vegetables are rich in starch and sugar, but deficient in nitrogenous matters. Bread is nitrogenous, amylaceous, and inorganic, but lacks fat; while Indian-corn contains less of the nitrogenous element, but a large amount of starch, and eight or ten per cent. of fat. As no one article of food, therefore, contains these four classes of materials in the proportions requisite to a perfect diet, we are obliged to mix our various food-stuffs. Confinement to a single alimentary principle, or to any one class of them alone, is sure to be followed by disease. It has been shown, by repeated experiments, that dogs confined to the exclusive use of either starch, fat, or albumen, soon die of starvation. Like experiments begun upon men were productive of a corresponding disturbance, and doubtless, if carried out, would have ended in the same way.

The proteids are first in importance, as much the larger part of the mass of the body is derived from them, and, when given alone, they sustain its powers longer than any other class of aliments. Hence, it is easy to see why exhaustion follows so much more quickly when they are withheld, than when other kinds of food are unsupplied. But the amyloids, fats, and minerals, are also requisite, and the body feels the want of them sooner or later, even though the proteids are furnished in abundance.

SECTION II.—*Animal Foods.*

Foods may be conveniently divided into three classes: animal food, vegetable food, and auxiliary food. Substances derived from animals, such as milk, eggs, and meats, are examples of the first class.

430. Milk.—As this liquid contains all the elements necessary for complete nutrition, it has been regarded as the type of composite foods, but, as just remarked, it is only completely adapted to a certain stage of animal life. A hundred parts of cow's milk contain of casein, 4.48; of butter, 3.13; of milk-sugar, 4.47; salts, .60; and of water, 87.32. This, however, is only an average statement, as no two cows give milk exactly alike in composition, while the milk of the same cow varies with the food. The milk of goats and ewes is richer in solids than that of the cow. Human milk is poorer in casein, and contains a larger proportion of sugar than cow's milk; this is the reason why the latter is diluted and sugared when employed as food for infants.

In cities, milk is often adulterated with water. If much water has been added, it may be detected by applying the specific-gravity test. The specific gravity of unadulterated milk ranges from 1.026 to 1.033; the average is about 1.030. Two parts water to eight parts milk will reduce its specific gravity to 1.024; four parts water to six parts milk, to 1.018. Good milk should be of a full white color, perfectly opaque, without deposit, and free from any peculiar taste or smell. It should give a neutral reaction, and have a specific gravity of at least 1.028.

431. Butter and Cheese.—These furnish the nutritive constituents of milk in a concentrated form. Butter is habitually associated with substances which are deficient in fat, and is held to promote their digestibility. All butter contains casein, which is derived from the milk skimmed off with the cream, but the less it contains the less liable it is to become rancid. Rancidity is chiefly owing to changes in the oil produced by decomposition of the casein. Butter in this condition is unfit for food, as it is indigestible, and has been known to produce dyspepsia and diarrhœa. Cheese is rich in nitrogenous material, and when fresh is regarded as excellent food. It is very liable, however, to undergo chemical change, and when this is once set up it becomes irritating and indigestible, especially if eaten in considerable quantity. The peculiar flavor of old cheese arises from this commencing decomposition, and it often disturbs weak stomachs. In this condition, however, it is said to promote the digestion of other substances, and for this reason is sometimes taken in small quantities as a condiment.

432. Eggs.—These are both nitrogenous and fatty, and, when properly cooked, are easily digested and highly nutritious. They contain no starch or sugar, and should therefore be eaten in connection with such articles as supply these aliments. Eggs are most wholesome when boiled sufficiently to coagulate the white without hardening the yolk. Hard boiled or fried eggs digest with difficulty. And eggs that have been kept long, though not spoiled, are less digestible than fresh ones.

433. Meats.—Whatever their source, these are essentially the same in constitution, that is, they all contain a large amount of nitrogenous matter, in union with much fat and various important salts. Their advantage as a diet is, that they contain a large amount of nutriment in a highly-concentrated form, are easily digested when properly cooked, and admit of ready assimilation.

Fresh meat varies in quality with different animals, and with the age, sex, and condition of the individual from which it was obtained, as well as with the character of the food upon which it was fattened. Stall-fed cattle make the finest beef, and corn-fed swine the best pork. The nicest mutton is obtained from sheep fattened on fresh, succulent pasturage. In all cases the animal should be free from disease, and of medium fatness, to make its flesh a healthly and economical food. The muscle should be of a firm yet not sodden consistence, of a pale-reddish color, somewhat lighter toward the centre than at the surface, and show no disposition to tear across its fibres. The fat should be white, or but slightly tinged with yellow, and also firm to the touch. The pale, moist muscle marks the young animal; the dark colored, the old one. The meat should be free from any disagreeable odor, and the muscles, when cut across, should present a uniform solidity. Any marbling, or points where the knife passes more easily than at others, indicates commencing decomposition. As a rule, the flesh of young animals is tenderer and more easily digested than that of old ones; veal, however, is an exception, so far as digestibility is concerned. The flesh of young animals contains more water than that of old ones, consequently it is more juicy, but, bulk for bulk, less nutritious.

434. Salt Meat.—Beef and pork are commonly preserved for future use by salting, and in this condition are largely employed as food. Salting, however, reduces the nutritive value of meat, detracts from its flavor, and renders its digestion more difficult. It does this by extracting a portion of the juices, which remain dissolved in the brine, thus leaving the fibres of the meat harder and consequently less easily acted upon by the fluids of the stomach.

435. Poultry and Game.—Meat of this kind is more easily digested than that just considered, but is regarded as less nutritious. It is not so juicy as butcher's meat, and as a rule contains less fat. Broths made from it have a delicate flavor, and contain considerable nutriment, hence they make an excellent food for convalescents.

436. Fish.—The flesh of fish is very similar in composition to that of other animals. It is somewhat poorer in nitrogenous matter, but richer in important salts, and contains a larger proportion of water than butcher's meat.

It is generally of easy digestion, but it should not be used exclusively, nor for a long period together, as it is liable to produce a scorbutic state of the system. The flesh of fish undergoes rapid decomposition; and is then highly injurious. It should be eaten only when it is perfectly fresh. Salt fish, like salt beef or pork, is much inferior to fresh, and extremely indigestible.

437. Crabs and Lobsters.—The flesh of these animals resembles that of fish, but it is less easily digested. It is peculiarly prone to decomposition, and when eaten in this state often produces sickness which sometimes proves fatal.

438. Clams and Oysters.—Clams, either raw or cooked, are difficult to digest. Oysters are much less so. They are most easily digested when raw, and, if cooked, should be either stewed or roasted.

SECTION III.— *Vegetable Food.*

439. Wheat.—Of vegetable food-stuffs, the most important and widely-used are the cereal grains. Among these wheat ranks first, both in point of nutritive value and in the ease with which it is digested. With the exception of milk, it approaches more nearly the standard of a perfect food, and will sustain the powers of the body for a longer period, than any other single article of diet. It contains from ten to fifteen per cent. of gluten; from sixty to seventy per cent. of starchy matter, and a small proportion of fat, besides certain important alkaline and earthy phosphates. Its proportion of water is very low, averaging about twelve per cent.; bulk for bulk, therefore, it is richer in solids than any other food. The starchy elements of the seed exist most abundantly in and about its centre, while its glutinous, fatty, and mineral constituents, are found in greatest quantity towards the surface. The coat immediately beneath the husk is especially rich in gluten, and therefore highly valuable as food. In the process of grinding, this is often lost by passing into the bran, the result being a whiter but much less nutritious flour. The soft wheats yield the whitest flours, as they contain more starch and less gluten than the hard or flinty varieties. Good wheat should yield at least eighty per cent. of flour.

The quality of wheaten flour may be best determined by the practical test of baking. Still, something may be told by its appearance. It should contain very little bran, and its starch should be white, or with the very slightest tinge of yellow. The flour ought not to be lumpy, or, if so, the lumps should readily give way under the slightest pressure. Grittiness indicates that the starch-grains are changing, and such flour will give an acid bread. When compressed in the hand, good flour will adhere in a lump, and retain the imprints of the fingers longer than that of inferior grade. If cast against the wall, a portion should stick firmly to its surface. The dough made with good flour is ductile and elastic, and may be drawn out into long strips, or rolled into thin sheets without breaking.

Flour becomes whiter with age, but it is at the expense of flavor, sweetness, and nutritive value. The greater the proportion of gluten, the sooner will this deterioration take place. Flour is sometimes contaminated by the presence of fungi or insects, and they always indicate inferior quality. It is also occasionally adulterated with the flour of other grains, which can only be detected by the microscope.

440. Rye.—This comes next to wheat in nutritive value, though it furnishes less flour to the bushel, and that of a decidedly darker color. Its gluten appears to contain more casein and less vegetable fibrin than that of wheat, consequently it is less tenacious. Owing to this quality, bread made from rye-flour does not rise well, and is liable to become heavy on cooling. Rye-bread soon becomes acid, and with many is not easily digested.

441. Buckwheat.—This is poor in nitrogenous and fatty constituents, but rich in starch. Bread made from buckwheat-flour does not rise well, owing to its deficiency in gluten. It is, therefore, chiefly consumed in making griddle-cakes, which, while warm, are light and palatable, but not well received by weak stomachs.

442. Indian-corn contains a much larger proportion of fat than any other grain in common use. It is also rich in starch, but has far less nitrogenous matter (zein) than either wheat or rye. This principle is not of a glutinous, adhesive nature, and hence maize-flour, or meal, will not make a dough, or fermented bread. In the preparation of articles of food from Indian-meal, long cooking is necessary, when it makes both a palatable and highly-nutritious food, which is easily digested.

443. Oatmeal is rich in gluten and fat, and also contains a fair proportion of starch and sugar. It does not make good bread, but is commonly cooked by stirring with boiling water until it has the consistence of hasty pudding. It should be thoroughly cooked, when it is palatable and highly nutritious. It is less digestible, however, than wheaten products.

444. Rice.—As an article of diet, rice possesses the advantage of an extremely digestible starch-grain. It has, however, but small proportions of nitrogenous matter, fat, and salts; hence, in rice-eating nations, it is habitually taken with such other food as will best supply these wants.

445. Peas and **beans** are much alike in composition, and both rich in nitrogenous constituents, often containing as high as twenty-six per cent. of vegetable casein, or *legumen.* They also contain much sulphur and phosphorus, together with an average proportion of salts, and but a small quantity of water. They are, therefore, very nutritious, and rank first among concentrated, strength-imparting foods. But they are somewhat indigestible, and liable to produce flatus. When eaten, it should be in small quantity, and only by those of an active habit of body.

446. Succulent Vegetables.—Of these, potatoes are the

most valuable and most extensively used.   They contain in
100 parts—

Water	74
Proteids	1.5
Fats	.1
Amyloids	23.4
Salts	1

They are thus seen to abound in amylaceous materials and
salts, but contain a low proportion of nitrogenous matter,
and very little fat.   Owing to this deficiency, we habitually
associate them with meat, when they form an easily digested
and valuable food.

Turnips, beets, carrots, parsnips, etc., contain more
water than potatoes, and are not so easily digested.   Their
solid portions consist mainly of starch and sugar, with a
small percentage of fat and salts.   They each possess a peculiar volatile principle, which adds much to their flavor,
and causes them to be eaten more as a relish than as a
strength-giving food.

Onions and cabbage are more watery than the preceding, but their solid parts contain a very large proportion
of nitrogenous matter.   They are relished chiefly for their
pungency, but should be eaten only at intervals, as they are
likely to cause flatus and indigestion.

447. The Fruits.—These consist mostly of water and
cellulose, with varying amounts of fruit-sugar, and small
quantities of potash, soda, and lime, in combination with
certain organic acids.   Their juices contain a gelatinous
substance termed *pectine*, which forms the basis of the various jellies.   Fruits are prized more for those qualities
which relate to their taste than for nourishing and strength-
ening power.   Nevertheless, they are valuable as sources
of the alkaline and earthy carbonates, and useful when eaten
in moderate quantity, as safeguards against constipation.
They are most wholesome when cooked, but in all cases the

skins, seeds, and cores, should be rejected, as indigestible, and prolific sources of irritation.

Section IV.—*Auxiliary Foods.*

448.—Auxiliary foods comprise a class of substances very extensively employed to give relish to other dietary compounds, to provoke the digestive organs, and for nervous stimulation, rather than for any nutritive properties of their own. Useful when taken with care, they are liable to prove most injurious when too freely indulged in. Under this head come the various condiments and beverages.

449. The Condiments.— *Vinegar* is essentially a solution of acetic acid in water. Good vinegar ought to contain at least five per cent. of the acid. Commercial vinegar is often largely adulterated, and some samples which pass under the name are made of sulphuric acid and water, colored with burnt sugar, and without a trace of acetic acid in their composition. Vinegar in small quantities, by augmenting the acidity of the stomach, may reënforce the gastric juice, and promote the digestion of the proteids.

Black pepper consists of an active principle (*piperin*), a pungent essential oil, and an acrid resin. It is a powerful stimulant of the digestive organs, increasing the flow of saliva and gastric juice in a marked degree. In the powdered state it is frequently adulterated with linseed-meal, starch, mustard, buckwheat-bran, etc. These may be detected by the microscope; but it is safest to purchase the berries and grind them as wanted.

Cayenne pepper resembles black pepper in properties, but is a much more powerful stimulant. Its habitual use, therefore, cannot be recommended, and, if taken at all, it should be only in the smallest quantity.

The sharp, acrid smell and taste of *mustard* are due to the volatile oil it contains. Used in small quantities, it is a gentle stimulant; in large doses, it acts as an emetic.

Like all articles of its class, it is subject to sophistication. Among the substances added, the most common are turmeric and some form of starch. Sulphate of lime and chalk are also sometimes used as adulterants.

450. Beverages.—TEA.—This consists of the leaves of the tea-shrub, grown and prepared chiefly in China. Many varieties are known in commerce, the differences between which are due probably to different modes of culture and preparation.

The substances for which tea is most prized as a beverage are—*first*, a peculiar volatile oil, which gives the tea its agreeable flavor; *second*, a vegetable alkali, rich in nitrogen, and known as *thein*—the active principle of tea; and *third*, tannic acid, which gives the tea its astringent quality. Of the first, tea contains less than one per cent.; of the second, from one and a half to six per cent.; and of the tannic acid, which is in combination with the thein, from fourteen to sixteen per cent. It contains, besides, about twenty per cent. of gluten, and is also rich in salts, but these last ingredients are not usually obtained in the beverage.

In making tea, it is desirable to obtain from the leaves the largest possible amount of matter, without destroying its flavor. If the tea is boiled, the volatile oil is driven off with the steam—and yet a boiling temperature is required to dissolve the compound of thein and tannic acid, the most important constituent of the leaf. To preserve the one and obtain the other is the principal object, and this is best attained by pouring boiling water upon the leaves in close vessels, and allowing them to steep for a time, with the temperature slightly below the boiling-point.

Tea acts as a gentle stimulant to the nervous system, without producing subsequent perceptible depression. It also quickens the pulse somewhat, and increases the amount of pulmonary carbonic acid exhaled. It produces an astringent effect upon the bowels, but not to any harmful extent. It hastens digestion and is invigorating, but should not be taken in excess, as it is apt to induce wakefulness and an irritable state of the system. *Green tea* is more injurious than black, often giving rise to nervous tremors.

Tea of all sorts is liable to the grossest adulteration, green teas being worse in this respect than the black varieties. The Chinese heighten the color of the leaves or *face* them, as it is termed, by the addition of Prussian blue, indigo, turmeric, gypsum, and China clay. A bright-green color is to be looked upon with suspicion, as the pure article always presents a dull, faded green appearance. The leaves of other plants are often mixed with tea. Sometimes, also, exhausted tea-leaves or *grounds* are bought up, astringency imparted to them by the addition of catechu, and, colored with black lead, or logwood, they are sold again as genuine tea. Another fraud of great prevalence consists of mixing inferior qualities of tea with better sorts, and cheating the purchaser by selling the compound at the price of the best article.

In selecting tea, it should be but little broken up, or mixed with dirt, and the leaves should vary somewhat in size and color. The best teas contain portions of the stalk and flower. Old teas do not possess so rich a flavor as fresh, owing to the loss of a portion of their volatile oil.

451. Coffee.—Coffee, like tea, contains a volatile oil, a vegetable alkali (*caffein*), and tannic acid. It also contains from twelve to fifteen per cent. of amylaceous material, in the shape of sugar and gum, and nearly the same quantity of nitrogenous matter, in various forms, besides being rich in salts. But very small quantities of these latter substances find their way into the beverage.

The agreeable flavor of coffee is due to its volatile oil, which is present in very minute proportions, and requires the action of heat to develop it. This is done by the process of torrefying. The caffein is almost identical in composition with the thein of tea, and, like it, is the active principle of the beverage. It is present in small quantity, rarely reaching one per cent. The quantity of tannic acid is usually less than six per cent., consequently coffee is not so astringent as tea.

The action of coffee upon the system is similar to that of tea. It is a stimulant, and promotes the digestion and assimilation of food. It both enlivens the mind and invigorates the body, relieving the depression of fatigue, and in this way undoubtedly tends to diminish the liability to disease.

There is a peculiar physiological effect exerted by coffee and tea, and probably also by alcoholic beverages when taken in small amount—a retardation of destructive metamorphosis. The renal products of muscular waste are found to be diminished after their use; while experience has shown that they may replace, in diet, a certain amount of ordinary food. De Gasparin, in his observations upon the regimen of the Belgian miners, found that "the addition of a quantity of coffee to the daily rations enabled them to perform their arduous labors on a diet which was even below that found necessary in prisons and elsewhere, where the article was not employed." The comparative effects of coffee, tea, and alcohol, in enabling men to endure cold and hardship, are thus stated by Dr. Hayes, in describing the experiences of arctic exploration: "Dr. Kane's parties, after repeated trial, took most kindly to coffee in the morning, and tea in the evening. The coffee seemed to last throughout the day, and the men seemed to grow hungry less rapidly after taking it than after drinking tea, while tea soothed them after a day's hard labor, and the better enabled them to sleep. They both operated upon fatigued and overtaxed men like a charm, and their superiority over alcoholic stimulants was very marked."

In the process of roasting, the coffee should be first

carefully dried in an open pan, over a gentle fire, until it becomes yellow. It should then be scorched, in a covered vessel to prevent the escape of aroma, taking care, by proper agitation, to prevent any portion from being burnt, as a few charred grains communicate a bad odor to the rest. The operation should be continued until the coffee acquires a deep cinnamon or chestnut color, and an oily appearance, or until the peculiar fragrance of roasted coffee is sufficiently strong. Unroasted coffee may be kept for any length of time, and grows better with age. After roasting, it is constantly losing flavor; hence, it is well to roast but a small quantity at once, and this ought to be kept in close vessels, and ground as it is wanted for use. This course necessitates the purchase of the berry and home preparation, but the additional trouble is more than compensated by the superior beverage thus obtained. The finer it is ground, the more readily, of course, will it yield its soluble constituents.

Ground coffee is very extensively adulterated; another inducement for purchasing the whole berries. Various substances are employed as adulterants, such as roasted peas, beans, corn, turnips, carrots, potatoes, etc. But the substance most commonly used is chiccory, which has a large white parsnip-like root, abounding in a bitter juice. A little of this, when roasted, gives as dark a color and as bitter a taste to water as four times the quantity of coffee, and, as it only costs about one-third as much, the temptation is very strong to mix it with ground coffee. So great is the demand for chiccory for this purpose, that it is itself adulterated with roasted barley and wheat grains, acorns, mangel-wurzel, sawdust, peas, and beans. Venetian red is sometimes added to give it a coffee-color, and even this is cheapened by the addition of brick-dust. The microscope detects many of these foreign substances, while some can be identified only by chemical means.

In the preparation of the beverage, we are met by the

difficulty that was encountered in the case of tea; that is, a high heat will drive off the aroma, while yet it is requisite to the extraction of the active principle—caffein. To obviate this, take two portions of coffee, boil the first for five minutes in the required amount of water; then, after settling a moment, decant the water upon the second portion, and allow it to steep for a few moments without additional heat. After it has settled, pour off the liquor for use, and retain the grounds for the next day's boiling. A fresh portion furnishes the aroma, and can in its turn be subjected to the boiling process.

452. Cocoa and Chocolate.—These are prepared from *cocoa-beans*, which are derived from a fruit resembling a short, thick cucumber, grown upon the small cocoa-tree of the West Indies, Mexico, and South America. The bean is brittle, of a dark-brown color internally, and has a slightly astringent but decidedly bitter taste. In preparing it for use, it is roasted in the same way as coffee, until the aroma is fully developed. The bean is now more brittle, lighter in color, and less astringent and bitter than before. The beans contain about fifty per cent. of fatty matter, called *butter of cocoa*, and from twenty to twenty-five per cent. of albuminous and starchy material. They also contain a peculiar nitrogenous substance called *theobromin*, similar in nature and properties to thein and caffein. The beans, crushed to a paste between hot rollers, and mixed with starch, sugar, etc., form common *cocoa*. Chocolate is made by grinding the recently-shelled beans to paste, mixing this with sugar, and flavoring it with vanilla, cinnamon, and the like. When used as a beverage, the chocolate or cocoa is scraped into powder, mixed with water and milk, and brought to a boiling heat. As thus prepared, chocolate is refreshing to the spirits, and highly nutritious.

SECTION V.—*Culinary Preparation of Foods.*

453. Cooking has a twofold object—*first*, to soften the food, and thus facilitate its solution in the digestive juices; and *second*, to develop its flavor, and thus render it more agreeable to the palate. When the operation is properly performed, both these purposes may be attained, and yet by improper management both may be defeated. For example, in cooking meats, it is desirable to retain their flavor, preserve their juices, and soften their texture, and, with the requisite care, all this may be accomplished; yet how often does careless or improper management give us a hard, dry, tasteless mass, as indigestible as it is unpalatable ! Over-cooking should be specially avoided, as it results in waste and loss of sapidity, without in any respect improving the character of the food.

454. Cooking of Meats. — *Boiling.* — Meats lose from twenty-five to thirty-five per cent. of their weight by this process. If it is desired to retain their juices and flavor, the pieces should be cut large, and, when first put in, the water should be boiling. This coagulates the albumen near the surface of the piece, and thus prevents further escape. After boiling three or five minutes, the heat should be lowered to about 160°, and maintained at that point until the completion of the process. If the temperature is kept above 170°, the muscular tissue shrinks, and becomes hard and indigestible. In making broth, the object is to extract the juices; hence the meat should be cut into small pieces and placed in cold water. After standing a little time, it may be slowly heated to about 150°; never much above this. Coagulation of the albumen is thus prevented, and the contained juices extracted. A nutritious beef-broth, or *beef-tea*, may be made without heat, by adding to a pint of cold water half a pound of finely-cut, fresh, lean beef and four or five drops of hydrochloric acid. Slight heat and a few drops more acid considerably increase the amount of extract.

Roasting is one of the best methods of cooking meat. It not only develops the flavor, but preserves the juices, and leaves the meat in a condition to be easily digested.

The loss is about twenty-five per cent., and is chiefly water. The process should be commenced with an intense heat, in order to coagulate the albumen of the surface and form a thin superficial crust. Afterwards it should be done very slowly, so as to avoid hardening the inner portions.

Stewing is analogous to roasting, only the meat is cut up, and continually moistened with its own juices. Like boiling and roasting, it should be done at a low heat. Tough meat is best cooked in this manner. Baking requires to be conducted with great care, or there is danger of drying up the meat. Constant basting prevents this to some extent, but the method is inferior to roasting. Frying is the worst possible way in which meat can be cooked. The oil or fat requiring a high temperature to bring it to the boiling-point, the meat is thus rendered extremely hard and the fat not unfrequently burned. Broiling is to be preferred to frying. It has much the same effect as roasting, and, like that process, should not be carried too far—a high heat at first, sufficient to incrust the outside, and then a low temperature to complete the work.

455. Cooking of Vegetables.—These are usually boiled, and are best cooked by this means. Care should be taken not to overdo them. Thorough softening is sufficient, as, when the process is carried beyond this, their structure is rapidly broken down, and a large proportion of their salts and juices lost in the water. The quality of the water employed exercises an important influence. Soft water exerts a much more powerful extractive action than hard, hence food boiled in it is oftentimes rendered insipid by the loss of its salts and juices. When it is desirable to obtain these in a liquid form, as in making soups, broths, or infusions, soft water is to be preferred. In those cases where it is not the object to dissolve out the contents of a structure, but rather to preserve it firm and entire, hard water is the best. To prevent the over-dissolving action of soft water, salt is often added, and proves quite effectual.

Section VI.—*Injurious Effects of Bad Diet.*

456. Effects of Excess in Diet.—The influence of food upon health is immediate and powerful, and is manifested in various ways. Imperfect diet is chiefly injurious by its excess, by its deficiency, by the wrong proportions of its elements, and by the unwholesome condition of the articles consumed.

The quantity of food that it is proper to take, varies, of course, with different circumstances: those thinly clad and exposed to cold require more than the well protected; those in active exercise more than the sedentary or persons of inactive habits; while the growing need, proportionally to their size, more than adults. But whatever the circumstances, if the quantity of food taken exceed the demands of the system, evil consequences are certain to follow. The immediate results of over-eating are lethargy, heaviness, and tendency to sleep. Overtaxing the digestive organs soon deranges their functions, and is a common and efficient cause of dyspepsia. If the food is not absorbed from the digestive apparatus into the system, it rapidly undergoes chemical decomposition in the alimentary canal, and often putrefies. Large quantities of gas are thus generated, which give rise to flatulence and colicky pain. Dyspepsia, constipation, and intestinal irritation, causing diarrhœa, are produced. If digestion be strong, and its products are absorbed, an excess of nutriment is thrown into the blood, and the circulation overloaded. If food is not expended in force, the natural alternative is its accumulation in the system, producing plethora and abnormal increase of tissue. This is accompanied by congestion of important organs, mal-assimilation of nutritive material, and increased proneness to derangement and diseased action. The excretory processes are likewise certain to be disturbed, which often leads to the retention of waste products, with perversion and poisoning of the blood, and a train of evil consequences.

457. Effects of Deficient Diet.—As food is the source alike of the material organism and of the power it exerts, if a due supply of it is withheld, there is defective nutrition, which reduces the structures and impairs the strength. Habitual insufficiency of food lowers the vital powers and depresses the functions. There is loss of mental vigor and muscular energy, and a tendency to digestive disturbance, anæmia, and the development of those maladies which result from debility and undervitalized conditions. The resistance of the system to the numerous causes of disease is diminished: typhus and typhoid fevers are peculiar diseases of the poorly-fed. In childhood, lack of sufficient food is often the cause of stunted growth and chronic disease, and in later life the parent of depraved appetites and moral perversities.

Of the effects of stinted food upon mind and character, Dr. Moleshott observes: "There is another instinct by which the vigor of mind is vanquished in a more melancholy way. Hunger desolates head and heart. Though the craving for nutriment may be lessened to a surprising degree during mental exertion, there exists nothing more hostile to the cheerfulness of an active, thoughtful mind, than the deprivation of liquid and solid food. To the starving man, every pressure becomes an intolerable burden; for this reason, hunger has effected more revolutions than the ambition of disaffected subjects. It is not, then, the dictate of cupidity or the claim of idleness which prompts the belief in a natural human right to work and food."

458. Amount of Food daily required.—Although this is variable in different circumstances, yet definite standards have been reached when dealing with large bodies of men in given cases. It has been shown that generally, in the case of the adult male, from ten to twelve ounces of carbon and from four to five ounces of nitrogenized matter (estimated dry) are daily discharged from the organism, and that, to replace this, there is required a daily consumption of from two to three pounds of solid food. Dr. Dalton says: "From experiments performed while living on an exclusive diet of bread, fish, meat, and butter, with coffee and water for drink, we have found that the entire quantity of food required during twenty-four hours, by a man in full health, and taking free exercise in the open air, is as follows:

Meat	. 16 ounces, or 1.00 lbs. avoirdupois.
Bread . . .	. 19 " " 1.19 " "
Butter, or fat . .	. 3¼ " " 0.22 " "
Water . . .	. 52 fluid-oz. " 3.38 " "

That is to say, rather less than two and a half pounds of solid food, and rather over three pints of liquid food."

"It is undoubtedly true that the daily ration has frequently been diminished considerably below the physiological standard in charitable institutions, prisons, etc.; but, when there is complete inactivity of body and mind, this produces no other effect than that of slightly diminishing the weight and strength. The system then becomes reduced without any actual disease, and there is simply a diminished capacity for labor. But in the alimentation of large bodies of men subjected to exposure, and frequently called upon to perform great labor, the question of food is of vital importance, and the men collectively are like a powerful machine, in which a certain quantity of material must be furnished in order to produce the required amount of force. This important physiological fact is most strikingly exemplified in armies; and the history of the world presents few examples of warlike operations in which the efficiency of the men has not been impaired by insufficient food.

"The United States army-ration is the most generous in the world; and the result has been that, in the recent civil war, scurvy and other diseases which are usually so rife in

armies subject to the exposure and fatigue incident to
grand military operations, have been comparatively rare.
In some of the long and arduous campaigns of the war,
the marches made by large bodies of troops, and the labor
performed, showed an amount of endurance heretofore
unknown in military history. The excellent physical
condition of the men was further evidenced by the remarkable percentage of recoveries after serious wounds and
surgical operations, and the slight prevalence of the
ordinary diseases, except those of malarial origin."—(Dr.
Flint.)

The following is the army-ration of the United States
soldier :

Bread or flour	22	ounces.
Fresh or salt beef (or pork or bacon, 12 oz.)	20	"
Potatoes (three times per week)	16	"
Rice	1.6	"
Coffee (or tea, 0.24 oz.)	1.6	"
Sugar	2.4	"
Beans	0.64	gill.
Vinegar	0.32	"
Salt	0.16	"

459. Effects of a badly-constituted Diet.—There may be
sufficient bulkiness in the food taken, but such a dispropor-
tion among its elements as to pervert the functions and
give rise to various maladies. The several elements of
food-stuffs are not replaceable. Deficiency of the proteids
results in muscular debility and prostration ; while, if too
great a quantity be taken, they charge the system with
imperfectly-assimilated compounds and wrongly-changed
products of decomposition, which produce a gouty state of
the constitution. Deficiency of the fats induces defective
nutrition and leanness; while excess of them not only
tends to produce obesity, but, if more be taken than can be
stored or consumed, the burden of disposing of the excess
falls upon the liver, which may itself become diseased from

over-action, or its secretions be thrown into the blood, giving rise to a bilious condition of the system. If the saline elements are withheld, softening, or deformity of the bones, or rickets, is the legitimate consequence. If the supply of fresh vegetable food is cut off for a lengthened period, a scorbutic condition of body is produced. Hence, for the preservation of health, mixed food and a various well-balanced diet are indispensable.

In the case of infants and children, where food subserves the double purpose of maintaining activity and growth, there must be extra provision in the diet for the development of muscular and bony tissues. Milk, though a liquid, by its abundance of salts and casein, is adapted to this end. But too frequently, after weaning, the food of children is given with no reference to this important condition. Sago, tapioca, arrow-root, and jellies, which rank lowest in nutritive value, with perhaps other substances less objectionable, but still inadequately nourishing, are frequently made use of, to the serious injury of the growing constitution.

460. Effects of a Deficiency of Fat.—It is believed that a lack of oleaginous elements in diet predisposes to consumption. The immediate cause of this disease, as has been already observed, is an abortive or perverted nutrition, tubercle being produced instead of healthy tissue. The seeds of consumption are most generally sown in the system in youth, when there is a double demand upon nutrition, for current waste and steady growth. There is, however, sufficient proteid matter present to nourish the structures; some other condition must, therefore, be wanting. Eminent physiologists have lately maintained that the faulty nutrition which results in tubercle is caused by a deficiency of oily substances, and therefore such of these bodies as are easiest digested and absorbed have been indicated as remedies. Cod-liver oil has come into use for this purpose. Dr. Hughes Bennett, who first introduced this oil to the notice of the public, states that butchers, cooks, oilmen, tanners, and others who are constantly coming in contact with fatty matter, are less liable than others to tubercular disease; and Dr. Simpson has observed that children and young persons employed in wool-factories, where large quantities of oil are daily used, are generally exempt from scrofula and pulmonary consumption. These facts would indicate that even the absorption of fatty matter through the skin may powerfully influence nutrition. Dr. Bennett says that, to prevent consumption during youth, indulgence in indigestible articles of food should be avoided, especially pastry, unripe fruit, salted provisions, and acid drinks; while the habit of eating a certain quantity of fat should be encouraged, and, if necessary, made imperative.

Dr. Carpenter observes: "There is a strong tendency and increasing reason to believe that a deficiency of oleaginous matter, in a state fit for appropriating by the nutritive processes, is a fertile source of diseased action, especially that of a tuberculous character; and that the habitual use of it in large proportions would operate favorably in the prevention of such maladies, as cod-liver oil unquestionably does in their cure."

Dr. Hooker, in a report on the diet of the sick, says: "1. Of all persons between the ages of fifteen and twenty-two years, more than one-fifth eat no fat meat; 2. That of persons at the age of forty-five, all except less than one in fifty habitually use fat meat; 3. Of those who have abstained, a few acquire an appetite for it, and live to a good old age, while the great proportion die of consumption before forty-five; 4. Of persons dying of consumption between the ages of fifteen and forty-five, nine-tenths, at least, have never used fat meat."

461. Unwholesome Foods.—Articles of food differ in digestibility, some being readily dissolved and assimilated, while others are changed in the stomach with such diffi-

culty as to irritate and injure the organ. Animal food is
more easily digested than vegetable, as it represents vegetable food that has been already once digested, and its
insoluble portions separated. But the chief cause of un-
wholesomeness in foods is their bad condition. The qualities which render them easily digestible within the system,
make them readily changeable without it; hence their
tendency to "spoil," and the facility of injurious culinary
changes. Bread, sour and heavy from unskillful working or
damaged flour, butter rancid and offensive, potatoes sodden,
and meat tainted or diseased, are examples of unwholesome diet, which produce disturbance in the system and
often serious disease. Meat that has entered upon decomposition, or the flesh of diseased, immature, or over-driven
animals, is unfit for use. They are liable to produce gastric
disturbance and diarrhœa, or they may be actively and dan-
gerously poisonous.

462. Flesh Parasites.—The disease of the pig, known
as "measles," is due to little parasitic animals which infest
the flesh. When pork is thus affected, there are found
scattered through the areolar or connective tissues numerous opaque or whitish points, which consist of little membranous bags, or *cysts*, each containing a small embryonic
animal, known as the *Cysticercus cellulosus.* These microscopic creatures are developed from the eggs of the common tape-worm (*Tœnia solium*).

Dr. Küchenmeister fed a number of cysticerci to a criminal at different periods before his execution, varying from
twelve to seventy-two hours, and, upon *post-mortem* examination of the body, no less than ten young tænia were
found in the intestine, four of which could be distinctly
recognized as specimens of *Tœnia solium* (Dalton).

The cysticerci are sometimes found in the organs of the
human body as well as in those of the lower animals. They
are most likely to be met with in the voluntary muscles,
but have been observed in the tissue of the heart, and,

what is more remarkable, in such organs as the eye and brain. Their presence in the muscles is not known to be harmful, inasmuch as they have been found in considerable numbers in the muscular tissues of individuals who were accidentally killed while in a state of apparently perfect health.

The *Trichina spiralis* is another parasite which infests the muscles of the pig, and is also found in those of the human subject. A muscle containing trichinæ appears as if thickly beset with small whitish specks. Each speck is in reality a cyst, which contains a single trichina, a minute, worm-like animal, coiled up in a spiral form. When straightened out, it measures about $\frac{1}{30}$th of an inch in length, and about $\frac{1}{700}$th of an inch in diameter. Like the cysticerci, these animals find their way into the human stomach, and thence, by means of the circulation, to the muscles, where they occasionally exist in immense numbers. They have been discovered in the muscles of persons who died by accident, and were otherwise apparently healthy; and also, and much more frequently, in subjects who have died from slow and debilitating disease. Within a few years past, it has been determined that the presence of these parasites not unfrequently gives rise to a peculiar disease, which has received the name of *Trichiniasis*. This affection is said to be highly febrile, often resembling typhoid or even typhus fever, and attended with excessive pain in the limbs, and œdema.

In selecting meat, if the lean flesh looks speckled or blotched, it should be suspected. When the cysticerci are in great numbers, the flesh crackles as its fibres are cut across. The trichinæ, if inclosed within cysts, are easily seen with the naked eye; but, if not, the microscope alone detects them. They may be effectually destroyed by thorough cooking.

18

CHAPTER XVIII.

CLOTHING AND HEALTH.

SECTION I.—*Properties of Clothing Material.*

463. Purposes to be subserved.—The principal object of clothing being to defend the body against the effects of heat and cold, it is obvious that the qualities best suited to these purposes are what we are to seek in the selection of fabrics for wearing apparel in different seasons and climates, and at different times. These qualities are chiefly connected with the relations of fabrics to heat and moisture. The body is constantly losing heat both by conduction and evaporation. In cold weather, the object is to prevent this loss as far as possible; in warm weather it is desirable to promote it; hence, we select our clothing with a view to these different purposes, wearing the free conductors and ready absorbers in summer, and the non-conductors and slow absorbers in winter. As far as is consistent with these primary objects, clothing should be light, durable, and readily cleansed. It should also be of such a character as will allow the free escape of the exhalations from the skin, and yet not be readily absorbent of moisture from without. Imperviousness is a very objectionable quality, and may, by retaining the cutaneous excretions in contact with the body, lead to serious disease.

464. Linen as an Article of Clothing.—This is a good conductor, and thus favors the escape of animal heat. It is also a rapid absorber of moisture from the surface of the body, and readily gives it off again by evaporation to the external air. For this reason, it produces a rapidly-cooling effect, even in hot weather, and is thus well adapted for summer use. It should not, however, under any circumstances, be worn next the skin, as it not only quickly cools the surface itself, but is incapable of preventing sudden chills from other causes.

465. Cotton as an Article of Clothing.—This is a poorer conductor of heat than linen, and consequently warmer. It is likewise less absorbent of moisture, and is therefore preferable for under-garments, or when it is desirable to avoid the cooling action produced by the evaporation of moisture from a material in contact with the body. It ranks next to linen as a fabric for summer wear, being a much better conductor of heat and absorber of moisture than either silk or wool.

466. Woolen as an Article of Clothing.—Woolen fabrics, owing to their coarseness and porosity, are capable of detaining within their meshes considerable amounts of air, and this makes them slow conductors of heat. It is upon this property of imprisoning air within its interstices that the warmth of clothing in a great measure depends. The air itself is an excellent non-conductor of heat, and, when materials are worn which have the power of entrapping its particles, the body is virtually encased in a garment of air, and its heat thereby prevented from escaping. The denser the fibre and the closer the texture, the less air there will be retained, and, hence, the cooler the clothing. The converse is equally true, though to a more limited extent. In any clothing, if warmth is the object, the texture must be sufficiently close to prevent the passage of currents, but up to this point the more open it is, the better.

Woolens also possess a great capacity for moisture, though they take it up and give it out very slowly. This is another valuable quality, giving them great advantages as articles of clothing. Every one may have noticed how readily linen and cotton become wet, while woolen in the same length of time is scarcely more than dampened. The former will also dry rapidly, while woolen parts with its moisture at a much slower rate. It is, therefore, a better protection against wet than either linen or cotton, and much warmer while wet, as the evaporation from its external surface is not nearly so rapid as from the surfaces of other materials. The water absorbed by different fabrics penetrates their fibres, and is also held between them in the interstices of the cloth. The latter can be wrung out, and is called water of *interposition.* The former is only got rid of by evaporation, and is termed *hygroscopic* water. Woolen greatly exceeds either linen or cotton in this power of hygroscopic absorption, taking up at least double the amount of water in proportion to its weight, and quadruple in proportion to its surface.

"This property is a most important one. During perspiration, the evaporation from the surface of the body is necessary to reduce the heat which is generated by exercise. When the exertion is finished, evaporation still goes on, often to such an extent as to chill the frame. When dry woolen clothing is put on after exertion, the vapor from the surface of the body is condensed in the wool, and gives out again the large amount of heat which had become latent when the water was vaporized. Therefore, a woolen covering, from this cause alone, at once feels warm when used during sweating. In the case of cotton and linen, the perspiration passes through and evaporates from the external surface without condensation; the loss of heat then continues. These facts make it plain why dry woolen clothes are so useful after exertion."—(Parkes.)

As an equalizer of the temperature and protector of the surface against sudden chills, wool stands at the head of all our usual wearing fabrics, and, when it can be tolerated, should be constantly worn next the skin.

467. Color influences the relations of clothing to *solar* heat, though it does not affect it in regard to non-luminous heat, such as that emitted from stoves. Black clothes absorb heat in a sunny day; while white clothes reflect more of it. The power of absorption decreases as the shade grows lighter. Thus, black absorbs the most, blue next, then green, yellow, and lastly white. Color also affects the relations of cloth to moisture, the darker-colored materials absorbing more moisture than the light - colored. Black will absorb nearly as much again as white.

SECTION II.—*Manner of dressing the Body.*

468. Its Importance.—Much more depends upon this than upon the materials used. The best fabrics improperly put on may be the source of all sorts of diseases, while the poorest, if used with judgment, are capable of conferring a goodly degree of comfort.

469. The Clothing should be light. — All garments should be as light as is consistent with the main objects for which they are worn. Weight does not necessarily imply warmth, and it often becomes a source of excessive fatigue and discomfort. Warmth is better attained by putting on several layers of light, loose-fitting garments, than fewer layers of heavy clothing. As before stated, it is not the clothing itself, but the air imprisoned by it, which secures warmth; and the air is not only held within the meshes of the cloth, but a stratum is retained underneath each additional layer of clothing. It is, therefore, desirable to multiply the number of layers, which is only possible when light materials are used.

470. It should be loose.—Every one knows that loose clothing is warmer than that which fits the body closely, and this alone should be sufficient reason for adopting it. But tight-fitting garments are in other respects very injurious. They obstruct the circulation, restrict the natural motions and healthy exercise of the parts, and not unfrequently produce deformities of the worst character. Many have observed the effects of a tight-fitting head-dress in obstructing the flow of blood. Constricting the neck is even worse. The great veins which carry the blood from the head back to the heart lie very superficially in the neck, and, when any thing tight is worn about this part, their currents are obstructed, and venous congestion of the brain results.

471. Compression of the Chest and Abdomen.—It is, likewise, of the greatest importance that the motions of the chest and abdomen should not be interfered with. There is probably no part of the body where freedom of

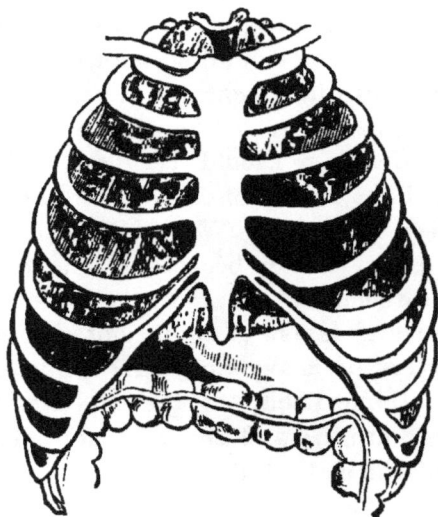

FIG. 129.

A diagram showing the natural form of the healthy chest, and the proper position of the organs which it contains.

action and of circulation is more absolutely required than here. At the junction of the chest with the abdomen are located the lower portions of the lungs, the spleen, stomach, liver, etc. There are also given off from the aorta at this point several large vessels, which carry blood to the adjacent viscera. The diaphragm, the most important muscle engaged in the process of respiration, is likewise found in this immediate vicinity. Every function of the body calls for the utmost freedom of movement in this important region. And yet it is the almost universal practice among females to bind down these parts often to half their natural dimensions. Reference to Fig. 129 shows this to be one of the roomiest portions of the body when left in its natural condition.

Fig. 130 shows the distortion which often results from compression. This deformity is not the worst of the evils which follow the practice of compressing these parts. The diaphragm is hampered in its actions, and the process of respiration thus directly interfered with. The lungs and heart are compressed, and the stomach and liver either forced out of place, or, what is worse, squeezed into much

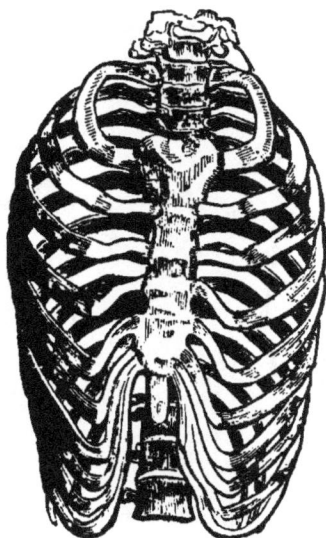

Fig. 130.
A diagram showing the deformity produced by compression.

less space than they would naturally occupy. The portal circulation is thus obstructed, and the viscera, like the brain in the former case, become the seat of venous engorgement.

It is hardly necessary to add that the troubles induced by this state of things are of the most serious character.

Diseases of the liver, dyspepsia, and consumption, are among its legitimate and certain results, while other disorders of a less definite character are, no doubt, traceable to the same efficient cause. The compression, when early applied, as it usually is, finds the bones of the chest soft and yielding, so that they readily give way. If the constriction is continued, as it is likely to be, for fear of losing "beauty of form," the bones, as age advances, harden and conform to the unyielding limitations without, and thus arise permanent and life-long deformity of the chest and continued restraint of its important organs.

472. Compression of the Feet.—This is a common practice, which often results in distortion and is always attended with great discomfort. Fig. 131 shows the de-

Fig. 131.   Fig. 132.

formity produced by compression, while Fig. 132 gives the natural shape of the foot. In walking with the feet unrestrained, each foot, as it receives the weight of the body, broadens slightly, and lengthens to the extent of half an inch or more. Freedom of motion in the foot itself is thus seen to be a natural requisite, and without it an easy, graceful walk is out of the question. Compression by the boot or shoe not only prevents this freedom of action, but also gives rise to deformity of the feet. The sole of the boot should be as wide as and somewhat longer than the foot when the weight of the body is resting upon it. The up. per-leather requires to be soft and yielding, and not so tight as to pinch the foot down upon the sole. The boot should be wide in front, leaving the toes perfect freedom of movement. If too narrow, they are made to override each other, thus producing ingrowing toe-nails, corns, bunions, etc. The heels should be low and broad, so as to furnish a firm support. High heels throw the feet forward toward the points of the boots, and tend to produce flattening of the arch of the foot.

473. Clothing should favor Uniformity of Temperature. —In health, all parts of the body have an average temperature of about 99° Fahr., and this is regulated and maintained by the circulation of the blood. This uniformity of temperature throughout the body is of the utmost importance, and, as it is controlled through the circulation, any thing which disturbs this should be carefully avoided. Clothing may do it in various ways, producing local results often of a very injurious nature. Compression obstructs the flow of blood, and at the same time forces out what the part already contains. It thus causes paleness of the parts, and is attended with an immediate lowering of the temperature. Hence the cold feet and hands, caused by tight boots and tight gloves. Over-clothing particular points leads to the accumulation of heat and consequent relaxation of the vessels, when more than the normal supply of blood flows in, and congestion results. A lack of clothing, by affording insufficient protection, permits the rapid escape of heat, and thus the temperature may fall below the healthy standard, while the surface-blood is driven inward, producing congestion of the internal organs. Both these causes of disturbance are generally operating: while one part is overheated by a superabundance of clothing, another part may at the same time be suffering from cold. This is often the case with children, who may be seen in cold weather loaded with clothing about the chest and

neck, while the legs and lower portions of the trunk are hardly more than covered.

474. Disturbance of Vascular Parts.—Certain organs of the body are more vascular than others; that is, their blood-vessels are larger and more numerous, and they receive a proportionately larger supply of blood. The throat, the lungs, the liver, and kidneys, are examples. Owing to their extreme vascularity, these organs are peculiarly liable to become the seat of engorgement if overheated by clothing or otherwise, especially when other regions are at the same time imperfectly protected. The region of the kidneys is commonly overdressed by the lapping at this point of the garments which clothe the trunk and lower extremities. In this way, two or three extra thicknesses are commonly obtained, and a tendency is thus created towards the accumulation of blood in these important organs.

Muffling the throat is very common, particularly among children, and it is often remarked that those who wrap it the most are the ones who suffer most from its disorders. This practice is perhaps responsible for more sore-throats, coughs, and croups, than all other causes put together; and, when such overdressing of the neck is supplemented, as it commonly is in children, by short dresses and thinly-clad extremities, the conditions are most complete for the production of all sorts of throat and lung affections.

475. Flannel next the Skin.—Uniformity of temperature is greatly promoted by constantly wearing next the skin some non-conducting material, such as flannel or silk. This prevents sudden chilling of the surface, which, in our variable climate, is liable to take place at any time, unless specially guarded against. Flannel is found by experience to be best for this purpose; but, in those cases where it irritates the skin, cotton-flannel or silk may be conveniently substituted. Linen should never be used. The good effects of wearing flannel next the skin the year round are unquestionable. In both cold and hot climates it is found to be an efficient safeguard against disease ; and there are few who cannot soon become accustomed to its use.

476. Clothing of Children. — Erroneous notions upon this subject lead to wrong practice, which is followed by the most pernicious consequences. Many entertain the idea that the constitutions of children may be hardened by exposure ; but, instead of any such vague benefit, specific and positive injuries are produced. Clothing, diet, and healthy growth, are intimately correlated. Food is the source of all bodily function and power, and the supply of force from this source is necessarily limited. Each day's bodily exercise, each day's mental exercise, each day's waste, repair, and growth of all the organs, and the definite amount of heat required to maintain the system at 99° during the twenty-four hours—each and all are at the expense of the food daily digested, and any overtaxing in one direction involves corresponding deficiencies in others. If the body is insufficiently clothed, there is extra loss of power through waste of heat, and a necessary reaction upon the constitution. The waste of heat entails a lowering of vital processes, and body and brain fail to reach a vigorous development. Thus, the naked legs and arms of children, which so please the vanity of silly mothers, are at the cost of their perfected constitutions.

477. Clothing in Advanced Age.—As the bodily functions decline in vigor with advancing life, the protecting influence of clothing becomes more necessary. The incapability of the aged to resist cold is well known, and fatal consequences frequently follow from persisting in old habits, and neglecting the indications of Nature for increased warmth and abundance of apparel.

CHAPTER XIX.

EXERCISE AND HEALTH.

SECTION I.—*Labor and Exercise.*

478. Man intended for Action. — Anatomy and Physiology alike proclaim that the purpose of the human constitution is activity. The provision for varied and complex movement is seen in the jointed skeleton, the contractile muscles, the controlling nerves, and the power-supplying apparatus of digestion and circulation. Thus the whole economy of the organism testifies that its end is action. Moreover, the circumstances of life involve the *necessity* of action. Effort must be put forth for the maintenance of existence, and for the gratification of the various faculties of our nature.

479. Labor.—This great end of our being finds its legitimate and natural expression in *labor*, which is human action applied to various materials and objects, for the attainment of some productive or useful result. The necessity of labor is thus doubly provided for in the construction of the human fabric and the order of external Nature, and, when performed with due regard to the laws and rights of our being, it is in every respect a benefit and a blessing. But, when pursued to excess, as has unhappily been too common in the past history of mankind, it is perverted into degrading drudgery, and then becomes a curse.

As skillful and effective labor involves intelligence, time and thought are needed to secure aptness in its performance, and the narrower the range of effort, the greater is the facility attained. This restricts the individual to specific pursuits, and gives rise to that diversified system of division of labor which has grown to such vast complexity in modern society. The tendency of this system is to call into intense exercise a portion—perhaps but a small portion—of the activity of the individual, and to leave the remainder of his powers unused. In many vocations the hands only are brought into requisition, while the body is unexercised; in others, the muscular system alone is involved, while the brain remains unoccupied; in other cases the brain is active and the body at rest, or perhaps a portion only of the brain is exerted, as in numerical computation and managing accounts.

480. Exercise.—Thus the tendency of modern life is to overwork a narrow portion of the human constitution and underwork the remainder, so that a large part of it is not called into the activity for which it was designed, and which is necessary to health. There are few persons whose habitual activities are so complete that they do not require to be supplemented by various artificial exertions, while this need is still more imperative with those of sedentary habits and the classes of leisure. To meet these various emergencies, and give to the unused portions of the human system their requisite action, is the object of *exercise*.

SECTION II.—*Effects of Regulated Exercise.*

481. Transformation of Physiological Forces.—All those vital processes which are essential to life, as digestion, circulation, respiration, secretion, are carried on independently of the will, and give rise to a large and constant amount of activity in the system. But labor and exercise are performed by calling into action an additional system of agencies—those of the voluntary muscles—and, to maintain these in a state of activity, involves an extra requisition upon the various involuntary organs. As the materials of the body are derived from the substance of the food, so all vital power is derived from the force stored up in the food. Organic matter is in a state of molecular tension, and, when decomposed, these tensions are given out in the form of

physical forces. Food is organic matter, suited to undergo assimilation, and then to give out its molecular tensions
in various forms, as animal heat, muscular power. It follows that in work, or exercise, the voluntary muscular system draws upon the involuntary functions for its supply of
energy; and hence, in proportion to the force expended, is
the general exaltation of the vital processes.

482. Exercise, Waste, and Repair.—Bodily exertion thus
increases atomic changes, and quickens that metamorphosis of tissue in which health essentially consists. Exercise
is at the expense of waste; waste involves repair, and
these augmented processes call into higher action the whole
apparatus of supply and excretion. Habitual exercise is
thus the cause and condition of that vital renovation of
parts which is the source and measure of constitutional
vigor.

483. Effect upon the Circulation.—As the circulation
ministers immediately to all the functions, its energy rises
and falls with their activity. Exercise increases the movements of the heart in both force and frequency, and accelerates the flow of blood through all parts of the body. The
circulation is also aided by the contractions of the voluntary muscles, which, by pressing upon the walls of the veins,
tend to force along the current of blood. Moreover, this
increased activity of the circulation meets the increased
demand of the muscles for new material, to renew the disin-
tegrated structures; and it also effects the speedy removal
of all waste products, by rapidly transferring them to the
proper eliminating organs. Thus, the complex stream
from which nutritive materials are constantly drawn, and
into which waste matters are constantly poured, is directly
affected, both in its composition and rate of movement, by
the state of action of the voluntary muscles.

Exercise also, it is well known, increases the production of heat. It is through the increased activity of the
circulation that the body is warmed by exercise. This is

the reason why walking is so effectual in warming the feet, and why exertion of any kind raises the temperature of the parts employed.

484. Effect upon Respiration.—Circulation and respiration are accelerated together by exercise, as whatever quickens the pulse hastens the breathing. It being the office of respiration to furnish the prime mover of vital changes—oxygen—and to rid the system of the chief product of such change—carbonic acid—this process is doubly subservient to the great dynamic objects of the organism. It follows that a fundamental condition of exercise is unimpeded respiration. If the pulmonary circulation and the elimination of carbon are in any way interfered with, the power of continued exertion rapidly declines. As thus muscular movement depends immediately upon the excretion of carbonic acid from the system, and as this, in turn, depends upon the state of the air itself, we see that an impure atmosphere is unfavorable to vigorous and healthful exercise. This explains the lassitude and indisposition to effort in unventilated houses, workshops, and factories. Exercise should, therefore, as much as possible, be carried on in the open air, or in places which admit of the freest ventilation.

485. Effects upon Digestion.—As power comes from food in the case of the living machine, increased expenditure of power, of course, implies increased consumption of food; hence, exercise sharpens the appetite. In those who indulge in active and regular exercise, digestion is effected with greater ease, and the process is more rapidly and more thoroughly completed than in those of inactive habits. In many cases, where the digestive function has become impaired, either from habitual inactivity or a too close application of the mind, relief can easily come through systematic and judicious exercise. Immediate exertion after a full meal is injurious, for several reasons. The distended condition of the stomach interferes with the free movement of the diaphragm and heart, and thus both respiration and circulation are mechanically impeded, while the diversion of blood and nervous force to the muscles withdraws them from the digestive organs and hinders their functions.

486. Effect upon the Skin.—With exercise, the skin becomes redder and hotter, from the increased amount of blood it receives. During exertion, heat is rapidly developed within the body, but its accumulation is prevented by the escape of water through the skin. No amount of external cold is able to prevent this outward passage of fluid, though it may slightly hinder evaporation. There is, therefore, little danger of chill during active exercise; but, when exertion is over, there is great danger of it, for the heat of the body rapidly declines, while evaporation continues, which still more reduces the temperature. During exertion, the skin may be exposed without danger; but, during the intervals of rest, it should be covered sufficiently to prevent the least feeling of coolness of the surface.

487. Exercise should be regular.—Like eating and sleeping, exercise should become a regular and persistent daily habit. It is an imperative necessity of the system, and, as an element of personal hygiene, is indispensable. If it be resorted to in any form of bodily training, as in military drill, rowing, or other athletic effort, it is found that the periods of exertion must not be less than half an hour, in order to take hold of the system, and produce the positive effect of bodily discipline.

488. The Mind in Exercise.—Exercise, or simple muscular movement, whatever may be its value for health, has in itself very few attractions, and will be avoided rather than practised, unless there is connected with it something capable of calling the mind into pleasurable activity. When taken merely from a sense of duty, or "because the health requires it," exercise becomes a drag and a bore, without vigor and of little benefit. When, however, it can be made the means of enjoyment, by associating with it something agreeable and exhilarating, it becomes at once spontaneous, vigorous, and hearty, and its value to the health, both of mind and body, is in a great degree increased.

SECTION III.—*Excessive and Insufficient Exercise.*

489. Effects of Over-exertion.—With the proper amount of exercise, the muscles increase in size, hardness, and elastic vigor, until the equilibrium of waste and repair is carried to its highest point. Exercise is at the expense of the part in action; in vigorous exertion, decomposition prevails over renewal. The muscles can bear this for a certain length of time, and then demand rest, in which repair prevails over waste, and restores the balance. If exertion be pushed still further, the equilibrium is lost; destructive changes prevail over reparative, and the muscle begins to degenerate and lose power. Prolonged exertion, without sufficient rest, impairs nutrition, and renders the muscular fibres soft and flabby. Nature thus provides for the rhythm of activity and repose. The involuntary muscles, as we have seen—those of the heart and chest—act in this intermitting way, and are thus kept up to a constant state of vigor. The law is equally imperative for the voluntary muscles, and the proper rest is to be secured either by ceasing from activity, or by calling different sets of muscles into alternate exercise.

When the muscles are weak, repair goes on more slowly than when they are "in condition." Hence, in any effort at acquiring strength by exercise, either after sickness or prolonged sedentary occupation, the exercise should at first be very light, and of short duration, with long intervals of rest. As the strength slowly increases, the exercise may be increased, but exhaustion in all such cases is to be carefully avoided.

Excessive exercise often produces palpitation, and sometimes hypertrophy and valvular disease of the heart. During exertion, if the heart is not oppressed, its movements, though rapid and forcible, are regular and equal; but when it becomes embarrassed, the pulse-beats are quick, unequal, and at last become irregular, indicating injury to the organ. All great or sudden efforts should be avoided, as they not only affect injuriously the muscular system, by direct over-strain, but it is at such times that blood-vessels are ruptured, and that the walls of important cavities give way.

. Rest after exertion is one of the indispensable conditions of health. Work or exercise carried habitually to the length of exhaustion, by lowering the bodily vigor and depressing the powers of the constitution, not only diminishes resistance to the encroachments of disease, but greatly reduces the capability of recovery in cases of sickness. Particularly in childhood, when the bones are yet incompletely ossified, and the muscles undeveloped, excessive labor or exertion is liable to entail permanent injury. If persisted in, arrested development of either body or mind can hardly fail to result. From the age of fifteen to twenty-five, although full growth may have been reached, the powers of endurance have not attained their maximum, and all exhausting tasks require to be avoided. Young soldiers break down under the toils and privations of the camp sooner than mature men. This is also true in civil life, where the young and immature are called upon to match their powers with those in the maturity of manhood; and the remark is equally applicable to the female, under the spur of competition with the male sex. The consequences are seen in broken-down constitutions and premature decay.

490. Effects of Insufficient Exercise.—Inaction contravenes the supreme design of the human constitution, and is therefore adverse to its health. As bodily vigor results only from active and well-regulated exercise, the absence of such exercise must entail bodily debility. As exertion favors nutrition and the healthy development of active parts, inaction impairs nutrition, reduces the size of the muscles, and gives rise to feebleness. The amount of injury in the case may, however, depend much upon accompanying circumstances. If abstinence from exercise be attended by abstinence in diet, there will still be loss of power, low vitality, and diminished resistance to morbific influences; the evils will be rather of a negative character. But, if deficient exercise be accompanied by a free indulgence of the appetite, perverted nutrition and positive disease will be the necessary consequence. Nutritive materials that would be reduced and excreted through bodily exertion, accumulate in the system, clogging its movements, deranging its functions, and deteriorating its structures. Not only is there an abnormal accumulation of fat, amounting to actual disease, but a disturbance of the nutritive forces, that undermines the healthy structure of the tissues. Nor is this muscular deterioration limited merely to the parts that are unused; the involuntary mechanism becomes implicated. Deficiency of exercise often leads to fatty degeneration of the heart, with loss of power and derangement of the circulation. In short, as vigorous and systematic exercise is a prime condition of the general health, so the want of it favors the approach of disease, which may take many forms, according to the circumstances of the constitution.

491. Amount and Conditions of Exercise.—As to the amount of exercise necessary to meet the requirements of the healthy individual, no precise rules can be given; the quantity will vary with many circumstances. Persons of sedentary habits would be seriously injured by attempting to perform an amount of work which, to others of a more active turn, would hardly exceed the bounds of recreation. The inmate of the workshop or factory would be speedily exhausted by the ordinary tasks of the out-door laborer. In any given case, the amount of exercise should be determined and regulated by the state of the constitution. That exercise is deficient which does not engage the vigorous action of the chief muscles of the system for a considerable period each day; and that too great which, passing beyond the point of simple fatigue, is prolonged to the period of exhaustion.

The sedentary, if they would acquire strength, must begin with light exertion, limited to short periods, and take ample time for rest. Nothing is more erroneous, and, if carried into practice, more injurious, than the notion that great exertion will augment the strength of those unaccustomed to active exercise. The growth of muscle, in both substance and power, is a gradual process, and one that is retarded rather than hastened by overwork. If exhaustion or restlessness follows exercise, we may be certain that it has been overdone, and will be productive of weakness rather than strength.

As has been stated in a previous chapter, an abundant supply of pure air is at all times a vital necessity of health; but the demands of the system in this respect are greatly increased during active muscular exertion. As the diminution of waste products is a result of oxidation, it is hindered by breathing an impure atmosphere. For this further reason, open-air exercise is much superior, as a health-promoting agent, to that carried on within the walls of a gymnasium or other confined area.

492. Remedial Influence of Exercise.—If exercise is an essential condition of health, and the want of it a fruitful source of disease, it is obvious that only by the reëstablishment of the needed exercise can health be regained. But in many cases the diseases induced make the required effort either impossible or very difficult. What is known as the *movement-cure* is a kind of dynamic treatment, in which the patient is subjected by the physician to various kinds of artificial exercise. In many cases of local weakness and partial paralysis, by the help of skillfully-constructed mechanical contrivances, these parts are gradually brought into action, and healthy power slowly recovered.

The principle in this case is valuable, and, important as a remedial agency, its employment has accomplished much good, and more is to be expected from its further development.

CHAPTER XX.

MENTAL HYGIENE.

Section I.—*Relations of Mind and Body.*

493. Mental Health a Physiological Question.—Thus far we have confined attention mainly to the influences which act on the bodily health, but the principles of hygiene have a still higher application. The mind has its states of health and vigor, of debility and disease, like the body, and these states are influenced by definite causes in the former case as well as in the latter. Mental philosophy, as commonly understood, explains to us the operations of thought and feeling as we discover them in the working of our own minds, and takes little account of the part played by the corporeal system in the control of these processes. But, if we would understand the conditions of mental health, and the nature and causes of mental impairment, the body must at once be taken into account. The study of mental phenomena in their corporeal relations thus becomes the business of the physiologist. He sees that mind is not only intimately dependent upon the body, but that the two have close and powerful reactions; states of body determining conditions of mind, and states of mind influencing conditions of body. Nature presents the problem, not of mind separate, but of mind and body bound up in a living unity, and the physiologist must take the question as he finds it.

494. The Brain and the Mind.—It is now universally admitted that the brain is the grand nervous centre of thought and feeling—the material instrument of the mind, and that all mental actions are accompanied and conditioned by physiological actions. From the high complexity of composition of nervous matter, it is extremely unstable and prone to change. The brain is therefore not only, like all other parts of the body, subject to the double metamorphosis of waste and repair, but the transformations take place in this organ with more rapidity than in any other part of the system. Upon these changes the mental operations are vitally dependent, and, if in any way they are interfered with, there is disturbance of the intellectual processes. If the cerebral circulation is lowered, mental activity is diminished; if accelerated, the mind's action is exalted. Various foreign substances introduced into the blood-stream alter the course of thought, some affecting it one way and some another, but each, through its specific action, producing characteristic psychological effects. Inflammation of the brain induces delirium, while different diseases of the organ, or perversions of the blood circulating through it, give rise to various forms of insanity.

It is important to note, not only that mind and body are both governed by laws, but that they are to a great extent governed by the *same* laws. Whatever improves the physical qualities of the brain, improves also the mind; whatever deteriorates the brain, impairs the mind. They have a common development, are equally increased in vigor, capacity, and power, by systematic and judicious exercise, and are alike injured by deficient or excessive effort. The brain is exhausted by thinking, as much as the muscles by acting, and, like the exhausted muscles, it requires time for the restoration of vigor through nutritive repair. As thus the mind is dependent upon the conditions of the brain, while the brain is controlled by the bodily system, we see how impossible it is to deal with the mental powers in a practical way, without taking the material organization into account.

495. Mental Health and Disease. — The observations made in regard to the true nature of disease (368, 369)—that it is nothing more than perverted physiological action— need to be here repeated with emphasis. Those who habitually think of the mind as a separate entity merely co-existing in some vague way with the body, will naturally look upon mental derangements as disorders of this entity —diseases of an abstraction. But this view has proved misleading and injurious in the extreme. So long as maladies of the mind were regarded as demoniac possessions, or as " fermentations taking place in a spiritual essence," all rational causality was excluded, and the arts of relief and prevention were impossible. When, however, it became established that mind depends upon definite physiological conditions, there was no escape from the conclusion that physiological perversions are causes of mental derangement. " Fair weather and foul equally depend upon the laws of meteorology ; health and disease equally depend upon the laws of animal life." As mental health is dependent upon the due nutrition, stimulation, and repose of the brain, mental disease is to be regarded as resulting from the interruption or disturbance of those conditions.

In showing that mental weakness is a concomitant of bodily debilty, and mental aberration a consequence of bodily disorder, the physiologist lays the sure foundations of a practical *Mental Hygiene*, the province of which is, to consider the various causes which disturb the harmony and impair the vigor of mental actions. Taking note of the multiplied forms and degrees of disturbance and degeneracy to which the mental nature of man is subject, it traces them to their numerous causes, and discloses the extent to which they are avoidable. As bodily and mental health depend to a great degree upon the same conditions, all that has been said in the foregoing chapters concerning the sanitary influences which affect the corporeal system has likewise its bearing upon health of mind. But the mental aspects of the subject are so generally overlooked as to demand special consideration.

Section II.—*Causes of Mental Impairment.*

496. Insanity the Result of Concurring Influences.—As the organ of the mind is the most delicate and complex of all parts of the living system, while its manifestations are so varied as to comprehend the whole circle of human thought and feelings, it is natural to suppose that the causes of cerebral impairment will be varied and complex in an equal degree. These causes are usually regarded as twofold, *moral* and *physical.* The former are those which take effect through the mind, as anxiety, over-study, or reverses of fortune; the latter are those which act directly upon the physical system without the intervention of the mind, as blood-poisoning by fever or narcotics, or an injury to the head. Another division is into *predisposing* and *exciting* causes. Predisposing causes are such as act remotely, or by slow degrees, to undermine the mental health; while exciting causes are those untoward events which immediately precede the breaking down of the mind. It is a common error to assign some shock or calamity as the efficient and adequate cause of an insane outbreak, whereas the real causality lies further back, and the occurrence in question is only the *occasion* of its development. The germ of the insanity may have been deeply latent in the constitution, and a long train of influences may have been at work to impair the cerebral vigor, while some event, perhaps of slight importance in itself, serves to bring on the final catastrophe. When it is said that a person has become insane through disappointment or religious excitement, we are not to suppose that this is the whole statement: the question arises, How is it that others in quite similar circumstances are unaffected? The human mind is not so constituted as to snap by a sudden strain, like cast-iron; insanity suddenly produced by the action of a single cause is of the rarest occurrence. Only by a "conspiracy of conditions," internal and external, proximate and remote, is the fabric of reason usually overthrown.

We will first notice the immediate physiological actions by which health of mind is destroyed, and this will prepare us to understand how the remoter causes of mental impairment take effect.

497. Nutrition of the Cerebral Structures.—If the mind is dependent upon the brain, it follows that each act of mind has its physical conditions, and this conditioning must of course be in accordance with the structure of the organ. The mental mechanism consists essentially of millions of cells and fibres, the former of which are the generators and the latter the transmitters of force. In thinking and feeling, these are called into exercise, and according to its intensity exhausted; while their functional power is restored by nutritive assimilation. The structure of the parts being perfect, mental coherency, energy, and health, depend upon their perfect nutrition. On the other hand, disordered mental manifestations are due to incapacitated structures which are immediately caused by imperfect nutrition. It is here, in their disturbance of the nutritive operations of the brain, that most of the causes of mental impairment take effect. "We attribute a large share of mental disease to pathological conditions of the brain whose most prominent characteristic is defective nutrition of the organ. In a very large proportion of cases this deficient nutrition is manifested after death in an actual shrinking of the brain—a shrinking which is coextensive with the duration and the degree of the loss of mental power. This loss of power marks all instances of cerebral decay, and is consequently a condition of most chronic cases of excitement " (Bucknill and Tuke).

The effect of impaired nutrition is, to produce derangements of structure, and these take many forms in the various cases of cerebral disease. The microscope has done

19

much to elucidate the pathological changes of the brain, but such is the marvelous delicacy of the organ that micro-scopists are still intensely occupied in making out the subtle details of its normal structure. Many physical indications of nervous disorder no doubt remain to be discovered; but, from the peculiar complexity and difficulty of the case, a large amount of infirmity of nerve-element will probably never be detected by physical means. Nutrition results from a relation between nerve-tissue and the blood; the causes of its perversion are therefore to be sought in various disturbances of the circulation as well as in the nerve-element itself.

498. Disturbance in the Cerebral Circulation.—Nutrition is dependent upon the supply of blood; in the brain, perhaps, more closely than in any other organ. The gray substance of the cerebral convolutions, which are devoted to the higher mental operations, is richly supplied with minute blood-vessels which impart to the cells the material of their renewal, and remove the waste products of their activity. The quantity and quality of the blood they transmit must therefore exert a determining influence over the functions and health of the organ.

499. Congestion and its Effects.—As mental action depends upon the interchange taking place between the blood-capillaries and the nerve-cells, it follows that increased excitation and interaction of ideas is accompanied by increasing interchange and demand for more blood. Or, if, from any cause, there is excessive brainward determination of blood, the plethora of the capillaries gives rise to increased mental excitement.

If this heightened activity is prolonged beyond due limits, and especially if the brain is weakly organized, a state of morbid congestion is induced, and over-stimulation is followed by stagnation of ideas, head-swimming, and emotional depression and irritability. "There are few students who are not practically conversant with the slighter

symptoms of cerebral congestion. Absorbed in some intellectual pursuit, the student's head becomes hot and painful,
and his brain even feels too large for his skull. With exhausted powers of thought and attention, he retires at a
late hour, as he hopes, to rest, but he finds that he cannot
sleep; or, if he does, his repose is unrefreshing and disturbed by dreams. An hour's freedom from thought before
retiring to bed would have enabled the partly-congested
brain to recover itself."

The stagnation of the cerebral currents and imperfect
removal of noxious products, with the irregularities of excitement and depression which are the results of frequent
brain-congestion, produce defective nutrition, which tends
to impair the soundness of the organ.

500. Anæmia, or bloodlessness, the opposite state of
congestion, produces similar mental effects. Insufficiency
of healthy blood, whether caused by its actual loss from
the system, or by poverty and dilution of the fluid through
want of food, imperfect digestion, or any of the numerous
anti-hygienic influences, by impairing the nutritive powers,
enfeebles the organ and powerfully predisposes to insanity.
In hyperæmia, with hot head and fullness of the cerebral
vessels, the mental functions are discharged with slowness
and difficulty. In anæmia, with pale face, cool head, and
weak pulse, the cerebral organs are in a state of irritable
weakness, easily excited to action; the action, however,
being powerless and irregular.

"The blood itself may not reach its proper growth and
development by reason of some defect in the function of
the glands that minister to its formation, or, carrying the
cause still further back, by reason of wretched conditions
of life; there is, in consequence, a defective nutrition generally, as in scrofulous persons, and the nervous system shares
in the general delicacy of constitution, so that, though
quickly impressible and lively in reaction, it is irritable,
feeble, and easily exhausted. In the condition of anæmia

we have an observable defect in the blood, and palpable
nervous suffering in consequence; headaches, giddiness,
low spirits, and susceptibility to emotional excitement,
reveal the morbid effects. Poverty of blood, it can admit
of no doubt, plays the same weighty part in the production
of insanity as it does in the production of other nervous
diseases, such as hysteria, chorea, neuralgia, and even epilepsy. The exhaustion produced by lactation is a well-
recognized cause of mental derangement; and a great loss
of blood during childbirth has sometimes been the cause
of an outbreak of insanity " (Dr. Maudsley).

501. Perversions of the Blood.—Although the blood is a
compound of wondrous complexity, and undergoing incessant change by active influx and drainage, yet in health its
constitution is preserved in such exquisite balance, that the
cerebral engine of thought and emotion is kept in harmonious and perfect action. This harmony is disturbed not
only by excess or deficiency of the vital stream, but in a
marked degree by the presence in it of various impurities.
Every grade of mental disease, from the mildest depression to the fury of delirium, may be produced by the accumulation in the blood of the waste matters of the tissues.
The presence in the blood, for example, of unexcreted bile,
so affects the nervous substance as to engender the gloomi-
est feelings, from which the individual cannot free himself,
although he knows that the cause of his depression is not
in the actual condition of external circumstances, but is
internal, and of a transient nature. But it only requires
the prolonged action of this cause to carry this morbid
state of nerve-element to that further stage of degeneration
which shall result in the genuine melancholia of insanity.
So also the non-evacuation of urinary products in the blood
of a gouty patient acts upon the brain to produce an irritability which the mind cannot prevent; and this, too, if
not arrested by medical resources, is liable to pass on to
maniacal excitement.

In like manner, suppressed discharges, the morbid products of typhus and typhoid fevers, the organic poisons generated in the system by small-pox or syphilis, and not promptly eliminated, are often efficient causes of nutritive perversion in the brain which result in various forms of mental disorder.

Various substances introduced into the blood, as opium, hashish, belladonna, take effect upon the brain, each perverting the mental functions in a manner peculiar to itself. Ingested alcohol produces an artificial insanity, in which the various types of mental disease are distinctly manifested. Its first effect is a gentle stimulation and a mental excitement, such as often precedes an outbreak of mania. This is followed by a rapid flow of ideas, an incoherence of thought and speech, and an excitement of the passions, which disclose automatic disturbance and diminished voluntary control, as in delirium from other causes. A condition of depression and maudlin melancholy succeeds, as convulsion passes into paralysis—the last scene of all being one of dementia and stupor.

502. Nutritive Repair of the Brain.—But, independent of the quantity or quality of the blood supplied to the brain, that organ is liable to certain conditions of exhaustion and nutritive degeneracy to an extent far greater than the other organs of the body. These other organs have various means of escape from overtasking; if they cannot increase their power so as to endure the burden imposed, they can refuse to act, or throw the excess of labor upon some other part. Overworking the stomach destroys appetite, and the task is no longer imposed. If the muscular system is worked beyond its power, it does not itself break down, but the excessive strain is thrown upon the nervous system, which receives the injury. The overtasked lungs throw part of their burden upon the skin and liver, and the overworked liver is relieved by the kidneys. But the economy of the organism affords the brain no vicarious relief;

if overburdened, it must suffer alone. Excessive exertion of the brain produces an excitement, which, instead of ceasing, is augmented by the very debility which it causes. The exhaustion continues the overwork, which again increases the exhaustion. The degeneration of nerve-element thus proceeds at a rapid rate of increase, which results in permanent perversion and degradation of the mental functions.

The conditions of rest and nutritive renovation of the mind's organ are provided for in the mechanism of the solar system, by which the quietude of night, darkness, and silence alternates with the stimulation of light and day. The recovery of its tone through nutritive repair undoubtedly takes place in the brain during the suspension of its functional activity in sleep. That sleep should be sound in quality and sufficient in quantity is one of the first conditions of mental health and vigor, and the want of it, as all have observed, reacts powerfully upon the state of the feelings. "The ill effects of insufficient sleep may be witnessed on some of the principal organic functions; but it is the brain and nervous system that suffer chiefly and in the first instance. The consequences of a very protracted vigil are too well known to be mistaken; but many a person is suffering, unconscious of the cause, from the habit of irregular and insufficient sleep. One of the most common effects is a degree of nervous irritability and peevishness which even the happiest self-discipline can scarcely control. That buoyancy of the feelings, that cheerful, hopeful, trusting temper, which springs far more from organic conditions than from mature and definite convictions, give way to a spirit of dissatisfaction and dejection; while the even demeanor, the measured activity, are replaced either by a lassitude that renders any exertion painful, or an impatience and restlessness not very conducive to happiness."

Such are the effects upon the healthy constitution of

that slight disturbance of brain-nutrition which accompanies insufficient repose; but, when this state of things is much protracted or takes effect upon a weakly-organized nervous system, the mental integrity becomes endangered. Sleeplessness is both a symptom and an immediate cause of cerebral disorder. Bucknill and Tuke observe: "Want of refreshing sleep we believe to be the true origin of insanity dependent upon moral causes. Very frequently, when strong emotion leads to insanity, it causes in the first instance complete loss of sleep."

The quality of the sleep, moreover, that is, whether it be total or partial, is of the first importance. In painful and harassing dreams the emotional perturbation continues, and the individual awakens exhausted rather than invigorated. It is probable that in such cases, when the mind is abandoned to fantasy, and the control of the judgment is lost, the wasteful activity of certain parts of the brain may exceed that of the waking state. Various cases are mentioned in which patients have ascribed their attacks of mania to the influence of frightful dreams.

We thus see in what mental impairment, in its various degrees, really consists. To the physiologist the question of healthy mental activity resolves itself into that of the soundness of nerve-element, and of the vigor and completeness of nutrition; while mental impairment is seen to result from instability of the nerve-structures conseqnent upon defective nutrition. In this view, therefore, all causes, physical or moral, immediate or remote, which influence the nutritive operations of the system, have a bearing, more or less direct, upon mental conditions and character.

We will now pass to some of the remoter influences by which mental health is impaired.

503. Hereditary Transmission.—The living constitution is powerfully influenced by many slow-working agencies. The causes of mental deterioration produce effects in time, and through successive generations. Hereditary transmission thus becomes a leading factor in the problem of mental impairment, and accounts for many of the agencies by which it is produced.

Bodily defects and diseases are transmissible. Consumption, gout, asthma, cancer, leprosy, scrofula, apoplexy, unsoundness of teeth, and even long-sight, short-sight, and squinting, are liable to be inherited. Of course these diseases are not transmitted in all cases of their occurrence, nor do they always psss directly from parent to offspring; one or two generations may be skipped, and the malady appear in the distant descendants. Hence, strictly speaking, it is not the disease that is hereditary, but a predisposition to it, which may either be neutralized and disappear, remain dormant, or break out, according to circumstances.

There is, perhaps, no form of constitutional defect more markedly hereditary than morbidities of the nervous system. Esquirol observes that, of all diseases, insanity is the most hereditary. The proportion of cases in which this malady is ascribed to predisposition has been variously estimated at from one-fourth to nine-tenths; probably at least one-half of all these cases of disease have this origin. Extensive and careful inquiry has led to the conclusion that predisposition to insanity on the part of the mother is more liable to be transmitted to children than a like tendency on the part of the father, but it is the daughters that are most exposed; the maternal defect, while it is equally dangerous to the sons as the paternal, is twice as dangerous to the daughters.

The common notion, that insanity is inherited only when madness in a parent reappears as madness in the child, is a most serious error. That which is transmitted is nervous infirmity, which may assume an endless variety of forms. Parental nervous defect may issue in one member of the family in unbalanced character, which is manifested in violent outbreaks of passion and unaccountable impulses, while another may go smoothly through life without exhib-

iting a trace of it, and a third will break down into mania
upon some trying emergency.   As features are modified by
descent, so are diseases, and none assume so wide a diversity of aspect as those of the nervous system.

"If, instead of limiting attention to the individual, we
scan the organic evolution and decay of a family—processes which, as in the organism, are sometimes going on simultaneously—then it is made sufficiently evident how close
are the fundamental relations of nervous diseases, how artificial the divisions between them may sometimes appear.
Epilepsy in the parent may become insanity in the offspring, or insanity in the parent epilepsy in the child; and
chorea or convulsions in the child may be the consequence
of great nervous excitability, natural or accidental, in the
mother.   In families in which there is a strong predisposition to insanity, it is not uncommon to find one member
afflicted with one form of nervous disease and another with
another; one suffers, perhaps, from epilepsy, another from
neuralgia or hysteria, a third may commit suicide, and a
fourth become maniacal.   General paralysis is a disease
which is usually the result of continual excesses of one sort
or another; but it may unquestionably occur without any
marked excesses, and when it does so there will mostly be
discoverable an hereditary taint in the individual" (Dr.
Maudsley).

504. Debilitated Stock a Source of Criminality.—How
the running down of stock through loss of vital power by
hereditary influences should swell the ranks of the dependent classes, or those incapable of self-support, is obvious;
but this cause is equally powerful in reënforcing the dangerous classes who fill our jails and prisons.   Immoral
training and vicious associations are undoubtedly among
the potent agencies by which these are educated for a
career of vice and crime, but a coöperating cause of far
greater power is low organization or defective cerebral
endowment.   They begin life with a nervous system inca-

pable of the higher controlling functions. The children of paupers generally inherit a lack of bodily and mental vigor, while the offspring of criminals have transmitted to them a disturbed balance of constitution—an activity of certain propensities, with a congenital weakness of the restraining sentiments. Upon this point a writer of large observation and experience of these classes, Dr. S. G. Howe, observes:

"There is a common opinion that in classes and individuals of low organization the purely animal appetites are apt to be fierce and ungovernable, but it is not so: on the contrary, as a general rule, the whole nature is let down and enfeebled; and persons in this condition are docile and easily governed. Sometimes, indeed, there is fearful activity of the animal nature in persons of very low organization, which impels them to commit shocking outrages; but these are exceptional cases, and the passions are usually the consequences of drink, or of insanity, rather than of intensity of nature. As a rule, in the classes marked by low and degenerate organization, the animal instincts and impulses are not stronger than in the others. On the contrary, the classes of higher bodily organization and vigor have more fire and potency even of animal appetites; and their superiority comes, not from lack of impulses and temptations, but from greater activity and power of the restraining faculties of reflection and of conscience."

In the light of these facts, the causes of mental impairment acquire a new and startling significance. The various agencies which are adverse to health not only shorten the duration of life, but they degrade its quality; while deteriorated life involves debilitated intellect and perverted moral powers. The general causes of impaired health which have been noticed, impure air, overcrowding, bad water, insufficient food, exposure to weather from inadequate clothing, want of exercise, or exhausting labor, and the whole array of bad physical conditions, by undermining the bodily vigor and lowering the nutritive operations, become powerful and extensive causes of mental impairment, and stand in close relation to the evils and vices of society. Their baneful influence, however, is not measured by their immediate effects upon the individual; their power is multiplied by transmission, for they inflict upon his posterity the curse of a bad descent. Evil habits and bad conditions of life may not in the first case reach the extent of mental derangement, but they so impair the vital stamina that their victim bequeathes to his children enfeebled and degenerated nervous organizations, which are incapable of withstanding the strains and shocks of social experience. The lowered vitality and perverted nutrition of the parent become feeble-mindedness or insanity in the offspring.

Hence, "for the moral and intellectual elevation of the race, we are to look not exclusively to education, but to whatever tends to improve the bodily constitution, and especially the qualities of the brain. In our schemes of philanthropy we are apt to deal with men as if they could be moulded to any desirable purpose, provided only the right instrumentalities are used; ignoring altogether the fact that there is a physical organ in the case, whose original endowments must limit very strictly the range of our moral appliances. But, while we are bringing to bear upon them all the kindly influences of learning and religion, let us not overlook those physical agencies which determine the efficacy of the brain as the material instrument of the mind" (Dr. Ray).

505. Overtasking the Emotions.—Increase of insanity is undoubtedly a concomitant of advancing civilization. The savage state is marked by simple and unchangeable social institutions, uniformity of manners and habits, limited wants, the discipline of privation, imperturbable resignation, feeble affection, and few emotions. The savage rarely laughs and rarely sheds tears. The mental disorders to which he is liable correspond to his imperfect development; they are idiocy and imbecility — the mental diseases of children. On the contrary, in the civilized state there is a high and varied development of the emotions: all the circumstances of refined society conspire to intensify the feelings. Pride, ambition, fear, grief, domestic trouble, speculation, reverses of fortune, great successes, and great failures, exemplify the excitement and intoxication of the emotions to which a highly-civilized people are continually subjected. In this country the intense and universal passion for wealth, the periodical convulsions of politics, and the stimulation of free competition for place and profit, carry to a high point the strain 'upon the feelings. Worse than all, our education, instead of being a training to self-control, and a systematic discipline of the emotions through a calm cultivation of the sciences of Nature, is too generally conducted in the same spirit of excitement: studies are pursued under the spur of sharp competition for the prizes and applause of public examinations, and, in place of sober and solid attainment, our culture degenerates into a mere preparation for trade and politics. This state of things is far from favorable to mental stability. The victims of overtasked and perverted emotion fill our asylums, and it is impossible to view the increasing tendencies to social and public excitement without grave solicitude for its future effects.

506. Overtasking the Intellect.—This is an extensive cause of mental derangement, though perhaps less so than that just considered. The baneful effects of cerebral exhaustion have already been noticed (502), and that study is often carried to this injurious length is notorious. Moderate use undoubtedly develops and strengthens the brain, and it is equally certain that, if the amount of work is carried much beyond this point, the organ is endangered. Among the causes of insanity tabulated in insane-asylum reports, excess of study figures as an inconsiderable item; but this belongs to the class of causes which mainly act by paving the way to a mental break-down. Cases like that of Hugh Miller, where, after an intense and protracted strain, the brain at last gives way, are by no means infrequent; but in many an over-stimulated child or overworked student there may be only sown the seeds of future mental disease, while some other circumstance, such as loss of rest, grief, or disappointment, may cause the seed to germinate, and itself be taken as the cause, whereas it is in reality only the occasion.

It has been objected to this view that the lunatic asylums are chiefly peopled with inferior rather than highly-cultivated minds; but inferior minds are just those most likely to be injured by excessive study. The more highly developed the brain, the greater is its capacity of endurance. In his testimony before the Parliamentary School Commission, Dr. Carpenter announced his conviction, as a physiologist who had specially studied the question, that the children of the educated classes are capable, without injury, of twice as many hours of school-study as the children of the uneducated classes.

What amount of labor the brain will endure without overstraining, depends upon various conditions, such as age, original vigor of constitution, habits as to physical exercise, and intensity of application. The brain of the adult will bear, unharmed, an amount of labor which would be most injurious to a young person, and men of active habits can endure, without fatigue, mental application which would be dangerous to the sedentary. Probably six hours a day of close brain-work is the maximum that the organ will endure without detriment. Mental labor may be prolonged, it is true, to double this length of time without apparent injury to the brain; but in most cases the quality of the work performed will be found to indicate a lack of strength, vigor, and spontaneity.

In order to disprove the unhealthfulness of this kind of exertion, attention has been called to the full ages reached by successful brain-workers who have achieved eminence in the various departments of mental activity. The collated results, however, have little value, for in the first place no one doubts that the cultivated brain is capable of a vast amount of labor, extending through a long lifetime, if judiciously exercised. In the second place, the biographies of eminent brain-workers actually show a vast amount of ill health and suffering due to excessive study, while the number of those who achieve distinction as thinkers, and then pass to premature graves as a consequence of it, is by no means small; and, in the third place, such a report is necessarily one-sided, as it deals only with the successes, and takes no account of the multitudes of failures of which the world never hears.

It is not to be forgotten, however, that there are evils of mental under-action as well as of over-action. While there is no evidence that in the case of uncultured savages the brain is liable to become diseased from lack of exercise, the same thing cannot be affirmed of the cultivated races. The progress of civilization in these races is accompanied by a higher development and increasing complexity of cerebral organization, and this higher condition can only be maintained by a correspondingly higher degree of functional exercise. Without that activity which its greater perfection implies and requires, the brain of the civilized man degenerates. A well-constituted organ *demands* exercise, and there can be no doubt that pleasurable, productive brain-work can be pursued to a great extent, in the form of close and severe mental labor, without injury. It is the evil accompaniments that generally work the mischief; the poisoning of the blood in the stagnant air of close, unventilated apartments; the resuming of work directly after dinner, and prolonging it into the late hours of the night; the provocation of stimulants and irregular habits; the hard, repulsive taskwork continued without recreation, and the unrelieved tension of anxiety that frets and strains and softens the delicate gray matter of the brain, and ends at last in paralysis or imbecility.

507. Early Symptoms of Mental Impairment.—Of all the calamities to which man is liable, none is so appalling as the loss of reason, and, when the diseases which cause it are far advanced, they are mostly beyond the reach of restorative measures. But a calamity so terrible does not come unheralded. Mental disease has its gradual beginning — its period of incubation, as physicians term it— which is accompanied by various signals of impending difficulty; and it is important that these early indications should be understood by all.

One of the greatest warnings of approaching cerebral disease is debilitated attention and loss of memory. When an individual begins to fail in his customary power of keeping his mind to a subject, or forgets the names of familiar persons and objects, or is unable to make simple numerical calculations with his usual facility and accuracy, or oddly transposes his words in conversation, there is serious ground for apprehending softening of the brain or apoplectic seizure. Slight deviations of the facial features, the trifling elevation of an eyebrow, the drawing aside of the mouth a hair's breadth, or a faint faltering of the speech, are dangerous intimations of the advance of paralysis.

The more active forms of mental disease have also their early symptoms. Preternatural acuteness of the senses, causing exaggerations of sight, hearing, and smell, is the frequent precursor of a maniacal outbreak. The sensibility is not only exalted, so that the individual sees, hears, feels, and smells more keenly than in health, but it is often vitiated; he sees double, agreeable odors become disgusting, and pleasant tastes offensive. A prickling sensation, or a sense of coldness, or grittiness in things touched, is sometimes experienced. In the case of a man who died of apoplexy, there was for some time previous to his illness a feeling in both hands as if the skin were covered with minute and irritating particles of dust and sand. The approach of mental disease is also foreshadowed in the conduct. Singularity or eccentricity of deportment is not, in itself, to be taken as evidence of mental alienation. A large margin must be allowed for individual peculiarities; there are naturally crooked sticks as well as straight ones. Whatever be the bent of the character, it is in the *deviations* from it that we are to watch for evidence of morbid action. When a person, who is well known to a circle of friends, begins to manifest unaccountable singularities of behavior; when a quiet and modest man becomes noisy and boastful; when a cautious man begins to embark in wild and reckless schemes; when a person of a serious turn suddenly becomes hilarious, or one of a lively and buoyant disposition sinks into despondency; when an affectionate person turns jealous and suspicious with no apparent reason, or one of usually steady, industrious habits becomes idle, neglectful of business, and takes to running about—in such cases there is reason to believe that trouble is brewing. These deviations from customary habits "are the switch-points which indicate that the mind is leaving the main line, and that, if left to itself, it will speedily career to destruction."

Sometimes the earliest symptoms of cerebral derangement are manifested in the consciousness itself, and, while no indications of disorder are disclosed in the outward behavior, the individual finds himself becoming the victim of morbid thoughts, which he cannot banish. A patient, writing to Dr. Cheyne, observed: "I am not conscious of the decay or suspension of any of the powers of my mind. I am as well able as ever I was to attend to my business. My family suppose me in health; yet the horrors of a mad-house are staring me in the face. I am a martyr to a species of persecution from within, which is becoming intolerable. I am urged to say the most shocking things; blasphemous and obscene words are ever on my tongue."

508. Hints and Precautions.—It is a serious error to suppose that, because there may be a predisposition to insanity in a family, therefore the members of it are to regard their danger in the light of a fatality from which there is no escape ; on the contrary, these are preëminently the cases in which, to a wise discretion, forewarning is forearming. The instances are probably very few in which latent tendencies are developed into actual disease in spite of all precaution. It will generally be found that the outbreak is due to some immediate disturbing agency which might have been avoided.

Where such a tendency exists, the education, occupation, and habits, should be ordered with the strictest reference to it: the establishment of strong bodily health should be a paramount consideration. The physical education should be specially directed to strengthen the nervous system and diminish its excitability. Much study, bodily inaction, confinement to warm rooms, sleeping on feathers, are all favorable to undue nervous susceptibility.

In the education of children thus circumstanced, that is, in their brain-exercises, it is of the first importance to remember that whatever tends in any degree to impair the mental health, acts with redoubled power when coöperating with morbid tendencies. While the brain is yet plastic and pliable, a little mismanagement—the humoring of precocity, the repression of physical and nervous activity, or over-stimulation of thought—may awaken the germs of mental disorder, and lead to the most injurious consequences.

To persons thus predisposed, steady and agreeable occupation, which does not try the patience or the temper, or involve much responsibility, excitement, or exhaustion, is in the highest degree desirable. Religious, political, and reformatory gatherings, where the passions are aroused and the sympathies excited, should be carefully avoided, together with all excitements which tend to disturb the

sleep. In respect to the mental habits, in such cases, Dr.
Ray has the following excellent practical suggestions :

" Persons predisposed to mental disease should carefully
avoid a partial, one-sided cultivation of their mental powers—a fault to which their mental constitution renders
them peculiarly liable. Let them bear in mind that every
prominent trait of character, intellectual or moral, every
favorite form of mental exercise, is liable to be fostered at
the expense of other exercises and attributes, until it becomes an indication of actual disease. Here lies their
peculiar danger, that the very thing most agreeable to
their taste and feelings is that which they have most to
fear.

" There is another disposition of mind to be carefully
shunned by the class of persons in question—that of allowing the attention to be engrossed by some particular interest to the neglect of every other, even of those most nearly
connected with the welfare of the individual. The caution
is especially necessary in an age whose intellectual character is marked by strife and conflict, rather than calm
contemplation or philosophical inquiry ; and in which even
the good and the true are pursued with an ardor more in-
dicative of nervous excitement, than of pure, unadulterated emotion. The prevalent feeling is, that whatever is
worth striving for at all, is worthy of all possible zeal and
devotion ; and, supported by the sympathy and coöperation
of others similarly diposed, the coldest natures become, at
last, willing to go as far and as fast as any.

" Where the mind of a person revolves in a very narrow circle of thought, it lacks entirely that recuperative
and invigorating power which springs from a wider com-
prehension of things, and more numerous objects of interest. The habit of brooding over a single idea is calculated to dwarf the soundest mind ; but, to those unfortu-
nately constituted, it is positively dangerous, because they
are easily led to this kind of partial mental activity, and

are kept from running into fatal extremes by none of those conservative agencies which a broader discipline and a more generous culture naturally furnish. The result of this continual dwelling on a favorite idea is, that it comes up unbidden, and cannot be dismissed at pleasure. Reason, fancy, passion, emotion—every power of the mind, in short—are pressed into its service, until it is magnified into gigantic proportions and endowed with wonderful attributes. The conceptions become unnaturally vivid, the general views narrow and distorted, the properties of time and place are disregarded, the guiding, controlling power of the mind is disturbed, and, as the last stage of this melancholy process, reason is completely dethroned."

509. Medical Management.—Although diseases of the higher nervous centres, when they become seated, are, to a great extent, incurable, yet, in their incipient stages, they are in most cases quite amenable to treatment. But, unhappily, those instances where delay is fraught with the greatest danger, are, of all others, most liable to be neglected in their earlier stages. If the liver or the lungs get out of order, there is usually incontinent haste to consult the physician; but, if the organ of reason is in danger of giving way, a mystery is made of it, and the dictates of common-sense are unheeded.

Nor is mere neglect the worst aspect of the case; false notions of delicacy frequently become hinderances to early and decisive action. The ancient superstition, which connected insanity with special Providential disfavor, descends to us in the shape of prejudices which speak of it still as a "taint," and lead to a culpable obliquity in dealing with it. Physicians of the largest experience attest that, even when they are consulted in these cases, there is often the greatest difficulty in getting at the real conditions, both the patient and his friends studiously concealing or flatly denying the facts.

The progress of medical science and the impulses of

public philanthropy have called into existence those noble institutions where alone physical and moral medication can be best united, and which are generally administered by physicians of the largest experience in this department of practice.   When, therefore, an individual begins to manifest symptoms which excite the apprehensions of his family or friends, no time should be lost in procuring the best professional advice and securing the advantages which those establishments offer; and ,if the patient is placed in an asylum, the friends, remembering that time is generally an all‑important element of recovery, should largely trust the discretion of the medical superintendent in regard to the proper duration of his confinement.

QUESTIONS.

PART FIRST.

CHAPTER I.

1. How are the bodily actions studied ?
2. What facts may we thus obtain ?
3. Describe the ice-chamber experiment. What does it show ?
4. How is the strength restored and the loss made good ?
5. In what form is matter excreted from the body ?
6. What is said of the absorption of oxygen ?
7. What is meant by the physiological balance ?
8. How may it be maintained ? What conditions disturb it ?
9. What determines the amount of force set free ?
10. Give an outline of the bodily structure. What is meant by bilateral symmetry ?
11. Describe the vertebral column. What cavities do the bodies of the vertebræ separate ?
12. What does the spinal canal contain ? How is the ventral cavity divided ? What canal traverses the two ventral chambers ? What else does the abdomen contain ? What the thorax ?
13. Describe the head. What are contained within its cavities ?
14. What does a longitudinal section prove ? What is shown by transverse sections ? What is said of the limbs ?
15. Describe the layers of the skin.
16. How does the skin differ from mucous membrane ?
17. What is connective tissue ?
18. What is said of the muscles ?
19. What constitutes the skeleton ? How many bones does it contain ? How are they fastened together ?
20. What enables us to stand upright ?
21. What of the relation of the mind to the muscles ?
22. What organs control the actions of the muscles ? What special power does the cerebro-spinal axis possess ?
23. What is meant by "special sensations ?" Name the organs which receive only certain kinds of impressions ? What are they called ?
24. What is said of the renewal of tissues ?

25. What are the organs of alimentation?
26. Name the organs of distribution?
27. What is meant by the exchanges of the blood?
28. Name the principal excretory organs. In what respects do they resemble each other?
29. What important additional purpose do the lungs fulfill?
30. What part does the nervous system play?
31. What is meant by "life" and "death?"
32. What is "local death?"
33. What is "general death?"
34. How does death result?
35. What becomes of the body after death? What forms may its matter subsequently take?

CHAPTER II.

36. Describe the capillaries. What is their function? How are they distributed?
37. Of what are the capillaries continuations? How do they differ from the small arteries and veins?
38. How are the muscles of the small arteries disposed?
39. What does their contraction effect?
40. How is their contraction regulated?
41. Wherein do the arteries and veins differ?
42. Describe the valves of the veins. How may their action be demonstrated? What arteries possess valves?
43. Describe the lymphatics. Where are they distributed? Where do they discharge their contents?
44. What are the lacteals? What is their function?
45. What large trunks pour venous blood into the heart? From what great trunk do most of the arteries spring? What vessels carry blood to and from the lungs? Into what parts of the heart do these various trunks open?
46. What vessels supply the substance of the heart?
47. What great vessel carries venous blood from the abdominal viscera to the liver? What vessels conduct the blood from the liver to the heart?
48. What is the average size of the heart? What its shape and position? By what membrane is it inclosed?
49. Describe the cavities of the heart? What are they called?
50. What is their relative amount of work?
51. What tissue makes up the walls of the heart? What membrane lines the cavities of the heart? How are the communicating apertures strengthened? What are attached to these rings?
52. Describe the structure and attachments of the heart-valves. What valves close the right auriculo-ventricular aperture? What the left? How are the free edges of the valves supported? What is the action of these valves? What valves are situated at the commencement of the aorta and pulmonary artery? What is their action? How may the action of the valves be demonstrated?
53. What is said of the rhythm of the heart? What is meant by "systole" and "diastole?"

54. Describe the working of the heart.
55. What is the action of the arteries ?
56. What constitutes the beat of the heart ?
57. What is said of the sounds of the heart ?
58. What constitutes the pulse ?
59. Why does the blood jet from cut arteries ?
60. Why are the capillaries pulseless ?
61. What causes the steady capillary flow ?
62. What is said of the velocity of the blood-current ?
63. Trace the course of the blood from the right auricle. How is the heart itself supplied ?
64. What is the shortest complete circuit the blood can make ? The longest ?
65. How does the nervous system affect the circulation ?
66. What happens in blushing ?
67. How may this be proved ?
68. What relation has this nervous control to disease ?
69. What relation does the heart bear to the nervous system ?
70. How may the movements of the heart be directly observed ?
71. What is the proof that the blood circulates ?

CHAPTER III.

72. How may we obtain blood for examination ?
73. How does it appear to the naked eye ? How under the pocket-lens ? What takes place when a drop is left to itself ? What is the effect of salt upon it ?
74. How many kinds of corpuscles does the blood contain ?
75. Describe them.
76. What is the structure of the red corpuscles ?
77. What are the peculiarities of the white corpuscles ?
78. How may the real nature of the corpuscles be determined ?
79. What is supposed to be their origin ? What is said of the corpuscles of the lower animals ?
80. What occurs to the corpuscles when the blood dies ?
81. How are blood-crystals formed ?
82. What is meant by coagulation ?
83. Into what constituents does the blood separate ?
84. What is the buffy-coat ?
85. What conditions influence coagulation ?
86. What is the nature of the process ? What causes the blood to coagulate ?
87. Name some of the physical properties of the blood.
88. What is its chemical composition ?
89. How does age influence the blood ? Sex ? Food ?
90. What is the total amount in the body ?
91. What is the function of the blood ? To what does it owe its vivifying influence ? What is said of the transfusion of blood ?
92. What of the lymph ?

CHAPTER IV.

93. What gives the blood its complex composition ?
94. How is the blood changed in the capillaries ?
95. In what respects do arterial and venous blood differ ?
96. What is said of the diffusion of gases ?
97. Why does the blood change color ?
98. How is this change explained ?
99. Describe the capillaries of the lungs.
100. Trace the air-passages from the mouth to the air-cells.
101. What is said of this mechanism ?
102. What are inspiration and expiration ?
103. State the difference between inspired and expired air.
104. What quantity of air passes through the lungs in twenty-four hours ? To what extent is it vitiated ? How much carbon and water is eliminated in twenty-four hours ?
105. What mechanism carries on the respiratory movements ? What is said of the elasticity of the lungs ?
106. How do the bronchial tubes facilitate the movement of air ?
107. Describe the action of the chest-walls. Explain the action of the intercostal muscles.
108. What is the diaphragm ? Explain its action.
109. What occurs when the diaphragm acts alone ? What if only the chest-walls are brought into play ?
110. What other muscles aid the process ?
111. How does the respiration differ in the sexes ?
112. What is meant by residual air ? Supplemental air ? Tidal air ?
113. What constitutes the stationary air ? What part does it play in respiration ?
114. What is the composition of the stationary air ?
115. How is the nervous system related to respiration ?
116. In what are respiration and circulation analogous ?
117. What are the secondary phenomena of respiration ?
118. What is said of the respiratory murmurs ?
119. How does respiration assist the circulation ?
120. What are the facts relating to this point ?
121. How does expiration affect the circulation ?
122. How may the action of the heart be arrested ?
123. What circumstances modify the respiratory function ?
124. What occurs when a man is strangled ?
125. How is life destroyed by this means ?
126. What is said of respiratory poisons ?
127. What is slow asphyxiation ?
128. Why is ventilation so important ?

CHAPTER V.

129. Describe the distribution of arterial blood throughout the body.
130. What great organs are constantly draining the blood ?
131. What is said of its losses in the liver and lungs ?
132. What are the intermittent sources of loss and gain to the blood ?

133. What are the incessantly active and intermittently active sources of loss and gain to the blood ?

134. Give the position and anatomy of the kidneys.

135. What is the composition of the renal excretion ?   What is its average daily amount ?   Its average specific gravity ?

136. In what respects are the lungs and kidneys alike ?

137. Describe the structure of the kidney.

138. What is said of its filtering mechanism ?

139. From what source are the kidneys supplied with blood ?   How do they change the blood ?

140. How is the excretory action of the kidneys controlled ?

141. What does the blood lose through the skin ?

142. What quantity of matter is thus lost ?   What is the composition of the sweat ?

143. Give the conditions of its escape.

144. What is said of the sweat-glands ?   What of their distribution ?

145. How is the action of the sweat-glands controlled ?

146. What conditions increase the amount of perspiration ?

147. In what respects are the lungs, kidneys, and skin alike ?

148. What does the blood lose in the liver ?   What does it gain ? Describe the liver.   With what great vessels is it connected ?   Give its internal anatomy.   What route does the blood take in its passage through the liver ?   What is said of the liver-cells ?

149. What is their function ?

150. What is the daily quantity of bile excreted ?   Its composition ?

151. What is the source of the bile ?

152. What organs furnish the blood with oxygen ?

153. What does the blood gain in the liver ?   What does it lose ?

154. How may the sugar-forming power of the liver be proved ?

155. What does the blood gain from the lymphatics ?   What of the " ductless glands ? "

156. What is said of the spleen ?   What is its supposed function ?

157. Through what channels does the body lose heat ?   What is the source of bodily heat ?

158. How is the heat of the body equalized ?

159. How does evaporation affect the temperature ?

160. What relation has the nervous system to temperature ?

161. What is said of the action of the glands ?   What is the duct of a gland ?   What are racemose glands ?   What determines the activity of certain glands ?

162. In what way are the salivary glands called into action ?   What is the character of their secretion ?

163. What does the blood gain from the muscles ?

CHAPTER VI.

164. What is another great source of gain to the blood ?

165. How much solid material does a man daily receive ?   How much oxygen ?

166. What is the daily loss of dry solids ?   In what shape does the balance leave the body ?

167. How are foods classified ?   What are Proteids ?   Give examples.

20

What is the composition of fat? What are Amyloids? Give some examples. What is meant by "vital food-stuffs?" What are mineral food-stuffs?

168. What is the composition of the vital food-stuffs? The mineral food-stuffs? What constitutes a permanent food?

169. What occurs if protein is not supplied? What is said of the necessity of other food-stuffs?

170. What is meant by nitrogen starvation?

171, 172. What are the disadvantages of a purely nitrogenous diet?

173. Why is a mixed diet desirable?

174. What constitutes a mixed diet?

175. What is said of the intermediate changes of the food?

176. What are the objections to the ordinary classifications of food?

177. What is the purpose of the alimentary apparatus?

178. Describe the cavity of the mouth and pharynx. What organs do they contain? Name the openings into the pharynx.

179. Give the names and positions of the different salivary glands. How does the saliva affect the food?

180. Describe the teeth.

181. Describe the working of the jaws.

182. What occurs to the food during mastication? Describe the operation of swallowing?

183. How are fluids swallowed?

184. Describe the stomach. What is the character of its lining membrane? What glands does it contain? What fluids do these glands pour out? - What are the properties of the gastric juice?

185. What is meant by artificial digestion?

186. Describe the process of osmosis.

187. By what routes does the food leave the stomach?

188. What is said of the intestines? How are they divided? Where is the ileo-cæcal valve situated? What is the cæcum? The vermiform appendix?

189. What glands are found in the intestinal mucous membrane? What other structures?

190. What is peristaltic contraction?

191. What glands pour their secretions into the duodenum? What is said of the chyme?

192. What is chyle? How does it differ from chyme? What changes does the chyme undergo in the intestine? What juices effect this change? In what way does the chyle reach the blood?

193. What is going on in the large intestine?

CHAPTER VII.

194. What is meant by the "vital eddy?" What maintains the active powers of the body?

195. In what way are the activities of the body manifested? What is locomotion? Name the organs of motion.

196. Describe the cilia. How do they act? Where are they situated?

197. How do the muscles give rise to motion? Into what two groups may the muscles be divided?

198. What is rigor mortis?

199. What is the chemical composition of muscle?

200, 201. What muscles are not attached to solid levers? What is the character of their fibres? What is said of their contractions?

202. What muscles are attached to solid levers? What is a lever?

203. How many orders of levers are described? What is a lever of the first order? Of the second order? Of the third order?

204. What levers of the first order are found in the human body?

205. What of the second order?

206. What of the third order?

207. How may a single part of the body represent the three kinds of levers?

208. How many kinds of joints are found in the human body?

209. What are imperfect joints?

210. Describe the structure and movements of a perfect joint?

211. What are inter-articular cartilages?

212. What are ball-and-socket joints?

213. What are hinge-joints?

214. What is a pivot-joint? Give an example from the human body. Describe the bones of the forearm. How are they articulated together? What is meant by pronation and supination?

215. What are ligaments? How do the ligaments differ in the different joints? What is said of the hip-joints?

216. What different movements are the joints capable of executing?

217. How are these movements effected? In what way are they limited?

218. What is meant by the origin and insertion of a muscle? How are the muscles attached to the bones? What direction does the axis of a muscle usually take? The exceptions?

219. Describe the operation of walking.

220. When does a man walk with least effort?

221. What is said of running and jumping?

222. What conditions are essential to the production of voice?

223. Describe the vocal chords?

224. What cartilages enter into the structure of the larynx?

225. To what are the vocal ligaments attached?

226. Describe the muscles of the larynx. What does their action effect? How are musical notes produced?

227. When will the musical note be low? When high? Upon what does range of voice depend? Upon what the quality of voice?

228. What is speech? How is the voice modulated?

229. What is said of the vowel sounds? What of consonant sounds? What sounds require blocking of the air-current? What are explosive consonants?

230. How are speaking-machines constructed?

231. What is said of tongueless speech? What example is given?

CHAPTER VIII.

232. How are the muscles made to contract?

233. What calls the nerves into action?

234. What is reflex action? What is a sensation? With what are sensations classed?

235. What are subjective sensations ?

236. What is said of the muscular sense ? How may its existence be demonstrated ?

237. What is said of the higher senses ?

238. Give the general plan of a sensory organ.

239. Where is the organ of the sense of touch located ? What are papillæ ? What is a tactile corpuscle ?

240. What is interposed between it and external objects ?

241. What is said of varying tactile sensibility ?

242. What gives rise to the feelings of warmth and cold ?

243. Where is the organ of the sense of taste found ? Describe the papillæ of the tongue.

244. Where is the organ of the sense of smell located ? Describe the nasal passages. The nasal chambers. What do these nasal chambers contain ?

245. How are odors brought in contact with the olfactory apparatus ?

246. Where is the organ of hearing situated ? Of what does it essentially consist ? What bodies are found in the membranous labyrinth ? In the *scala media* ?

247. What part of the ear is called the vestibule ? What are the semicircular canals ? What the ampullæ ? What fluids form a part of the mechanism ?

248. Where is the *scala media* situated ? What part is known as the *scala tympani?* The *scala vestibuli?* What peculiar mechanism is found within the *scala media?*

249. What is the bony labyrinth ? What fenestræ does it contain ?

250. What part of the ear is known as the *drum?* How is this separated from the external *meatus?* In what way does the drum communicate externally ?

251. What are the *auditory ossicles?* What two points do they connect ? What is their purpose ? How are the perilymph and endolymph set vibrating ?

252. What muscles are connected with the tympanic membrane ?

253. What is the *concha?*

254. What conditions are necessary to the production of sound ? How is sound transmitted to the ear ?

255. How do the aërial vibrations affect the tympanic membrane ? Into what two kinds of vibrations may bodies be thrown ?

256. Which are supposed to transmit the impulses of the aërial waves ?

257. Describe the actions of the auditory muscles.

258. What part of the ear is supposed to recognize the intensity of sounds ? What part is concerned with the quality of sounds ?

259. What is the probable function of the fibres of Corti ?

260. What is the purpose of the Eustachian tubes ?

CHAPTER IX.

261. Describe the general structure of the eye.

262. What is seen on the centre of the retina ?

263. Describe the microscopic structure of the retina.

264. What is the function of the retina ? What is said of the sensation of light ?

265. In what respects do different parts of the retina differ? What is the blind spot?

266. What is said of the duration of luminous impressions?

267. Can the retina become exhausted? What are complementary colors?

268. What is color blindness?

269. What appearances are produced by pressure upon the eyeball?

270. What is the function of the rods and cones? What are *Purkinje's figures?*

271. What is said of the formation of visual ideas?

272. What physical agent gives rise to vision? What is a convex lens? Describe the experiment with the candle and lens.

273. What is meant by the "focus?" What is adjustment of the eye? When does the lens give a distant picture? What is the effect of moving the object?

274. What follows from varying the convexity of the lens? What relation does convexity bear to the focus? How does a convex surface affect the rays of light? Describe the experiment with the watch-glass and water-box. What is a camera obscura?

275. What organs must the light pass through to reach the retina? Give the structure of the eyeball.

276. What are the humors of the eye? By what organ are the humors separated? Describe the crystalline lens.

277. Describe the *choroid* coat. What is its position? Where are the *ciliary* processes situated?

278. Describe the *iris.* Where is it situated? What of the ciliary muscle? What relation has the iris to the lens?

279. What is the ora serrata?

280. How does the eyeball resemble a water-camera?

281. How is the focus adjusted in a camera obscura? How in the eye?

282. Describe the experiment. What does it show?

283. What is said of the mechanism of adjustment? What are the facts of adjustment? What explanations of the process have been offered? Which is the most probable?

284. What limits the power of adjustment?

285. Name the muscles of the eyeball. What are their respective positions? What does their action effect?

286. Describe the structure of the eyelids? What muscles move them?

287. Where is the *conjunctiva* situated? Describe the lachrymal apparatus? What is the source of the tears?

CHAPTER X.

288. What is meant by a simple sensation? What is the character of most of our sensations?

289. What sensations are the simplest?

290. Of what does a tactile sensation consist?

291. What is said of complex sensations and judgments?

292. Why are delusions of the senses impossible? What is said of delusive judgments?

293. What are subjective sensations? What examples are given?

294. Relate the case of Mrs. A——. What senses were implicated? To what class did her peculiar sensations belong?

295. What conditions seemed to favor their development? What prevented her forming false judgments?

296. Were her senses really at fault?

297. How may outside causes give rise to delusive judgments? Give an example.

298. What is said of optical delusions?

299. What is meant by the *optic axis?* How is the position of a phosphene accounted for?

300. What is said of the inversion of visual images?

301. How do objects and their visual images correspond in number? What is the action of multiplying-glasses?

302. Upon what does *perspective* depend?

303. How does the distance of an object affect its visual image? How do convex and concave glasses affect it?

304. Why do the sun and moon look larger near the horizon?

305. What is said of the judgment of form by shadows?

306. What is the principle of the *thaumatrope?*

307. What is the explanation of squinting?

308. Give the principle of the *pseudoscope.*

309. What of the *stereoscope?*

CHAPTER XI.

310. Of what is the bulk of the nervous system made up?

311. What two systems constitute the nervous apparatus?

312. Describe the structure of nerve-fibres and nerve-centres.

313. Where is the *cerebro-spinal axis* located? What membrane separates it from the bone? What other membranes surround the brain and cord?

314. Describe the spinal cord. How is it divided? Describe the roots of the spinal nerves.

315. What does a transverse section of the cord show?

316. How do gray and white matter differ?

317. What follows the irritation of a spinal nerve?

318. What are the functions of the anterior and posterior roots?

319. What results from cutting the anterior root of a spinal nerve? The posterior root? Both roots?

320. How are impressions propagated along the nerves? What is an *afferent* nerve? What is an efferent nerve?

321. In what respects are they alike?

322. What occurs when the spinal cord is cut across? What when the end remote from the brain is irritated?

323. What power does the cord possess independently of the brain?

324. What is said of the distribution of reflex effects?

325. Do all parts of the cord possess a like conducting power?

326. What is said of the conducting power of the gray matter?

327. What special functions have certain regions of the cord?

328. Describe the *medulla oblongata.* What cavity does it contain? What overhangs this cavity? What is the *pons Varolii?* Into what

parts do the fibres of the medulla pass ? What elevations are found between the crura cerebri ? Where is the third ventricle situated ? Into what masses of nervous matter do the crura cerebri pass ? Where is the *pineal gland* located ? The *pituitary body?* Where are the *lateral ventricles* situated ? What forms the floor of the lateral ventricles ? What is said of the hemispheres of the brain ? How are they connected ? What is said of the outer surfaces of the hemispheres ?

329. How are the white and gray matter arranged in the medulla oblongata ? In the cerebellum and cerebral hemispheres ?

330. How many pairs of nerves are given off from the brain ? Name the first pair. The second. The third. In what muscles is the third pair distributed ? Where are the fourth and sixth pairs distributed ? Describe the origin and distribution of the fifth pair. In what muscles does the seventh pair terminate ? The eighth pair terminate ? What is the function of the ninth pair ? What organs does the tenth pair supply ? Describe the course of the eleventh pair. Give the origin and distribution of the twelfth pair.

331. What is said of the olfactory and optic nerves ?

332. What effects follow injuries of the medulla oblongata ?

333. What direction do the afferent impulses take in the medulla oblongata ? Give the course of the fibres in the anterior pyramids. What would be the effect of dividing one of the crura cerebri ?

334. What is the function of the cerebral hemispheres ?

335. What is said of the reflex action of the brain ?

336. What takes place in reading aloud ?

337. What is meant by "artificial reflex actions ? "

338. What is said of the *sympathetic system ?*

CHAPTER XII.

339. What is said of the microscopical analysis of the tissues ?

340. What is the early primitive structure of the body ?

341. What is the character of the epidermis and *epithelium ?* How do these tissues grow ? What is *squamous* epithelium ? What kind of epithelium lines the alimentary canal ? What is ciliated epithelium ?

342. From what kind of tissue are the nails developed ?

343. Of what are hairs composed ? Describe their growth. How are the hairs kept supplied with oil ? What is meant by *horripilation*, or "goose-skin ? "

344. What is the structure of the *crystalline lens ?*

345. Of what is cartilage composed ?

346. What is the structure of *connective tissue?* How is it affected by being boiled in water ? How does acetic acid affect it ? What is *fibro-cartilage?*

347. Describe the structure of ligaments and tendons.

348. Describe fat-cells.

349. What are pigment-cells ?

350. Describe the minute structure of bone. What are *lacunæ?* *Canaliculi?* What were the lacunæ once supposed to be ? Describe the *Haversian* canals. What is *periosteum ?* What is found in the cavities of the bones ?

351. How do bones grow ? What are sutures ? In what kind of

material are bony matters first deposited? What is meant by *centres of ossification?*

352. Of what are the teeth composed? Name the different parts of a tooth. What is the character of *dentine?* What is the structure of *enamel?*

353. How are the teeth developed? Which are the deciduous, or milk-teeth? When do they appear?

354. How are the permanent teeth formed? How divided? When do they begin to appear? How long before the set is completed?

355. What two kinds of muscles are found in the body? Of what are the striated composed? What is a *fascia?* The *sarcolemma?* What does it inclose? Of what is the contractile substance made up? What is the structure of smooth muscle?

356. What are the elements of nerve-tissue? Describe the structure of a nerve-fibre. How do the nerve-fibres terminate?

357. What is a *tactile corpuscle?*

358. What is the structure of the olfactory nerves?

359. Where are *ganglionic corpuscles* found? What is their structure?

CHAPTER XIII.

360. Give the weight of the different parts of the body. How much of the body is water? How much solid matter? What do the solids consist of? What would be the losses of such a body in twenty-four hours? Through what organs would these losses occur? How much does the body gain in twenty-four hours?

361. What substances, and how much of each, does the body daily require? In what forms could these be conveniently obtained?

362. How much blood passes through the heart per minute? At what rate does it flow in the large arteries? In the capillaries? What is the daily work of the left ventricle?

363. How much air passes through the lungs in twenty-four hours? How is it changed in the passage? What does the body lose by respiration in twenty-four hours? At what rate does the respiration of a single person vitiate the external air?

364. How much matter is lost through the skin in twenty-four hours?

365. How much by the kidneys?

366. What is the velocity of a nervous impulse?

367. What is the size of the blood-corpuscles in man? What the thickness of his muscular fibres? What the breadth of nerve-fibres? Of connective-tissue fibrils? Of epithelium-scales? Of capillary blood-vessels? Of the cones in the yellow spot? How long are the cilia of the windpipe?

PART SECOND.

CHAPTER XIV.

368. Of what practical value is a knowledge of physiology? What is said of its importance?

369. What were some of the old notions regarding disease? How did such views affect the community?

370. What is the true idea of health and disease? How is this illustrated in the case of gout?

371. When do the agencies of health become sources of disease? What is the chief value of hygienic knowledge?

372. Name some of the results that have followed its application?

373. What is said of its value as a remedial means?

374. What are the chief sources of ill health?

CHAPTER XV.

375. Name the chief constituents of the atmosphere?

376. What are its minor constituents?

377. What is the office of the air in respiration?

378. What is said of it as a purifying agent?

379. How is the air rendered impure?

380. How do atmospheric impurities affect the senses?

381. What is said of carbonic acid as an impurity? In what proportion is it thrown out from the lungs? From what other sources does the air of apartments receive it? What does an excess of it denote?

382. What is the effect of air saturated with moisture? Of dry air?

383. In what form is organic matter found in the air? What are some of its sources? By what means may we determine its presence? What is said of its presence in the air of sick-rooms and hospitals? How does it affect the system?

384. What suspended impurities are common in the air?

385. What impurities enter it from sewers and cesspools?

386. What contaminations are found in the air of marshes?

387. What is said of the air of cellars?

388. What is the general effect upon the body of impure air?

389. What is said of impure air and consumption?

390. What effect has impure air upon the scrofulous? Relate the case of the Norwood School.

391. How does air contaminated by certain trades affect the health?

392. What is the effect of inhaling air containing organic impurities?

393. How does impure air affect the course of disease? What is of the first account in the treatment of febrile complaints?

394. What are the effects of a sick-room atmosphere?

395. What is the effect of impure air upon the mind?

396. How does Nature purify the air?

397. What is the object of ventilation? How may pure air be best

obtained? What quantity of air is required? How may its movement be controlled? What is said concerning its temperature?

398. When are other means of purification required? What substances are most efficient as disinfectants?

CHAPTER XVI.

399. What proportion of water do the various tissues contain?

400. What duties does it perform in the economy?

401. What leading property fits it for this office?

402. The average daily consumption of an adult?

403. What is said of its excretion?

404. What gives rise to the several varieties of water?

405. What is said of soft water?

406. How is hard water formed? What are mineral waters? Give the characters of limestone-water. What is said of sand and gravel waters? What are the foreign ingredients of alluvial waters? The impurities of surface and subsoil waters? What is said of marsh-water? What is the general character of river-water? What is said of sea-water?

407. How may perfectly pure water be obtained? What water may be regarded as most healthy?

408. What is said of the organic impurities of water?

409. How is water affected by contact with lead?

410. What kinds of impurities are likely to produce dyspepsia?

411. What kinds of water are said to produce diarrhœa?

412, 413. Are dysentery and cholera ever caused by impure water?

414. What is said of the spread of enteric fever?

415. How are malarious fevers often produced?

416. What is the supposed cause of goitre?

417. What animals may pass into the body with the drinking-water?

418. Are the senses alone trustworthy in the examination of water?

419. What is said of distillation as a means of purification?

420. What is the effect of boiling and freezing?

421. What chemical substances are sometimes used as purifiers?

422. What is said of filtration?

CHAPTER XVII.

423. Into what four groups may food be classed?

424. What is said of the proteids?

425. What of the fats as articles of diet?

426. What substances belong to the amyloid group?

427. To what uses are these various food-stuffs applied?

428. What are the mineral aliments?

429. Why is a mixed diet necessary?

430. What is said of milk as food?

431. Of butter and cheese?

432. What is the composition of eggs, and how should they be cooked?

433. What is said of the various meats?

434. Why is salt inferior to fresh meat?

435. What peculiarity do poultry and game present?
436. How is the flesh of fish regarded as food?
437, 438. What is said of crabs and lobsters? Clams and oysters?
439. Why is wheat such a valuable food?
440. How does rye compare with wheat?
441. What of buckwheat?
442. How does Indian-corn differ from wheat and rye?
443. What are the properties of oatmeal?
444. What advantage does rice possess over other foods?
445. What is said of peas and beans?
446. Give the composition of potatoes. Why should the succulent vegetables be eaten with meat?
447. What is said of the fruits?
448. What are auxiliary foods?
449. What substances come under the head of condiments?
450. Why is tea valuable as a beverage? How should it be made? What is its action? How is it adulterated?
451. What is the composition of coffee? How should the beverage be prepared?
452. What is said of cocoa and chocolate?
453. What should cooking aim to accomplish? Why should over-cooking be avoided?
454. How does boiling affect meat? How should the process be conducted? What is said of roasting? Stewing? Frying?
455. How should vegetables be cooked?
456. What are some of the effects of over-eating?
457. What are the effects of deficient diet?
458. What amount of food is daily required?
459. What results from a badly-constituted diet?
460. What is said of a diet deficient in fat?
461. What constitutes unwholesome food?
462. Give an account of the cysticercus cellulosus. Of the trichina spiralis.

CHAPTER XVIII.

463. What is said of the purposes for which clothing is worn?
464. What of linen as an article of clothing?
465. How does cotton differ from linen?
466. What are the properties of woolen clothing? Its relations to moisture?
467. How does color influence the character of clothing?
468. What is of more importance than the character of the fabric?
469. Why should clothing be light?
470. Why should it be worn loose?
471. What is said of compressing the chest and abdomen?
472. What results from compressing the feet?
473. How is uniformity of temperature to be maintained?
474. How is a part affected when habitually overheated? Why is over-dressing the throat pernicious?
475. What is said of wearing flannel next the skin?
476. How should children be clothed?
477. Why should the aged be well protected?

CHAPTER XIX.

478. What renders it evident that man is intended for action?

479. What is said of labor? What causes division of labor? How does it affect the individual?

480. How does exercise remedy the evil?

481. Describe the transformation of physiological forces.

482. Why is habitual exercise invigorating?

483. How does exercise affect the circulation? How the temperature?

484. What is its influence upon respiration? Why should we exercise in pure air?

485. How does exercise affect digestion? Why is immediate exercise after a full meal injurious?

486. What is the effect of exercise upon the skin?

487. How should exercise be regulated?

488. What are the most favorable conditions for exercise?

489. Why is over-exercise injurious? How is proper rest to be secured? How should exercise be managed after sickness? How does over-exercise injure the system? Why does it particularly injure the young?

490. What are the consequences of insufficient exercise? Describe its operation in different circumstances.

491. What is said of the amount and conditions of exercise? What course should the sedentary pursue? Why is pure air specially necessary during exercise?

492. What is the value of the "movement-cure?"

CHAPTER XX.

493. Why is mental health a physiological question?

494. What is said of the office and changes of the brain? What is the effect of disturbing its normal movement? Describe the mutual relations of the mind and brain. What is remarked as to materialism?

495. What constitutes *disease?* What error is to be guarded against? How is mental disease to be regarded? On what is mental hygiene founded? What is its province?

496. Why are the causes of cerebral impairment varied and complex? How are they usually divided? What are predisposing causes? Exciting causes? What error is mentioned? In what way is insanity usually caused?

497. What is said of each mental act? What are the composition and action of the mental mechanism? What are the results of its perfect or imperfect nutrition? Repeat the remarks of Bucknill and Tuke. What further effect is due to impaired nutrition?

498. What is said of the blood transmitted to the brain?

499. What are the relations between mental excitement and the brainward flow of blood? How is congestion induced, and what are its effects?

500. What is anæmia, and how caused? What are its effects as compared with those of hyperæmia? Give Dr. Maudsley's remarks upon the subject.

501. What keeps the brain in harmonious action? How may its harmony be further disturbed? Mention examples of perversion of blood. How does alcohol affect the brain?

502. How does the brain differ in action from other organs of the body? How does Nature renovate the brain? What is a prime condition of mental health? What are the effects of insufficient sleep? What of disturbed sleep? In what does mental health consist? From what arises mental impairment? Hence, what causes influence mental character?

503. Give the estimates relative to the transmission of insanity. What is transmitted, and how? Repeat the remarks of Dr. Maudsley.

504. How is debilitated stock a source of criminality? What is Dr. Howe's opinion upon this subject? Name some of the causes of mental impairment and their operation. Give the observations of Dr. Ray.

505. What comparison is made between the savage and the civilized man? What are our peculiar perils as a nation?

506. What is said of overtasking the intellect? Repeat the testimony of Dr. Carpenter. What conditions control the amount of healthful brain-work? How is the argument against the unwholesome effect of excessive brain-work met? In what respect does the brain of the savage and the civilized man differ? What usually works the mischief in cerebral application?

507. How is cerebral disease heralded? How the more active forms? In what manner is the conduct affected? The consciousness?

508. What hints and precautions are given? How should children thus predisposed be managed? How adults? What is Dr. Ray's advice when there is a predisposition to mental disease?

509. What is said of medical management?

INDEX AND GLOSSARY.

Changes of the food, 175.

Charcoal as a deodorizer, 398.

" filters, 422.

Check ligaments, ligaments limiting rotation of the skull. 215.

Cheeks, 242.

Cheese, 431.

Chest, the cavity containing the lungs and heart; the thorax, 10.

" bones of, 19.

Chewing, 182.

Chloride of potassium, 428.

Chloride of sodium, common salt, 428.

Chlorine as a disinfectant, 398.

Chocolate, 452.

Cholera, effect of hygienic measures on, 372.

Cholera, spread of, 392, 413.

Cholesterin, a crystalline constituent of the bile, having a pearl-like, fatty appearance, 150.

Chondrin, a nitrogenous substance, which may be extracted from cartilage by boiling, 167.

Chordæ tendi'neæ, fibrous cords connecting the valves of the heart with the papillary muscles of the walls of the ventricles, 52.

Chords, vocal, organs in the larynx by which voice is produced, 100, 222, 225–227.

Choroid, the vascular membrane of the eyeball, lying between the sclerotic and retina, 277.

Chyle, the milk-like fluid taken up by the lacteals from the small intestine, 44, 192.

Chyme, the food as it passes from the stomach into the small intestine, 187.

Cilia, minute filaments attached to cells, and which, during life, are capable of motion, 196.

Ciliary ligaments and muscles, 278.

Ciliated epithelium, 341.

Circulation affected by exercise, 483.

" compared to a river, 93.

" course of, 63.

" evidence of, 70.

" organs of, 26, 36–53.

" and respiration, analogies of, 116.

Circumduction, that movement of a limb by which it describes a conical surface when rotating around an imaginary axis, 216.

Circumvallate, walled around, 243.

" papillæ, 243.

Cistern of the chyle, 44.

Clams as food, 438.

Clavicle, the collar-bone, 19.

Clothing, absorption of moisture by, 464–467.

Clothing, for children and the aged, 476, 477.

Clot, the jelly-like mass formed by the coagulation of the blood, 83.

Coagulation of the blood, 82, 85.

Coccyx, the last four vertebræ of the spinal column consolidated into a single bone, 19.

Coch'lea, a conical cavity of the internal ear, 248.

Cochlear nerve, 259.

Complex sensations, 288.

Cocoa, 452.

Cod-liver oil, 460.

Coffee, 451.

Cold, 157.

Cold and heat, feeling of, 242.

Colon, middle portion of large intestine, 188.

Color-blindness, inability to distinguish certain colors, 268.

Color of the blood, 130, 133.

Colum'næ car'neæ, column-like fleshy elevations of the substance of the walls of the ventricles, 52, 54.

Combination of actions, 20.

Complementary colors, 267.

Complemental air, 112.

Conjunctiva, the mucous membrane lining the eyelids and covering the external portion of the eyeball, 287.

Cones of the retina, 263, 270.

Connective tissue, tissue made up of a net-work of filaments, or fibrous threads, and which serves to connect the different parts of the body together, *fibrous tissue, areolar tissue,* 17, 346.

Compression of the chest, 470.

" " feet, 471.

Concha, the external ear, 253.

INDEX AND GLOSSARY.

THE END.

www.ingramcontent.com/pod-product-compliance
Lightning Source LLC
Chambersburg PA
CBHW031810270326
41932CB00008B/370